VIVA
la Cucina Italiana

Long live the Italian Cooking !
over 300 wonderful recipes from the North, Central & the South of Italy

Joe Famularo
with Cristopher Laus

Copyright © 2012
All rights reserved.

ISBN-10: 1470170434
EAN-13: 9781470170431

Library of Congress Control Number: 2012904052
CreateSpace, North Charleston, SC

VIVA
la Cucina Italiana

Other Books by Joe Famularo

The Joy of Pasta* (Barrons)

The Joy of Grilling (Barrons)

A Cook's Tour of Italy (Berkeley)

The Italian Soup Cookbook (Workman)

Celebrations (Barrons)

Vegetables* (Barrons)

The Festive Famularo Kitchen* (Atheneum)

Supermeals from Supermarkets (Barrons)

Healthy Pasta (Barrons)

Healthy Grilling (Barrons)

* with Louise Imperiale

CONTENTS

Grazie Mille	ix
Introduction	xi
Chapters:	
1. Antipasti And Soups	1
2. Pasta	59
3. Risotto And Polenta	111
4. Vegetables And Legumes	127
5. Fish And Sea Food	171
6. Poultry And Game	207
7. Meats (Beef, Pork, Veal, Lamb, And Others)	225
8. Salads	257
9. Cheeses	279
10. Breads And Pizzas	291
11. Desserts (Cakes, Tarts, Cookies, Fruits, Pudding, & Ice Cream)	315
12. Basics	373
Sources	381
Index	385

GRAZIE MILLE

I wish to thank the many friends, relatives, chefs, restaurants owners, and workers in Italy who always found time and patience to inform and instruct me. Many of their names have been included in the text or as part of a recipe title. In addition, I would like to thank Tiziana and Francesco Antonini (Bevagna), Ermenegildo Baggio at Hosteria Ca'Derton (Asolo), Walter and Emanuele Ascani (Bevagna), Rosalba Balestrazzi (Ostuni – Apulia), Bruno Boggione at Il Vicoletto (Alba), Gianrodolfo Botto (Pallermo), Giovanni Cappelli (Panzano in Chianti), Pina and Marco Carli (Naples), Paola Cavazziini and Maurizio Rossi (Parma), Corrado Costanzo (Noto-Sicily), Agata Pariella and Romeo Caraccio (Rome), Monseignor Divine (The Vatican), Piero and Pina Fassi (Asti), Luca Garrone at Ristorante Universo (Vignale Monferrato), Giovanni Gradassi and her son, Andrea Scotacci (Spoleto), Giorgi Intelesano (Taormino), Mariuccia at the Fiaschetteria Toscana (Venice), Fauto Monti (Florence), Emanuele Monzeglio and William Perrotta (Asti), Gabriele Moscati and her sons, Giuseppe and Filippo Saladini (Doglie-Todi), Georgianna and Armando Orsini (Asheville, NC), Fabio Picchi (Florence), Cristina di Piovani (Mantova), Angelo Ricci (Bari), Cinzia Ricci (Lucca), Nicoletti Ruggieri (Siracusa), Pietro and Angela Santi and Carmensita Poggianti of Hotel Brunamonti (Bevagna-Umbria), Antonio and Nadia Santini at Dal Pescatore (Canneto sull'Oglio-Mantova), Clotilde Treves (Monteporzio-Rome) and Benedetta Vitali (Florence). Thanks to HP Books (Penguin USA, 2003) for *"A Cook's Tour of Italy"* from which this book has been adapted.

I want to especially thank AnnaMaria and Maurizio Manciolli di Montefano for their invaluable help with the Italian recipe titles and other Italian expressions; Louise and John Imperiale and other family members, for joining me on many trips to Italy, to visit, sightsee, study, and, most of all, to cook; Keeshia Laus for her work on the manuscript; Phyllis Rose, a good friend who is one of the most creative people I know; David Schorr, a painter and graphic artist who created the magnificent cover for this book; David Wolkowsky (Key West, Florida), for his inspiration and long-term support over many years; and, without a doubt, Cristopher Laus, my assistant, for accompanying me to Italy on many major trips and whose good help in testing these recipes was simply wonderful and indispensable. To all of you, I dedicate this book.

INTRODUCTION

Going to Italy always reminds me of how we should be eating (and living) in the U.S. Italians seem to be more passionate about their food. They market daily, talk about it all the time, spend time in the kitchen — even close their shops to devote three hours a day to eat lunch for them, eating is a simple pleasure and eating the Italian way delivers a better quality of life. No one expects our lunchtime to increase, but I think there is agreement that most of us want (many crave) the Italian eating experience at home.

My love for Italian food began before my first visit to Italy. Growing up in New York in an Italian household taught me to appreciate homemade pastas and breads, fresh vegetables, delicious yummy soups, fish in simple preparations, and meats and stews in all their guises. When I did get to Italy, the food seemed better, the flavors were clearer; the perfume of the fresh fruit was outstandingly noticeable — eating in the trattorias and in friends' homes clearly showed how the various foods melded together, as in perfect harmony. Every time I returned from Italy, my goal was to recreate these food experiences. I so enjoyed them, and still do. Along the way, I learned that the Piemontese cook their way, the Umbrians their way, the Neapolitans their way, and so it is for all Italian regions. I learned, in fact, that each Italian has his own style. In spite of these differences, there is a fundamental truth that ties the various cuisines together: careful selection of ingredients, treating them separately and purely, striving for flavors that at the same time are both natural and powerful. This makes Italian cooking unique, and to recreate it outside Italy, one learns also that mediocre ingredients will not make the same dish. Italians market every day, sometimes two times a day — they inspect asparagus spears and artichoke leaves for freshness and imprint their thumbs on eggplants, snap green beans and pierce pea pods with their thumb nails, all in search of freshness. If an Italian doesn't have or can't get the ingredient it takes to make a dish, he'll move on to something else. That is also a reason why he markets frequently, in search of the best, freshest food to cook that day.

In our family kitchen, the message on a Florentine wall tile, painted in shades of blue and yellow, and sprinkled with years of heavy kitchen duty marks, reads: *"Il padrone di casa sono io, chi comanda e mia moglie!"* (I am the master of my household, but it is my wife who commands). No one in the family disputed mama's authority and it was witnessed in many ways. What I remember most of all was her daily shopping. She was a fabulous cook, with an uncanny sense for bread making, rolling out pasta, filling ravioli, and cooking her special stuffed chicken in broth

Americans love Italian cookbooks. Yet, few of them tell the reader how to bring Italian food to American tables. how to view taste, color, texture and, of course, substance. *Piatti alla buona*, everyday food, is included if for no other reason that they're easy, quick, simple family preparations. *Piatti domenicali*, Sunday food, is also included because it is more special and out of the ordinary.

Most of the recipes included here are souvenirs of my "working" trips to Italy; enjoying food there and writing about it is never work, whether I'm in the well-known cities or in remote villages. There is no question in my mind that the recipes have been tested over there and over here. But let me assure you that these talented, imaginative cooks of Italy have their own way of sharing a recipe: it is always a "little of this, some of that" (in the same way they give directions – it is always "*sempre diretto* – always go straight even if there is a "T" in the road, or roads that go left and right – it is always "*sempre diretto*". Sometimes, the recipe at home in the U.S. did not work for the American table. It was necessary to translate the little of this and some of that to get a good replication of the Italian dish. Flours, water, and many fish are only a few examples of the differing ingredients.

One must recognize that "*la nuova cucina*" was a disaster in Italy. Ties to family and land are so entrenched that trattorias, restaurants and food at home is unabashedly anti-urban. "*Mamma e Nonna*" is still stirring the polenta. In Montefalco, just north of Spoleto in Umbria, at the charming restaurant "Coccorone", and in fact all over the Italian boot, lamb and other meats are still slowly roasted in a wood-burning hearth, as it has been for hundreds of years. We all know the beauty of Italian cooking is startling simplicity and honest, direct flavors. At times, it seems Italy is light-years away from the concept of *alta*-casual dining. Culinary time seems languid and anything food wise, too far ahead of its time, has to fight for a generation to be born. On many trips over the last several years, however, I have felt a breeze floating through their kitchens. New cooks and others are defining the future by celebrating the past. In the countryside particularly, younger cooks are creating small revolutions by redefining their own regional tastes. An example in Asti, a short distance from Turin, at the splendid restaurant Gener Neuv, I enjoyed a dish of a half roasted red pepper wrapped around an ethereal tablespoonful of tuna mousse. Grilled peppers and tuna antipasti have always been traditional, but Gener Neuv was showing its concept of this "updated" cooking in Italy. Another example further south in San Remo on the Ligurian Sea, at the highly regarded Paolo e Barbara: the traditional "*stoccafisso*" (air-dried cod with potatoes) is given a major lift by the addition of the thinnest slivers of candied lemon peel. One has to taste it to appreciate this unpredictable touch.

INTRODUCTION

These updated, upscale, new wave recipes — call them what you will — are included here if they meet the test of simplicity, and honest and direct flavors. Many traditional recipes are adapted for American use by reducing portions, substituting easier-to-get ingredients, improving presentation and garnishment of the dish. I have traveled to Italy many times. I recently returned from a home in southern Tuscany. We shopped in Pienza, Montalcino, Sienna, Asciano, Montepulciano, Sarteano and Chiusi and a host of other fabulous villages and towns. Last year, I lived in Lucca and spent time in Viareggio, Pisa, Pietrasanta, Camaiore, and Empoli. Montelupo and Florence. On several other trips, I concentrated on the hill towns of Tuscany.

Before that I traveled from Montoporzio (a suburb of Rome) to Rome (for the twentieth time), to Frascati, Tivoli, Castel Gandolfo, Velletri and more. One springtime, I traveled through Umbria. I have been to La Spezia, S. Margherita, Rapallo, Portofino and others in Liguria on the Italian Riviera. Of course, I've spent time in Torino, Milano, Asti, Alessandria and the Italian towns bordering Switzerland, such as Bellinzona. Several trips were to Venice, to Padova, Verona, Treviso, Conegliano, Asolo (oh!, beautiful Asolo), Bassano (sad for the trees planted there in memory of deceased Italian war heroes), Vicenza and Bergamo (*alta* and *basso* – high for the old town and below for the new town), and Como, too. Longer stays were in Bologna, Modena, Parma (for one of the most delicious meals at La Greppia) and Ferrara. Another time: along the Adriatic coast visiting Ravenna, Rimini, Pesaro, Fano, Ancona, Pescara, Vasto (for a special homemade *brodetto*), and Brindisi (the end of the Appian way).

Many trips were made to Napoli, Capri and Ischia, and spending time in the southern towns of Potenza, Matera, Taranto and Lecce (a true melting pot location of the different Mediterranean people). I've circled Sicily, loving Siracusa, Agrigento and Erice. La Puglia, the region of Italy's 7th largest city, Bari, was explored food wise; another time, there were Monopoli, Molfetta, Trani, Barletta, Conversano and Alberobello – villages and towns surrounding Bari.

I am an American-Italian, proud of his Italian roots, its history, culture and food. I love eating Italian food.

Thirty years ago, on my first trip to Rome, I looked out of my hotel window and saw the local outdoor market. I was intrigued at the sight of the panorama of fruits and vegetables, the hustle of business, the view of Italians engrossed in their daily shopping. Although I was jet-lagged, and needed a nap, I had to visit the market first which proved to be a timeless experience. The month was May and the *primizia*, the produce anticipating the season was deliciously displayed. The freshly picked local fare was set up in architectural splendor – mounds of fresh green peas, layered paler green arugula, rectangles of light green asparagus, baskets of field greens, cornucopias of fragrant strawberries set on fern leaves, tubs of yellow and red peppers, a pyramid of long stemmed green and purple artichokes were everywhere. Italians were doing their daily thing — marketing for today's meal, exchanging recipes with vendors and sharing family gossip. In the U.S. markets, I now see more and more vegetables without plastic wrap, which was the only way to pack fresh vegetables a few years ago. Might this be Italian influence?

It may seem frivolous to say that Italian cooks emphasize color and contour in addition to flavor and texture, but it is not. The Italian sense of color and shape dominates their lives in many ways: the planning of a garden, the arrangement of vegetables and fruit in the open markets all over Italy, the way a meal is presented in the trattorias and restaurants and in their homes.

Italian cooking in this country has made major advances. Americans now know a lot more about the range of the Italian kitchen, well beyond spaghetti and meatballs and manicotti swimming in a tart tomato sauce. The food revolution of the 70s, thanks to Craig Claiborne, Julia Childs and Alice Waters helped tremendously to create food awareness. Specific Italian food awareness by outstanding teachers, restauranteurs, and food writers such as Lynne Rossetto Kasper, Marcella Hazan, Biba Gaggiano, Giuliano Bugiali, Lydia Bastianich, Mario Batali and others have helped make Italian food the number one cuisine preferred by Americans. I believe the appearance of fresh greens in markets across the country, the importation of many more Italian foodstuffs and the enlightened marketing practices of U.S. supermarkets which now feature a greater variety of Italian olive oils, cheeses, vegetables, herbs, condiments, and more, give the entire realm of Italian cooking a major push forward. Just look at the fresh Portobello and cremini mushrooms, Italian eggplant, broccoli rape, radicchio, curly endive, escarole and arugula in the supermarket bins (mostly sold fresh and loose — not shrink-wrapped). All of these means the full joy of Italian home cooking is within one's reach.

If you've been to Italy, this book will help you recreate some of your eating experiences there, and hopefully offer you some others. If you've not traveled there, read the introductory material before each recipe and hopefully, you will be transported there as you cook an Italian meal, here in your kitchen in the U.S. The goal of this book is to present simple Italian pleasures, fresh, fragrant and flavorful food from the joyful Italian table to yours in America. .

Joe Famularo
Key West, Florida

Chapter I

ANTIPASTI

*A*ntipasti means "before the meal", not "before the pasta" as is commonly thought. Italy, often thought of as the land of *"abbondanza"* – meaning "plenty, abundant, or bountiful" has also a measured pace of life that lends itself to small dishes eaten casually. Sometimes these may be midmorning snacks or *"sputini"* as the Italians call them. If a small plate of food comes in the afternoon hours, it's a *"merende"*. Most small dishes of food are known to us as antipasti and this small plate of food is the first course of a meal served in individual portions at the table or as a series of them grouped on a buffet. Antipasti can be a simple appetizer – melon or figs with prosciutto, or prosciutto by itself, fresh tomatoes with mozzarella and basil, anchovies with roasted peppers. It may include a squid salad, grilled or pickled vegetables, marinated olives, pie slices of omelets, called *"frittate"*, usually served at room temperature, zucchini or onions stuffed with meats, fish, or other vegetables and most surely homemade breadcrumbs with herbs and good olive oil. If you are preparing a "heavy" meal, think of a lighter antipasto, and remember that you can enjoy any of those presented here by them.

CAPONATA
Caponata

Serves 12

I am always amazed when by accident I learn something new. Such is the case with the Sicilian specialty dish of caponata, one of my favorite things to eat. Each Sicilian friend in the United States and in Italy claims to have the best way of preparing this dish. I have enjoyed it in each of their fashions, until one day in Palermo, I took a wrong turn walking and stumbled upon a small trattoria "Al Cancelletto Verde" – the green gate. It is located north of via Vittorio Emanuele in a toney shopping area known as Ruggiero-Settima.. This caponata was light, fresh, and not dark and heavy as some people prepare it. I was told by the owner that the" secret" is to sauté the eggplant cubes and set them aside. The onion, celery (after pre-cooking it), capers, tomatoes, oil, vinegar, sugar are then sautéed and combined with the eggplant after all the cooking is done. It may be served as an appetizer, (especially delicious on small pieces of toast), as a condiment to chicken, pork, beef, lamb, or scrambled eggs.

2½ pounds eggplant, peeled and cut into 1-inch squares
vegetable and olive oils (¾ vegetable; ¼th olive oil)
1 large onion, peeled and chopped
6 ribs celery (do not use outer stalks), cut into 1-inch pieces, steamed to pre-cook them
3 cloves garlic, minced
2 cups homemade – tomato sauce, see page 24
1-1/3rd cups green olives, pitted and halved
½ cup capers, rinsed and drained
½ cup finely sliced basil leaves
1¼ cups red wine vinegar
3 tablespoons sugar

1. Put the eggplant pieces in a large colander and sprinkle with salt. Allow to drain a minimum 30 minutes. Using paper or cloth kitchen toweling, dry the eggplant pieces.

2. Add vegetable and olive oil to a heavy skillet, filling it ½-inch, and heat. Add the dried eggplant and cook over moderate heat 10 to 15 minutes or until browned on all sides. Stir frequently. Drain on paper towels and set aside.

3. In the same skillet, without the eggplant, add the onion and celery and sauté, over medium heat about 10 minutes, stirring frequently. Add more oil if needed. After 8 minutes of cooking, add the garlic, stir, and finish cooking.

4. Stir in the tomato sauce, olives, capers and basil. Add some salt and freshly ground pepper. Bring to boil and add the vinegar and sugar. Simmer over low heat about 15 minutes. The vegetables should be cooked through but not be mushy. Drain off as much liquid as you can. Stir in the eggplant, adjust seasoning, and allow to stand at room temperature until ready to serve. Refrigerate if not ready to be served. When ready to serve, leave at room temperature 30 minutes and sprinkle a little more finely chopped fresh basil over the top.

GRILLED EGGPLANT WITH CAPERS & ANCHOVIES
Melanzane ai capperi

Serves 6

I had eggplant prepared this way since I was a child and have found it or something similar on almost every antipasto table in Italy. My friend, Al Panariello, said he had it in Capri, and I'm sure he did. What I like about this dish besides its flavor, is that it can be made one, two or three days ahead. I often serve it with drinks by putting pieces of it on crostini (dried pieces of bread) dotting with some cheese and heating them in the oven.

To prepare the eggplant:
2 small eggplants (about 3/4 pound each)
1/2 cup extra-virgin olive oil

To prepare the sauce:
6 tablespoons extra-virgin olive oil
3 tablespoons red wine vinegar
1 anchovy fillet
2 cloves garlic (peeled and minced)
4 tablespoons finely chopped Italian parsley
2 tablespoons finely chopped shallots
2 tablespoons drained capers

1. Cut the ends off each eggplant, but leave it unpeeled. Stand each eggplant on end, and cut it lengthwise into the thinnest possible slices. Salt each slice lightly, lay the slices flat in a colander, and allow them to drain 30 minutes. Dry each slice with a paper or tea towel.

2. In a large skillet, heat 2 tablespoons of the oil and sauté the first batch of slices slowly on both sides, until they are cooked through. Test doneness with the tines of a fork — if they go through the eggplant, it is done, but don't allow the slices to blacken (as they will be difficult to roll later). Eggplant absorbs lots of oil, so don't add more oil until ready to sauté the next batch. As you remove each slice, roll it and set aside to cool.

3. Combine the oil and vinegar and the anchovy. Mash the anchovy and dissolve it in the oil. Add the garlic, parsley, shallots, capers, and freshly ground pepper.

4. Place the eggplant rolls in a plastic or glass container with a tight-fitting cover. Pour the oil and vinegar mixture over the eggplant. Cover the container and marinate for several hours or overnight. To serve, it is best to bring this dish to room temperature; therefore, remove it from the refrigerator 1 hour before serving.

FOIE GRAS WITH HAZELNUTS
Fegato D'Oca Con Nocciole

Serves 4

Although we think of foie gras as strictly French, foie gras was an invention of the ancient Romans. And it is a popular dish in Rome today. Customarily, the foie gras is sautéed in butter, then put on top of bread also fried in butter and topped with a sauce that includes pine nuts and raisins. The appetizer below is lightened somewhat by serving it with a light arugula salad and optional slices of Italian bread, not fried. If you'd rather not deal with a fresh lobe of foie gras, use slices of chilled foie gras terrine or mousse, which is offered, in most delicatessens — these, of course are not to be sautéed.

1/4 – cup hazelnuts
3 tablespoons extra-virgin olive oil
1 tablespoon red wine vinegar
4 tablespoons finely chopped chives
1 bunch arugula, trimmed, rinsed and dried
4 cherry tomatoes, halved
1/2-pound foie gras, sliced in 4, see *n.b.*
2 tablespoons butter
4 to 8 thin slices Italian bread, optional

1. Preheat oven to 400 F. Bake the hazelnuts in a pie dish until lightly browned, 4 to 6 minutes. Remove, cool, and chop coarsely.

2. Combine oil and vinegar with some salt and freshly ground pepper in a bowl. Add the chives, arugula, tomatoes and hazelnuts. Toss lightly but well. Distribute among 4 plates.

3. Heat the butter in a skillet and when it bubbles, add the foie gras slices and sauté 2 to 3 minutes each side.

4. Lay a slice of sautéed foie gras on the plates, slightly overlapping some of the salad leaves and serves with thin slices of Italian bread.

Notabene: Some companies sell foie gras in convenient packages of 2 ounces, an ideal amount for an individual serving. See Sources, page 383.

A COUNTRY SPINACH PIE
Torta di spinaci e ricotta

Serves 6 to 8 as first course
Serves 4 as main course

This is a crustless tart, simply a blend of spinach, ricotta, onion, basil, and eggs, combined in a food processor and baked until the pie sets. To achieve a creamy tart, the ricotta should be drained as explained below.

1 pound ricotta cheese
12 ounces fresh spinach, stems removed
2 tablespoons butter
½ cup finely chopped onion
½ cup freshly grated Parmesan cheese

2 tablespoons freshly minced basil
¼ teaspoon freshly grated nutmeg
2 eggs, beaten
1 egg white, beaten

1. Wrap ricotta tightly in fine cheesecloth, place in a colander over a bowl, and let it drain, refrigerated, for a minimum of 3 hours, or overnight.

2. Prepare the spinach by thoroughly rinsing, draining, and spinning dry. Chop roughly and set aside.

3. Heat the butter in a small skillet and sauté the onions until opaque, 4 or 5 minutes.

4. Heat the oven to 350°F. Lightly oil a 9-inch glass pie dish.

5. In the bowl of a food processor, combine the ricotta, spinach, sautéed onions, the Parmesan cheese, basil, nutmeg, salt, and freshly ground pepper. Process until smooth. Add the beaten eggs with the extra white and blend a few seconds longer. Pour the mixture into the prepared dish and bake until set, about 40 minutes. To serve, let the pie rest about 5 minutes, loosen the edges with a knife, and cut into wedges. Add the following garnish:

4 to 6 large fresh spinach leaves, shredded, or 8 thinly sliced fresh mushrooms
¼ fresh red or orange bell pepper, trimmed and sliced thinly
1 tablespoon extra-virgin olive oil
1 teaspoon fresh lemon juice

1. Choose either the additional spinach or the mushrooms as a garnish, combine all ingredients in a bowl, and toss well. Add salt and freshly ground black pepper. Put some of the dressed spinach on each serving plate, placing it next to the spinach tart wedge, slightly overlapping.

BACON OMELET WITH PARSLEY
Frittata con gli zoccoli

Serves 6

Frittate are cooked until set on both sides (unlike the manner of the French, who fold them over) in a skillet, and they are always filled with a variety of foods, especially vegetables, herbs, meats, and cheese. They are often served at room temperature or cold, so they are ideal for picnics. They are served flat and cut into wedges or slices.

6 ounces unsmoked bacon (pancetta), cut into very small cubes
4 tablespoons extra-virgin olive oil
6 eggs, room temperature
3 tablespoons finely chopped parsley
¼ cup freshly grated Parmesan cheese

1. Sauté the bacon in 2 tablespoons olive oil in a large nonstick skillet, over moderate heat, until it begins to crisp, stirring frequently, about 5 minutes. Drain and set aside. Leave the skillet as is to receive the egg mixture below.

2. In a large bowl, whisk the eggs and add salt and freshly ground pepper. Add the parsley, cheese, and the cooked bacon.

3. Add 2 tablespoons of oil to the skillet in which you cooked the bacon, heat it, and pour the egg mixture into it. Cook over medium heat until the bottom of the frittata is lightly browned and the top begins to solidify, about 6 to 8 minutes. Place a large plate over the skillet and turn it onto the plate. Slide the frittata back into the skillet and cook several minutes longer. Slide it onto a plate and serve at room temperature.

Nota bene: If you feel unsure about turning over an omelet and returning it to the skillet, turn on the broiler and set the skillet under it to finish cooking. Do not overbroil.

PROSCIUTTO WITH CANTALOUPE
Prosciutto e melone

Serves 8

The reason Tuscan bread is not salted is because it is eaten most often with their salty ham preparations, such as Tuscan prosciutto. Because the ham is salty, it is a good match with the fresh, lemony cantaloupe. It also works well with other melons, such as crenshaw and honeydew. If fresh figs are in season, purple or green, use them instead of the melon—an excellent combination also. Some people like to peel the figs; that is up to you.

2 ripe cantaloupes, skin removed, seeded, and cut into 16 lengths
2 lemons, cut in 4 lengths each, trimmed of core and seeds
24 paper-thin slices of Tuscan prosciutto or Parma ham

1. Arrange 2 melon slices on individual plates and place a lemon wedge to the side. Liberally apply freshly ground pepper over the melon.

2. Drape 3 prosciutto slices over each, being sure to expose at least ½ of the melon. It is all right, and preferred, that the prosciutto lay on part of the plate also. If the melon and prosciutto have been refrigerated, leave at room temperature 15 minutes or so.

PROSCIUTTO WITH ROASTED PEPPER

Prosciutto con peperoni arrostiti

Serves 6 to 8

Italy was traditionally an agricultural country, so almost every rural family kept a pig and cured every part of it, from snout to tail, to provide food for the family throughout the year. In any Italian larder, a range of home-cured hams, sausages, and bacon would be found hanging from the ceiling. In many places, they still hang from ceilings. Not long ago, I met with Claudio Bonzagni, proprietor with his wife, Evelina, of the famous small, luxurious hotel in Ferrara, the Hotel Isabella Duchessa. In his private *salumeria*, he offers friends tasting of homemade salami, prosciuttos, and *culatellos* (very special small hams) accompanied by thick slices of yellow and red bell peppers in vinegar, which he urges you to try with a sprinkling of sea salt and extra-virgin olive oil. Cured ham and vinegar peppers are a classic food combination.

Nowadays, hundreds of different types of hams, cured meats, and sausages are commercially produced, many still using the old artisanal methods. Wherever you travel in Italy, you will find regional variations on the same theme. Slices of cured meats make excellent antipastos. The *affettati* antipasto of sliced hams and salame is a famous Tuscan dish, and it is often served with pickled vegetables (remember Mr. Bonzagni of La Duchessa in Ferrara served peppers in vinegar), which are designed to whet the appetite. Although the variety of these delicacies is infinitely greater in Italy, many are now available in the U.S.United States, especially in shops concentrating on imported foods. See Sources, page 383.

4 roasted red or yellow bell peppers, cut into strips
2 tablespoons extra-virgin olive oil
½ teaspoon balsamic vinegar
1 clove garlic, halved
2 tablespoons butter, softened
8 thin slices white bread
8 thin slices prosciutto

1. Combine pepper strips, olive oil, vinegar, and garlic with salt and freshly ground pepper. Allow mixture to stand 1 hour. Discard garlic.

2. Butter each slice of bread and lay the slices on a flat surface. Arrange 1 prosciutto slice on each piece of bread so that as little of the meat as possible hangs over the edge. Then arrange the pepper strips to cover the prosciutto, again with as little as possible overhanging. Trim the crusts on all 4 sides, cutting through the prosciutto and peppers to make clean edges. Cut each slice in thirds.

3. Serve as an hors d'oeuvre or as a first course. If made ahead, cover with plastic wrap to keep the bread from drying out.

CARPACCIO OF SEA BASS WITH HERBS
Carpaccio di branzino alle erbe aromatiche

Serves 4

The Cipriani's Harry's Bar in Venice is usually credited with the creation of *carpaccio*, a dish featuring thinly sliced raw meat. The term and procedure for carpaccio since its creation has extended itself to fish of all kinds. Here it is made with fresh sea bass. The very fresh sea bass is "cooked" with lemon juice, spiced with fennel, and served with a cream sauce.

1¼ pounds fresh sea bass fillet in 1 piece
4 tablespoons extra-virgin olive oil
5 tablespoons fresh lemon juice
1 cup light cream or half-and-half
Pinch of red pepper flakes
¼ teaspoon fennel seeds, crushed
1 small fresh fennel bulb with feather leaves

1. Slice the fish fillet into 4 pieces and then again into 8. Lay them flat on a dish or small platter and sprinkle them with the oil and 3 tablespoons of lemon juice. Season liberally with salt and freshly ground pepper. Cover with plastic wrap, refrigerate, and marinate for 4 to 5 hours.

2. Pour the cream in a bowl and fold in the remaining lemon juice, pepper flakes, crushed fennel seeds, salt, and freshly ground pepper.

3. Thirty minutes before serving, move the fish out of the marinade, draining it well. Lay the fish on a fresh plate or platter and pour the cream mixture over the fish.

4. Trim the fennel and slice into very thin julienne strips including the light green feathery leaves. Arrange some thin fennel slivers over the fish carpaccio and serve.

VAL D'AOSTA'S FONTINA FONDUE WITH STEAMED VEGETABLES

Fonduta con verdure

Serves 4

This is one of the most delicious Italian cheeses. There are American imitations of this great Italian cheese, but they do not measure up to the original. The real fontina comes from the Piedmont's Valle d'Aosta, a mountainous area south of Switzerland. Fontina looks like Swiss Gruyere; it has a rather light brown crust and comes in large wheels like Swiss cheese, but it doesn't have the network of holes.

Fontina is made from cow's milk and has a fat content of 45 to 50 percent; the flavor is delicate, somewhat fruity, and nutty, and is excellent with the light fruit wines of Piedmont. It is frequently melted, so it is excellent with vegetable and pasta dishes, especially for those which require cheese for stuffing and baking. When fully cured, it is hard, and used for grating. Italians, that is, those who cook at home, bake it with Savoy cabbage and bread because it melts easily and it is a simple, tasty, comforting way to use and enjoy it.

8 small white mushrooms, trimmed, cut in ½
2 cups 1½-inch broccoli florets
2 cups 1½-inch cauliflower florets
8 baby carrots, 2 to 3 inches long
1¼ cups milk, warmed
¾ pound thinly sliced fontina cheese
Freshly grated nutmeg
4 egg yolks
4 tablespoons butter, room temperature

1. Prepare the vegetables and steam the broccoli, cauliflower, and carrots. Set aside the mushrooms; they are to be served uncooked. Steam each vegetable 5 to 10 minutes, depending on thickness of stems, etc. Set aside all vegetables.

2. In the top of a double boiler pan set over simmering water, pour 1 cup milk. Add the fontina and some salt, white pepper, and a pinch of freshly grated nutmeg and stir all the time with a wooden spoon until the cheese has melted and the mixture is smooth.

3. Combine ¼ cup milk with the yolks, stir until combined, and add to the cheese mixture. Add the butter, 1 tablespoon at a time, stirring until the mixture is creamy and smooth. Remove the top pan to keep from cooking more.

4. To serve: Put the fonduta in a small bowl and center it on a large platter. Arrange the mushrooms, broccoli, cauliflower, and carrots in an attractive fashion surrounding the bowl and serve. Or, you can put the fonduta in 4 small bowls, centered on smaller plates, adding some of each vegetable to each plate, and serve individually.

OCTOPUS WITH WINE, GARLIC, OIL, AND PARSLEY
Polipo con olio, aglio, e limone

Serves 4

Octopuses, small and large, are appreciated by Italians all over the boot. Octopus is an ingredient in the well-known fish soup *zuppa di pesce alla gigliese*—meaning "in the style of Giglio," an island off the Tuscan coast where ancient Romans once built vacation villas. In Grossetto, also in Tuscany, it is combined with mussels and cooked in oil. Rome distinguishes its fish chowder by adding octopus, and in Emilia Romagna, octopus is given local dialect names according to size, from the very large to the smallest, which they call *polipetti* or *fragoline di mare*, meaning "sea strawberries," because of their rosy color. In the south, they cook *polipi alla Lucania*, in which the octopus is cooked a long time in a sauce of oil, parsley, and hot red pepper. In Lombardy, octopuses are cooked for salads and antipasti, and I've added some shrimp here more for American tastes (quite frankly, to help bring those Americans who shy away from octopus closer to eating it). In Como and elsewhere, it would be served alone or with squid or cuttlefish.

1 pound shrimp, shelled and deveined
1 small octopus, about 1 pound, no larger, cleaned by fishmonger, or see note below
1 large onion, peeled and chopped
1 large carrot, trimmed and cut into small dice
2 ribs celery, trimmed and strings removed, cut into small dice
4 lemons
⅓ cup plus 2 tablespoons extra-virgin olive oil
¼ cup finely chopped fresh Italian parsley
4 radicchio leaves, rinsed and dried

1. Prepare the shrimp and octopus.
2. Bring a large sauce pan of water (about 3 quarts) to boil, adding about ⅓ of the onions, ⅓ of the carrots, and ⅓ of the celery pieces, a good dash of salt, and 2 of the lemons, cut in 4 pieces each. When it has reached the boil, add the octopus and the shrimp. Remove the shrimp as soon as they are cooked and have turned pink, about 3 or 4 minutes. Do not overcook the shrimp or they will toughen. Remove the shrimp with a slotted spoon and set aside to cool.
3. Continue to cook the octopus and the vegetables until tender, about 45 minutes to over 1 hour. When the octopus is tender, remove it carefully and allow to cool. Discard the liquid and its contents.
4. While the octopus is cooking, heat 2 tablespoons oil in a medium skillet. Add the remaining onion, carrots, and celery pieces, and sauté until tender, about 10 minutes. Transfer to a bowl. Add salt and freshly ground pepper. Add the shrimp. Cut the octopus in small-bite pieces, ½ to ¾ inch, and add to the bowl. Squeeze the juice from the remaining lemon and add to the bowl with the olive oil. Toss lightly. Add the parsley and toss until well mixed.

Check for salt and pepper seasoning, and adjust the lemon and oil flavoring to your liking.

5. If individual servings are to be made, spoon some of the antipasto on a radicchio leaf, or put the radicchio leaves on a platter and spoon antipasto into them.

Nota bene: Most fish shops sell octopus pre-cleaned. If it isn't, ask your fishmonger to do it for you. If the answer is no, then you can prepare it yourself. Invert the octopus by turning it inside out, as you would a swimsuit. Remove the beak and the viscera from the mouth, and also the ink sac. Rinse it very well under cool, running water. Luigi Miroli, in Portofino, told me that there is a little trick to tenderizing octopus—after cleaning it, put it into boiling water, holding it by its mantle. Count to twelve and remove it. Do this two more times before adding it to the sauce pan as in step two above.

ROASTED PEPPER AND EGGPLANT PUREE APPETIZER

Purea di melanzane e peperoni

Serves 4 to 6

This delicious puree may be served in two ways: first, some of it may be put in an attractive bowl, surrounded by cucumber slices, and served as a dip. Or it may be served as a first course. On individual plates, put about a tablespoon of finely sliced spinach leaves on individual plates. Add 4 cucumber slices to each, and top each slice with ½ teaspoon of the puree. Add salt and freshly ground pepper.

1 medium eggplant
2 cloves garlic, halved lengthwise
2 red bell peppers
¼ teaspoon fennel seeds
4 tablespoons extra-virgin olive oil
2 tablespoons fresh lemon juice
12 to 16 thin slices of cucumber
4 tablespoons thinly sliced fresh spinach for garnish

1. Preheat the oven to 425°F. Make 4 knife slits into the eggplant, overall, and tuck in the garlic deeply. Grease a baking sheet and place the eggplant on it. Bake until the eggplant is soft, about 25 minutes.

2. Place the peppers directly on the grill or under a broiler and roast, turning, until the skins are blackened all over and the peppers are soft and cooked. Rinse them under running warm water to remove the charred skins. Remove the cores and seeds. Pat dry with paper toweling.

3. Toast the fennel seeds in a dry skillet until fragrant. Crush them in a mortar with a pestle, or put them on a counter and run a rolling pin over them.

4. Peel the eggplant and put the flesh in a food processor. Add the peppers, crushed fennel seeds, and salt and pepper to taste. Puree the mixture. While the motor is running, trickle in 4 tablespoons oil, which will be absorbed as in making mayonnaise. Add more oil, by tablespoon, if needed. Add the lemon juice, process briefly, and turn the puree into a bowl. Serve warm or cold on thin slices of cucumber.

SHRIMP AND SMOKED SALMON IN A SWEET AND SOUR SAUCE

Involtini di gamberi e salmone in salsa agrodolce con dadolada di legumi

Serves 4

Fresh lemon juice must be used. The shrimp can be cooked ahead by a day, dried carefully, and refrigerated. Sweet and sour sauces are particularly prevalent in this region of Italy—the sauce may be made ahead, but do not apply it to the dish until it is ready to be served.

1 pound large shrimp (16 to 20 count)
2 tablespoons fresh lemon juice
4 thin slices of smoked salmon, each large enough to make a cornet
1 clove garlic, coarsely chopped
⅓ cup white onion, coarsely chopped
1 teaspoon prepared mustard, Dijon type
3 tablespoons herbed vinegar
1 cup extra-virgin olive oil
1 teaspoon sugar
1 tablespoon cooked small green peas
1 tablespoon cooked baby corn niblets
2 tablespoons finely chopped fresh chives

1. Bring 4 cups water to boil in a medium sauce pan, add some salt, and put in the shrimp. Let the water come back to a boil, and cook until the shrimp turn pink, 2 to 4 minutes. Remove from the heat and add some cold water to stop cooking. Drain the shrimp, peel, devein, place in a small bowl, and toss with the lemon juice.

2. On individual plates, arrange a piece of salmon around 2 cooked shrimp, wrapping the salmon around them in cornet fashion (like a small ice cream cone). Add more shrimp as if coming out of the cone.

3. Put the garlic, onion, mustard, vinegar, 2 tablespoons of the oil, and the sugar in the food processor, and pulse to a count of 8. Pour remaining oil through the food tube while the motor is on. Add salt and freshly ground pepper. Stir in the peas and the corn. Do not refrigerate the sauce if using the same day.

4. Spoon some of the sauce on the shrimp in a flowing effect and dot with a sprinkle of chives.

ASPARAGUS WITH OIL, VINEGAR, AND HARD-BOILED EGGS ON RADICCHIO
Asparagi alla bassanese

Serves 4

Bassano del Grappa is a town in the Veneto that is known for its fat asparagus. The eggs here are boiled and worked into the sauce, and this is why it is called *alla bassanese*—Bassano style. Also, it is quite popular in Italy to fry eggs and lay them atop cooked asparagus with a little butter and cheese—this, in itself, can make a good lunch.

1 bunch fresh asparagus
2 hard-boiled eggs, chopped
3 tablespoons white wine vinegar
½ cup extra-virgin olive oil
1 head radicchio, preferably long Treviso style, or rounded head
2 tablespoons finely chopped white onion

1. Break each asparagus stalk at the tender point and discard the tougher end. If needed, pare the tender stalk and put into cool water. Steam them standing up in an asparagus cooker until slightly al dente, about 10 to 12 minutes. Drain right away. If you don't have an asparagus cooker, improvise by using a coffee pot with the inside parts removed. Dry the asparagus with paper toweling, being careful not to break off the tips. Set aside.

2. Put the chopped eggs into a bowl and add the vinegar. Mash with a fork. Add a little oil and mash more. Add salt and freshly ground pepper. Keep adding the oil and incorporating it until all the oil is used. Set aside.

3. Trim the head of long lettuce by removing any worn or tattered leaves. Cut off the stem end and separate the leaves. Rinse and dry them. If using the rounded head, trim it in the same way. Cut it in ½ and slice each ½ in slivers.

4. To assemble: Lay 1 or 2 long leaves on a plate, or a sprinkle of radicchio slivers. Arrange 5 or 6 asparagus spears on top of the radicchio, with the spears facing in the same direction, and spoon the sauce over the center portion of the asparagus. Sprinkle chopped onion over all. Add more salt and freshly ground pepper as you wish.

PARMESAN CUSTARD TART
Crostata di parmigiano

Serves 6

The eggs and cream are the perfect foil in this tart for the sharp, nutty, flavorful cheese. Its smoothness is only interrupted by the occasional bite of crisped pancetta or bacon. The flaky pastry adds to the richness and mouthwatering quality of the tart.

For the pastry:
6 tablespoons chilled butter, cut into ¼-inch pieces
2 tablespoons chilled vegetable shortening
1½ cups all-purpose flour
4 tablespoons ice water

1. Combine the butter, shortening, flour, and some salt in a bowl. With your hands or a pastry blender, blend until the mixture looks like coarse meal. Add the water 1 tablespoon at a time, toss quickly, and form a ball. If the dough is too crumbly, add another tablespoon of water. If too moist, sprinkle with a dash of flour. Dust with flour and wrap in plastic. Refrigerate for several hours until the dough is firm.

2. Preheat oven to 400° F. Remove the dough from the refrigerator several minutes before rolling it. Press by hand into a circle about 1 inch thick. Lightly dust both sides with flour and roll out to a 12-inch circle.

3. Butter the sides and bottom of a 9-inch tart pan with a removable bottom. Carefully arrange the pastry in it. Roll the rolling pin over the edge to remove any extra pastry. Prick all over the bottom and press a sheet of buttered foil over the dough in the tart pan to help keep the shape of the tart as it bakes 10 minutes. Remove the foil, and cook 2 or 3 minutes longer to brown the pastry. Remove the pan from the oven and lower the heat to 350°F.

For the filling:
2½ tablespoons butter
¼ cup small pieces (¼ inch) pancetta or bacon
2 whole eggs and 2 yolks
1¼ cups heavy cream
¾ cup freshly grated Parmesan cheese

1. Heat ½ tablespoon of butter in a skillet and sauté the pancetta or bacon until crisp. Remove to paper toweling. Discard the fat in the skillet or save for another use.

2. Beat the eggs, yolks, and the cream. Stir in the cheese and a pinch of white pepper.

3. Dot the bottom of the cooked tart shell with the pancetta or bacon and carefully pour in the cheese mixture. Do not overfill—pour up to ¼ inch of the top of the tart. Cut the remaining butter into small bits and sprinkle over the filling. Bake about 30 minutes, until the custard has firmed and browned. Remove from the oven. After resting for several minutes, remove the cooked tart from the tart pan. Serve hot, in wedges.

STEWED LENTILS WITH DUCK

Lenticchie in umido con filetti di anatra

Serves 8 to 10

In this recipe the lentils will absorb the flavor of the duck as they cook together. But an important part of the recipe requires crisping strips of duck to be added to the top of the dish. Look for the exquisite imported lentils from Umbria, small, medium, or large brown ones. Italian lentils seem to keep their shape better than their American counterparts.

To cook the duck:
2 small duck breasts, boned, with skin, ½ to ¾ pound
2 tablespoons finely chopped prosciutto fat (see note)
1 tablespoon butter
1 tablespoon extra-virgin olive oil

To stew the lentils:
1 pound lentils
¼ cup extra-virgin olive oil
1 medium onion, finely chopped
6 fresh sage leaves, cut into slivers and then minced
4 to 6 cups beef broth, warmed
2 cooked duck breasts, see above
2 tablespoons white wine vinegar
¼ cup finely chopped Italian parsley

1. Rinse the breasts and dry well.

2. In a medium skillet, cook the fat until it begins to crisp, 3 or 4 minutes over medium-high heat. Add the butter and oil, and when the butter is melted and begins to bubble, add the duck breasts, skin-side down. Sauté over medium-high heat 4 minutes. Turn and sauté the other side. Remove the skillet from the heat and transfer the breasts to a plate to cool. But be sure to keep the skillet with any liquid in it for a later step.

1. Put the lentils in a colander and, under running water, stir by hand and look for and discard any foreign matter such as stones that may be among them. Rinse well and transfer to a large bowl. Cover the lentils with fresh water and allow to stand 4 or 5 hours.

2. In a medium sauce pan, heat the oil and cook the onions over medium heat until they become translucent, 4 to 5 minutes. Stir in the sage and cook 1 minute, stirring. Drain the lentils well and add them. Stir well. Add some broth just to cover the lentils. Bring to a boil, lower the heat, cover, and simmer 30 minutes.

3. Cut the duck breasts carefully into very thin julienne strips, as thinly as possible. Take ½ of the strips and cut them into fine dice. Set aside the remaining duck strips, covered with plastic. Add the diced duck and the vinegar to the pan with the lentils and continue cooking until the lentils are tender, another 30 minutes. The total cooking time for the lentils should be about 1 hour, but it is best to taste a few to test for doneness. When the lentils are done, the liquid should have been absorbed. Add some salt and freshly ground pepper.

4. Reheat the skillet in which you cooked the duck breasts and add the remaining julienne of duck. Over very high heat, stir them in the skillet to crisp them. To serve, spoon some stewed lentils on individual plates, or put some in a bowl or platter, and arrange some crisped duck pieces on top. Sprinkle with parsley.

Nota bene: Anyone who sells prosciutto will give you some of its fat. Just ask for it to be cut off the whole piece of prosciutto. Two tablespoons chopped fat is about one-half ounce.

GRILLED ASPARAGUS AND PARMA HAM SALAD

Insalata di asparagi alla griglia con prosciutto di Parma

Serves 6

Italy is famous for its prosciutto crudo (salted and air-dried ham that needs no cooking), and the most famous is the prosciutto di Parma. The cognoscenti explain that the pigs in this area are fed mostly on the whey from the Parmesan cheese-making process. This makes the flesh sweet and rather mild. The pigs never roam outdoors, as they are kept in sheds to grow them fat and tasty. These hams are made from the hindquarters and dried at least one year and often up to two. Law protects the production of Parma hams to the area between the Baganza and Tara Rivers, where the air and humidity levels are considered near perfect for drying and curing. Some people think the San Daniele hams from the Friuli region (north of Venice) are as good or better, although a bit pricier because of smaller production.

Most rural families in Italy still keep a pig and cure every part of it to provide food through the year. Cured hams, pancetta, and sausages still hang in their larders. Today, of course, many of these products are produced commercially, often using the tried-and-true artisanal techniques.

One of the most typical antipasto dishes in Italy is a plate of sliced cured meats served with pickled vegetables to whet the appetite. When I was in Ferrara, a neighboring town of Parma, my hosts Claudio and Evalina Bonzagni, owners of the famed Hotel Duchessa, offered tasting of their homemade salami, prosciutto, and *culatello* (a small ham) in their private *salumeri* (larder for keeping their cured products), served with thick slices of yellow and red peppers in vinegar with a sprinkle of sea salt and extra-virgin olive oil. A memorable taste experience. This simple asparagus and Parma ham salad brings this part of Italy to you. There is nothing like Parma ham, but if you can't find it, use Black Forest ham instead.

2 pounds fresh asparagus
1 teaspoon sugar
4 tablespoons fresh lemon juice
¾ cup extra-virgin olive oil
2 scallions, finely chopped
1 tablespoon mustard, Dijon type
3 tablespoons red wine vinegar
⅓ cup finely chopped Italian parsley
6 cups baby lettuces
2 small bunches arugula
6 tablespoons freshly grated Parmesan cheese
1 pound thinly sliced Parma ham

1. Peel the lower parts of the asparagus stems with a vegetable peeler and test for the tough part of the stem by bending the asparagus. Cut off tough ends (opposite the tips) and discard. Blanch the asparagus for about 3 minutes in a sauce pan filled with enough water to cover them and into which has been added the sugar and ½ the lemon juice. Drain immediately to stop cooking the asparagus.

2. To make the dressing, combine ½ of the olive oil, remaining lemon juice, scallions, mustard, vinegar, and pepper. Mix well and set aside.

3. Prepare the grill or the broiler. Combine the partially cooked asparagus and the remaining oil and toss lightly so the asparagus are covered with oil. If using the grill, place the asparagus directly on the grill and grill approximately 2 minutes per side. If using the broiler, arrange the asparagus on a cookie sheet with sides and broil for 2 minutes; turn the asparagus and broil 2 minutes longer.

4. Just before serving, add the parsley to the lettuce and arugula leaves, toss with the dressing, and divide among 6 plates. Arrange the warm asparagus over the lettuce. Sprinkle Parmesan cheese over each plate. Top with slices of ham, sprinkle over all with fresh ground pepper, and serve.

PARMA HAM, MORTADELLA, AND PICKLED VEGETABLES

Prosciutto di Parma, mortadella, e verdure sott'aceto (giardiniera)

Serves 4

Mixed pickled vegetables are sold packed in olive oil and vinegar, both in Italy and across the United States. Often, the name on the jars in the United States is *giardiniera*, and the mixture includes an assortment of vegetables: zucchini, eggplant, onions, artichokes, carrots, celery, and peppers.

4 thin slices of Parma ham
4 thin slices of mortadella
¾ cup pickled vegetables

1. Lay a slice of Parma ham, without folding it, across ½ of a plate. Fold the mortadella slice in 2 or 4 (depending on its size), as you would a crepe, and place it along side the ham. Put a spoonful of the vegetables where the meats meet. Repeat this on other plates.

ANTIPASTI

THE PASTA STARS OF ITALY WITH TWO SAUCES
Stellette d'Italia col due salse

Serves 4

This is the light and charming pasta dish enjoyed in the Spoleto restaurant Appollinare, described above. It is served as a *primi piatto*. This dish has been adapted from the original recipe given to me by Andrea Scotacci, owner of the restaurant and a very creative cook. A fresh pasta is made, called *frascarelli*, using two pounds of white flour with five eggs and salt (this is enough for twelve people, but Andrea prefers making it in large quantities as he can use it over several days). He combines these ingredients, as in making pasta, and puts the dough into a large, stainless, flat steel pan, called an *acciaio*, whose bottom has small holes in it. The dough is rubbed by the palm of the hand in a circular movement to make ricelike forms. These are cooked in boiling water and will rise to the top rather quickly. They are removed with a slotted spoon and put in cold water for several minutes. They are drained and stirred with a little oil.

What is unusual about this dish is that the pesto sauce is put on the plate first, then covered with pasta, then topped with tomato sauce, Parmesan, and a light sprinkle of Umbrian oil. As the pasta is eaten and parted by a fork, the vivid green pesto at the bottom comes as a pleasant surprise of colors in celebration of the Italian flag. The taste is divine.

In winter, lamb is an added ingredient in the tomato sauce. "We are greatly influenced by the cooking of Rome," explains Andrea about adding lamb. One needs special equipment for this pasta, but the same end result can be achieved by using a very small type pasta, such as stellette, a pasta sold in boxes in most supermarkets in theUnited States; it is a popular pasta for children, who like it in chicken broth here and in Italy.

½ cup Umbrian pesto, see below
½ cup tomato sauce, see below
½ pound pasta stars, cooked al dente
⅓ cup freshly grated Parmesan cheese
¼ cup finely chopped scallions
Sprinkles of Umbrian olive oil

To make the pesto:
1 cup fresh basil leaves, tightly packed
⅓ cup pine nuts
2 large cloves garlic, coarsely chopped
½ cup Umbrian extra-virgin olive oil
(No cheese is used in Umbrian pesto)

1. Combine the basil, pine nuts, garlic, and 4 tablespoons of the oil in the bowl of a processor. Process to a count of 6.

2. Continue to process and immediately add the remaining oil. Add some salt to prevent discoloration of the pesto. If too thick, thin with a tablespoon or 2 of hot water. This entire process should not take more than a couple of minutes. Transfer to a small bowl and set aside, at room temperature.

To make the tomato sauce:
⅓ cup Umbrian extra-virgin olive oil
3 tablespoons butter
½ cup finely chopped onion
⅓ cup finely chopped celery
⅓ cup finely chopped carrots
2 pounds ripe plum tomatoes, or 2 cups canned Italian plum tomatoes, put through a food mill
½ teaspoon sugar

1. In a large skillet, heat the olive oil and butter until bubbly. Add the onions, celery, and carrots, and sauté 10 minutes over medium heat until the onions become opaque and the other vegetables begin to turn color. If the vegetables begin to scorch, turn the heat to low.

2. Add the tomatoes to the skillet with the sugar and add about 1 teaspoon salt. Cook uncovered at a bare simmer 30 minutes. The sauce should simmer, not boil. Remove from the heat.

To assemble the dish:

1. Place 4 plates on a work surface and on each, in the center of the plate, put 2 tablespoons of pesto. Spread the pesto with the back of a spoon to create a 4-inch circle.

2. Spoon the drained pasta over the pesto. Then top with 2 tablespoons of the tomato sauce, sprinkling some cheese and sliced scallions over all. Sprinkle a little olive oil over all, and serve right away.

GRILLED BREAD WITH OIL
Bruschetta

Serves 4

Once a poor man's dish, grilled garlic bread has become even more popular now that it is called by its Italian name, *bruschetta*, which comes from *bruscare*, meaning to roast over coals. I still like to grill the bread over a charcoal fire or a gas-fired grill, though it is much easier to broil it. Bruschetta is always made with fresh garlic, even when the bread is not roasted over coals. Ideally, bruschetta should be made with *pane integrale* (Italian whole-wheat bread), which is now available in many specialty food shops, not just Italian bakeries.

4 slices (each 1 inch thick) Italian bread, preferably whole-wheat
2 large cloves garlic, peeled and cut in ½
2 tablespoons extra-virgin olive oil

1. Preheat the grill or broiler.

2. Place the bread slices on the grill or broiler rack and grill until crisp and golden brown, 1 to 2 minutes per side.

3. Rub the cut side of the garlic over 1 side of each piece of toast, preferably the side that last faced the heat source.

4. Carefully brush the oil liberally over the garlic side of the toasts. Sprinkle with salt and pepper and keep warm until ready to serve, no more than 1 hour.

HOT ANCHOVY, MORTADELLA, AND FONTINA CANAPES
Stuzzica apetito (o assaggini)

Serves 4

This appetizer's common name, *stuzzica apetito*, comes from the expression *stuzzicare a'appetito*, which means to stimulate the appetite, and it does that exactly. These are really fun to make, and you can serve them as family and friends are enjoying a pre-dinner glass of wine.

8 thin slices white bread, preferably Pepperidge Farm's Very Thin White Bread
6 anchovy flat fillets packed in oil, drained, and sliced lengthwise
4 thin slices fontina cheese
4 thin slices mortadella
¾ cup olive oil
3 eggs
3 tablespoons heavy cream
1 tablespoon water
3 tablespoons freshly grated Parmesan cheese

1. Place 4 slices of white bread on a flat surface and arrange 3 anchovy strips on each. Cover the anchovies with a slice of fontina and then add a slice of mortadella. Don't fret if the meat and cheese overhang the bread a bit (if they overhang too much, fold over the meat or cheese into the "sandwich." Liberally add some freshly ground pepper and cover with the 4 remaining slices of bread.

2. With a sharp knife, trim the edges of the bread. Cut each sandwich into 4 triangles—easily done by cutting from southeast to northwest corners, then reversing and cutting from southwest to northeast corners.

3. Add the eggs, cream, water, and Parmesan in a bowl and whisk to combine them. Heat half of the oil in a large skillet.

4. Dip each small sandwich in this batter and fry them until browned all over. If you want to test for the proper heat of the oil, add a drop or 2 of the batter into it—if it sizzles quickly, the oil is hot enough. Move quickly to dip the sandwiches into the batter and to add them to the skillet. As they brown, remove them to paper toweling to drain. Heat remining oil and fry the remaining sandwiches.

5. These should be served soon after cooking. They may be passed during a cocktail or refreshment time, or 4 sandwiches can be plated and served at the table with a parsley sprig in the center of each plate as a first course.

BREAD TOASTS WITH TRUFFLES
Crostini al tartufo

Serves 12

Probably the most noteworthy food produced in Umbria is the truffle. Most people think of truffles as white (since white truffles are only found in Italy), which are a Piemontese specialty. However, the Umbrian truffle is black and very tasty. It is for sale all over Umbria, mostly packed in brine in small and larger jars. Truffles are an easy item to carry home. Spoleto and Norcia are the two major producers of Umbrian truffles. In Italian, the word "truffles" is *tartufi*, and this is often confused with another Italian term, *trifolati*—this is a term applied to any dish that is quite rich, such as kidneys or mushrooms or a combination of both. The derivation of the term is simply a tribute to the truffle meaning richness. Here is a simple way to get the essence of Umbria's truffle and still keep the cost within the family budget.

8 slices fine enriched white bread, toasted and crusts removed
⅓ cup extra-virgin Umbrian olive oil
2 cloves garlic, peeled and halved
1 anchovy fillet
2 small black Umbrian truffles, approximately 1 inch diameter, about 1 ounce, grated
2 tablespoons fresh lemon juice

1. Prepare the bread and set aside.

2. Heat the oil in a small skillet over medium heat with the garlic. When the garlic begins to turn color, mash it a bit with the tines of a fork and then discard the garlic. Add the anchovy and stir to dissolve.

3. Take the skillet off the heat. Stir in the grated truffle. Lower the heat (as low as possible) and put the skillet on for 30 to 35 seconds. The oil must not boil or the truffles will lose their aroma. Remove skillet and add the lemon juice.

4. Brush the oil and truffle mixture over the bread slices. Cut each slice in fourths to make squares and serve.

ANTIPASTI

MARINATED SALMON WITH RHUBARB
Salmone marinato con rabarbaro

Serves 12

Le Tre Vaselle is a posh inn in Torgiano, not far from Perugia, that is owned and operated by the well-known Lungarotti family, famous for their wines and wine museum. The inn's dining room is one place in Umbria that attracts the elite tourist. The food there is remarkable and somewhat expensive. Along with Japanese and German patrons, I remember this particular dish, perhaps because of the rhubarb condiment.

3 pounds salmon fillet, skinned and boned
½ cup extra-virgin Umbrian olive oil
½ cup fresh lemon juice (must be fresh)
1 cup light cream or half and half
Tabasco sauce to taste
Rhubarb sauce, see below
½ cup diced (¼ inch) red radishes

1. Ask your fishmonger to skin and bone the salmon. If he won't, here's how: Place the salmon skin side down on a flat surface. Hold the tail end securely with a cloth towel in your fingers (this makes it less slippery). Place the knife at a 15-degree angle and cut gently under the skin with a sawing motion. As you cut, pull the skin toward you and against the knife. Continue this motion toward the front, making sure you do not cut through the skin. To bone: Keep the salmon flat and run your hand and fingers carefully over the inside side of the fillet—you'll feel the bones. Use a pair of tweezers and pull out each bone. Discard them.

2. Slice the fillet crosswise as thinly as you can. It's easier to do this if the salmon is very cold—put it in the freezer 30 minutes and then slice. Arrange slices in a single layer on a large platter with a little depth. Spoon the oil all over the slices; do the same with 4 tablespoons of lemon juice. Add some salt and freshly ground pepper. Cover with plastic and refrigerate 4 hours.

3. Combine the cream with 2 tablespoons fresh lemon juice. Add salt and Tabasco to taste. Refrigerate until needed.

4. One hour before serving, transfer the salmon slices to a fresh platter, draining them well. Discard the original marinade of oil and lemon. Spoon the cream sauce over the salmon and leave it at room temperature. Serve either on individual plates with a dollop of rhubarb sauce and a sprinkle of red radish dice, or serve the platter as is but add a sprinkle of red radish over the salmon. Serve the sauce on the side.

<u>The Rhubarb Sauce</u>
Don't make this too sweet, as in a dessert. Here, tartness and sharpness are needed to reduce the oiliness of the salmon.

1 pound rhubarb stalks, trimmed and cut into 1-inch pieces
2 large pieces of lemon zest, each 1x3 inches
½ cup of white sugar

1. Put the 3 ingredients in a large skillet. Add ½ cup water and bring to a simmer. Cook, uncovered, stirring frequently, until the rhubarb is tender, about 20 minutes. Remove and discard the zest and allow the rhubarb to cool before sereving with the salmon.

FRESH FENNEL WITH PARSLIED OIL AND VINEGAR

Insalata di finocchi con olio al prezzomolo

Serves 6

Fresh fennel is on view in every supermarket I've been in, but that wasn't always the case. During my college days, friends who visited me at home would look at a fennel head and say, "What a strange piece of celery." Fresh fennel, Florence fennel, sweet fennel, or *finocchio*—call it what you will—will dry out more quickly than celery, so always cut off the stalks (they are great in soups and to flavor roasts) and store the bulbs in plastic in the crisper sections of the refrigerator until ready to use.

3 large heads fresh fennel
½ teaspoon sugar
2 tablespoons red wine vinegar
6 tablespoon extra-virgin olive oil
¼ cup finely chopped Italian parsley

1. Wash and dry the fennel, removing any blemished outer leaves. Cut each fennel in ½. Lay cut side on cutting board and slice each ½ as thinly as possible.

2. Combine the sugar, vinegar, and oil in a small bowl and whisk until blended. Add some salt and freshly ground pepper. Sprinkle the parsley over the fennel, and then pour the oil and vinegar over the salad. Toss lightly but surely to distribute the parsley and dressing over the fennel.

FRITTATA WITH PANCETTA, PASTA, AND PEAS

Frittata con pancetta, pasta, e piselli

Serves 4 to 6

Pancetta is the Italian equivalent of unsmoked bacon. It is rolled slices of pork belly that has been cured in salt and spices to give it a mild flavor. Pancetta can be eaten raw, but it is too fatty for most people's taste. It is probably best known as a key ingredient for the famous spaghetti *alla carbonara*, a pasta dish made famous by the Romans. There is a smoked version of pancetta, and it is sold in thin strips rather than being rolled.

This frittata is utterly charming and delicious. It can be prepared ahead and transported to a picnic. A beet salad with this dish makes a lovely lunch.

1 cup spaghetti broken into 2-inch pieces and cooked al dente
4 eggs, lightly beaten
1 cup freshly grated mozzarella cheese
6 very thin slices pancetta, cut into small pieces and cooked until crisp
1 cup fresh or frozen green peas, lightly cooked
⅓ cup freshly grated Parmesan cheese
3 tablespoons extra-virgin olive oil
2 small cloves garlic, minced

1. In a medium bowl, combine the cooked pasta, eggs, mozzarella, salt, and freshly ground pepper. Mix well and set aside. In another small bowl, add the crisped pancetta, peas, and Parmesan cheese. Toss gently until well combined.

2. In a 9- or 10-inch nonstick skillet, heat the oil over medium heat until hot but not smoking. Add the garlic and sauté 1 minute. Pour ½ the egg and spaghetti mixture into the skillet and top with the pancetta, peas and cheese. Cover with the remaining egg and spaghetti mixture. Turn the heat to medium-high and cook, pressing the frittata down lightly with a spatula. Cook for about 8 minutes, or until the underside is golden brown.

3. Invert the frittata onto a plate, add a few more drops of oil to the pan, and slide it back into the pan. Cook the underside for 5 minutes or until golden brown. If you are hesitant to turn over the frittata or think the contents are still too "runny," put the skillet under the broiler 2 to 3 minutes. Beware if the handle is made of wood; if so, wrap a piece of foil around it. Serve warm or let cool for later.

MARINATED CANNELLINI BEANS WITH OREGANO AND CRISP SALAMI
Cannellini con origano

Serves 6

If you are in Italy in summer or fall, you will surely see all kinds of beans in their pods. But you will also see dried beans as you do in this country. When you buy them dried, always check the date of sale on the package—if dried beans are old, they're hard, shriveled, and generally not good to look at (and this is before and after cooking them). I find canned cannellinis most acceptable (especially if you don't have time for the presoaking of dried beans), but be sure to rinse them in a colander before using them.

2 cans (16 ounces) cannellini beans or 1½ cups dried
1 teaspoon finely chopped fresh oregano or ½ teaspoon dried
⅓ cup extra-virgin olive oil
½ teaspoon aged balsamic vinegar
6 crisped very thin salami slices, see below
3 small celery hearts, root end trimmed, cut in halves lengthwise

1. If using canned beans, drain them well and put them in a bowl. If using dried beans, put them in a bowl and soak them in lukewarm water overnight, or for at least 8 hours, before cooking. Drain, put them in a sauce pan with water to cover by several inches, and bring the contents to a boil, covered. Lower the heat to achieve a simmer, and cook until the beans are done, 50 to 60 minutes. (Dried beans can always be cooked a day ahead and refrigerated in the cooking liquid until ready for use). Drain the beans and put in a bowl.

2. To the canned or cooked dried beans, add some salt and freshly ground pepper. If using canned, you may not need to add any salt. Stir in the oregano, ¼ cup of the olive oil, and the balsamic. Stir well and leave at room temperature for 1 hour, or longer in the refrigerator. But the dressed beans must be served at room temperature.

3. To crisp the salami slices, arrange the slices on 3 layers of paper towels and microwave on high for 30 seconds, or put them on a baking tray and bake at 350°F for 3 to 5 minutes, depending on thickness of salami slices.

4. To serve, place 3 full tablespoons of dressed beans in the center of a serving plate. Add a celery heart piece alongside the beans. Sprinkle the remaining oil over each serving, being sure to get some on the celery. Take a crisped salami slice and stick it upright into the beans.

PEPPERS WITH ALMONDS, BASILICATA STYLE
Mandorlata di peperoni

Serves 4

This southern Italian pepper dish, because of the sugar and vinegar ingredients responsible for creating the *agrodolce* (sweet-sour) taste, gives credibility to the school of thought that the origins of Italian cooking are Greek and Roman. The foods of those days were salty, probably because of preservation needs, so in their cooking they resorted to disguising the saltiness by adding vinegar and wines, honey, dried fruit, and so on. The *agrodolce* sauces are still popular in Italy, especially with venison, wild boar, and hare, but also with vegetables, as is evident here.

½ cup golden raisins
6 bell peppers, 2 red, 2 yellow, 2 green
2 tablespoons extra-virgin olive oil
½ cup slivered almonds
⅓ cup red wine vinegar
2 tablespoons sugar
2 tablespoons finely chopped fresh Italian parsley

1. Put the raisins in warm water to cover and let steep 15 minutes or so. Drain well.

2. Rinse and dry the peppers. Remove and discard stems, ribs, and seeds, then slice the peppers lengthwise in ½-inch strips. Set aside.

3. Heat the oil in a large skillet and add the peppers. Toss and sauté them over the lowest heat possible 20 minutes.

4. Add the raisins, almonds, vinegar, and sugar. Stir everything in the skillet. Add some salt and freshly ground pepper. Over very low heat, sauté the mixture uncovered for 20 minutes. The peppers should be very well done but not disintegrated. This may be served warm or at room temperature. Add a sprinkling of parsley before serving.

BAKED OYSTERS, TARANTO STYLE
Ostriche in forno, alla Tarantina

Serves 4

The oldest oyster beds in the world are those of Taranto. The Greeks, who established the oyster beds, later to be taken over by the Roman Empire, colonized the foot of Italy. Oysters seem to be grown today as they were in ancient times. These are oysters shipped all over Italy for home and restaurant use, and, as you may imagine, they are prepared in a variety of ways. In Taranto, they are mainly eaten fresh with a squeeze of lemon juice. But the Tarantini also have a simple way to bake them, and here it is.

2 dozen fresh oysters
½ cup finely chopped Italian parsley
½ cup freshly made bread crumbs
2 cloves garlic, minced
Extra-virgin olive oil for sprinkling
2 lemons, cut in wedges, seeds removed

1. Shuck the oysters as described below. Arrange the ½ shells carefully (do not spill any of the juices) in 1 layer in 1 or 2 large baking pans.

2. Preheat oven to 350°F.

3. Sprinkle some parsley over each oyster. Combine the bread crumbs and the garlic. Mix well, and sprinkle this over the oysters. Liberally sprinkle with freshly ground black pepper.

4. Carefully spoon about ¼ teaspoon olive oil into each shell. Bake 10 to 12 minutes. Serve 6 per person with 2 or 3 lemon wedges.

Nota bene: Oysters should be tightly closed and odorless. Fresh oysters should be consumed as soon as possible after buying them. If you need to keep them a short while, store them in plastic bags in the refrigerator, making small openings in the bag (snip with a scissors after tying the bag) to let air inside.

How to shuck oysters
Hold each oyster in your hand, which should be protected by a kitchen towel. The flat side of the oyster should be up and the hinge side should face out. Put the tip of an oyster knife into the hinge—twist carefully to free the top shell. To help do this, run the knife along the underside of the top shell. This will cut the muscle. Do *not* cut the small muscle that holds the edible oyster to the bottom shell, as it will cause the oyster to curl and lose its flavor. Discard the top shell.

Again, try to do this slowly and carefully to avoid losing the juices inside the shell.

GRILLED PEPPERS IN ANCHOVY SAUCE WITH ROASTED OLIVES

Peperoni alla griglia con salsa all'acciuga

Serves 4

In Ischia, an island in the Bay of Naples, a well-known fish dish is *alici all'ischiana* (anchovies, Ischia style). Fresh anchovies are sprinkled with olive oil, fresh lemon juice, and marjoram and then baked. Anchovies in Apulia appear in tart form with bread crumbs, parsley, and olive oil. Anchovies are appreciated in the north of Italy, especially in Liguria, where they stuff the little fish with bread moistened in milk, cheese, eggs, olive oil, and herbs, then bake them. At times, they deep-fry the stuffed anchovies after dipping them in egg and bread crumbs. Other times, they don't stuff them at all—the anchovies are scaled, beheaded, their tails and fins cut off, and just deep-fried. Many Americans are not as enthusiastic about anchovies as their Italian friends. Here is a good way to get them started.

To make the peppers:
2 bell peppers, preferably red and yellow
½ of a 2-ounce can of anchovy fillets, drained
2 cloves garlic
2 tablespoons chopped mixed fresh herbs: oregano, basil, and chives
4 tablespoons extra-virgin olive oil

1. Grill or roast the peppers as directed on page 14. Let cool. Peel and remove the seeds. Cut the peppers into long strips about 1 inch wide. Refrigerate until ready to use, but bring to room temperature before serving.

2. Combine the remaining ingredients in the bowl of a food processor and blend well. Arrange the peppers on individual plates, and spoon some of the sauce over them. Sprinkle freshly ground pepper overall. These may remain at room temperature for about ½ hour.

To make the olives:
½ pound Gaeta olives
2 cloves garlic, sliced
2 small sprigs fresh rosemary
¼ cup dry white wine
Pinch of red pepper flakes

1. Preheat the oven to 400°F. Place the olives in a small ceramic baking pan large enough to hold them in 1 layer. Add the remaining ingredients and bake 15 minutes. Cool before serving.

2. Add 3 or 4 olives to each plate alongside the bell peppers. Put remaining olives in a jar with a cover and refrigerate for another use, but always bring to room temperature before serving.

SCALLOPS AND PANCETTA ON CHICORY HEARTS AND RADICCHIO

Camesante e pancetta fritte su cuori di cicoria e radicchio

Serves 4

Pancetta and bacon are the same cut of pork, except that pancetta is not smoked as is bacon; it is cured in salt and spices, and it is shaped like a salami. As a rule, it is thinly sliced to order. It is available in some supermarkets and almost always available in specialty food shops. If you can't get pancetta, use thinly sliced prosciutto or, as a last resort, thinly sliced bacon.

3 tablespoons raisins
½ cup vin santo (a traditional Tuscan dessert wine) or white wine
2 small heads radicchio
2 small heads chicory
16 large fresh sea scallops
16 small slices of pancetta (or 8 cut in ½ lengthwise) or its substitute, to fit around the curved side of each scallop
4 tablespoons extra-virgin olive oil
½ teaspoon finely chopped fresh rosemary
⅓ cup walnut pieces, toasted
4 fresh lemon wedges, seeds removed

1. Combine the raisins and the vin santo or wine in a small bowl and allow to stand for 1 hour to plump the raisins. Drain, reserving the wine, and set the soaked raisins aside. Trim the radicchio heads of their first layer of outer leaves, core the heads, and cut them in ½. Slice each ½ very thinly. Remove the green leaves from both heads of chicory to reach the yellowish-white inner hearts. Cut off the stem ends and finely slice the hearts. Set aside.

2. Rinse and dry the scallops. Add some salt and freshly ground pepper to them and wrap a piece of pancetta around each scallop, securing with a toothpick.

3. Heat 3 tablespoons of oil in a large skillet. Add the rosemary and stir, sautéing it about 1 minute. Add the scallops and cook until the pancetta begins to brown. To do this, put the scallops in the skillet on their sides, rotating every now and then, to brown evenly. Also, sauté the scallops on their flat sides. Sautéing the scallops should not exceed 5 minutes, and it is necessary to stay at the stove during this procedure. Transfer the scallops to a dish and set aside for a minute. Do not clean the skillet.

4. Add the remaining oil in the same skillet. Add the radicchio and chicory slices, the walnut pieces, and the raisins to the skillet. Toss constantly over medium-high heat to wilt the greens. If the mixture seems too dry in the skillet, add a teaspoon or 2 of the reserved wine. Sautéing the greens from start to finish should take about 3 minutes.

5. To serve, remove the toothpicks from the scallops. On each of 4 plates, add a portion of the sautéed greens. Arrange 4 scallops on each plate, on top of the greens. Add more salt and pepper and serve with a lemon wedge.

EGGS WITH TUNA MAYONNAISE
Uove sode tonnate

Serves 6

A simple, classic Italian appetizer or first course which by itself will make an excellent light luncheon dish if served with a freshly made green salad. The flavors are very Sicilian—tuna, capers, anchovies, and lemon juice. Yes, you can use prepared mayonnaise, but the dish is noticeably different (and significantly better) if homemade is used.

To make the tuna sauce:
1 can (6 ounces) Italian tuna, packed in olive oil
3 anchovy fillets
2 tablespoons fresh lemon juice
1 tablespoon capers, rinsed well, drained, and dried
¾ cup mayonnaise, see below
6 large eggs, room temperature

1. Put the tuna and the oil it is packed in into the container of a food processor. Add the anchovies, lemon juice, and capers and process until smooth. Transfer to a medium-size bowl.

2. Fold in the mayonnaise and add some salt and freshly ground pepper. Refrigerate for 1 hour or longer, but remove from refrigerator 15 minutes before using.

3. Boil the eggs until they are hard, about 12 minutes. Cool them by running under cold water. Peel the eggs and slice in ½ lengthwise. Arrange them on a serving dish and spoon the sauce over them. If you wish, add more anchovies by cutting some in ½ lengthwise, placing them on top of the egg, and sprinkling more capers on top.

To make the mayonnaise:
Makes about ¾ cup
1 egg yolk, room temperature
1 teaspoon fresh lemon juice
1 teaspoon prepared mustard, preferably Dijon
⅔ cup vegetable oil

1. In a small bowl, large enough to hold while whisking, combine the yolk, lemon juice, and mustard and whisk until well combined. Add the oil a tablespoon at a time, until ⅓ of the oil is amalgamated, then add the remaining oil all at once, whisking all the time. Whisk until smooth, cover with plastic wrap, and refrigerate until ready for use.

SOUPS

*I*talian cuisine is among the richest and most imaginative in the world. The same spirited flair for improvisation in the arts is present in Italian kitchens. The cook begins in the market, selecting the freshest ingredients for the meals, including importantly soups, which will be a triumph of colors and flavors. I have felt for a long time that the satisfactions in making and eating a homemade soup are deep and inexhaustible for every member of the family.

In Italy's open-air markets, the aroma of garlicky sausages and sublime smoked hams beckons shoppers. The vividly colored, bountiful tumble of herbs and produce, harvested only a few hours earlier from the warm, fertile valleys, will soon simmer gently in an enormous soup pot in a snug kitchen where a garland of hot red peppers hangs drying nearby.

Italians say, *"La zuppa fa sette cose."* This means, "Soup does seven things." It quenches your thirst, it satisfies your hunger, it fills your stomach, it aids your digestion, it makes your teeth sparkle, it colors your cheeks, and it helps you sleep. If this is true, and I believe it is, who wouldn't welcome a bowl of good homemade soup with Italian freshness and flavor? There is nothing more satisfying to make, to eat, to enjoy. How wonderful to reheat, after flavors have blended more so, and serve again. Soup is a comfort food, above all else. All people, not just Italians, feel better for eating soup.

EMILIA MASTRACCI'S ROMAN MINESTRONE
Minestrone all' Emilia

Serves 4, two times

Each region, each city, each village, each person has a unique version of this famous, classic soup. For example, in Milan, you'll find potatoes, zucchini, cabbage, peas, rice, and red kidney beans. In Emilia-Romagna, the beans are white and fresh green beans are added, and the rice is left out. In Piedmont and other northern areas, the inclusion of rice is traditional, but you'll find that Umbrians and Tuscans are wedded to beans, and plenty of them, rather than rice. The minestrone made in the south of Italy are flavored with oil, garlic, and tomatoes, and, more so than not, pasta is added. Fresh herbs predominate in these soups in the Italian Riviera. The Roman preparation is based on beef broth, cooked beef (especially if any is left over), red beans, red wine, and pastina, a tiny pasta we used to call baby food.

¼ cup finely chopped pancetta or bacon, about 1 ounce
2 medium onions, cut into ½-inch dice
2 large cloves garlic, minced
1 can (15½ ounces) red kidney beans, drained and rinsed under fresh water
8 cups beef broth
¼ cup extra-virgin olive oil
2 large carrots, peeled and thinly sliced
3 medium potatoes, peeled and cut into ½-inch cubes
1 small zucchini, scrubbed and cut into ¼-inch slices
1 rib celery with leaves, thinly sliced
1½ cups thinly sliced cabbage
1 cup dry red wine
1 can (14½ ounces) plum tomatoes with juice, seeded and chopped
2 tablespoons finely chopped basil or 1 teaspoon dried
⅓ cup pastina
1½ cups chopped cooked beef (4 ounces rare roast beef)
¾ cup freshly grated pecorino cheese, such as Romana

1. Sauté the pancetta and the onions in a large soup pot over medium-high heat until most of the fat is rendered, about 5 minutes. Add the garlic and cook until lightly browned, about 2 minutes.

2. Add the beans and the beef broth. Bring to a boil, then reduce the heat to a very slow but steady simmer and cook, covered, for 10 minutes.

3. Heat the oil in a large skillet over medium-high heat. Add the carrots, potatoes, zucchini, celery, and cabbage and sauté, stirring several times, until the vegetables brown a bit, about 10 minutes. Transfer these vegetables to the soup pot, then add the wine, tomatoes, and basil, and cook, uncovered, to cook off some of the wine, about 30 minutes.

4. Stir in the pastina and the cooked beef. Add salt and freshly ground pepper to taste and cook, partially covered, until the pastina is softened, 10 minutes. Serve with pecorino.

ASPARAGUS AND LEEK SOUP WITH CRUSHED AMARETTI AND CRISPED LEEKS

Crema di asparagi e porri

Serves 8

This is delicious. Make it ahead by two days, but add the amaretti and crisped leeks just before serving. This makes an excellent lunch dish if you add a salad with some sliced beets, cooked broccoli, or other vegetable.

4 leeks
4 tablespoons butter
3 or 4 boiling potatoes, peeled and diced in ½-inch pieces to make 2 cups
2 cups asparagus pieces, 1 inch long, using tender parts only
1½ quarts chicken broth
1 to 2 cups light cream or half and half
4 amaretti cookies, crumbed
Oil for deep-frying leeks for garnish

1. Cut the leeks in ½ lengthwise, and wash them well, separating the leaves with your fingers as you rinse them under cool running water, to remove any sand. Drain the leeks, and cut them crosswise into thin slices to make 2 cups thinly sliced. Reserve about ¼ cup for garnish.

2. In a large sauce pan, melt the butter, and sauté the leeks very lightly. Dry the potato cubes and add them to the sauce pan, toss them with the leek pieces, and sauté them 4 minutes. Add the asparagus pieces, the broth, and a little salt and freshly ground pepper. Bring to boil, lower the heat, and simmer 30 to 40 minutes until the vegetables are tender.

3. Put the mixture through a food mill, or rub it through a fine sieve. Return the pureed mixture to the sauce pan and add the cream to achieve a desired thickness. Simmer until the mixture is warmed.

4. To serve, heat some oil in a small sauce pan and fry the ¼ cup leeks until crisp. Remove with a slotted spoon to a kitchen paper towel. Ladle some soup into individual warmed bowls, sprinkle a bit of the crumbed amaretti to the center, and top with a bit of the crisped leeks. Serve right away.

KALE SOUP IN THE TUSCAN STYLE
Zuppa di cavolo nero con crostini

Serves 6

Peasant-style cooking continues to predominate in Tuscany, and it is usually described as "pillars of tradition"—plain, simple, and wholesome—just like this soup. Kale is another green leaf vegetable liked by the Tuscans, and they have told me that the tenderest, tastiest kale leaves are those that have been zapped by frost and cold weather. What is really strange about this soup is that there are no beans in it. But it is made with other essentials, and every ingredient counts. Its flavor depends on the tenderest kale, Tuscany's extra-virgin olive oil, and a generous sprinkling of Parmesan cheese.

1½ pounds fresh kale, thick stems removed
3 cups each beef and chicken broth, or 6 cups mixed broth on page ____
12 thick slices (1½ inches) whole-wheat Italian bread
3 large cloves garlic, halved, for rubbing bread
½ cup Tuscan extra-virgin olive oil
½ cup freshly grated Parmesan cheese

1. Rinse, drain, and thinly slice the kale. Put it in a large sauce pan and add the broth. Bring to a boil over medium-high heat, then lower the heat to a slow, steady simmer and cook, partially covered, until the kale is tender, about 30 minutes.

2. Preheat the broiler. While the kale is cooking, place the slices of bread in a single layer on a broiler tray and place 5 inches below the heat source to toast both sides, approximately 2 minutes per side. Rub both sides of the toasted bread with the garlic halves.

3. Drain the kale, reserving the broth. Carefully dip each toast slice into the hot liquid and quickly put 2 slices into 1 of 6 rimmed soup bowls. Repeat until all toast slices have been dipped and placed in the bowls. Drizzle 1 teaspoon of the olive oil over each toast slice. Add salt and a liberal sprinkling of freshly ground pepper.

4. Spoon some kale over each slice and add a few more drops of olive oil over the kale, adding more salt and pepper. Ladle some of the broth into each bowl and serve. Pass the grated cheese.

THE YELLOW PEPPER SOUP OF CIBREOS IN FLORENCE
Passato di peperoni gialli alla Cibreo (Firenze)

Serves 6 to 8

This soup is an almost indescribably warm and inviting yellow. It was created by Fabio Picchi, a superstar chef and owner, with his wife, Benedetta Vitali, of the famous restaurant Cibreo in Florence. It is one of his signature dishes. Fabio adds milk to smooth out the acidity of the peppers and to give them a more even consistency. In the raw, the peppers should be brightly colored, without wrinkles, and shiny. They should be firm to the touch and feel heavy for their size when you heft one in the palm of your hand. There is a huge outdoor market next to Cibreos, and when you see ripe yellow peppers (the color you see on some palazzi walls), with no streaks of green whatever, you are looking at the peppers used in this soup. The unique garnish of crushed amaretti cookies and grated Parmesan cheese should be sprinkled on top of the soup for quite an intriguing and eye-catching presentation—a superb, visual, tasty treat.

2 tablespoons extra-virgin olive oil
1 medium red onion, cut into ½-inch dice
2 medium carrots, peeled, cut lengthwise in ½, and thinly sliced crosswise
1 medium celery rib, thinly sliced
8 large yellow peppers, stemmed, seeded, and ribs removed, cut into 1-inch pieces
2 pounds potatoes, peeled and cut into ½-inch dice
3 cups canned low-sodium beef broth, or more if needed
1 cup water, or more if needed
2 bay leaves
2 to 3 tablespoons crushed amaretti cookies
2 to 3 tablespoons freshly grated Parmesan cheese

1. Heat the oil in a large soup pot over medium heat. Add the onions, carrots, and celery, and sauté until the onion turns golden, about 5 minutes. Stir often.

2. Add the bell peppers and potatoes, and sauté until lightly softened, stirring often during 5 minutes' cooking. Add 3 cups beef broth and 1 cup water, and don't be alarmed if they don't cover the vegetables. Add a pinch of salt and bring to boil. Reduce the heat to a slow and steady simmer. Cook, partially covered, 20 minutes, or until the vegetables are tender. Remove from the heat.

3. Puree the soup in batches, using a food mill. For a smoother soup, put the puree through the food mill again. Do not use a food processor, as it will pulverize the pepper skins. Return the puree to the pot.

4. Add the milk and the bay leaves and reheat the soup without boiling, or it will lose some of its bright yellow color. Remove the bay leaves and add more salt if you

wish. The soup should be thick, but you may thin it with more broth and/or water, but only ½ cup at a time. In Florence, this is a thick soup.

5. Ladle the soup into warmed bowls and top each with a scant teaspoon of crushed amaretti cookies to 1 side and a scant teaspoon of Parmesan cheese to the opposite side.

POACHED EGGS AND PARMIGIANO IN BROTH

Zuppa alla Pavese

Serves 6

This is a famous Italian soup created in Pavia, a city in Lombardy, in 1525 for a king who was ruling the region at the time.

Some people poach the eggs before adding them to the soup so that they can be sure the eggs are cooked. Others place the eggs raw into the bowl; if the broth is boiling hot, the eggs will cook in it as long as the broth is gently poured over the eggs to avoid breaking the yolks. I think you will find it easier to poach the eggs first. Remember, butter takes over for oil in Lombardy, so the soup is enriched by butter, not oil, and butter is used to brown the bread.

4 tablespoons (½ stick) butter, melted
12 slices Italian bread, each 1-inch thick
4 cups each beef and chicken broth, or 8 cups mixed broth, page 176.
1 teaspoon distilled vinegar
6 eggs
6 tablespoons freshly grated Parmesan cheese

1. Preheat oven to 350°F. Butter all the bread slices on both sides and place them on a baking sheet. Toast the bread in the oven, turning once, until golden on both sides, about 10 minutes total.

2. Bring the 2 broths to boil in a medium-size sauce pan over medium heat. Cover the pan, lower the heat, and simmer.

3. In a nonreactive skillet, add water to fill ¾ full. Add the vinegar and bring to a boil. Lower the heat to simmer. Break an egg into a saucer and slip it into the skillet. Add 2 more eggs. Poach 5 minutes or until the whites are set and the yolks semisoft. Carefully remove the eggs with a slotted spoon to 3 layers of paper towels. Repeat this for the other 3 eggs. Then trim off the ragged egg white, leaving ½ to 1 inch of white around each egg.

4. Place 2 slices of the toasted bread into 6 warmed wide bowls, arranging the slices side by side. Place a poached egg over the bread slices and sprinkle with 1 tablespoon grated cheese. Carefully ladle the hot broth into the soup bowls. Add salt and freshly ground pepper.

LENTIL SOUP
Zuppa di lenticchie

Serves 4

The flavor of the onions, carrots, and celery, and of the oil and butter, will be absorbed by the lentils to make a delicious-tasting soup. This soup seems to taste better after it sits for a day or two.

1 tablespoon extra-virgin olive oil
3 tablespoons butter
½ cup finely chopped onions, carrots, and celery (about 3 tablespoons of each)
2 tablespoons finely chopped prosciutto or pancetta
1 large clove garlic, minced
1 cup canned Italian plum tomatoes with juice, seeded and chopped
1 cup lentils, picked over
3 to 4 cups combined beef and chicken broth
6 tablespoons or more freshly grated Parmesan cheese

1. Heat the oil and 1 tablespoon butter in a medium sauce pan over medium heat. Sauté the onion, carrot, and celery, stirring often, until the onion begins to turn golden, about 5 minutes.

2. Add the prosciutto or pancetta and sauté until lightly browned, 2 minutes. Add the garlic and cook 1 minute longer. Add the tomatoes and continue cooking 10 minutes.

3. Add the lentils and 3 cups of broth. Liberally sprinkle with freshly ground pepper. Bring to a boil, then lower the heat to a slow, steady simmer. Cover the sauce pan and cook until the lentils are tender, 35 to 40 minutes. If the soup appears too thick, add some or all of the remaining broth. Remove from the heat and stir in 3 tablespoons of the cheese. Serve and pass more cheese.

A NOTED CHEF'S VEGETABLE SOUP FROM THE RIVIERA

Zuppa con verdura alla Genovese

Serves 6

Chef Gilberto Pizzi, who created this recipe, uses fresh beans, which are best, but if this is not possible, use frozen.

4 ounces fresh lima beans, or frozen
10 cups water
7 tablespoons extra-virgin olive oil from Liguria
4 medium potatoes, peeled and cut into ¼-inch dice
3 small zucchini, scrubbed and cut into ¼-inch dice
2 medium carrots, peeled and cut into ¼-inch dice
2 medium celery ribs with leaves, thinly sliced
2 large, fresh, ripe tomatoes, peeled, seeded, and cut into ¼-inch dice
½ medium onion
4 ounces fresh green beans, trimmed and cut into ½-inch pieces
½ cup fresh or frozen green peas
1 large leek, white part only, cut in ½ lengthwise, well rinsed, and thinly sliced crosswise

For garnish:
2 or 3 teaspoons extra-virgin olive oil from Liguria
12 small leaves fresh basil, chopped

1. If using frozen limas, thaw and set aside. Bring the water, the oil and a pinch of salt to boil in a large pot over medium-high heat. Add the potatoes, zucchini, carrots, celery, tomatoes, onion, green beans, peas, leek, and the lima beans. Return the liquid to a boil.

2. Reduce the heat to a lively simmer and cook, covered, until the vegetables are almost tender, about 25 minutes. Let the soup rest off the heat 15 minutes or so to gain flavor.

4. To serve, ladle into warmed soup bowls. Lightly drizzle some olive oil in the shape of your initial over each serving, then top with a sprinkle of the chopped basil.

ANTIPASTI

PIETRO TECCHIO'S FRESH ASPARAGUS SOUP

Zuppa di asparagi alla Vicentina

Serves 6

This is a lovely soup and can be made with green asparagus only. I like it best served warm with garlic bread, but since it can be made ahead by several days and refrigerated, you might like to try it served cold, or at room temperature.

2½ pounds fresh asparagus, ½ green, ½ white
8 cups broth: 4 chicken, 4 beef, or 8 cups mixed broth, page 176
2½ tablespoons semolina
½ cup freshly grated Parmesan cheese
12 thin slices grilled garlic bread, see page 301

1. Carefully bend each stalk of asparagus and break off and discard the tough end. Using a vegetable peeler, pare the skin on the lower end of the tender stalk and rinse. Cut off the tips and reserve. Repeat with all the stalks. Thinly slice the tender stalks without tips.

2. Bring the broth to boil in a large sauce pan over medium-high heat. Slowly sprinkle the semolina into the broth with 1 hand while stirring all the time with a wooden spoon in the other hand. Cook until lightly thickened, about 10 minutes.

3. Add the sliced asparagus pieces (not the tips) and cook until tender. Once the boil has been reached, lower the heat and simmer. Total cooking time should be about 20 minutes. Add the asparagus tips and cook, uncovered, 5 minutes longer. Add salt and freshly ground pepper.

4. Serve sprinkled with cheese and accompany each serving with 2 slices of the garlic bread.

HOMEMADE TORTELLINI IN BROTH
Tortellini in brodo alla casalinga

Serves 8 to 12

Tortellini are hat-shaped, meat-filled little pasta that are usually served floating in broth. This is one of the most famous dishes of the Emilia region, especially in Bologna at Christmastime. Fillings vary greatly, even in Bologna. Some preparations add ground veal to the pork, some use capon instead of chicken or turkey, and others prefer prosciutto to Parma ham. They are all delicious, but I like this one, which combines pork, chicken or turkey, and Bologna's most famous sausage, mortadella, which is available in the United States.

6 tablespoons butter
2 ounces pork loin, minced
2 ounces chicken or turkey meat, minced
2 very thin slices prosciutto, minced
4 very thin slices mortadella, minced
1¼ cups freshly grated Parmesan cheese
2 large eggs, lightly beaten
Pinch of freshly grated nutmeg
Fresh pasta recipe, see page 104
8 cups broth made up of 4 cups beef and 4 cups chicken

1. Melt the butter in a medium-size skillet over medium heat. Add the pork and chicken or turkey and sauté, breaking up any meat clumps, until the mixture turns golden, about 5 minutes. Transfer the mixture to a food processor.

2. Add the prosciutto and mortadella to the processor and pulse until the mixture resembles medium-size bread crumbs. Transfer the mixture to a large bowl. Stir in ¾ cup of the grated cheese and the eggs. Add a little salt, freshly ground pepper, and the nutmeg.

3. Prepare the pasta. Roll out, then cut the dough into rounds with a 2-inch cutter (you should get about 80 rounds) and keep covered, to keep the pasta from drying out.

4. Add ½ teaspoon of the filling in the center of each pasta round. Fold over to form ½ moons. Press the edges of the ½ moons with the tines of a fork to secure the filling. Bend each ½ moon around your index finger and press 1 end over the other. Set aside.

5. Bring the broth to boil in a large soup pot over medium heat. Add the tortellini, stirring gently to prevent them sticking to each other, and cook until the pasta rises to the top, 2 to 4 minutes. Ladle into warm bowls, dividing the tortellini evenly, and serve with the remaining ½ cup grated cheese.

POTATO AND ZUCCHINI SOUP FROM A NOTED RESTAURATEUR IN BARLETTA
Zuppa di patate e zucchini alla pugliese

Serves 4 plus

When I first described this soup to a good friend, the response was, "Potatoes, zucchini, and water—where is the flavor?" I made the soup anyway since I had enjoyed it with Frank Ricatti, who at the time was in Rome, and I knew it would be delicious. My friend now claims it is one of her favorite soups. Again, sheer simplicity. The little bit of pasta is the binder, and let me warn you not to overcook and disintegrate the potatoes or zucchini—they should be cooked to the point of perfection (tender and keeping their shape) and, when eaten as a soup, they will simply dissolve in your mouth.

4 cups water
6 medium potatoes, peeled and cut into ½-inch dice
6 small zucchini, scrubbed and cut into ½-inch dice
2 tablespoons plus 6 teaspoons extra-virgin olive oil
4 ounces dried vermicelli, broken into 2- to 3-inch pieces
6 tablespoons freshly grated Parmesan cheese

1. Bring the water to boil in a large soup pot over medium-high heat. Add some salt and the potatoes. When boiling again, reduce the heat to a very slow but steady simmer, and cook, covered, 5 minutes.

2. Add the zucchini and return to the boil.

3. Add 2 tablespoons olive oil and the pasta. Stir well, then cook, uncovered, until the pasta is al dente (tender but still firm to the bite) and the vegetables are tender, about 10 minutes.

4. To serve, ladle the soup into warmed bowls, adding a teaspoon of olive oil to each bowl along with freshly ground black pepper and a tablespoon of the grated cheese.

CALABRIAN ONION SOUP WITH POTATOES
Minestra Licurdia

Serves 4

This soup is typical of the Cosenza district, and the term *licurdia* refers to both a soup and a sauce. It is a peasant dish, as is most of the cooking in this region, and here it has been uplifted by the use of butter and chicken broth—originally, the butter would not be used and water would have been used in place of the broth. As the region slowly opens up to tourism, the restaurants and some home cooking are seeing change. This is especially true in the area of Reggio Calabria, where people seem to eat better, probably because the economy is better (thanks to the production of bergamot used in perfume production), and surely because it's closer to Messina, just across the strait, where the art of preparing food is more developed.

1½ pound onions, thinly sliced
1 pound potatoes, peeled, diced ½ inch
6 tablespoons butter
1 tablespoon sugar
6 cups chicken broth, boiling
¼ cup grappa or brandy
4 slices Italian bread, lightly brushed with oil, both sides grilled, rubbed with a clove of garlic, see page 301
¾ cup freshly grated pecorino
4 teaspoons extra-virgin olive oil

1. Prepare the onions and potatoes and set them aside.
2. In a large sauce pan, heat the butter and sauté the onions and potatoes until they take on some color and the onions become translucent, 8 to 10 minutes. Add the sugar, stir, and cook 2 minutes longer.
3. Add the boiling broth, and when it has returned to the boil, lower the heat to a steady, slow simmer and cook, covered, 25 minutes.
4. Add the grappa or brandy and cook 5 minutes over medium heat, uncovered.
5. To serve, add a piece of bread to a soup bowl, pour in some soup, add a spoonful of pecorino to the top, and pour 1 teaspoon of oil over the cheese. Most Italians do this by writing the initial of their first name in oil.

Chapter 2

PASTA

Pasta is the most omnipresent component of Italian cuisine, a remarkable food, made in so many sizes and shapes that even food historians have lost count of the variations.

Until I was a teenager, I didn't know pasta could be bought in a store. In my home, and the homes of friends and relatives, a long wooden pole draped with pasta was as permanent and as important a piece of furniture as the sturdy kitchen table. Like the family's cleavers and knives, the pasta board received special care and safekeeping. Our board had been specially made for us by an Italian carpenter. It was quite thick and heavy, almost four feet square, and on it, my mother rolled out sheet after sheet of pasta, each one lightly folded over and cut into strips or shapes designed to hold delicious fillings. I noticed at an early age that neighbors and relatives compared pasta boards with as much concern and care as they did pasta quality—or automobiles.

Times have changed, yet I am always surprised when some who has invited me for dinner is serving homemade fettucine. What a joy!

This change has been facilitated by the use of an inexpensive pasta machine that does most of the work. If you don't have one, you should consider the purchase of one. Another real change has been the appearance of "fresh pasta" in cool cabinets in most supermarkets. They have improved greatly in quality since being introduced some years ago. Dried pastas, many coming from major Italian pasta manufacturers, are always on the shelves in all grocery shops. I have included here some of my favorite pasta recipes.

Good luck, and be sure to have fun and to enjoy.

PASTA

SWEET MACARONI WITH CHEESE
Maccheroni con la ricotta

Serves 6

It is rare in Italian pasta dishes to add sugar and spices, but that is exactly what gives this Roman dish a special appeal. Romans are people who cannot help but express their character in their cooking, where their inspiration bursts forth. Romans love newly born lamb and pecorino cheese, but there is something else they love from sheep, and that is ricotta cheese. The macaroni/ricotta preparation below is as simple as the combination can get, but Roman individuality offers other ways of pairing these two foods—one example is to mash the ricotta with two egg yolks, two or three tablespoons of pasta water, and a dash of cinnamon powder. No other city in Italy has as many restaurants, *trattorie*, or inns, as Rome. *Alta cucina* didn't fare well in Rome because Romans stick loyally to their traditions.

Since this particular dish is so simple, there's no need to prepare it ahead. You can make this in the kitchen; your family or guests will not wait long.

Nota bene: If you cannot get really fresh ricotta, use the store-bought variety, but instead of using milk in the recipe, use half-and-half instead.

1 pound penne, fusilli, or small rigatoni
1½ cups fresh ricotta
⅔ cup warm milk
3 tablespoons sugar
Several pinches ground cinnamon and some for garnish
¼ cup finely chopped chives

1. Bring a large pan of salted water (be liberal with the salt) to boil, and let it boil rapidly. Add the macaroni and cook according to package directions, usually about 10 minutes, until tender.

2. While the pasta is cooking, combine the ricotta, warm milk, sugar, and cinnamon in a large bowl (large enough to receive the cooked macaroni) and whip together until smooth.

3. Drain the macaroni and add it to the bowl with the ricotta mixture. Toss to coat the macaroni. Divide among 6 plates. Add another dash of cinnamon and top each serving with a sprinkle of chives. Serve right away.

GNOCCHI, ROMAN STYLE
Gnocchi alla Romana

Serves 4

Gnocchi are usually eaten as a first course *(primo piatto)*, but here, for the American table, they are the main course. They are usually made of flour or potatoes, or both, and sometimes may be combined with other foods, such as spinach. The shapes vary from cook to cook, region to region. What makes these gnocchi Roman is that they are made with semolina flour (cooked in milk), with eggs added to make a rich spread of "dough" that is cut into rounds (the squares are creative license), layered with some overlap and sauced with butter and Parmesan cheese and baked. Some gnocchi are called *strangolopreti* (priest-stranglers); others may be shaped small and added to broths or soups, casseroles, and stews. In Italian dialect, *gnocco* (the singular term for gnocchi) means "dumb-head," as one would use "pudding-head" in England or "tete de lard," lard-head, in France. Gnocchi were made in Italy as early as Renaissance times, but they were made with crustless bread. They are made this way—with bread—in the very north of Italy (Trentino-Alto Adige) even today, and they are called *canderli*. But let's have them the Roman way today.

4 cups milk
6 tablespoons butter
Pinch freshly grated nutmeg
1 cup semolina or white cornmeal
4 eggs, beaten
1 cup freshly grated Parmesan cheese

1. Butter 2 cookie trays and set aside.
2. In a sauce pan, combine the milk, 2 tablespoons butter, some salt and freshly ground white pepper, and the nutmeg. Bring to boil over medium heat. Slowly add the semolina *a pioggia*—like soft raindrops, as say the Italians—stirring all the time to prevent lumps from forming. Reduce the heat to low and cook until very thick, thick enough for a wooden spoon to stand in it. Remove from the heat.
3. Add the eggs and ½ cup of the Parmesan and mix well. Spread this mixture on 1 of the buttered cookie sheets, smoothing it off with a wet spatula, making a rectangle ½ inch thick. Place in the refrigerator to firm.
4. Preheat oven 350°F. Cut into rounds, 1½ to 2 inches wide, or in squares, if you wish. Arrange them in a row in the other buttered cookie tray (or large ovenproof platter), slightly overlapping each other. Make a second row until all of them are so arranged. Melt the remaining butter and drizzle over the gnocchi. Also sprinkle the remaining Parmesan cheese over them.
5. Bake 15 to 20 minutes or until golden and the butter is bubbling. Remove from the oven and let rest 5 minutes or so. Then serve them.

SPAGHETTI WITH A LEMON SAUCE
Spaghetti al limone

Serves 4

This is an unusually creative way to prepare spaghetti—it is one of my favorites. The lemon intoxicates the cooked cream that envelopes the pasta strands, and every forkful is delicious.

2 cloves garlic, minced
2 tablespoons butter
1 cup light cream (half-and-half)
1 teaspoon finely minced lemon zest
Up to 1 tablespoon fresh lemon juice
½ pound spaghetti

1. In a large skillet (large enough to hold the pasta when cooked), sauté the garlic in the butter until it just begins to turn color, 2 or 3 minutes.

2. Add the cream and the zest and cook over medium heat, uncovered, 3 or 4 minutes, stirring most of the time with a rubber spatula—the cream should thicken a little. Add salt and freshly ground pepper.

3. Cook the pasta, drain it, and add it to the sauce. Add ½ of the lemon juice, and toss the pasta lightly but well, cooking it 1 to 2 minutes over heat. Taste for lemon flavor, and add more lemon juice if you feel it needs it.

LASAGNA SQUARES WITH BRAISED BROCCOLI RAPE

Quadrati di lasagna con broccoletti

Serves 8

Without question, this is a favorite dish of mine. I make it also by replacing the broccoli rape with fresh ricotta, spiked by a tablespoon or two of freshly grated Parmesan cheese, and adding *besciamella (a white sauce)* and pesto sauces over each serving.

2 bunches fresh broccoli rape
3 tablespoons extra-virgin olive oil
2 large cloves garlic, minced
A pinch of red pepper flakes
24 fresh pasta squares, each about 4 inches square, see page 104
2 tablespoons butter, melted
1 to 1½ cups fresh ricotta cheese
Nutmeg

1. To prepare broccoli rape, wash it well and trim the ends. Remove the strings on the larger stalks as on large celery. Cut the larger leaves in ½ and let them stand in cool water until ready to cook them. Heat 2 or 3 cups of water in a large sauce pan. Add 1 teaspoon salt and bring the water to a rapid boil. Add the rape and cook until just tender; depending on size and freshness of stalks, this may take 5 to 10 minutes. Drain well.

2. Heat 3 tablespoons oil in a large skillet. Add the minced garlic and cook 1 minute. Add the rape and move it around in the oil and garlic. Add the pepper flakes and cook 2 or 3 minutes longer. Remove from heat. Keep warm.

3. Bring water to boil in a large sauce pan. Add a tablespoon of salt just before boiling. Cook the pasta squares until al dente, 6 at a time. After a few minutes, they will rise to the top, and that indicates they are cooked. Using a slotted spoon, remove the pasta, drain well, and place in a large bowl Add the butter to the bowl and stir the pasta to coat it. Repeat this until all the pasta is cooked.

4. To serve, set out 8 plates (shallow bowls with rims are best) and put a buttered square of pasta in each plate. Add a good tablespoon of ricotta to each square and cover each with another square. Put a tablespoon broccoli rape over each and cover again with a pasta square. Add a bit more butter to the top and a sprinkle of nutmeg. Serve at once.

SPAGHETTI WITH PECORINO CHEESE AND BLACK PEPPER IN ROME
Spaghetti al pepe e pecorino

Serves 4 to 6

This dish can be enjoyed in the many excellent trattorias in Rome, and in most Roman homes. Like most other pastas, it makes an easy, yet wonderful one-dish meal with a hearty salad, probably one with some vegetables (steamed broccoli, green peas, steamed zucchini, or sliced red ripe tomatoes and basil dressed with oil, vinegar, and some salt) and some good crusty bread.

Pecorino Romano is probably the best pecorino available, and therefore it is used widely in and around Rome. It is found all over Italy and in the United States (every supermarket I have been into in this country has had block or grated pecorino cheese). I have made this dish with the Sardinian *pecorino pepato*, peppered Pecorino cheese, and it works well also.

1 pound spaghetti
¼ cup pasta cooking liquid
1 cup freshly grated pecorino cheese
Freshly ground black pepper

1. Bring 4 quarts of water to boil and cook the pasta until al dente, 8 to 10 minutes. It is a good idea to check the boxed instructions offered by the manufacturer of the pasta you have chosen to use. Drain the pasta, but reserve 1 cup of the water in which the pasta boiled. Transfer the pasta to a large, decorative bowl and add ¼ of the cup of cooking liquid.
2. Add the cheese and a very liberal amount of black pepper and toss well. If too dry, add more cooking liquid by the tablespoon, but this pasta should be fairly dry. Serve right away with the salad and bread.

Wine Bars in Rome
Wine bars in Rome have proliferated, and one of the early initiators was the wine merchant's shop Bleve, which now offers, in addition to wine, an exciting array of appetizers, pastas, and desserts. Although Rome is known for its *cucina povera* (poor man's cuisine), the number of simple trattorie offering these simple dishes is disappearing, and fancier establishments using more costly ingredients appear to be taking over. Yet, even in these more chic restaurants, there are offerings of simple pasta dishes such as the one presented here. So imagine yourself at the glamorous restaurant Ar Galletto, in the Piazza Farnese, surely one of Rome's most beautiful squares, eating this baked pasta dish while looking at a movie star who has driven up in a silver Mercedes convertible.

BAKED PASTA WITH ZUCCHINI, HERBS, AND TOMATOES

Pasta al forno con zucchine ed erbe aromatiche

Serves 6

5 zucchini, 1x6 inches each
1 medium onion, chopped
2 scallions, thinly sliced
1 celery heart, thinly sliced
¼ cup finely chopped fresh basil
¼ cup all-purpose flour
2 ripe plum tomatoes, cored, finely chopped
6 tablespoons extra-virgin olive oil
1 pound small rigatoni, or penne, cooked al dente
Good pinch of red pepper flakes
1 cup freshly grated pecorino cheese

1. Rinse and dry the zucchini. Cut off the ends and cut in halves to make 1x3-inch pieces. Slice each piece lengthwise into ¼-inch sticks.

2. Preheat oven to 425°F. Combine the zucchini, onions, scallions, celery, and basil in a bowl. Add salt and freshly ground pepper, and sprinkle the flour over all. Toss well. Add tomatoes and toss again.

3. Use 1 tablespoon of oil to coat a 9x13x2-inch baking pan. Transfer vegetable mixture to the pan. Sprinkle 2 tablespoons olive oil over all and bake 10 minutes, stirring 2 times during this period.

4. Remove pan from the oven (keep the heat on), add the cooked pasta and the red pepper flakes, and toss well. Add remaining 3 tablespoons oil over all and sprinkle grated pecorino over the pasta and vegetables. Add more salt and a liberal amount of freshly ground pepper.

5. Return to the oven and bake 15 minutes. Remove from the oven and allow to rest 5 minutes. Serve with a crisp salad of mixed lettuces dressed with oil and vinegar.

FETTUCCINE WITH SMOKED SALMON ALL' ORSINI

Fettuccine con salmone affumicato all' Orsini

Serves 4

Almost all the smoked salmon eaten in Italy is imported, and therefore expensive, as it is in this country. The amount of salmon needed in this recipe is minimal, and therefore affordable. The first time I enjoyed this dish was at the Tuscan home of Armando and Georgianna Orsini in Radda in Chianti. They owned the Orsini restaurant in New York, famous for many years and frequented by Hollywood, political, television, and publishing people. This particular dish is not basically regional in character, for as far as can be discerned, it appeared on Italian menus a short while ago. It can be found in better restaurants in major cities all over Italy, and may be considered an international or national type dish that has cut across the regions.

In cooking this dish, be sure all ingredients are ready to be used: the salmon is cut into pieces, the cheese is grated, and so on. The dish must be prepared quickly and served almost at once.

½ pound fettuccine, fresh or dried
4 tablespoons butter
¼ pound thinly sliced smoked salmon, cut in 1-inch squares
2 tablespoons cognac
½ cup half-and-half or heavy cream
⅓ cup freshly grated Parmesan cheese

1. Bring 4 quarts of water to a rolling boil. Add a tablespoon salt. Add the pasta and cook until al dente.
2. While the pasta is cooking, heat the butter in a large skillet. Add the salmon and cook quickly, only until the salmon loses its pink color, a minute or 2. Add the cognac and stir well. Add the cream and bring to a boil.
3. Drain the pasta well and add it to the skillet. Taste for salt seasoning. Add black pepper and the cheese. Toss quickly over heat and serve while very hot.

THE RESIDENT COOK'S PENNE PASTA IN TIMBALE, LUCCA STYLE
Timballo di penne con il sugo alla Lucchese

Serves 6 to 8

This is a typical dish from Lucca that is country style, a good, hearty dish that is served as a first course, or it can be a main dish. It will serve more than four persons, but it is a good leftover and will reheat, or it can be eaten at room temperature.

Pastry for pie, see below
½ pound penne pasta, or other short pasta such as fusilli, cooked al dente and cooled
2 cups tomato sauce made with meat, see below
1 cup besciamella sauce, see below
½ cup freshly grated Parmigiano
1 egg, beaten

To make the pastry:
2 cups sifted all-purpose unbleached flour
½ cup sugar
8 tablespoons butter, softened
2 eggs
½ teaspoon lemon zest

1. Add the sifted flour, sugar, and a pinch of salt together and sift again; put on a work surface. Make a well in the center. Put the butter, eggs, and lemon zest in the well and incorporate these ingredients with your hands. Do not add any water. When smooth, shape into a ball, wrap in waxed paper, and chill for a minimum of 30 minutes.

To make the tomato sauce (makes 2 to 3 cups):

1 can (28 ounces) plum tomatoes, chopped coarsely, with juice
2 teaspoons tomato paste
1 teaspoon sugar
1 large onion, chopped
2 celery ribs, chopped coarsely
¼ cup extra-virgin olive oil
¾ pound ground beef
¼ cup quality red wine
1 tablespoon butter

1. Put the plum tomatoes, tomato paste, sugar, onion, celery ribs, and 2 tablespoons olive oil with salt and freshly ground pepper in a sauce pan. Cook over medium heat 15 minutes. Put this mixture through a food mill. Leave the sauce pan as is.

2. In a large skillet, heat 2 tablespoons olive oil and add the ground meat. Break up the meat with a wooden spoon and cook over medium heat until the meat has changed color and looks half-cooked, about 6 minutes. Transfer to the reserved sauce pan, adding the strained tomato mixture and the wine. Bring to a boil, lower the heat, and simmer, partially covered, 40 minutes. Add the butter and check for salt and pepper seasoning.

<u>To make the besciamella (makes 1 cup):</u>
3 tablespoons butter
3 tablespoons all-purpose unbleached flour
1 cup light cream
Pinch nutmeg

1. In a small sauce pan, melt the butter over medium heat, add the flour, and stir well.

2. Add the cream and beat with a whisk to dissolve the flour. Bring to a boil, lower the heat, and cook 3 minutes. Taste to see if the taste of raw flour is gone. If it isn't, cook another minute or 2. Add salt and freshly ground pepper, plus the nutmeg. When the sauce is thick and smooth, 2 or 3 minutes, remove from the heat.

<u>To assemble the pie:</u>

1. Preheat the oven to 400°F. Cut the pie dough in 2 pieces, ⅔ and ⅓. Roll out the larger piece and fit into a deep 9-inch baking pan, about 1½ inches deep.

2. Add the cooled, cooked pasta to the tomato sauce, stir well, and transfer into the pastry shell. Then pour the besciamella sauce over the pasta, and sprinkle the cheese over all.

3. Roll out the smaller piece of dough and fit in over the filling, bringing the upper and lower pastry together by uniting them with the tines of a fork. Make a leaf, star, or other cutout from leftover dough to add to the center of the top crust. Brush the top pastry with the beaten egg and bake for 30 minutes. If the crust has not browned, cook further.

4. Allow to rest 4 or 5 minutes before cutting into wedges.

CHIARA'S LASAGNETTE WITH MEAT SAUCE

Lasagnetta di Chiara con ragu di manzo

Serves 8

This will serve eight persons and more. Any leftovers will keep well up to a week, refrigerated, and may be reheated.

To make the pasta:
2 cups all-purpose unbleached flour
1½ cups semolina flour
4 large eggs
1 tablespoon extra-virgin olive oil, preferably Tuscan
2 tablespoons cold water

1. Sift both flours together with a good pinch of salt onto a flat work surface for kneading dough. Using your hands, make a well in the center.

2. In a small bowl, combine the eggs, oil, and water. Whisk until combined and pour into the well. Start incorporating the flour into the well by using a fork in 1 hand and steadying the flour wall with the other. Keep doing this until all the flour has been mixed in. Then flour your hands and start to knead the dough for 8 to 10 minutes until the dough is smooth.

3. Using a pasta machine (see page 104.__), roll out first in the widest opening, lightly flour each strip, and put aside until all 6 have been put through the wide opening. Cut each in ½ crosswise. Put them through the next-to-narrowest opening. Cut these lengths of dough into squares—these are called *lasagnette*. Don't be too serious about all the squares being equal in size. If the pasta is 4 inches as it is cranked through the pasta machine, feel free to cut the pasta into 4x6-inch rectangles; if the pasta width is 5 inches, cut the "squares" 5x5, or 5x6, or 5x7. Put these pasta pieces on lightly floured towels, cover with another cloth, and set aside until ready to cook them. If they sit more than 30 minutes, refrigerate until ready.

To make the meat sauce:
¾ cup extra-virgin olive oil, preferably Tuscan
1 medium onion, minced
2 carrots, trimmed and minced
2 ribs celery, strings removed, and minced
¼ cup finely chopped basil
2 fresh sage and 2 bay leaves
2 cloves garlic, minced
2 pounds lean ground beef
1 cup white wine
1 large can (35 ounces) plum tomatoes, chopped with juice
Good pinch of nutmeg

1. Heat the oil in a large heavy sauce pan and sauté the onions, carrots, celery, basil, sage, and bay leaves over medium heat, uncovered, 8 to 10 minutes, stirring frequently. After 8 minutes, add the garlic and cook a bit longer.

2. Add the beef and break it up with a wooden spoon. Cook over medium heat, uncovered, until the meat loses its color, about 10 minutes. Stir frequently. Add the wine and let it cook off, about 5 minutes.

3. Add the tomatoes and their juices, raise the heat, and bring to boil. Lower the heat, cover the sauce pan, and simmer 20 minutes. Stir 1 or 2 times. Add the nutmeg and salt and freshly ground pepper.

To make the besciamella:
3 cups milk, preferably whole
1 cup unbleached all-purpose flour
½ teaspoon freshly grated nutmeg
3 sticks butter, softened

1. In a medium, heavy sauce pan, bring the milk just to the boiling point. Whisking all the time, add the flour and nutmeg and salt and freshly ground pepper. Cook over medium heat, stirring all the time, until the sauce thickens, about 10 minutes. If needed, turn the heat to below medium during this time.

2. Add the butter a spoonful at a time until all of it is incorporated.

To assemble the lasagnette:
Besciamella sauce, above
Meat sauce, above
Pasta, above
1 to 1½ cups freshly grated Parmesan cheese

1. Preheat the oven to 350°F. Bring a large pot of water to boil. Add a teaspoon of salt, and add the pasta. Bring back to a boil, cook 3 minutes, and immediately drain the pasta and put it in cold water to stop cooking. Drain the pasta, lay it on cloth towels, and pat dry with paper toweling.

2. In a large, squarish baking dish, size 10x12x2 inches, make layers as follows: spoon some besciamella first, then spoon some meat sauce, then layer with the lasagnette pasta and some Parmesan. Continue this layering until 6 layers of pasta have been used. You may have a few pieces of pasta left over—cover them, refrigerate, and use later in soup and so on. Top the pasta with meat sauce, then besciamella, and finally some Parmesan. Bake ½ hour. Remove from the oven, let sit 5 to 10 minutes, then serve.

SPAGHETTI WITH CHEF GILBERTO PIZZI'S GENUINE BASIL PESTO

Spaghetti al pesto di Gilberto Pizzi

Serves 6

Pesto purists will mash garlic and salt in a marble mortar with a wooden pestle, adding a few basil leaves at a time; they work the pestle to pulverize the basil, adding pine nuts and mashing them. Then they add grated Parmesan and pecorino cheeses to form a thick paste. To finish off the pesto, extra-virgin olive oil is added to thin the paste. Of course, this is an excellent way to prepare it, but most people resort to blenders and food processors. I find a good compromise is to process the basil, nuts, and garlic with a little oil and the cheeses, and then add the remaining oil slowly while the machine is running. I almost always have to thin the paste a little with some hot water. It is important to add some salt at the appropriate time. See below.

80 small fresh basil leaves
¼ cup pine nuts
4 large cloves garlic, coarsely chopped
½ cup freshly grated Parmesan cheese
¼ cup freshly grated pecorino cheese, such as Romano
¾ cup plus 2 tablespoons extra-virgin olive oil from Liguria
¼ cup hot water
1 pound spaghetti

1. Combine the basil, pine nuts, garlic, both cheeses, and 7 tablespoons of the oil in a food processor. Turn on the processor, and as the ingredients become minced and well combined with the oil (count to 15), pour the hot water and some salt and freshly ground pepper in through the feed tube. Adding salt at this point is important, for it will prevent discoloration of the pesto. Add little salt, as the cheeses are salty. More salt can be added later if needed.

2. While the motor is running, add the remaining olive oil slowly through the feed tube until all is absorbed into the pesto (about a count of 10); the whole procedure should take less than 3 minutes. Transfer the pesto to a large bowl or platter, large enough to receive the pasta.

3. Cook the spaghetti according to the package directions; drain well, setting aside a cup of the hot salted water. Put the cooked pasta into the bowl or platter with the pesto and toss lightly and well. If it seems dry, add some of the hot water, by tablespoons, until you achieve a desired thinness of sauce. Serve right away.

PASTA WITH CABBAGE, CHEESE, AND POTATOES

Pasta con verza, formaggio, e patate (Pizzocheri)

Serves 6

This is a gutsy, earthy dish from the northern part of Italy which has traveled to many other parts of the country. I first learned of it at home, as it was a dish my father enjoyed making. For whatever reason, he loved cooking Savoy cabbage, which was always available in Italian markets in New York. These days, it is in every greengrocer section of most supermarkets. The cabbage adds a lot to the taste of this dish, but it is as tasty as it is because of the pecorino cheese, which is strong in taste but seems to marry well to these other ingredients.

This recipe is an adaptation of the Ligurian dish called *pizzocheri*, which is made with buckwheat *(grana saracena)* pasta served with cabbage, potatoes, cheese, butter, and sage.

3 medium potatoes, peeled and diced ½ inch to make about 3 cups
1 small head of Savoy cabbage, about 1 pound, trimmed, cored, and sliced thinly as for slaw
1 pound fresh fettuccine
1½ sticks butter, sliced into thin pats
4 large cloves garlic, peeled and halved
8 sage leaves
1½ cups freshly grated pecorino cheese
Freshly ground black pepper

1. Bring 4 quarts water to boil; add some salt, the potatoes, and cabbage and cook 12 minutes. Stir frequently. Add the fresh pasta and cook until the pasta is al dente, up to 5 minutes. Drain well and transfer to a large serving platter. Add ⅓ of the butter and toss with the pasta, cabbage, and potatoes.

2. Melt the remaining butter in a skillet and brown the garlic with the sage leaves, about 4 minutes. Remove the garlic, discard it, and spoon the flavored butter and sage over the pasta. Add the pecorino over the top and dust liberally with the black pepper. Serve now, or hold as in step 3.

3. Put the cooked ingredients into a baking dish and keep warm in a low oven—250°F. If prepared ahead, put in a baking dish and reheat in a 350°F oven until heated through, about 15 minutes. Serve with a freshly made arugula or curly endive and sliced tomato salad, or sliced cucumbers and finely chopped Italian parsley dressed lightly with oil and vinegar.

THIN SPAGHETTI WITH CLAMS, CHERRY TOMATOES, AND BASIL
Vermicelli con vongole, pomodoro, e basilico

Serves 4

Cherry tomatoes do not have to be peeled or put through a food mill and therefore make this sauce quite easy to prepare. They are not cooked very long, so they keep their shape. You can cook the sauce as you cook the pasta, and this dish can be made in less than fifteen minutes.

4 tablespoons extra-virgin olive oil
4 cloves garlic, minced
1 pound cherry tomatoes, washed, trimmed, and cut in ½
3 cans (6 ounces) chopped clams, drained, liquid reserved
½ cup finely sliced fresh basil leaves
12 ounces thin spaghetti or vermicelli pasta
1 cup freshly grated Parmesan cheese
3 to 4 tablespoons fresh lemon juice (1 lemon)

1. Heat the oil over moderate heat in a large skillet. Add garlic and sauté until garlic just begins to turn color, 2 minutes, stirring all the time. Add tomatoes and cook 5 minutes.

2. Add the drained clams and the basil, stir well, and cook 2 minutes. Set aside.

3. Cook the pasta al dente according to manufacturer's instructions, drain well, and return to pot in which it cooked. Add the clam sauce from the skillet, the cheese, and the lemon juice. Toss lightly but well over moderate heat until all is heated through. Add the reserved clam liquid a little at a time. Season with salt and freshly ground pepper and continue cooking, tossing all the time, 2 or 3 minutes, to marry the sauce with the pasta.

RICOTTA GNOCCHI WITH LIGHT PICCANTE TOMATO SHRIMP SAUCE

Gnocchi alla ricotta in salsa di gamberi e pomodori "piccante"

Serves 6

These lovely gnocchi are some of the easiest and lightest ones to make. Follow these steps carefully and you will be surprised at the simplicity and ease of the dish.

To make the gnocchi:
2 cups fresh ricotta cheese
1 cup freshly grated pecorino cheese
1 egg, beaten
1½ cups all-purpose flour

1. Combine the ricotta and the cheese in a large mixing bowl with the help of a rubber spatula. Blend in the egg to make a smooth mixture. Do not add salt as the cheese is salty enough.

2. Before measuring the flour, put 1½ cups of flour into a large bowl and aerate it by tossing lightly with a fork. Then spoon and measure the flour, always topping off the measuring cup with a straight-edged knife. Put the flour on a flat work surface, as in making dough. With your fingers, make a well in the center of the flour. Add the ricotta mixture to the well. Work in the flour a little at a time to make a dough—do this with your fingers or a fork. This will only take a minute or 2 and a light dough will be formed.

3. To test the dough before cooking, cut off a tiny piece and form a little ball, about the size of a small marble. Add it to boiling water, and if it keeps its shape, the dough is fine. If it breaks up, a little more flour should be added to the dough—this shouldn't happen, but if it does, this is the trick.

4. Form a large disk of the dough, flattening it out to about 2 inches in height. Cut the disk into ½-inch slices and then cut the slices lengthwise. On a lightly floured surface, roll with splayed fingers to form a ½-inch rope. Cut the rope into 1-inch lengths and put them on a lightly floured cloth that has been placed in a cookie sheet or pizza pan. Repeat until all the ropes are rolled and cut. If not using right away, cover them with another cloth and let rest ½ hour, or longer in the refrigerator.

To make the sauce:
3 tablespoons butter
¼ cup finely chopped onions
1 clove garlic, minced
1 cup heavy cream
½ cube fish bouillon
½ cup fish or clam broth
1 teaspoon tomato paste
Pinch red pepper flakes
1 cup finely chopped cooked shrimp, preferably fresh

1. Heat the butter in a large skillet and sauté the onion until limp, 4 or 5 minutes. Add the garlic and cook 1 minute. Add the cream. Dissolve the bouillon in the fish broth, and add it. Bring the broth and the cream to boil. Lower the heat immediately, and simmer to reduce the sauce to thicken it, a little more than heavy cream, about 10 minutes. Stir all the time, especially around the edges—using a rubber spatula is helpful here.

2. Stir in the tomato paste and combine it well. Add the pepper flakes, salt, freshly ground pepper, and the shrimp. Cook until the shrimp are thoroughly heated.

To bring the sauce and pasta together, and to add the squash:

1. Cook the gnocchi in boiling water and, as they rise to the top, remove them with a slotted spoon. Drain them well and add them immediately to the skillet with the sauce. Toss lightly but well. Serve right away.

TAGLIATELLE IN PARMA HAM/SAFFRON SAUCE

Tagliatelle con salsa al prosciutto e zafferano

Serves 8 to 10

Noodles, sometimes called string pasta, come in a number of varieties and with different names according to those who make and eat them. Probably the best known Bologna noodle is *tagliatelle*, and it is supposed to be as thin as possible and cut approximately one-quarter inch wide. The Bolognese think there is nothing better, especially if it is homemade.

Tagliatelle made with 3 eggs and 2¼ cups all-purpose flour (see page 104), or 1 pound dried
¼ teaspoon saffron threads
½ cup butter
4 slices prosciutto, each individual slice finely chopped
1 cup heavy cream
Pastry garnish, see below
1 cup freshly grated Parmesan cheese

1. Make the pasta and set aside.
2. Combine saffron with ¼ cup warm water and stir to dissolve.
3. In a large skillet, melt the butter, and when it is bubbly, add the prosciutto and sauté for several minutes to crisp it. Add the cream and saffron, and stir over moderate heat until the sauce is combined and hot. Add some salt and freshly ground pepper.
4. In boiling, salted water, cook the tagliatelle; if it is freshly made it will take 2 minutes—if it is dried, about 8 minutes. Drain the pasta and add to the sauce in the skillet. Toss lightly but well—try to coat the noodles with the sauce and keep over a flame 1 to 2 minutes while tossing. Before garnishing with pastry stars, sprinkle the parmesan cheese over the pasta.

<u>To make pastry stars:</u>
This is an extra step you may wish to pass on. Paola Rossi, the chef, delighted in making this tasty garnish. One time, she added a puff pastry bow, tied.

1 sheet frozen puff pastry, thawed
Butter for bake sheet

1. Preheat oven to 400°F. Using a small 1-inch star-shaped pastry cutter, cut stars out of the puff pastry. You can make as many as the sheet will allow and freeze what you don't use, or make 2 stars per person and reserve the remaining pastry for another use. If you don't have a star-shaped cutter, use a 1-inch round shape, or a crescent shape, or any other decorative shape. But do not make them larger than 1 inch.

2. Place the stars on a buttered cookie sheet, spacing them 1 inch apart. Liberally add freshly ground pepper over the pastry cutouts. Bake 10 minutes or until they turn golden. If you are serving the pasta in a large platter, surround the pasta with the stars. If you are serving individual portions, lay 2 stars on top of each serving.

TAGLIATELLE WITH A BUTTERY TOMATO SAUCE
Tagliatelle al sugo di pomodoro e burro

Serves 4

This pasta sauce is a simple combination of butter and tomatoes flavored with an onion and carrot. No garlic, no olive oil, no tomato paste, no long cooking; it is fresh and light and may be considered the ultimate Italian pasta sauce for anyone's taste. The freshness, tenderness, and crispness of the curly endive and fennel matchsticks give balance to the texture side of the meal and provide a needed counterpoint in taste to the buttery sauce.

2 pounds ripe plum tomatoes or 2 cups canned Italian plum tomatoes
¼ pound butter, cut into 8 pieces
1 medium onion, peeled and quartered
1 medium carrot, peeled and quartered
½ teaspoon sugar
2-egg recipe for tagliatelle, see below
¼ cup finely chopped fresh Italian parsley
½ cup freshly grated Parmesan cheese

1. If using fresh tomatoes, wash them well, cut each in ½, and cook over low heat in a covered pan for 15 minutes. Put them through a food mill to have a fine puree. If using canned tomatoes, measure 2 cups into a food mill along with about ½ cup liquid from the can and process for a fine puree.
2. In a medium sauce pan, place the butter, onion, and carrot pieces, sugar and 1½ teaspoons salt. Add the tomato puree. Over low heat, simmer these ingredients 40 minutes, partially covered. Stir frequently and be sure the simmer does not turn to a boil.
3. While the sauce is cooking, cook the pasta and drain.
4. To serve, remove onion and carrot pieces from the sauce, and adjust for salt seasoning. Add the cooked pasta to the sauce, toss well, and divide among individual plates. Add a piece of cooked vegetable, if you wish, and sprinkle some chopped parsley overall. Pass the Parmesan

To make fresh tagliatelle pasta for 4 persons: 1½ cups all-purpose flour
2 large eggs, beaten

1. Put the flour on a flat surface or in a bowl and form a well deep enough to hold the eggs. Put the eggs in the well. With a fork or with your fingers, begin to pick up a little of the flour from inside the well. Incorporate the flour so the mixture is no longer runny. A good technique for mixing, if the flour is on a flat surface, is to incorporate with 1 hand and, with the other, hold or support the outside wall of flour. By gently pushing the outer edge of

the flour wall with your hand, some of the flour will fall into the well. If the dough is sticky, add a little more flour.

2. With both hands, bring all the flour from the outside of the well toward the center and make a ball with the dough, including the crumbs of flour caked on the working surface (use a pastry scraper). Put the ball of dough on a flat surface, and push down firmly in the center with the heel of your hand. Give the dough a slight turn and push down again. Dust your hands with flour, because the dough is likely to stick in the beginning. Knead for 6 or 7 minutes until the dough becomes smooth and satiny. Cover with a kitchen towel or a bowl, and let it rest 10 to 15 minutes.

3. Roll out by hand or use a pasta machine. Pasta machines are fitted with smooth rollers that will produce several thicknesses of "sheet," which is what pasta is called when it has been rolled out by hand or machine. A knob can be turned to widen or narrow the opening between the rollers. Most machines have 6 settings. Cutting rollers, which can be attached to the machine, slice the sheet to various pasta widths. Only 1 pasta width can be cut at a time. Tagliatelle are ¼ inch wide, so use the appropriate cutter.

4. Before using the machine, cut the dough into 6 equal pieces. Cover 5 of them and run the sixth 2 times through the widest opening. Then run it through a narrower opening. It is not necessary to run the pasta through every opening. For example, on a 6-notch machine, roll the dough through setting 6, the thickest, 4, 2, and 1 (the thinnest). Lightly, very lightly, flour each strip of dough after it is rolled. After sprinkling the dough with flour, rub the palm of your hand up and down the dough strip to cover it lightly with flour. Lay the pasta strips on cloth toweling while completing the task. Repeat procedure with the 5 other pieces of dough. Cut into tagliatelle size, loosen the pasta with your hands, as if unraveling them, and place carefully on towel to dry for about ½ hour before cooking.

LASAGNA BAKED WITH MEAT SAUCE, BOLOGNA STYLE
Lasagna al forno alla Bolognese

Serves 8 to 10

The Italian sense of quality and freshness in food can be seen best in their pasta preparations. Few will deny that Italian cuisine is among the richest and most imaginative in the world. The same high-spirited flair for improvisation we find in the Italian arts is in their pasta and sauce making also.

The Italians begin to cook in the market, selecting the freshest ingredients for a meal that will be a triumph of colors and flavors, because Italian food must be as beautiful as it is delicious. Combining tomato sauce and grilled red peppers to create an opulent, scarlet-colored dish is as uncanny as the seventh Italian sense. They combine spinach and egg pasta in *paglia e fieno*—straw and hay—because Italians love color. Take the beautiful spinach gnocchi in Tuscany or the *lasagne verde* in Bologna with their delicate sauces and you begin to imagine the Italians' feeling for their food. This is why it is said that if there is one dish that sums up the essence of Italian cooking, it must surely be pasta and its sauces.

In Italy, pasta is an essential part of every full meal and does not, as a rule, constitute a meal on its own. The pasta course is called *il primo*, and it is eaten between the antipasto and *il secondo*, the main course.

Italians say that pastas tend to taste alike, but they declare that each is given a life of its own when served with the proper sauce. The ultimate success of a pasta dish depends on the sauce with which it is served. Classic Italian sauces are easy to prepare, especially when compared to French sauces; they have fewer pitfalls and possess a freshness that many sauces lack.

The great trinity of Bologna pastas is tortellini, tagliatelle, and lasagna. The first two pastas have been covered elsewhere; see pages 54 and 80. The third, lasagna, is a classic preparation not only in Bologna and elsewhere in Emilia-Romagna, but also all over Italy, and now in many other countries as well. Lasagna, which is made in broad sheets, is claimed by the Bolognese to be a pasta of their own; actually, it is a pasta of olden times, as far back as the Roman Empire, where it was called *laganum* and possibly derived from the word for a cooking vessel, *lasanum*. In Calabria today, lasagna is called *lagana*.

What makes this particular dish of lasagna Bolognese is the use of a rich, green spinach pasta. The preferred way to cook lasagna is baking in an oven after it has been parboiled, transferred to cold water, drained, and dried. In Italy, depending on where you are, fillings for lasagna are as varied as one can imagine. The most frequently used fillings include mozzarella and Parmesan or pecorino cheeses, ricotta, and tomato sauce. But then there are also pesto fillings, sausage, vegetables such as asparagus, artichokes, and I recently cooked a delightful one with radicchio and besciamella. The classic Bologna version insists on fresh spinach pasta, the Bolognese ragu tomato and meat sauce, besciamella, and, of course, Parmigiano-Reggiano cheese. And in this case, it can be served as a main dish in Italy, and it is ideal on the American table.

To assemble, bake, and serve the lasagna:

5 fresh spinach lasagna sheets, about 5x24 inches each, see below
5 cups ragu Bolognese, see below
2 cups besciamella sauce, see below
Soft butter for the baking vessel, about 2 tablespoons
1¼ cups fresh grated Parmesan cheese

1. Before assembling, be sure the spinach pasta, ragu, and besciamella are made and ready to be incorporated here. Also, set a large bowl with cold water in it for cooling the pasta. Then set the oven to 450°F.

2. Bring water to boil in a large sauce pan. Add 1 teaspoon salt. Put 1 sheet of the pasta in the boiling water and let cook briefly. It will float to the top in less than a minute. Remove right away to the bowl of cold water. When it has cooled a minute or so, remove it to a damp cloth towel and cover with another damp towel. Repeat this procedure until all 5 sheets are cooked, cooled, and dried. If 1 of the strips should break, don't fret. Take the pieces and do exactly what you are to do with them.

3. Liberally butter a squarish baking dish, approximately 10x12x2½ inches. Fit in a single layer of spinach pasta, covering the bottom of the dish. Use a sharp knife or scissors to help fit the pasta, patching where needed.

4. Layer the lasagnas in this way: add ⅓ of the ragu over the bottom layer of pasta and sprinkle ¼ cup of the cheese over the ragu; add another layer of pasta, covering it with ⅓ of the besciamella, and sprinkle ¼ cup of the cheese; add another layer of pasta and, over it, another ⅓ of the ragu and an additional ¼ cup of the cheese; add the fourth layer of pasta and spread over it ⅓ of the besciamella with ¼ cup of cheese sprinkled over it; lastly, another layer of pasta with the remaining ragu over it, then the remaining besciamella and the remaining cheese.

5. Bake the lasagna 15 to 20 minutes, until it bubbles around the edges. Insert a wooden skewer in the center of the lasagna and feel the tip of the skewer to see if it is hot. If so, remove the lasagna from the oven and let it rest for 10 minutes or so before serving.

To make spinach pasta:

To make green, or really spinach, pasta, cooked, finely chopped spinach that has been thoroughly squeezed dry is added to eggs. The spinach and eggs are carefully beaten together and then added to the flour to make a dough. The amount of cooked and squeezed spinach is:

One-egg pasta—add 1 tablespoon spinach
Two-egg pasta—add 2 to 3 tablespoons spinach
Three-egg pasta—add 3 to 4 tablespoons spinach
Four-egg pasta—add 4 to 5 tablespoons spinach

The color and amount of spinach will determine the color of the pasta.

To make the ragu, Bologna style:

With its base of chopped prosciutto, onion, celery, carrots, and the beef, pork, and chicken livers, all slowly simmered in beef broth and wine, this classic Bologna sauce has the vigor and character to stand up assertively to any heavy pasta in addition to pasta for lasagna. To soften its impact somewhat, the Bolognese will enrich the ragu with heavy cream or use it in tandem with besciamella. Few pasta dishes are as luxurious and opulent as this lasagna dish, immersed in ragu Bolognese, masked with a nutmeg-flavored besciamella, and gratined with a golden crust of freshly grated Parmigiano cheese.

This will make more than the five cups needed for the lasagna, so keep the remainder for another use. It will keep in the refrigerator for three days and may be frozen for up to sixty days.

2 mediums onions, peeled and chopped to make 2 cups
2 medium celery ribs, trimmed and chopped to make 1 cup
1 medium carrot, trimmed and chopped to make ½ cup
¼ pound prosciutto, chopped
6 tablespoons butter, 4 for sautéing ham and vegetables and 2 for sautéing chicken livers
1½ pounds ground meat: 1 pound lean beef chuck, and ½ pound lean pork, ground finely by the butcher or in food processor
1 cup dry white wine
1½ cups milk, warmed
3 cups light beef broth
3 cups canned plum tomatoes, without juice, put through food mill
2 tablespoons finely chopped fresh Italian parsley
½ pound fresh chicken livers, fat removed, livers cut into ¼-inch dice
Freshly grated nutmeg

1. On a chopping board, combine the onions, celery, carrots, and prosciutto, and mince them together as finely as you can with a large, sharp knife. The Italians call this mixture *soffritto*. Melt 4 tablespoons butter in a large sauce pan, and sauté the soffritto over medium heat until the vegetables and

ham are lightly browned, about 8 to 10 minutes.

2. Add the ground meat, mashing it with a large wooden spoon. The lumps of meat should dissolve and be completely broken up. Raise the heat for a few minutes to lightly brown the meat. Add the wine, stirring all the time, and let it cook off (evaporate), about 5 minutes. Add the milk and let it cook off, stirring frequently and still over medium-high heat, about 10 minutes.

3. Stir in the beef broth, tomatoes, and parsley, bring to boil, lower the heat to a simmer, and cook, half covered, 2 hours.

4. Melt the remaining butter in a small skillet and sauté the chicken livers. When they are browned, transfer them to the ragu sauce pan. Taste the sauce for seasoning, adding salt, freshly ground pepper, and nutmeg as needed. Cook 5 minutes longer.

5. Measure out 5 cups for the lasagna and put the rest aside for another use. You will appreciate having the extra on hand for later use.

<u>To make 2 cups besciamella:</u>
This sauce has been in use in Italian kitchens for hundreds of years. It is used to bind many pasta and vegetable dishes, and when it is used also as a topping, as in this lasagna, it helps to prevent it from drying out.
3 tablespoons butter
4 tablespoons sifted all-purpose flour
2 cups milk, warmed
Freshly grated nutmeg

1. Heat the butter in a sauce pan over medium heat. Add the flour and whisk continuously 2 minutes without letting it brown. Add the warmed milk slowly, whisking all the time. Add some salt, freshly ground pepper, and nutmeg, and whisk for 10 minutes or longer, until the mixture looks like heavy cream.

CANNELLONI FROM PEPPINO'S IN PIACENZA
Cannelloni alla Peppino (Piacenza)

Serves 4 to 6

Piacenza is a city in the food-rich region of Emilia-Romagna. It is an important center built by the Romans at the end of their Via Emilia on the south bank of the Po River. Piazza Cavalli is the center of the old city, named for its pair of bronze horse statues (*cavalli* means horses) of the dukes Alessandro and Ranuccio Farnese. In the same square is the fine Gothic Palazzo del Comune, called Il Gotico, begun in 1280. The remarkable twelfth-century Lombard-Romanesque cathedral (Il Duomo) is down the street from the square. This charming city is only thirty-five miles from Parma and about fifty from Milano. Food there is exquisite. Look for the restaurants Antico Osteria del Teatro, via Verdi 16, Il Gotico in Piazza Gioia, 3, and Peppino's on via Roma, 183, where you can delight in cannelloni and other pasta specialties of the area.

To make the pasta:
1¾ cups all-purpose flour
2 medium eggs plus 2 more egg yolks, whisked
4 tablespoons melted butter
1¼ cups whole milk

1. Sift the flour and a pinch of salt into a bowl. Add the eggs and the yolks, and 1 tablespoon of the butter. Stir in the milk slowly and stir until a smooth batter is formed. Let stand for 20 to 30 minutes.

2. Heat a small, nonstick, 6-inch skillet, add a little butter, and cover the bottom of the skillet with the butter by swirling with a paper towel. Stir the batter thoroughly and add 3 tablespoons of it to the skillet. Tilt the pan to cover the bottom of the skillet with the batter. Cook 2 or 3 minutes or until lightly golden. Turn over the "pasta," cook 1 minute longer, and empty onto a plate. Continue making the "pasta" circles until all the batter is used. Trim each circle into a square. These squares will be the packages to receive the cannelloni filling.

To make the filling:
2 pounds fresh spinach, large stems removed, washed well, cooked, squeezed dry, and finely chopped
⅔ cup each fresh ricotta and freshly grated Parmesan cheese
½ cup softened mascarpone cheese
2 small eggs, whisked
¼ cup loosely packed, finely chopped Italian parsley
Pinch of freshly grated nutmeg

1. Put all the filling ingredients and a pinch of salt in a bowl and delicately combine until thoroughly mixed.

2. Lay the pasta squares on a flat surface and divide the filling among them by placing spoonfuls of it in the middle of each square. Fold the squares into parcels by folding over 1 side, folding over the other, then folding both ends over. Place the seam sides down in 1 layer in a heavily buttered baking pan.

To bake the cannelloni:
½ cup freshly grated Parmesan cheese
4 pats of butter, cut into 4 squares each

1. Preheat oven to 375°F.

2. Sprinkle the Parmesan over all and dot with the butter pieces. Bake on a middle shelf 20 to 30 minutes until the tops turn golden. These are best served piping hot. Serve with sliced tomatoes and cucumbers tossed in extra-virgin olive oil and fresh lemon juice, with a sprinkle of finely chopped fresh basil.

PASTA WITH MASCARPONE, SAGE, AND TOASTED BREAD CRUMBS
Pasta con mascarpone, salvia, e pane macinato

Serves 4 to 6

This is a favorite way I prepare spaghetti. It makes a great one-dish meal and needs only a green salad topped with a tomato slice. Be sure the mascarpone cheese is at room temperature and that the bread crumbs are made fresh. You will love this dish.

2 tablespoons butter
½ cup fresh bread crumbs
1 tablespoon finely chopped fresh sage leaves
8 ounces mascarpone cheese, room temperature
1 cup freshly grated Parmesan cheese
1 pound thin spaghetti

1. In a large skillet, heat the butter and sauté the bread crumbs and sage with some salt and freshly ground pepper until lightly browned, about 3 minutes. Set aside.

2. In a large bowl, combine the softened mascarpone and Parmesan cheeses.

3. Cook the pasta and drain, reserving about 1 cup of boiling pasta water. Add the pasta to the bowl with the cheeses. Toss lightly and well. Check for salt seasoning and add black pepper. If sauce is too thick, thin with some of the hot water.

4. To serve, divide the pasta among individual plates and sprinkle each with a full tablespoon or more of bread crumbs, or put the pasta on a large platter and sprinkle bread crumbs on it.

TAGLIOLINI BAKED WITH TWO CHEESES
Tagliolini al forno con formaggi misti

Serves 6

It is difficult to be in Emilia-Romagna and not eat pasta every day—I go there because of *la sfoglia* (the sheet), which refers to the delicious, thin, almost transparent pasta made with eggs and cut into tagliatelle, a star of the kitchen there, as are all the pastas, whether string or not. I've had a dish similar to this in Rome and elsewhere.

Combining pasta with cheese and oven baking it is everywhere Italian, but in Emilia-Romagna, it is the quality of the pasta that makes the difference. If you have the time, make the pasta on page 104, to serve six persons.

1 pound tagliatelle, preferably homemade
6 tablespoons butter, soft
¼ cup freshly grated Parmesan cheese (do not substitute here)
1 cup heavy cream
1 pound fontina cheese, cut into small cubes, less than ½ inch
½ cup fine bread crumbs
1 egg
¼ cup finely chopped Italian parsley and scallions (white and light green parts only)

1. Preheat oven to 350°F.

2. Bring at least 4 quarts of water to a raging boil, add a teaspoon of salt just before adding the pasta, and cook al dente. Drain the pasta well and return it to the pan in which it cooked. Add all the butter and toss lightly but well.

3. Add the Parmesan cheese, the heavy cream, fontina, and a liberal amount of freshly grated pepper. Toss lightly but well.

4. Butter an oval ovenproof glass baking vessel, about 9x13x2 inches. Use glass as it is helpful to be able to see through the baking container during baking time. Add 4 tablespoons of the bread crumbs to the buttered dish and move it around to coat the entire inside. Lay out a piece of waxed paper and turn out any extra crumbs onto it.

5. Put the egg in a small bowl and beat it well. Pour it into the crumbed dish and swirl it around by tilting to cover the inside of the dish (that is, over the bread crumbs). Add the remaining 4 tablespoons bread crumbs and move the dish again to accomplish a second coat of crumbs. Turn out to empty any excess crumbs.

6. Transfer all the pasta with the help of a rubber spatula into the double-crumbed baking dish. Bake 15 minutes, or until the crumbs turn golden and brown. You will be able to see through a glass dish if you have used one. When nicely browned, remove the dish from the oven and allow to rest at least 10 minutes. Choose a beautiful platter, preferably one with an interesting border, or a plain white one, and turn out the molded dish after loosening the edges all around the inside of the baking dish. You will need mitts or potholders to do this, and be careful. I lay the inside of the platter on the top of the baking container and turn over in one fell swoop, but I have to be very careful doing this.

7. When the molded dish is turned out, add the chopped greens in a decoration to your liking; I usually center them in the middle or try to get a little all around the edge of the dish. Be sure to serve this with a large green salad filled with fresh tomatoes, cucumbers, curly endive, and cooked beet batons (add these at the very last minute).

PENNE PASTA WITH COGNAC FROM CITTA DI CASTELLO
Penne al cognac (Trattoria dalla Lea in Citta di Castello)

Serves 8 to 12

Citta di Castello, a town of about forty thousand inhabitants that happens to be the most northern city in Umbria, is not in every guidebook. That can be a fortunate thing. The last time I was there, only two other tourists (from Scotland) were there—I joined them for a noonday drink at a local bar. We agreed that we liked the streets and architecture without teeming tourists, and that the service in the restaurants was ideal. Friends of mine who live and work there (they own the Trattoria dalla Lea), Lea and Anontonio Giambanelli and their son Cristiano, made this pasta dish for me one evening. With the help of Cristiano, I was able to get them to share this recipe.

2 cups tomato sauce, see page 24
¼ cup cognac
2 pounds penne pasta
½ cup light cream or half and half
¼ cup finely chopped fresh Italian parsley
1 to 2 cups freshly grated pecorino cheese

1. In a heavy sauce pan (large enough to hold 2 pounds cooked pasta), heat the tomato sauce. Add the cognac and simmer for 10 to 15 minutes to cook off the alcohol.

2. Put the pasta water to boil. Before adding the pasta, add 1 teaspoon salt to the water. Cook the pasta al dente according to package directions.

3. Add the cream to the tomato sauce and simmer 10 minutes without bringing the sauce to a boil. Check for salt seasoning, adding more if necessary. Add some freshly ground pepper.

4. Drain the pasta well and add it to the sauce pan with the tomato/cream sauce. Toss well and transfer to a large serving bowl. Sprinkle the parsley over all and pass the pecorino.

SPAGHETTINI WITH CLAMS, CARROTS, AND WINE
Spaghettini alle vongole

6 small servings

There is no single way to prepare spaghetti or linguini with clam sauce except to use the best ingredients you can get and to respect the traditions of the dish, which comes from Naples and the Amalfi coast. This is where the real *vongole veraci* clams are to be found—they are tender, tiny, and sweet. But I have tasted *arselle* clams in Genoa, called *vongole* in Rome, and it's difficult for me to see or taste the difference. Manila clams, or small clams such as littlenecks, cockles, or Cedar Key (Florida)—sometimes called littleneck pasta clams—work best in the United States. The purists may take me to task for using canned or jarred clams, minced, but they make a tasty substitute. The carrot adds color and a touch of sweetness, as in *vongole veraci*.

5 dozen Manila or littleneck clams, or 3 cans (7½ ounces) of minced clams
2 cloves garlic, minced
½ cup extra-virgin olive oil
4 tablespoons butter
1 carrot, trimmed, cut lengthwise in 6 pieces and chopped finely
½ cup finely chopped scallions
1 cup clam juice in addition to cooking liquid from fresh clams or liquid from canned clams
1 cup dry white wine
¼ cup finely chopped Italian parsley
1 pound spaghettini (thin spaghetti)

1. If using fresh clams, scrub the clams thoroughly with a stiff wire brush, rinsing them several times. Soak clams in cool, fresh water 30 minutes or longer to remove any sand that may be in them. Remove the clams by hand from the bowl or pan in which they soak. The sand will have settled in the bottom, and removing the clams by hand helps prevent stirring the sand. Place the clams in a heavy sauce pan with a cover, along with ½ the garlic pieces and 3 tablespoons olive oil. Cover and cook over medium heat until the clams open, 10 to 15 minutes. Discard and clams that have not opened. When you separate the clams from their shells, do so over a bowl so you can catch all the juices, which will be used later. Chop the clams and set the clams and the juice aside.

2. In a large skillet, heat the remaining oil (if you used some with the fresh clams, or all of it if you did not) and the butter. Heat both, and add the carrots. Sauté them 5 minutes. Add the scallions and remaining garlic pieces (or all of them if you are using canned clams) and cook 3 minutes Add all the juice from the cooked clams (or from the canned clams), the additional 1 cup clam juice, and the white wine. Cook to cook off the wine, about 10 to 15 minutes. Add some salt.

3. Cook the pasta to al dente and drain well. While the pasta is cooking, heat the sauce to be sure it is hot. As soon as the pasta is done, add the chopped clams, fresh or canned, to the sauce and cook until the clams are heated through, 2 to 3 minutes.

4. Add the cooked pasta to the sauce and, over heat, toss to bring the pasta and sauce together. Check for salt seasoning and liberally add freshly ground pepper. Transfer to a large platter and sprinkle parsley over all. This can rest for a few minutes.

PENNE WITH PORK TOMATO SAUCE
Penne al ragu di maiale

Makes about 6 cups

This sauce should be made ahead and the fat should be removed. The pork shoulder can be served separately with a vegetable and salad. If you decide against the pasta and just want to use some of the sauce with the pork, refrigerate remaining sauce for several days or freeze for several weeks. It is very tasty and hearty and wonderful over pasta.

3½ pounds boned pork shoulder (may be in 1 or 2 pieces)
2 medium cloves garlic, minced
1 cup finely chopped Italian parsley
6 tablespoons olive oil
1 large onion, finely chopped
7 cups plum tomatoes (after putting them through a food mill)
½ teaspoon red pepper flakes
1 pound penne pasta

1. Lay the meat flat on a work surface and add the garlic and parsley. Roll it and tie it with string. If 2 pieces of meat are used, do this for both, dividing the amount of garlic and parsley.

2. Heat the oil in a large, heavy pot and sauté the rolled pork over medium heat, uncovered, until it is browned all over, about 10 minutes. Add the onion and sauté 2 or 3 minutes, stirring several times. Add the tomatoes and the pepper flakes and cook, covered, over low heat about 2 hours. Taste for salt and add some if it is needed.

3. Remove the pork and set aside for later serving. If sauce appears thin, keep over heat and cook down to desired thickness, up to 20 minutes.

4. Cook the pasta according to package directions, drain well, and add 1 to 1½ cups of tomato sauce.

5. Serve the penne with the sauce first. Then slice the pork to serve as a separate course. If you are omitting the pasta course, add 2 tablespoons sauce to each portion of meat when serving with the carrots and salad.

FRESH ANGEL HAIR PASTA IN CUSTARD MOLD FOR LUNCH
Sformato di pasta in besciamella

Serves 8

This is a delightful preparation; it is tasty and easy to prepare and serve. Just add a salad of asparagus, green beans, or a variety of green lettuces with sliced plum tomatoes in wine vinegar and extra-virgin olive oil.

1½ cups ricotta
3 large eggs, beaten
3 tablespoons finely chopped chives
1 teaspoon finely chopped fresh rosemary
1½ cups milk
Pinch red pepper flakes
6 ounces fresh angel hair pasta (if nested, use 3 of them)
4 tablespoons butter

1. Preheat oven to 350°F. Mix the ricotta, eggs, chives, rosemary, milk, red pepper flakes, and some salt in a large bowl. Combine well and set aside.

2. Cook the pasta in boiling salted water until al dente. Fresh pasta cooks in less time than dried, so this should take about 3 minutes. Drain well and return the pasta to the sauce pan in which it cooked. Add 3 tablespoons butter and toss to coat. Transfer the pasta to a well-buttered 1½-quart baking dish.

3. Cover the cooked pasta with the ricotta mixture, season with freshly ground pepper, and dot with the remaining tablespoon butter. Bake 1¼ hours. Remove from the oven and let cool 10 to 15 minutes. Loosen the edges with a small knife, and cut into squares and serve. Sprinkle some more chopped chives over each serving.

PASTA WITH GINGER AND GARLIC
Pasta allo zenzero e aglio

Serves 4

Ginger and garlic suit each other like bacon and eggs. I have substituted candied ginger for the fresh ginger and get good results. This dish is a conversation piece. It is important to "marry" the sauce and the cooked pasta; you do this by keeping both over heat for two or three minutes, tossing all the time.

1 pound pasta, spaghettini, vermicelli, or spaghetti
½ cup extra-virgin olive oil
½ cup finely diced carrot
1 tablespoon minced fresh garlic
2 tablespoons finely chopped fresh ginger
2 tablespoons finely chopped fresh scallions
1 teaspoon dried oregano, crushed
¼ to ½ teaspoon dried red pepper flakes
½ cup dry vermouth
4 tablespoons butter
¾ cup freshly grated Romano cheese

1. Heat the water in a large sauce pan in which the pasta will cook. Meanwhile, heat the oil in a skillet and add the carrot. Cook 3 minutes, stirring occasionally. Add the garlic, ginger, scallion, oregano, pepper flakes, and vermouth. Add some salt if you wish. Cook 5 minutes. Add a cup of water to thin the sauce, bring to a boil, lower the heat, and simmer; in total, do not cook the sauce more than 15 minutes.

2. Cook the pasta in salted, boiling water until it is *al dente*. Drain the pasta, return it to the pan in which it cooked, add the butter, and stir. Add ¾ of the sauce and toss again. Serve in warm plates or bowls, adding another tablespoon of sauce to the top of each serving. Pass the cheese separately.

SPAGHETTI WITH GARLIC AND CHILI
Cifutti

Serves 4

Cifutti is a dialect name given to this dish by the Calabrians because they say the word sounds like the noise the cooked spaghetti makes when it is added to the skillet with the hot oil and chili pepper.

½ pound spaghetti
4 tablespoons extra-virgin olive oil
2 cloves garlic, minced
½ teaspoon red pepper flakes
½ cup freshly grated pecorino cheese
Finely chopped Italian parsley for garnish

1. Bring water to boil in a large sauce pan. Add a teaspoon of salt just before adding the spaghetti. Cook to the al dente stage, 8 to 10 minutes. It is always best to consult the pasta manufacturer's instructions about cooking time, but it is also important to test along the way by forking a strand of pasta from the pot and tasting it. It should have "bite" between the teeth.

2. While the pasta is cooking, heat the oil in a large skillet. The garlic and pepper are to be added just before adding the spaghetti. Drain the pasta, reserving ½ cup of the boiling water. Then quickly add the garlic to the hot oil, cooking it less than a minute. Remove from the heat, add the red pepper flakes, stir, and add the spaghetti. Toss lightly but well, putting the skillet back on the heat. Add a tablespoon or more of the cooking water to the skillet while tossing the pasta Add salt and freshly ground black pepper if you wish.

3. Serve on individual plates, topping with some freshly grated pecorino cheese and a sprinkle of parsley. Pass more cheese.

RIGATONI WITH EGGPLANT IN A CREAMY CURRY SAUCE
Rigatoni con melanzane in salsa al curry

Serves 6

In Sicily, Naples, and other parts of southern Italy, round, hollow pasta is used more often than the other pastas. Generally, this kind of pasta is called macaroni. Bucatini or perciatelli is a thick version of spaghetti (with the hole through it). Ziti, also hollow like the rigatoni and bucatini, are only two inches in length, whereas rigatoni are longer and larger tubes with rigati (grooves) on the outside. Rigatoni seem popular elsewhere in Italy. I recall a dish away from the south called *rigatoni del Curato*—rigatoni in the style of the rustic priest. They are sold dried, made of durum wheat, and are on all supermarket shelves. In this recipe, they are prepared with a hint of curry, which found its way into Italy through early spice routes, especially located in southern Italy. This is also true of ginger.

1 (1-pound) eggplant, diced
½ cup extra virgin olive oil
¾ pound zucchini, diced
1 medium onion, diced
2 cups pureed tomatoes
1½ cups heavy or half-and-half cream
1 tablespoon curry
1 pound rigatoni
1 cup fresh basil, finely chopped
½ cup freshly grated Parmesan cheese

1. Sprinkle salt over the eggplant (in a colander) and drain for about 1 hour. Dry eggplant with kitchen toweling and sauté in ¼ cup of oil, using a large skillet. Drain on paper towels and set aside.

2. Sauté zucchini in remaining oil, drain on paper towels, and set aside.

3. Sauté the onions in the same skillet until they become transparent, 6 to 8 minutes. Add the tomatoes, some salt, and freshly ground pepper. Cover and cook 8 minutes over medium heat. Remove from the heat and stir in the cream and the curry.

4. Boil the rigatoni until al dente, drain, and add it to the skillet. Add the eggplant, zucchini, and the basil. Mix well over high heat for several minutes to bring the sauce and pasta together. Serve right away with Parmesan on the side.

ROTELLE PASTA SALAD WITH CUCUMBER SAUCE
Insalata di rotelle

Serves 12

Rotelle are little pasta wheels and look like the wheels on antique Sicilian carts. They are a popular pasta throughout Italy, and they appear on most supermarket shelves. This particular way to cook them was talked about by Giuseppe Calafiore, a man with a taxi, who drove me from Palermo to Marsala, on to Mazara del Vallo, and then on to Agrigento. Giuseppe would return home to Palermo and his family after each of my stops and come back to drive me on to the next location. In addition to being a good driver, he knew a good deal about food and the Mafia. In the middle of a sentence about preparing pasta or tuna, he would interrupt himself to show me a statue, from the taxi window, built in memory of one or more citizens who were gunned down by the Mafia. I did not want to part with Giuseppe, but I thought it was short of ridiculous for him to come from Palermo each time, especially so when it was halfway across Sicily. The idea for this pasta salad is his.

4 small cucumbers, Kirby preferred, peeled and pureed; if using other cucumbers, seed them after peeling
¼ cup white wine vinegar
½ cup extra-virgin olive oil
1 cup diced red onion (about 1 medium onion)
1 cup diced red bell pepper
¾ cup finely chopped fresh basil
3 cloves garlic, minced
4 plum tomatoes, peeled, seeded, and chopped
1 tablespoon sugar
1 pound rotelle pasta
1 tablespoon crushed, dried oregano

1. Combine all the ingredients except the pasta and the oregano in a large bowl, and stir with a fork until well mixed. Add some salt and freshly ground pepper. Also add a bit more sugar if the sweet/sour taste is not to your liking.

2. Cook the pasta in boiling water, after some salt has been added to the boiling water, until al dente. Drain and immerse the colander in ice-cold water to stop the cooking. Drain the pasta really well by shaking the colander to remove as much liquid as possible.

3. Add the pasta to the sauce and stir to coat it with the sauce. Sprinkle with some crushed, dried oregano and serve. This is excellent at room temperature.

TIMBALE OF EGGPLANT AND PASTA
Timballa di pasta e melanzane

Serves 6

Sicilians are very fond of timbales, and it doesn't matter whether the container is made of pastry, vegetables, or pasta. I particularly like this one, a pasta filling with an eggplant shell, as it reminds me of the macaroni pie that was served to selected citizens of Donnafugata in Lampedusi's *The Leopard*. Try to include the grated caciocavallo cheese to make the dish authentically Sicilian. Caciocavallo is bound with a cord as is provolone, and bottle-shaped. It is inclined to be salty, so watch the amount of salt you use otherwise.

Mala insana, meaning "the raging apple," was the name given to eggplant *(melanzane)* for hundred of years because of its bitterness. People thought it had poisonous drippings. This is the reason it is necessary to salt eggplant and let it rest for thirty minutes or so. This is especially the case with the larger-size eggplants. Buy smaller-size ones with lovely green, capelike bracts and stems firmly attached. Loose bracts are an indication of aging and spoiling. The eggplant should be firm.

1 eggplant, about 1 pound
Vegetable oil for frying
1½ cups tomato sauce, see page 24
½ pound small pasta, such as penne, elbows, or shells, cooked al dente
4 large eggs, hard-boiled, peeled, and coarsely chopped
1 tablespoon finely chopped fresh oregano or 1 teaspoon dried
¾ cup combined grated caciocavallo and pecorino cheeses
2 tablespoons butter

1. Remove the top and bottom of the eggplant, leaving the skin on, It should be able to sit upright. Slice lengthwise into very thin slices. Salt each slice and put it in a colander set over a plate to drain, 30 minutes. Discard any liquid. Pat dry each slice and set aside.

2. Liberally brush each eggplant slice with oil and arrange them in a flat baking container, such as a jelly-roll pan, and broil them on both sides until they take on some color, about 4 minutes per side. Do not broil too closely to the heat source—about 6 inches from the broiling element is fine. Broil in batches if necessary. Remove the slices when cooked to paper toweling to drain.

3. Preheat the oven to 375°F. In a large bowl, combine the tomato sauce, cooked pasta, chopped eggs, oregano, all but 2 tablespoons of the cheese, and some salt and freshly ground pepper.

4. Butter a 2½-quart ceramic soufflé dish or a rounded glass ovenproof bowl and line it with ½ or more of the eggplant slices, making an attractive arrangement by overlapping each slice (imagine this as it will be turned out). The slices should overlap the baking dish, as they will later be turned over to close in the top side. Transfer the pasta mixture to the lined mold, fold over the overhanging eggplant slices, and add any remaining slices to fully close the mold.

5. Bake 30 to 40 minutes until heated through and bubbling. Remove from the oven, allow to rest 6 to 8 minutes, loosen the edges with a sharp knife, lay a flat plate over the mold, and turn it over. Carefully remove the baking dish. Dot the mold with butter and add the remaining cheese over all.

PASTA
HOW TO MAKE IT, COOK IT, SAUCE IT, AND EAT IT

<u>Making Pasta:</u>

This is about homemade pasta, pasta *fatta in casa*, as contrasted to the factory-mass-produced kind. It is only recently, the last twenty years or so, that pasta shops have opened, making fresh pasta daily. People began making the fresh pasta also at home, especially since the roller-type, inexpensive pasta machines came on the market. Fresh pasta and dried pasta may seem to be similar, but they are not and are used in different ways in Italian cooking. Rarely would someone sauce dried pasta such as spaghetti with the Bolognese ragu sauce; such a sauce is more suitable to freshly made lasagna. Neapolitans prefer their pasta dried, and they manufacture it for distribution not just all over Italy, but also all over the world. In the United States, Gia Russo brand pasta is imported from Naples, as are some other brands. Of course, there are other places in Italy besides Naples where excellent dried pasta is made (Del Verde in Abruzzo, DeCecco in Fara San Martino, also in Abruzzo, and Barilla in Lombardy, just to mention a few of them).

On most packages of factory-made pasta, the words *pasta di pura semola di grano duro* will appear, and this means that the pasta is made from the fine flour of the cleaned endosperm, or heart of the durum (hard) wheat grain. This is the cream of wheat, and in buying pasta, it is best to purchase brands with this claim.

Italians in Emilia-Romagna show a preference for fresh pasta, which they cut into tagliatelle or roll out for tortellini. In making fresh pasta, experience will count, because formulas do not always fit exactly when the flours differ (they absorb eggs differently), and eggs vary in size. There is a general guideline, however, and my basic rule in making pasta is for every egg, add three-quarters of a cup of flour Basically, just use flour and egg with pinches of salt. Many of my friends in Italy, especially those living in rich olive-oil-producing areas, such as Lucca, will add several tablespoons of their oil, or more. Since many of the sauces include olive oil, it is left out of these guidelines. However, you may add

one to two teaspoons of olive oil to one- and two-egg pastas, and a tablespoon to three- and four-egg pastas. You should try making pasta with and without the olive oil and make your own determination about the ease of kneading, rolling, cutting, cooking, and eating it.

One-Egg Pasta
Makes about ½ pound, enough for 2 full servings

¾ cup all-purpose unbleached flour
1 egg
¼ teaspoon salt
1 teaspoon olive oil, optional

Two-Egg Pasta
Makes about ¾ pound, serving 3 or 4

1½ cups all-purpose unbleached flour
2 eggs
½ teaspoon sea salt
2 teaspoons olive oil, optional

Three-Egg Pasta
Makes about 1 pound, for 5 or 6 servings

2¼ cups all-purpose unbleached flour
3 eggs
¾ teaspoon sea salt
1 tablespoon olive oil, optional

Four-Egg Pasta
Makes about 1½ pounds, for 7 or 8 servings

3 cups all-purpose unbleached flour
4 eggs
1 teaspoon salt
1 tablespoon olive oil, optional

1. Put the flour on a flat surface or in a bowl and form a well deep enough to hold the eggs. The sides should be kept high enough to prevent the eggs from running out. Break the eggs into the well, add the salt, and the optional oil, with a small whisk or fork, beat the eggs lightly and, in so doing, begin to pick up a little of the flour from inside the well with the whisk or fork. Incorporate the eggs into the flour until no longer runny. A good technique for doing this is to hold the wall of flour with 1 hand while whisking with the other.

2. When all the flour has been incorporated, make a ball with the dough. Put the ball on a flat surface and start kneading. With the heel of your hand, push down firmly into the center, giving the dough a slight turn and pushing down again. Dust your hands with flour as you knead, especially if there is some stickiness. A 1-egg recipe will take 5 minutes of kneading, up to about 10 minutes for the 4-egg recipe and varying amounts in between.

3. The dough should rest for a minimum period of 15 minutes. Cover with a cloth or a bowl. You can roll out a ball of dough made with 2 eggs if you have a large, flat work surface or a large pasta board. Otherwise, cut the ball of dough in 2.

4. To roll by hand, lightly flour the surface on which the rolling will take place. Flatten the dough with a rolling pin by rolling first forward toward you and then

backward, away from you. With each roll, turn the dough by ¼. Try to keep the dough as round as possible. The sheet of pasta (this is what rolled out dough is called) about ⅛ inch thick. Don't flour the dough too much, as it will toughen it.

5. To make any of the string pastas, such as tagliatelle or fettuccine, roll up the pasta as you would a jelly roll. Hold the roll with 1 hand and slice with the other hand the thickness of pasta you wish. Open out the cut pasta with both hands and put it on a lightly floured towel to dry for several minutes. Cornmeal may be used in place of flour.

How to use the smooth-roller pasta machine:

The smooth rollers of a pasta machine will produce several thicknesses of pasta by turning a knob to widen or narrow the opening between the smooth rollers. Most of these machines have six settings. Run each ball of dough (a three-egg pasta after resting should be cut into six pieces that are to be formed into balls and put through the rollers) through the opening two times without folding it. Some people fold the dough, but that seems to distort the shape. It is not necessary to put each piece of dough rolled out through each of the openings. On a six-notch machine, roll the dough through opening six, then four, and then two. For very thin pasta, roll through the thinnest opening, number one. Very lightly flour each strip of dough after it is rolled; try to do this with a brush.

Cooking the Pasta:

The rules are simple.

1. Use 4 quarts of water for each pound of pasta. The water should come to a rolling boil before adding anything.
2. Add 1½ tablespoons coarse salt for every 4 quarts of water.
3. Put the pasta in right away and all at once. Stir with a wooden fork.
4. Cook to al dente stage (firm to the bite) and remember that fresh pasta cooks in a matter of 2 to 4 minutes. At no time run the cooked pasta under cold water (this may be called for as an exception when making pasta salads).
5. When draining, put the pasta in a colander, shake it to remove as much water as possible (some recipes call for reserving 1 or 2 cups of the boiling liquid, so be sure to check this out before pouring it down the drain), and return the pasta to the pan in which it cooked, or follow the specific direction of the recipe. Many recipes call for returning the cooked pasta to a skillet with sauce in it to marry the pasta and sauce. If the pasta is to be held—usually it is not—add a tablespoon of good olive oil or butter and stir—this will help keep the strands from sticking together.

6. Most Italians combine part of their sauce with the just-drained pasta, toss it well, and then add more sauce on top. Rarely is pasta put on a plate with the sauce spooned over it.

How to Eat Pasta:

Italians do not use forks and spoons to eat pasta. Table settings do include the spoon and fork, but that is for tossing the pasta and sauce at the table, not for eating it. Put the fork into a few strands of spaghetti. Let the tines of the fork rest against the curve of the bowl or the curved indentation of the plate, and twirl the fork around, giving it brief, quick lifts to prevent too much pasta from accumulating. If pasta is cooked properly, it will twirl easily around the fork and some of it will dangle, but not much of it.

Bread is always on the table in Italy with pasta and other food, and there is always more cheese in a bowl. As for putting cheese on pasta with fish sauces, it is a matter of taste. I think you should do what pleases you.

CASONCELLI (RAVIOLI), BERGAMO STYLE
Casonsei alla Bergamasca

Makes 40 to 50 ravioli

These ravioli are made basically the same as most others, except for the filling, which combines pork, chicken, and salami. It is difficult to find this particular type of ravioli in food shops, or even Italian specialty stores in theUnited States, so they have to be homemade. Because the filling is somewhat complex in taste and texture, they are dressed simply in melted butter and sage with the delightful crisped crumbs.

To make the pasta:
1½ to 2 cups unbleached all-purpose flour
2 eggs, lightly beaten
1 tablespoon extra-virgin olive oil

1. To make the pasta, put 1½ cups flour in a bowl or on a flat work surface. Make a well in it and add the eggs, 1 tablespoon of oil, and some salt. Mix with a fork, holding the outer rim of the flour to keep its shape while mixing in the center. Keep doing this until most of the flour has been absorbed. If too moist, add a little more flour. Knead the dough, pushing down with the palms of your hands to make a smooth, satiny dough, kneading 4 or 5 minutes, resting 1 or 2, kneading some more. Cover with a damp cloth and let rest for 30 minutes.

To make the filling:
4 tablespoons extra-virgin olive oil
¼ pound ground pork and chicken (equal amounts)
2 tablespoons finely chopped salami
2 tablespoons each finely chopped carrots, shallots, and celery
2 tablespoons freshly grated Parmesan cheese
3 tablespoons fresh bread crumbs
1 large egg, lightly beaten
1 tablespoon finely chopped Italian parsley

1. Heat 2 tablespoons oil in a sauce pan and sauté the pork, chicken, and salami until they are browned, about 6 minutes. Add the carrots, shallots, and celery and sauté 10 minutes, stirring every few minutes.

2. Remove the sauce pan from the heat, allow to cool 5 minutes, and then add the cheese, bread crumbs, egg, parsley, and the remaining olive oil. Mix lightly but well. Adjust salt and pepper seasoning as needed. Set aside.

To make the ravioli

1. Cut the dough in four 4 pieces and roll through a pasta machine, working up to the next to last setting. The strips should be at least 4 to 5 inches wide. Lay a strip of pasta on a flat work surface and spoon a scant teaspoon of filling onto the pasta, making 2 rows at least 2 inches apart down the middle, and between each filling, the length of the strip. Dip a very small brush in warm water and brush around each spoonful of filling. Cover with another sheet of pasta. Press down with your fingers, going around each filling to secure the 2 pastas together. Use a ravioli cutter and cut into individual ravioli. Set aside on very lightly floured cloth towels if ready to cook them within ½ hour. If not, put them on a plate, cover with damp towels, and set in the refrigerator for several hours or overnight.

2. Cook the casoncelli in rapidly boiling salted water until they come to the top, about 4 or 5 minutes. While they are cooking, make the sauce.

To make the sauce:

8 tablespoons butter
10 fresh sage leaves
3 tablespoons fresh bread crumbs

1. In a large skillet, heat the butter and add the sage leaves. Brown the butter slightly to cook the sage. Drain the ravioli well and add to the skillet. Stir carefully to coat the ravioli. Transfer to a large platter and sprinkle with the bread cumbs. Serve right away.

PASTA BOWS WITH FRESH SPINACH, MUSHROOMS, AND CREAM
Farfalle primaverile

Serves 4 to 6

Primaverile means springlike, and it would be wonderful if this dish could be made when spinach is as fresh from the garden as it can be. However, this dish can be made anytime of the year, as spinach is almost always available in the markets. Purchase young, fresh spinach or, if packaged, baby spinach. I believe Giulietta (and Romeo) would have preferred this dish to potato gnocchi. When I was staying at Giorgio and Ilaria Miani's home in Contignano, south of Sienna, I cooked this dish because it's easy, and easy to double for a large group. I had invited eleven nieces and nephews to join me. Ivana Fabbrizzi, the Mianis' treasured cook and housekeeper, liked the idea of this dish and its springlike nature—she saw the pasta bows as things little girls put in their hair, only as Italians can imagine, and asked if she could be the twelfth niece.

1 pound cremini or button mushrooms
¼ cup fresh lemon juice
6 tablespoons butter
2 cloves garlic, minced
¼ cup marsala wine
1½ cups heavy cream
1 pound pasta bows
4 cups finely shredded fresh spinach leaves
½ cup freshly grated Parmesan cheese

1. Wipe the mushrooms with damp kitchen toweling, cut off the stem ends and discard, and slice the mushroom caps thinly. Put in a bowl with the lemon juice and toss well.

2. Melt the butter in a large skillet and add the garlic and the marsala. Cook about 3 minutes and add the mushrooms. Stir well and cook 8 minutes longer. Add the cream and bring the mixture to boil. Season with salt and freshly ground pepper. Keep this sauce at a simmer, about 5 minutes, and then remove from the heat.

3. Cook the pasta al dente according to directions on the package. Drain and return the pasta to the pan in which it cooked. Add all the shredded spinach except about ⅓ cup, and the cream sauce. Toss lightly but well. To serve, apportion the pasta and add a heaping tablespoon of Parmesan over the top. Garnish with some shredded spinach over the cheese. Serve right away.

Chapter 3

RISOTTO AND POLENTA

The best known rices of Italy are medium grain and are much valued for their soft-cooked texture. Italian rice, grown in the Piedmont and Lombardy regions, includes *arborio, carnaroli, vialone nano,* and *baldo*—use the "superfine" grade. American medium-grain rice can be substituted for these, although the Italian types are now found in most American supermarkets.

Risotto is Italy's contribution to the art of rice cooking. A technique as well as a dish, risotto exists in no other culture. It is creamy yet resilient to the bite, and with full flavors, a risotto is not merely cooked, it is built. Always use the best broth, rice, and cheese possible.

Polenta is a grainy, yellow flour, a type of meal made from ground corn, usually sold in coarse or fine varieties. Its versatility is seen in first courses, vegetable dishes, main courses, cookies, and cakes. American-made polenta is quite satisfactory for the dishes presented here (Arrowhead Mills and King Arthurr both have good yellow cornmeal).

Northern Italy loves polenta, but nowhere is it loved more than in the Veneto. It can be cooked in hundreds of ways, as it blends so easily with meats, poultry, fish, all kinds of vegetables; it can be sauced, but it doesn't have to be; it can be fried, baked, grilled, or served just plain hot from the sauce pan in which it cooked. It is amazing to think that a food that came from America could take hold this way in the northern regions of Italy. The great ships of the Venetian Republic came from Turkey and its empire by sea, and from the day they brought their first sack of maize to the Rialto Market in Venice, maize was called *granoturco*—Turkish corn—thinking it came from Turkey, not America.

RISOTTO WITH CHICKEN LIVERS, TUSCANY STYLE

Risotto coi fegatini di pollo

Serves 6

1 pound chicken livers
4 tablespoons extra-virgin olive oil
1 large onion, finely chopped
1⅔ cups Italian rice (arborio, vialone nano, or carnaroli)
1 cup light tomato sauce, see page 24
3 to 4 cups chicken or vegetable broth, heated
6 tablespoons butter
½ cup freshly grated Parmesan cheese
2 tablespoons finely chopped fresh sage

1. Rinse the chicken livers and cut away fat and connecting tissues. Rinse again and pat dry. Salt liberally and chop each liver lobe into 2 or 3 pieces. Set aside in a bowl.

2. Heat the oil in a sauce pan over medium heat and sauté the onions until they become translucent, about 5 minutes. Add the rice and stir well to combine the rice with the oil and onions. Lower the heat.

3. Add the tomato sauce and ½ cup broth, bring to boil over increased heat, lower the heat again to to achieve a steady simmer, and cook 20 minutes, stirring most of the time, adding additional broth ½ cup at a time until the rice is tender.

4. While the rice is cooking, melt ½ of the butter in a skillet and sauté the chicken livers over medium heat until nicely browned, 6 to 8 minutes. When the rice has cooked about 20 minutes, add the livers to the sauce pan, scraping the skillet with a rubber spatula. Continue simmer to cook the rice, up to 30 minutes. Taste for doneness and for seasoning. If more salt is needed, add it; also add a liberal amount of freshly ground pepper. Fold in the remaining 3 tablespoons butter.

5. Combine the cheese and sage in a small bowl. Serve the rice and livers in a bowl, on a platter, or on individual plates with a good sprinkle of Parmesan and sage.

POLENTA AND FONTINA CHEESE WITH TOMATOES AND ROASTED RED PEPPERS
Polenta con formaggio fontina e peperoni

Serves 6

Fontina, one of the most celebrated of Italian cheeses, comes from the celebrated Val d'Aoste region in the northwestern part of Italy. The breathtaking views of the Alps are a match for the taste of the straw-colored cheese with small holes. In this recipe, the cheese is strewn over polenta, cooked with tomatoes and roasted red peppers, and topped with fresh basil, a combination of foods made in heaven. Just add a fresh green salad dressed with extra-virgin olive oil and fresh lemon juice.

3 large red bell peppers
1 tablespoon olive oil
1 can (15 ounces) ready-to-use chopped tomatoes
1 polenta recipe—see below
1½ cups (6 ounces) shredded fontina cheese
½ cup finely chopped fresh basil

1. Broil the peppers on all sides until blackened. Put them in a paper bag, close the bag, and let rest 10 minutes. Peel, core, and seed the peppers, patting them dry with paper towels. Cut them into thin strips and set aside.

2. Heat the oil in a large nonstick skillet and cook the tomatoes and their juices 3 minutes. Add the pepper strips and cook 5 minutes over low heat. Set aside.

3. Preheat the oven to 350°F.

4. Put ¼ of the tomato/pepper sauce in an ovenproof dish (9x12x2). Arrange polenta squares over the sauce. Spoon the remaining sauce over the polenta. Add the fontina cheese over all and bake 20 to 30 minutes until the sauce is bubbling and the polenta is heated through. Sprinkle basil over the top and serve hot.

<u>To make the polenta:</u>
1 pound polenta
2 tablespoons butter

1. Bring 2 quarts of water to boil. Add 1½ teaspoons salt. Add the polenta a little at a time, stirring always with a wooden spoon to prevent lumping. When the polenta thickens, 20 to 30 minutes, add the butter and let stand several minutes. Pour into a flat dish or pan with a 1-inch rim to cool and solidify. Cut into 3-inch squares and use as suggested above.

RISOTTO, THE MILAN WAY
Risotto alla Milanese

Serves 6

Americans love risotto, but many of them fear cooking it. There is no mystery to cooking this if one follows the cardinal rule that the liquid should be added to the pan in small amounts and the rice should absorb it before adding more liquid. This rice is almost always served with veal shanks.

¼ cup dried mushrooms
½ pound butter
1 small onion, finely diced
2 tablespoons dry white wine
1 pound arborio, carnaroli, or vialaone nero rice
5 cups chicken broth
¼ teaspoon saffron threads, soaked in ¼ cup chicken broth
¾ cup freshly grated Parmesan cheese

1. Put the mushrooms in a large strainer and run under cool water to rid them of any dirt that may be there. Rinse several times until they are thoroughly clean. Then put them in a small bowl with about ½ cup warm water to soak, preferably for 2 hours, but minimally for 1. (Do not soak mushrooms beyond several hours.) Drain and have ready for use.

2. Melt the butter in a large sauce pan and sauté the onions until golden, about 5 minutes. Add some white pepper. Add the wine and, over high heat, cook, uncovered, until the wine evaporates, 2 to 3 minutes.

3. Add the rice, stir well to coat the rice, and cook 5 minutes. Stir in the drained mushrooms.

4. Add the broth, ½ cup at a time, stirring all the time. When the broth is absorbed, add another ½ cup. Keep doing this until the broth is used up, about 20 minutes. When the rice is al dente, add the saffron and its liquid. Add ½ cup of the cheese and stir. The saffron will make the rice a wonderful yellow color.

5. To serve, put all the rice in a shallow bowl, or put some on each of 6 plates alongside the veal shanks, and top with the remaining cheese.

POLENTA IN BERGAMO
Polenta Taragna

Serves 4

It is best and easiest to use Arrowhead Mills Yellow Corn Grits, organically produced, to make this polenta. It is available in most supermarkets. Also use the buckwheat flour made by Arrowhead Mills. The original recipe calls for local Italian cheese called *formaggio di monte grassi*, which is difficult to find in most cheese shops, so I have found it easy to use taleggio or fontina as a satisfactory substitute.

6 cups water
1¼ cups yellow corn grits (preferably Arrowhead Mills)
¼ cup buckwheat flour (preferably Arrowhead Mills)
½ cup taleggio or fontina cheese, cut in small pieces
4 tablespoons butter
6 fresh sage leaves, 4 chopped finely, 2 cut in halves lengthwise

1. In a medium sauce pan, bring the water to boil. Add some salt.

2. Slowly, stir in the grits and the buckwheat flour. Bring to a boil, lower the heat, and simmer, uncovered, over low heat, 5 minutes, stirring often.

3. Remove the pan from the heat. Add the cheese, butter, and finely chopped sage leaves. Stir to melt the cheese and butter. Then transfer to a flat-type bowl. Arrange 4 half sage leaves to resemble a flower with 4 petals in the center and top of the polenta. Serve now or keep warm in a 250°F oven up to ½ hour or so.

THE DOGE'S RICE AND PEA "SOUP"
Risi e Bisi alla Veneziana

Serves 6

A good Venetian friend with whom I shared many meals in Venice was Hedy Giusti. This is her recipe. I saw a lot of Venice through Hedy's eyes and heard even more via her tongue. She was fierce in her opinion if it had anything to do with Venice. I dare not alter the recipe. This is probably the most famous of all Venetian rice dishes. The doges, the city's rulers, served it on April 25 each year at a banquet held to celebrate the feast day of Saint Mark, the patron saint of Venice. The spring banquet was held just as the first sweet, tender young peas, this dish's main ingredient, were harvested. Hedy only made this when fresh peas were in season. It may be cooked out of season by using frozen baby peas.

8 tablespoons (1 stick) butter
1 medium onion, cut into ½-inch dice
2 slices prosciutto, finely chopped
3 pounds (in the shell) fresh peas, shelled, or
1 package (16 ounces) frozen small peas
4 cups each chicken and beef broth
2 cups arborio, vialone nero, or carnaroli rice
2 tablespoons finely chopped Italian parsley
1 cup freshly grated Parmesan cheese

1. Melt the butter in a large sauce pan over medium heat. Add the onion and prosciutto and sauté until the prosciutto crisps, about 5 minutes.

2. Add the fresh peas, and some salt if you wish, and cook 2 minutes, stirring all the time. Add the broth and bring to boil, then reduce the heat to simmer and cook, uncovered, 10 minutes (see note). Add the rice and parsley, then reduce the heat to a slow and steady simmer. Cover and cook until the rice is al dente, tender but still firm to the bite, about 15 minutes.

3. Remove the sauce pan from the heat and stir in the cheese. Taste and adjust the seasoning, adding salt if needed, and ladle into warmed bowls.

Nota bene: At this point, if using frozen peas, add them when the liquid reaches the boil, but do not cook ten minutes; instead, add the rice and parsley and continue with the remainder of step two.

LAYERED, BAKED POLENTA, VENETIAN STYLE
Polenta Pasticciata alla Veneziana

Serves 6

Venice in winter is the home of the grandiose Carnival; in summer it boasts the historic regatta on the Grand Canal. But the best times in Venice can be spring and autumn, when some feeling of tranquility may be possible. Walk slowly through the shopping streets (called the *Mercerie*) leading to the Rialto Bridge—along the way, see the greengrocer and fishmonger shops that receive their goods by boat. Think of the trattorie along the beach and recall Thomas Mann's *Death in Venice*. Feast on squid, eels, mussels, clams, and calf's liver, roasted quail with butter and herbs, and, yes, on layered, baked polenta, Venetian style.

To make the polenta:

Serves 10 to 12

This method uses American-made polenta, called yellow corn grits, organically produced by Arrowhead Mills.

6 cups water
2 cups yellow corn grits
1 teaspoon salt

1. Bring water to boil in a large sauce pan. Add salt. Pour in the cornmeal with 1 hand while stirring with the other, using a wooden spoon. The cornmeal should be added *a pioggia*—which means "like a gentle rain." Cook and stir 20 to 25 minutes or until a spoon stands up by itself.

2. Pour into 2 oiled loaf pans, each 5x9x2½ inches, or 1½ quarts) and cool in the refrigerator 2 hours. Unmold and slice, and proceed as described below.

To make the sauce:

¼ pound salt pork, finely chopped
1 medium onion, finely chopped
1 medium carrot, finely diced
1 rib celery, trimmed and finely diced
½ cup imported dried mushrooms, soaked ½ hour in warm water, water reserved
1 can (14½ ounces) diced tomatoes

1. Sauté the salt pork in a sauce pan over medium heat, and when it has rendered some fat, add the onion, carrot, and celery and sauté until the vegetables take on some color, about 8 minutes.

2. Drain the mushrooms and finely chop them. Add to the vegetables and cook 2 or 3 minutes, stirring most of the time. Add the tomatoes and some freshly ground pepper. Taste for salt seasoning and add some if needed (remember that the salt pork is quite salty). Add ½ cup of the mushroom water and cook 15 minutes. Set this sauce aside.

To assemble the dish:

Sliced polenta, as above
Sauce, as above
8 tablespoons butter
½ cup freshly grated Parmesan cheese

1. Preheat oven to 375°F.

2. Butter a baking dish deep enough to hold 3 layers of polenta: oval dish, 10x15x2½ inches). Arrange a layer of polenta in the bottom of the baking dish. Spoon ½ of the sauce over it. Dot with 2 tablespoons of butter and 3 tablespoons of the Parmesan.

3. Make another polenta layer, add the remaining sauce, 2 tablespoons butter, and some Parmesan. Add a third layer and just dot with the remaining butter and Parmesan.

4. Bake until the top is golden, about 40 minutes. If the top isn't browned enough, run under the broiler. Remove from the oven, let sit several minutes, and serve with any 1 of the green salads in this book.

RISOTTO WITH SHRIMP, SEA BASS, AND SAFFRON

Risotto con gamberi e bronzino allo zafferano

Serves 6

Giuseppe Mazzoti, the Italian gastronomic writer, said there's not much difference between a risotto and rice soup, and that the people of Venice like risotto *all'onda*, or wavelike (it seems natural that a city of navigators would prefer it this way). What this really means is that Venetian risotto, unlike that of Milan, should not only be creamy, it should be almost liquid, or, as they say, *ondoso*, meaning wavy. There is an infinite variety of rice and fish dishes in the Veneto—almost every imaginable fish out of water, if fresh, can be added to rice.

When I prepare this dish, I see gondolas in the canals or moored to the tall barbershoplike posts called *briccole* near the Paglia Bridge, home for the gondolier's Madonna. There are gondolas for every purpose, even funeral ones with black pompoms. I see the sailor jumpers and straw hats with gay ribbons. I hear the soft hums of the songs they sing, and smell the risotto that they and I will eat a bit later.

1 pound fresh shrimp (16 to 20 count), shelled (reserve shells for broth) and deveined
4 cups fish/shrimp broth at boiling point, see page 379
2 small zucchini, 1x6 inches
1 stick butter
½ cup finely chopped shallots
2 cups Italian rice, preferably vialone nano
1 cup dry white wine
½ teaspoon saffron threads
4 tablespoons freshly grated Parmesan cheese
½ pound fresh sea bass fillets (or similar white fish fillets), rinsed, dried, cut in 1- to 2-inch squares.

1. Rinse the shrimp and pat dry with paper towels. Set aside. (If you have forgotten to heat the fish broth, do so now.)

2. Rinse zucchini. Cut off ends and slice each zucchini in ½ lengthwise. Cut each ½ again lengthwise. With a small, sharp knife, cut away and discard seedy pulp. Cut the strips crosswise in ¼-inch pieces. Set aside.

3. In a large sauce pan, melt 4 tablespoons butter over medium heat. Add the shallots, stir frequently, and cook until they begin to take on some color, about 4 minutes. Add the rice and stir to coat it, 1 to 2 minutes.

4. Add the wine, zucchini, and shrimp. Cook until the wine evaporates, about 5 minutes. Add some hot fish broth, ½ cup at a time, waiting for the rice to absorb the liquid before adding the next cup of broth. Stir most of the time to prevent sticking.

5. When the rice has cooked 10 to 12 minutes, add the saffron and 2 tablespoons Parmesan cheese. Keep stirring and adding more broth as it is absorbed by the rice. Add the pieces of bass or other fish and stir gently.

6. The rice should be cooked properly in 25 to 30 minutes. The rice should be firm, not appear dry, and tender to the bite (al dente). The whole dish should appear "wavy," so add a little more broth to make this *ondoso*, as they say in Venice. If more salt is needed, add it now.

7. Remove from the heat. Stir in the remaining 4 tablespoons butter and 2 tablespoons Parmesan cheese, stir, and let rest for several minutes before serving. Transfer to a serving dish and top with a liberal grinding of pepper, and more Parmesan cheese.

CHICKEN RISOTTO WITH VEGETABLES, VENETIAN STYLE
Risotto alla sbiraglia (Veneziana)

Serves 6

In northern Italy, rice is served as a first course, but this dish lends itself to serving as a main course—all it takes is the addition of a salad and a loaf of good Italian bread. Adding the butter and Parmesan at the end of its cooking time is an important finishing step, so add them then. When I am asked if I reheat risotto, I sheepishly admit that I do so in a microwave for a minute or two, depending on quantity, after adding a few drops of water over the rice and covering it with plastic wrap.

4 tablespoons extra-virgin olive oil
1 onion, finely chopped
1 carrot, finely chopped
1 rib celery, finely chopped
1 pound skinless, boneless chicken breasts, cut into ½-inch dice
½ cup dry white wine
1 cup tomato puree (do not use tomato paste)
4 to 6 cups chicken broth, heated
2¼ cups Italian rice
6 tablespoons butter, softened
1 cup freshly grated Parmesan cheese

1. Heat the oil in a large sauce pan and sauté the onions, carrots, and celery 5 to 6 minutes, stirring frequently until they take on some color.

2. Add the chicken pieces and cook 5 minutes, stirring all the time. Add the wine; let it boil and cook away, about 5 minutes.

3. Add the tomato puree, along with salt and freshly ground pepper. Bring to a boil, lower the heat to achieve a slow, steady simmer, partially cover the pan, and simmer 15 minutes. During this period, check to see if the mixture is too dry; if so add ½ cup of hot broth.

4. Add the rice, and stir thoroughly. Adding ½ cup of hot broth at a time, add the broth to the rice, stirring carefully so that the rice absorbs the broth. Continue doing this for 20 to 25 minutes, adding more broth when the rice has absorbed it. When the rice is tender (it is always best to taste a little of it to test for doneness), add a little more hot broth to make the risotto *ondoso*, wavy, as the Venetians like it.

5. Remove the pan from the heat and fold in the butter and ½ cup of the Parmesan cheese. This should be served right away, passing more Parmesan. Add a fresh baby spinach salad to complete the one-dish meal.

SPICY POLENTA WITH CHEESE, BROCCOLI DI RAPE, AND SAUSAGES

Polenta piccante con formaggio, rapini, e salsicce

Serves 6 to 12

This will make more than enough for six people, but it is delicious reheated and served the next day. It will keep in the refrigerator five or six days. This preparation can be made ahead and frozen up to a month.

3 quarts water
1 medium potato, peeled and cut into 4 pieces
1 pound broccoli di rape, trimmed, washed, and cut into 2-inch lengths
2 teaspoons salt
2½ cups polenta or yellow corn grits
1 tablespoon olive oil
4 Italian pork sausages (about 1 pound)
5 cups pork tomato sauce, see page 24 (2½ cups for making the polenta dish and 2½ cups for extra saucing)
¼ teaspoon red pepper flakes
1 cup freshly grated provolone or scamorza cheese (or 1 cup grated Auricchio)
½ cup freshly grated pecorino cheese
2 tablespoons butter

1. Combine the water and the potato in a large soup pot and cook the potato until tender, about 10 minutes. Remove and mash the potato and return it to the boiling water.

2. Add the broccoli di rape and the salt and cook 2 minutes. Add the polenta (or the cornmeal) in a steady flow—*a pioggia*—like a gentle rain, stirring all the time to avoid lumping. Lower the heat and cook about 25 minutes until the polenta comes away from the sides of the pot. Do not let it stick to the bottom of the pot, and beware of burning. Pour the cooked polenta into 2 oiled glass loaf pans. Let cool 2 to 4 hours, or overnight.

3. Heat the olive oil in a skillet and sauté the sausages until browned, about 8 minutes. Remove the sausages, cool them, and slice as thinly as possible.

4. Turn out the cooled polenta and slice thinly, about ⅓ inch. Butter a baking dish (9x12x2 inches) and pour a thin layer of the pork tomato sauce on the bottom. Lay ⅓ of the polenta slices over the sauce, adding ½ the amount of sliced sausages, ½ of the pepper flakes, and the cheeses as follows: ½ of the scamorza or provolone and ⅓ of the pecorino. Continue making another layer, like lasagna. Make a third layer with the remaining polenta slices, and sprinkle the remaining ⅓ cup pecorino on the top, dotting with butter.

5. Bake for about 1 hour in a preheated 375°F oven. Cool 5 minutes before serving.

Chapter 4

VEGETABLES AND LEGUMES

If I had to choose one family of food to live with for the rest of my life, I would choose vegetables. The variety is infinite: there are so many vegetables and so many ways to cook them. Moreover, I can't think of more beautiful things to look at. What can compare with the shape, color, or gleam of a bright red tomato? A smooth-as-silk, deep purple eggplant? The pure white cap of a mushroom? A bunch of carrots, with their fernlike ends? Lacy celery hearts? Fresh, pale green dandelion leaves? A majestic artichoke? A family of garlic cloves? The regal leek? The beauty and mystery of the inner rings of an onion?

ARTICHOKES COOKED IN A SAUCE PAN
Carciofi al tegame

Serves 6

Artichokes are a part of the most typical Roman meal. I particularly like this preparation because of its simplicity and taste. An Italian woman who sells artichokes at a vegetable stand in the Campo dei Fiori, where Roman chefs go early in the morning to do some of their major food shopping, gave this recipe to me.

12 baby artichokes, without chokes, trimmed
½ cup finely chopped fresh mint leaves plus 12 whole mint leaves
¼ cup finely chopped Italian parsley
3 cloves garlic, minced
⅔ cup extra-virgin olive oil plus 6 teaspoons
2 cups water

1. To prepare the artichokes, tear off the outer leaves and remove the stalk. Press down on each artichoke with the palm of your hand, adding a little pressure to open it up. Immediately plunge into acidulated water to keep them from turning dark. When ready to cook them, drain well and dry.

2. Combine the mint, parsley, garlic, salt, and pepper in a small bowl and mix well. Open the center of each artichoke and put in some, dividing the mint mixture appropriately.

3. Arrange the artichokes side by side in a heavy sauce pan with a cover. Pour ⅔ cup oil over all the artichokes, and then slowly add the water. Cover the pan and simmer over low-moderate heat for 1 hour. Remove the cover, and continue to cook over high heat to reduce the liquid, about 10 minutes.

4. Place 2 artichokes on each plate; pour 1 teaspoon of oil onto the plate crisscrossing the artichoke. Add 2 mint leaves to the side for garnish. Pass more salt and pepper.

FAVA BEANS, COUNTRY STYLE
Fave alla campagnola

Serves 6

Fava beans, sometimes called broad beans, look like large lima beans. Their texture is mealy and granular with an assertive flavor. Favas are very popular in Italy; they are eaten raw with Parmigiano or pecorino cheese. Their thick skins have to be peeled before eating. At certain times of the year, it is difficult to find fresh favas in theUnited States, so use canned beans. They must be drained and rinsed several times before adding other ingredients. This is a simple preparation with a great taste.

2 cans (15 or 16 ounces) fava, broad, or lima beans, drained and rinsed several times
½ cup extra-virgin olive oil
1 tablespoon finely chopped fresh oregano or 1 teaspoon dried
⅓ cup finely chopped chives

1. After rinsing the beans to rid them of their saltiness, drain well. Pat dry with paper toweling as best you can. Set aside.
2. In a medium-size sauce pan or large skillet, heat the oil. Add the beans, stir, and cook until the beans are heated through. Add the oregano and the chives, stir well, and cook 2 minutes longer. Add salt and freshly ground pepper. Remove from heat. These may be served hot or at room temperature, and will keep unrefrigerated for several hours, or refrigerate for 1 or 2 days and reheat.

Nota bene: Hungry Sultan is the name of the canned fava beans used in this preparation, but there are others.

SLOW-COOKED ROASTED PLUM TOMATOES
Pomodori al forno

Serves 8

At times, it is incredible to think that the tomato is a native South American plant that was brought to Europe in the sixteenth century, and that it wasn't until the nineteenth century that it was accepted as a food. In Italy (and in America), they say the best tomatoes are grown in San Marzano, an area of exceedingly rich soil, south of Rome toward Naples. Plum tomatoes, known as Italian or Roma, are meatier and less juicy than slicing tomatoes, so they are ideal for making sauces. Here they are slow-cooked and used as a condiment for the lamb. There are many canned plum tomatoes to choose from: Progresso, Pastene, and Vitelli—read the labels to be sure the tomatoes come from San Marzano, Italy.

½ cup extra-virgin olive oil
1 small onion, finely chopped
2 cloves garlic, peeled and minced
1 tablespoon finely chopped fresh rosemary leaves
¼ cup finely chopped fresh Italian parsley
2 cans (28 ounces) plum tomatoes, drained, seeded
2 tablespoons sugar

1. Preheat the oven to 275°F. Put 4 tablespoons oil in a ceramic or glass baking dish. Add the onions, garlic, rosemary, and parsley. Toss well and spread on the bottom of the baking pan.

2. When the tomatoes are drained, snip off any visible stem end and gently squeeze each tomato in the palm of your hand to release the seeds and excess juices. It helps to puncture the tomato with a paring knife to create the opening for the seeds and juice to escape. Fit the tomatoes, side by side, in a single layer in the baking pan. When all the tomatoes are in, sprinkle the remaining oil over all. Also sprinkle the sugar over everything, along with salt and freshly ground pepper.

3. Bake for 3 to 3½ hours. Serve warm.

CHICORY AND SMOKED MOZZARELLA ON THE GRILL
Cicoria e mozzarella affumicata alla griglia

Serves 6

Lavagna is the Italian word for slate, and this black stone from Liguria, when heated, is often used in Italy instead of grilling something on a gas-fired flattop. I was surprised to see it in use in New York City at the restaurant Il Cantinori on East 10th Street in Manhattan. The slate is first oiled, then heated in a broiler until almost red hot. Then it is put on a heatproof countertop, and there, vegetables of almost any description can be grilled. The lavagna stays hot for about thirty minutes. Chicory is used in this recipe, but the method works also for radicchio, sliced fennel, turnips, leeks, sliced eggplant, or zucchini.

As interesting as the lavagna cooking may be, use your gas-fired flattop grill if you have one; otherwise, use a large skillet on the stove.

6 small heads of green chicory
6 tablespoons extra-virgin olive oil
6 thin slices of smoked mozzarella

1. Remove the green leaves from each head of chicory so only the hearts are left. Trim each head and, if necessary, wash them and drain well.

2. Heat a gas-fired flattop until very hot. Place the chicory hearts on the grill and sprinkle each with a tablespoon of oil. With a spatula, press down on each head and cook until lightly browned, a minute or 2. Quickly turn them over and press down with a spatula again. Add salt and freshly ground pepper.

3. Just before removing, cover each head with a mozzarella slice. When the cheese melts, remove the chicory to a serving plate.

4. If using a skillet, heat the skillet with a little oil in it, place the chicory in it, pour more oil over the heads, and follow the remaining steps above.

ROASTED BROCCOLI AND CAULIFLOWER
Broccoli e cavolfiore arostiti

Serves 4 to 6

The discussion of the simplicity of Italian food may seem overdone, and it is not my aim to persist in it; however, here is another classic example of the subject of such discussions: the simplicity of Italian food. For me, the deliciousness of this simple preparation cannot be surpassed. It is, without question, one of my favorite dishes in this book, and it is perfect on any American table.

4 cups broccoli florets, including tender stems (1 bunch)
3 cups cauliflower florets (1 small to medium head)
½ cup extra-virgin olive oil
¼ to ½ cup freshly made bread crumbs, see page 302

1. After making the broccoli florets, take some of the heavy stems, cut away the bottom ½ of them, and discard. Pare the remaining stems, using a small, sharp knife, and cut in ½-inch widths. Use about 1 cup of these plus 3 cups of the broccoli florets to make 4 cups.

2. Put the broccoli and cauliflower pieces in a large bowl and pour the olive oil over them. Toss well to be sure to coat all the vegetable pieces, as this helps seal in their moisture.

3. Preheat the oven to 425°F. Arrange the vegetables in 1 layer in a baking pan. Bake for 8 minutes, turn over the vegetables and cook another 8 minutes. Check for doneness by putting a wooden skewer into a vegetable—if it pierces easily, the vegetables are done; if not, cook several minutes longer.

4. When done, remove the vegetables from the oven and salt them, and liberally add freshly ground pepper. Sprinkle a tablespoon or 2 more of olive oil. If ready to serve now, sprinkle with bread crumbs. If serving later, add the bread crumbs at the time of serving. These may be served lukewarm.

VEGETABLES AND LEGUMES

BAKED MUSHROOMS WITH HAZELNUTS
Funghi con nocciole al forno

Serves 6

It is amazing to discover the extent to which one ingredient can alter, or even glorify, the nature of a dish. In this case it is actually two ingredients—the hazelnuts and the bread crumbs (hopefully homemade)—that glorify the mushrooms.

12 large mushrooms
2 tablespoons fresh lemon juice
4 tablespoons butter
½ cup finely chopped hazelnuts
¼ cup fresh bread crumbs

1. Carefully remove the stem from each mushroom. If part of the stem is still attached to the cap, cut it away with a small paring knife. Reserve stems for another use or discard. Wipe each mushroom with a damp towel; do not wash. Lay the mushrooms on a tray and sprinkle with lemon juice. Add salt and freshly ground pepper.

2. Preheat oven to 375°F. Melt the butter in a skillet over medium-high heat, add the hazelnuts, and sauté 1 minute, stirring all the time. Remove from the heat.

3. Fill each mushroom cap with the hazelnuts. Sprinkle with the bread crumbs. Bake 15 minutes, or until golden brown, watching carefully for the last few minutes of baking; the mushroom caps should stay firm and not fall apart. Serve at room temperature.

MARINATED SWISS CHARD STALKS IN POOR BOY WRAPS
Coste di bietola nel sacco di mendiccante

Makes 12 packets

Swiss chard looks like oversized spinach with very long white or red stems. Italians love this vegetable and prepare it in many ways. When buying it, go for a deep green color with crinkly and crisp leaves. Many Americans discard the long white or red stems; Italians do otherwise and use them these ways: fried, steamed, baked, with marinades and salads, and just sautéed simply with the green leaves, olive oil, and garlic. This picnic from Pienza, as most other al fresco meals, requires something a little special, a little out of the ordinary. Here, we take the stalks, cook and marinate them, and put them in envelopes (some of which will be torn, thus the poor-boy connotation) made with the dark green leaves. At first, this will seem labor intensive, but if you read and re-read the recipe, you will see it's quite a simple procedure, and, best of all, they can be made ahead and travel well. This makes twelve packets.

12 large, fresh Swiss chard leaves, with stalks, red or white
¼ cup plus 2 tablespoons extra-virgin olive oil
1 large potato, peeled and diced ¼ inch
1 large or 2 small red onions, finely chopped
2 cloves garlic, minced
2 tablespoons wine vinegar, red or white
1 tablespoon honey
2 tablespoons finely chopped Italian parsley
Pinch red pepper flakes

1. Wash and dry the leaves and cut out the stems with a scissors or a small, sharp knife. If large, pare the stalks if they look stringy (as you would a celery stalk), trim the rough edges, and cut the stems into 1-inch lengths. Cook these stems in boiling, salted water until tender, 4 to 5 minutes. Drain well, dry with paper toweling and put in a bowl. In the same boiling water, cook the leaves whole until tender, 2 to 3 minutes. Drain into cold water to keep them from cooking further. Dry with paper toweling. Set aside.

2. In a small skillet, heat 3 tablespoons oil and sauté the potatoes and onions until they become tender and take on some color, stirring all the time, 6 to 8 minutes (both should be cooked, so test for doneness by tasting). Two minutes before they are done, add the garlic and continue cooking another minute or so. Transfer this to the bowl with the stems in it. In a small bowl combine the remaining oil with the vinegar, honey, parsley, red pepper flakes, salt, and freshly ground pepper, and pour over the stems. Mix lightly but well.

3. Carefully set 4 leaves of Swiss chard on a flat work surface. In the center of each, put a tablespoon of stems, and fold

the leaf into an envelope shape, first the flap closest to you, then the 2 sides, and then the top flap. Turn over and place it in a glass dish, 7x11x2 inches. Continue making the envelopes and put in the container, making 2 rows of packets. If any of the stem mixture is left, spoon it down the center of the dish lengthwise, between the rows of envelopes. Do not cover the packets with this. Any liquid remaining in the bowl should be poured all over the packages. Cover and refrigerate if not ready to use, but be sure these sit at room temperature for several hours before serving.

WHITE BEAN AND MUSHROOM CASSEROLE
Fagioli ai funghi

Serves 8

Everyone knows of Tuscany and its Chianti wine and its Fiorentina steak, but not everyone knows that the region's best-kept secret lies with its humblest ingredients—beans and bread. *Fagioli*, small white beans, are eaten in large quantities throughout the region, dressed up in many different ways at most meals. Their fellow countrymen know the Tuscans as *mangiafagioli*, often said in a somewhat uncomplimentary fashion. As a rule, the beans are served simply. In one of the most dramatic Tuscan recipes, beans are cooked in a wine flask—*fagioli nel fiasco*. They are actually cooked in an empty Chianti wine flask because the narrow opening of the bottles keeps steam from escaping, and the beans retain maximum flavor. They cool in the flask and are then served with olive oil, fresh lemon juice, and seasonings.

In the following upscale recipe, the beans are joined with mushrooms, onions, garlic, celery, and wine to make a one-dish meal, served over the ubiquitous slice of bread, toasted and rubbed with garlic and oil. The unusual personal touch here is to reserve some of the beans and marinate them to add as an extra layer of taste. This is a nourishing dish on its own; however, enhance it by adding a salad of sliced fresh oranges, papaya, or grapefruit with a splash of lemon juice and a sprinkle of freshly ground pepper.

16 ounces dried white beans (2 cups), soaked overnight in water, drained
6 tablespoons extra-virgin olive oil, preferably Tuscan
1 medium onion, finely chopped
2 cups thinly cut celery, including leaves
8 cloves garlic, minced
1 tablespoon white wine vinegar
1 teaspoon finely chopped fresh rosemary
2 pounds fresh mushrooms, wiped with moist paper towels, ends trimmed, sliced thinly
¼ cup dried mushrooms, soaked in warm water 30 minutes, drained, and finely chopped
½ cup white wine
2 to 3 cups vegetable broth
8 slices bruschetta, see page 301
1 cup freshly grated Parmesan cheese

1. Put the soaked and drained beans in a colander. Under cool running water, rinse and sort them to be sure there is nothing extraneous in them, such as a pebble. Set aside.

2. Heat 1 tablespoon olive oil in a large casserole that is stovetop and ovenproof. Add the onion, celery and garlic and cook them over medium heat until the onion becomes translucent, about 5 minutes.

3. Add the drained beans, 1 teaspoon salt, and 1 teaspoon pepper. Add water to cover the beans by 1 inch. Bring to boil, lower the heat to get a steady simmer, cover the casserole, and cook 1 hour, until the beans are tender. Remove 1 cup of beans and put in a bowl with 3 tablespoons olive oil, the vinegar, the rosemary, and ½ teaspoon pepper. Stir well and set aside.

4. Heat the remaining 2 tablespoons of oil in a skillet and add the fresh and dried mushrooms. Cook over medium-high heat, stirring frequently, until the mushrooms become tender, about 15 minutes. Add the wine, toss lightly but well, increase the heat, and cook until the wine is reduced by about ½. Set the skillet aside.

5. Puree the beans in the large casserole (these are the ones not marinating) in a processor and return them to the casserole in which they originally cooked. Add the mushrooms and their liquid and 2 cups of vegetable broth. Over medium heat, cook 15 minutes. If you think more liquid is needed, add some or all of the remaining broth, but remember the mixture should be thick.

6. To serve, put a bruschetta in each flat rimmed-bowl and spoon some of the bean mixture over the bread. Top with a tablespoon of the cold marinated beans. Sprinkle some Parmesan over all, and pass more of the cheese for those wanting it.

GREEN PEAS, GRANDMOTHER'S WAY
Piselli della nonna

Serves 6

When the early spring peas come into the markets, people rush out to buy them as quickly as they can, and they are often prepared homestyle (*casalinga*) or in mother's way or grandmother's style. Here is a recipe given to me by a vendor who happens to be a grandmother.

4 tablespoons butter
6 thin slices of prosciutto, cut crosswise into thin strips
½ cup finely chopped onions
1 teaspoon all-purpose flour
½ cup white wine or 1 cup chicken broth
2 pounds fresh peas, shelled, or 1½ packages (10 ounces each) of frozen peas, preferably tiny green peas
1 small packet of fresh herbs (basil, rosemary, and marjoram) or a pinch of each, dried

1. Heat the butter in a large skillet and, over low heat, sauté the prosciutto and the onion until the prosciutto crisps, up to 10 minutes. Remove the ham and onions, leaving whatever juices may be in the pan. Add the flour and stir to amalgamate.

2. Add the wine or the broth and bring to boil. Add the peas and the herb packet or dried herbs and cook 10 minutes if the peas are fresh; if frozen and thawed, cook only 3 or 4 minutes.

3. Add the cooked prosciutto and onions; cook a few minutes more, stirring. Remove the herb packet if there is 1 and serve.

VEGETABLE MATCHSTICKS, IN BUNDLES, WITH GREEN SAUCE
Bastoncini di vegetali con salsa verde all'italiana

Serves 4

Bastone in Italian means a stick, staff, cane, or baton. *Bastoncini* means little sticks, and this play on words is part of the Italians' spirit in their kitchens. These are fun to make, are tasty with the sauce, and add a touch of Italian chicness in presentation.

8 snow peas, trimmed
2 celery ribs, trimmed and strings removed
2 small zucchini, scrubbed with peel on, ends trimmed
12 green beans, trimmed
1 large green bell pepper, stemmed, ribbed, seeded, and cut into ¼x2½-inch lengths
2 scallions
Green sauce, see below

1. Cut the snow peas, celery ribs, zucchini, and green beans the same size as the bell pepper. If the zucchini has a seedy, limp center, cut it away and discard. Keep in mind that the vegetables are being cut to form bundles that will be tied with a scallion length.

2. Steam each vegetable, except the scallions, to the al dente stage. When all the vegetables are done, dry them.

3. Trim the scallions and carefully separate the leaves, keeping them as long as possible. Drop the raw scallion leaves into a skillet of boiling water. Immediately turn off the heat and remove the scallion lengths to a towel to dry. Preheat the oven to 325°F.

4. Place 1 scallion length on a work surface. Over it, arrange a variety of vegetables to make a bundle about 1 inch in diameter. Wrap the bundle with the scallion, typing it gently. Complete the procedure by making more bundles. Arrange the bundles in a shallow baking dish. When the bundles are assembled, spoon the green sauce over each bundle and warm in the oven 10 to 15 minutes before serving.

To make the Green Sauce (salsa verde):
¼ cup extra-virgin olive oil
1 large clove garlic, minced
2 anchovy fillets, minced
1 tablespoon finely chopped gherkins
1 tablespoon capers
1 tablespoon finely chopped Italian parsley

1. Combine all the ingredients, mix well, and set aside, or refrigerate if not needed now.

WEDGES OF SAVOY CABBAGE WITH FRESH LEMON

Verza al limone

Serves 4

Cabbage has been domesticated for over 2,500 years. It was in use in the eastern Mediterranean, and the Greeks and Romans loved it. Cabbage did not grow in compact heads as we know it today. It was during the Middle Ages that farmers in northern Europe developed compact-headed varieties. These cabbages are capable of thriving in cold climates. Savoy cabbage has crinkled, ruffly, yellow-green leaves that form a less compact head than other types. It is very popular in Italy. Italians advise not to pick a head of Savoy until it has been hit by the frost—for only then will it have reached full flavor.

1 small head of Savoy cabbage
Juice of 2 lemons
4 tablespoons butter
Freshly grated nutmeg

1. Core the cabbage and remove the outer green leaves, reserving 1 of the leaves. Cut the cabbage into 4 wedges and put in cold, salted water. Allow to stay in the water a minimum 30 minutes.

2. Place the wedges, after draining, in the top part of a steamer over boiling water. Cover the wedges with the reserved outer green leaf, which has been rinsed and dried—this will help keep in the steam. Cook until tender, 10 to 15 minutes.

3. In a large skillet, add the lemon juice and the butter. Heat until the butter dissolves. Add salt and freshly ground pepper and a sprinkle of freshly grated nutmeg. Spoon the sauce over the wedges and heat just long enough to immerse the wedges in the lemon sauce.

PIEDMONT BAKED BEANS
Tofeja (Fagioli di grasso)

Serves 6 to 8

This is a dish of baked beans with pork and herbs (called *tofeja*). In some parts of Italy, this dish is still made in a *tofeja*, a low terra-cotta cooking pot with four handles, but an ovenproof casserole will suffice. It is a rich, fragrant, marvelously thick preparation laden with velvety beans and meltingly tender pork, a treat for the senses in every respect.

The dish is traditionally served at Carnevale, and its richness is particularly appreciated because this celebration is the last opportunity to eat meat before the beginning of Lent. Years ago, the dish was flavored with pigs' feet and rolls of pork fat filled with herbs (especially rosemary) and spices, which was how my father made it. To keep up with current cooking trends in Italy and America, small chunks of lean pork shoulder are now substituted for the pigs' feet, and the amount of pork fat is substantially cut back to reduce the fat, but not the flavor.

Forget American pork and beans—there is no comparison to this Italian bean dish. To accompany this dish, cook up some vegetables, any kind you like, and mix them with oil, vinegar, salt, freshly ground pepper, and some finely chopped fresh herbs. Or, cook asparagus and combine them with a salad dressing, and serve with the beans.

1 pound dried Great Northern beans
2 large cloves garlic, minced
2 teaspoons rubbed sage leaves
1 teaspoon finely chopped rosemary
½ teaspoon freshly grated nutmeg
¼ teaspoon red pepper flakes
4 ounces fresh pork fat
2 tablespoons extra-virgin olive oil
1 pound lean pork shoulder, cut into ½-inch pieces, or 2 pigs' feet, cut into 2-inch pieces
1 large onion, diced ½ inch
4 bay leaves
2 medium carrots, peeled and thinly sliced
1 medium rib celery, thinly sliced
7 cups chicken broth
½ cup freshly grated pecorino cheese, such as Romano
¼ cup finely minced fresh chives

1. Pick over the beans, discarding any stones. Soak them overnight in cool water to cover by 2 inches. Drain and set aside.

2. Combine the garlic, sage, rosemary, nutmeg, red pepper flakes, salt, and freshly ground pepper in a small bowl. Set aside.

3. Thinly slice the pork fat to make 4 pieces, each about 3x2½ inches in size. Sprinkle about ½ of the garlic mixture over the slices of fat, dividing evenly. Roll up each slice and tie with string in 2 places. Set aside.

4. Preheat the oven to 350°F.

5. Heat the oil in a flameproof casserole over medium heat. Add the rolls and sauté until they lose color and become somewhat translucent and lightly browned, about 15 minutes. Fat splatters when very hot; use a splatter guard if you have 1. Remove the rolls and set them aside on a plate or paper towels. Add the pork shoulder or the pigs' feet to the drippings in the casserole, turning the pieces on all sides, about 10 minutes. Add the onion and the remaining garlic mixture. Sauté, stirring, until the onion softens, 3 to 4 minutes.

6. Add the beans, bay leaves, carrots, celery, reserved pork fat rolls, and broth to the casserole. Remove from the heat, cover tightly, and place in the oven. Bake for 1 hour without removing the cover. Reduce the heat to 300°F and cook until the beans are very tender and the mixture is very thick, about 2 hours more. Remove and discard the pork fat and bay leaf.

7. Combine the grated cheese and chives in a small bowl. Serve the beans with teaspoonfuls of the cheese mixture on top of each serving. Serve the remaining cheese mixture alongside.

BROCCOLI, BAKED WITH PROSCIUTTO
Broccoli con prosciutto al forno

Serves 6

I have never seen this dish served outside Italy, yet it is an ideal preparation for the American table. It is the way to serve broccoli to someone who may not be fond of it. Remember, this is a cooked broccoli dish—not one in which broccoli has been dipped in hot water and pulled out almost immediately. The prosciutto slice should crisp, allowing its juices and flavor to permeate the broccoli.

2 bunches fresh broccoli
2 tablespoons fresh lemon juice, plus 4 strips zest
¼ cup chicken broth
6 tablespoons butter
6 tablespoons Parmesan cheese
Sprinkles of nutmeg
6 thin slices of prosciutto

1. Trim the broccoli spears by removing all the leaves, keeping the florets in as large bunches as possible. Pare the stalks and cut off the bottom parts of the stem. (The way to do this is to use a paring knife and cut away 1 inch of the stem. You will feel it to be tender if it is; if not, keep removing pieces of stem until you reach the tender portion. Most Italians prefer the tender stems as much as the florets.) Rinse the trimmed broccoli and stems and drain.

2. Preheat oven to 400°F. Bring a large pot with water to boil. Add the broccoli, the lemon juice, and zest, and cook until tender, uncovered, over high heat, about 5 minutes. Drain.

3. In a large ceramic or glass baking dish, add the broth and the butter. Bake until the butter melts. Arrange the broccoli in 6 "bundles" and spoon the melted butter and broth over each. Add salt and freshly ground pepper. Sprinkle nutmeg and the cheese over each portion. Place a slice of prosciutto over each bundle and bake for 8 to 10 minutes. When serving, add some of the buttery juices remaining in the baking pan over each portion.

FRIED ZUCCHINI WITH CAPER AND CHIVE SAUCE

Zucchine piccanti

Serves 4

The secret to this dish is thoroughly drying the zucchini pieces before adding them to the skillet. If you would rather not use anchovies (I can't imagine why not, but some Americans are still squeamish about them), be sure to salt adequately. These must be served with fresh bread crumbs, and they should be added at the last moment.

4 zucchini, about 1x6 inches each

5 tablespoons extra-virgin olive oil

2 anchovy fillets, drained and dried

1 tablespoon each of chopped Italian parsley, capers (drained and chopped), and chopped chives

2 tablespoons white wine vinegar

¼ cup fresh bread crumbs, toasted

1. Rinse the zucchini and cut both ends off each 1. Cut each in ½ across the middle to make 2 smaller zucchini. Then cut these in ½ lengthwise. There should be 4 pieces from each zucchini. Dry with paper towels and set aside.

2. Heat 2 tablespoons oil in a large skillet and sauté the zucchini pieces on both sides until they are tender and lightly browned, 3 to 4 minutes per side. Leave in the skillet.

3. In a small bowl, combine the remaining oil and the anchovies, and, with a fork, mash the anchovies so they blend into the oil. Add the herbs and the vinegar. Liberally add freshly ground pepper. Taste for salt seasoning and add some if needed. Mix well and pour over the zucchini. Toss lightly but well. Transfer to a small platter and sprinkle with the bread crumbs.

STEWED SWEET PEPPERS, THE WAY THE GONDOLIERS LIKE TO EAT THEM
Papriche stufate

Serves 6

The market gardens of the Veneto coast are well known, and it's a joy to see the luscious peas, red ripe tomatoes, shiny yellow peppers, pale green curly-leafed cabbages, and especially the grand-looking, multicolored "baroque squashes" for sale. One can buy roasted slices, scalding hot from the booths, in the market of Venice. One of the most popular vegetable dishes is called, in dialect, *papriche stufato*—stewed sweet peppers, which are easy to cook.

4 yellow bell peppers
2 large cloves garlic, peeled and halved lengthwise
½ cup extra-virgin olive oil
2 pounds fresh plum tomatoes, peeled, seeded, and chopped, or 1 can (28 ounces) whole plum tomatoes, drained, seeded, and coarsely chopped
¼ cup finely chopped fresh Italian parsley

1. Rinse the peppers well, drain, and dry, and cut them in quarters lengthwise. Remove and discard the stem ends, ribs, and seeds. Slice the peppers in thin strips not wider than ¼ inch. Set aside.

2. Put the garlic cloves in a skillet with the oil. Over medium-high heat, sauté the garlic until it turns light brown. Discard the garlic. Add the pepper strips and cook them, stirring frequently, uncovered, 15 minutes.

3. Spoon the tomatoes over the peppers; add salt and freshly ground pepper. Continue to cook at a simmer, uncovered, until the tomatoes thicken, about 30 minutes. Sprinkle parsley over all and serve hot, or let it stand and serve at room temperature.

MARINATED AND SAUTÉED RADICCHIO

Radicchio marinato soltato in padella

Serves 4

There are two kinds of radicchio: the radicchio from Treviso, which is long, purplish red, and with definite cream-colored veins; and the radicchio from Verona, which is rounded. Both have a slightly bitter taste and can be cooked or used in salads.

½ cup balsamic vinegar
¼ cup extra-virgin olive oil
2 heads radicchio
1 cup beef broth
¼ cup finely chopped shallots
2 teaspoons grated lemon zest
1 teaspoon truffle oil

1. In a small bowl, combine the balsamic vinegar and the olive oil. Add salt and freshly ground pepper and mix well. Reserve ¼ cup of this mixture.

2. Cut each head of radicchio into 4 wedges. Place them in a large skillet and pour ½ cup of the balsamic and oil mixture over them, still reserving the ¼ cup. Set aside and marinate for several hours, 3 or 4.

3. In a small sauce pan, combine the broth, shallots, and the reserved ¼ cup balsamic/oil mixture, and cook over moderate heat 5 to 8 minutes, to reduce mixture to ½ cup. Add the lemon zest and the truffle oil and allow to cool. Season with salt and freshly ground pepper.

4. Put the skillet with the radicchio wedges over high heat and sauté until lightly browned. The radicchio will lose some of its color. Cook about 4 minutes per side. To serve, put 2 cooked wedges on each plate and pour over the sauce made in step 3. This should be served in the center of a dinner plate, with a quail on either side.

CUBES OF BUTTERNUT SQUASH WITH CINNAMON
Zucca alla cannella

Serves 6

This is a popular vegetable dish in northern Italy, especially in the Veneto. n this region. In fact, pumpkin and other winter squashes can be cooked the same way. Don't overcook the squash; it should keep its shape. I test with a wooden skewer, or a toothpick will do—just put it into the piece of squash and you will discover its state of tenderness.

1 butternut squash, about 1½ pounds
4 tablespoons butter
Dashes of cinnamon

1. Peel the squash after removing the stem and bottom ends. Cut it in ½ crosswise and again in halves, but this time lengthwise. Remove the seeds and cut all 4 sections into 1-inch pieces.

2. Steam them until tender, up to 20 minutes. Drain and put the pieces into a shallow bowl. Melt the butter, browning it a little. Add salt and freshly ground pepper and pour this over the squash. Use a rubber spatula to get all the butter transferred from the skillet to the squash. Sprinkle cinnamon over all and serve as described above.

FENNEL "SOUFFLÉ" WITH HERBS
Sformata di finocchio e besciamella

Serves 4

This is one of my favorites and will impress your family and friends. It is simply a white sauce (besciamella) joined with a puree of fresh fennel and combined with cheese and eggs. It is cooked in a water bath and will keep in the bath for up to an hour before serving.

1 (1-pound) fennel bulb with fronds, trimmed
2 cloves garlic, minced
2 tablespoons extra-virgin olive oil
1 teaspoon each finely minced sage, rosemary, and Italian parsley
½ teaspoon dried fennel seeds, toasted, crushed
½ cup butter
1 cup all-purpose flour
3½ cups milk, warmed
1½ cups freshly grated Parmesan cheese
6 eggs, separated
2 tablespoons anisette, optional
Butter and bread crumbs for pan

1. Use the bulb only and some of the soft green fronds. Chop these coarsely and put in salted boiling water with the garlic and oil and cook until the fennel is tender, about 15 minutes. Drain and dry; it is important to drain well. Transfer to a strainer and press down with the back of a wooden spoon to release excess liquid, or arrange in a cloth towel and slowly wring. Put in a food processor with the herbs and pulse to make a puree. Transfer to a bowl and set aside.

2. Preheat oven to 400°F. Melt the butter in a heavy sauce pan, add the flour, and whisk until all lumps dissolve and the mixture is smooth, about 5 minutes. Lower the heat and slowly add the warm milk, stirring until smooth and thick. Sample to be sure the taste of raw flour is gone; otherwise cook a bit longer. Transfer to a large bowl and cool slightly. Add the fennel puree and fold in the Parmesan with the help of a rubber spatula. Check for salt seasoning; add some if needed. Allow to cool.

3. Add 1 yolk at a time, whisking fully after each addition. Beat the egg whites until they hold peaks, and fold them into the mixture. Pour immediately into a buttered and crumbed oval baking dish, glass or ceramic, 15x10x2½ inches.

4. Put the baking dish into a larger pan and fill halfway up with water. This creates a water bath, or *bagnomaria*. Put in the oven and bake 1 hour and 10 minutes. As the top begins to brown, cover with a piece of foil to keep from browning too much. To test for doneness, insert a wooden skewer—it should come out clean. After resting 15 minutes or so, serve.

STEAMED GREEN BEANS WITH ONION SAUCE
Fagiolini con salsa di cipolle

Serves 8 to 12

Italians do not like cooked beans that are raw. If green beans are to be cooked, cook them. The best way to cook these is to steam them—that is, the green beans do not touch water.

1½ pounds fresh string beans, trimmed, washed, and left whole
1 clove garlic, coarsely chopped
⅓ cup chopped white onion
1 teaspoon prepared mustard, Dijon type
3 tablespoons herb-flavored vinegar
1 cup extra-virgin olive oil
8 to 12 fresh radicchio leaves, rinsed and dried

1. Steam the beans until tender, up to 15 minutes. Dry well and put them in a large bowl or platter.

2. Put the garlic, onion, mustard, vinegar, and 2 tablespoons of the oil in the food processor and pulse to a count of 8. Pour remaining oil through the food tube while the motor is on. Add some salt and freshly ground pepper.

3. Pour the sauce over the green beans. Toss lightly but well. Arrange some of the beans in radicchio leaves on individual plates. Serve beans warm or at room temperature—sauce always at room temperature.

INDIVIDUAL ARTICHOKE MOLDS WITH TALEGGIO SAUCE AND SAGE
Budino di carciofi in salsa di taleggio

Serves 8 to 10

Molds, especially vegetable molds, are popular all over Italy, and here is a special one I adapted from the well-known restaurant in Parma, La Greppia. They are cooked in a water bath and will keep in the bath, once the heat in the oven is turned off, for a half hour or longer.

8 fresh artichoke hearts or 1 can (13¾ ounces) or 1 package frozen (10 ounces)
2 cups chicken broth
1 cup milk, warmed
4 tablespoons butter, softened
½ cup freshly grated Parmesan cheese
3 eggs, beaten
Dash of freshly grated nutmeg

1. Preheat oven to 350°F. If using fresh artichoke hearts, chop them coarsely and cook them in the chicken broth, barely covered with liquid, until tender, about 10 minutes. If using canned, drain and rinse them several times in fresh water to remove as much salt taste as is possible. If using frozen, thaw and cook them in broth as with fresh. Drain artichokes and put them in a food processor. Add the warm milk and butter to the processor and pulse to a count of 10. Transfer this mixture to a bowl.

2. Fold in the Parmesan, eggs, and nutmeg with the help of a rubber spatula. Add some freshly ground pepper.

3. Spoon into 8 buttered timbales (5-ounce or ⅔-cup size), leaving ½-inch space at the top. Arrange these timbales in a baking pan and fill with warm water to ½ of the height of the timbales. Bake for 50 to 60 minutes or until the timbales have set. These will keep in the oven, heat off and door open, for 15 minutes or so.

4. To serve, run a knife around the edge of the timbale and turn out, either on individual plates or on a platter. Spoon 2 tablespoons of sauce, 1 on each side of the mold. Place a sage leaf upward, leaning against the mold. Serve right away

To make the taleggio sauce:
2 cups besciamella sauce, see page 70
8 ounces taleggio cheese, room temperature

1. Over low heat, warm the besciamella, add ¼ of the cheese, and stir to melt. Repeat, adding cheese until all of it has combined smoothly into a sauce. If you think the sauce is too thick, thin it with a little milk.

THE CLASSIC WAY TO COOK BROCCOLI: COOKED IN GARLIC-FLAVORED OIL

Broccoli saltati in padella: con aglio e olio (classico italiano)

Serves 4 to 6

Broccoli lovers think this is the only way to cook broccoli. Italians love this vegetable, and although this is considered a classic way to cook them all over Italy, there are many variations. For example, in Rome, they are not parboiled but added to the skillet with the oil and garlic. The leaves take longer to cook than the florets, so they are added first. Then two cups of white wine are added to the skillet and the broccoli cooks until tender. This method does have the extra step of parboiling, but that means less time in the skillet. Finishing off a vegetable in a skillet with olive oil and garlic is a popular and preferred way to cook vegetables the Italian way.

2 pounds broccoli
5 tablespoons extra-virgin olive oil
2 cloves garlic

1. Clean the broccoli by discarding the coarse leaves, retaining the tender ones, cutting off the bottom stems, peeling them, slicing the tender parts of the stems, and cutting florets off the stems. If not cooking them immediately, keep them in lightly salted, cold water and drain for cooking.

2. Boil some water in a pan large enough to hold the cut broccoli, and add some salt before adding the broccoli. As soon as the water returns to a boil, remove the broccoli and drain well.

3. In a large skillet, heat the oil and lightly brown the garlic cloves. With a fork, carefully press down on the cloves to break them a little. Remove the garlic before it turns dark brown. Add the drained broccoli and cook until tender, 4 to 6 minutes, stirring lightly. The broccoli should retain its bright green look and be cooked. Add more salt before serving if you wish.

GLAZED CELERY IN MUSTARD SAUCE

Sedano glassato alla crema di mostarda

Serves 4

Most people in the United States do not cook celery, but they may be interested in this cooked celery dish that combines the vegetable with cream and mustard. One advantage has to do with cooking the celery and saucing it ahead, and then broiling just before serving.

10 celery ribs
1½ cups chicken broth
2 tablespoons butter
2 teaspoons sugar
¼ cup plus 2 tablespoons heavy cream
2 teaspoons Dijon-style mustard

1. Rinse celery and remove any coarse strings with a vegetable peeler. Cut off the leaves, chop finely, and reserve. Cut the ribs into ½-inch-thick diagonal slices and place in a large skillet.

2. Add the broth, butter, and 2 teaspoons sugar, and bring to boil. Cook, stirring, until the liquid is reduced to a glaze, about 10 minutes.

3. Combine the cream and mustard and add to the skillet. Lower the heat and cook until the sauce is thickened, about 5 minutes. Season with salt and freshly ground pepper.

4. Preheat broiler. Divide the mixture between 4 individual ramekins. Sprinkle a little more sugar over the top of each. Broil until the top is flecked with brown. Sprinkle with the chopped celery leaves and serve.

VEGETABLE RAINBOW OF CARROTS, ZUCCHINI, ASPARAGUS, AND BROCCOLI RAPE
Arcobaleno di ortaggi

Serves 12

These vegetables can be cooked and left at room temperature until you are ready to make the rainbow arrangement. The sauce should be hot and added at the last minute. The lemon wedges are important to the taste of this dish, so don't try to skip them.

6 fresh zucchini, each about 1x6 inches long
1½ pounds fresh asparagus spears
6 large carrots
2 bunches fresh broccoli rape
½ cup extra-virgin olive oil
6 large cloves garlic, minced
Good pinch of red pepper flakes
3 lemons, cut in wedges, seeds removed

1. Wash and dry the zucchini; cut off the ends and pare any blemishes. Leave on as much skin as you can. Hold a zucchini upright and cut ¼ inch (from the outside to the inside) straight down the full length of the zucchini. Do this on 3 remaining sides. Discard pulpy center. Cut the zucchini length further into more strips, about ¼ inch thick. Steam them to al dente stage and set aside.

2. Take 1 asparagus spear in hand and bend it, far enough so it will snap and break (it breaks at the tenderest point). Discard the tough end. Repeat with all other spears. Wash them and steam to al dente. Set aside.

3. Trim the carrots by cutting off the stem ends and paring lightly with a vegetable peeler. Cut in halves lengthwise and cut again to get lengths about ¼ inch wide. Steam to al dente and set aside.

4. To prepare broccoli rape, wash it well and trim the ends. Remove the strings on the larger stalks as on large celery. Cut the larger leaves in ½ and let them stand in cool water until ready to cook them. Cut the rabe in 2-inch pieces. Heat 2 or 3 cups of water in a large sauce pan. Add 1 teaspoon salt and bring the water to a rapid boil. Add the rabe and cook until just tender; depending on size and freshness of stalks, this may take 5 to 10 minutes. Drain well.

5. Heat 3 tablespoons oil in a large skillet. Add ¼ of the minced garlic and cook 1 minute. Add the rape and move it around in the oil and garlic. Cook 2 or 3 minutes longer. Remove from heat.

6. Arrange a rainbow (*arcobaleno*) of vegetables on a large platter as follows: Place wide side of platter in front of you. On the left side, place the zucchini strips in a tight fan shape, spread more at the top than the bottom. Do the same with the carrots in the center of the platter, and then add the asparagus on the right side. Add the rape to the bottom across all vegetables. Add salt to taste.

7. In the same skillet, heat the remaining oil, the remaining garlic, and sauté the garlic briefly, just enough to take on a little color—1 to 2 minutes. Remove the pan from the heat. Add the pepper flakes, stir, and spoon over the zucchini, carrots, and asparagus. Serve with lemon wedges.

SPINACH WITH OIL AND LEMON
Spinaci all'agro

Serves 8 to 12

This is probably the most usual way spinach is served in Italy. It is an excellent partner with fish of almost any kind, and it doesn't have to be eaten hot, as in from stove to table. Take my advice about several rinsings of the spinach to rid it of sand—there is something un-American about grit on cooked spinach.

3 pounds fresh leaf spinach
6 tablespoons extra-virgin olive oil
2 cloves garlic, sliced lengthwise
4 tablespoons fresh lemon juice (1½ lemons)

1. Cut off the stem end of the spinach and trim any leaves needing it. Also remove any especially long stems. Rinse the spinach at least 3 times; it is best to soak it in a sink with a drain plug or a very large basin of water. Shake the spinach leaves in the water to dislodge any foreign matter. It is usually necessary to do this even with packaged fresh spinach supposedly sold as ready to use. Remove the spinach by hand, trying not to disturb the bottom of the sink or basin. Drain dirty water and start anew.

2. After properly cleaning the spinach, transfer it to a large sauce pan. No water is necessary—the water clinging to the spinach leaves is adequate. Add some salt, cover the pan, and cook over high heat, 6 or 7 minutes, stirring it several times. Remove from the heat, drain it, and press as much liquid out of the spinach as is possible. Chop it coarsely,

3. In a large skillet, heat the oil and sauté the garlic pieces. When they brown lightly, remove and discard them. Add the spinach and cook it over moderate heat, uncovered 6 to 8 minutes, stirring several times. Transfer to a serving platter and sprinkle the fresh lemon juice over all. Add more salt.

CARROTS WITH MARSALA
Carote al marsala

Serves 6

Carrots cooked in classic Italian style require them to be sautéed in butter with salt and pepper, sugar, and flour, and then some broth is added; this results in a vegetable with a slightly thickened sauce. The newer Italian chefs are abandoning the flour-thickening technique and going for a bit more flavor by adding a wine, such as marsala. The result is most satisfying.

4 tablespoons extra-virgin olive oil
6 medium carrots, trimmed and sliced on the bias
½ to 1 cup chicken broth
1 tablespoon sugar
¼ cup marsala wine
¼ cup finely sliced scallions

1. Heat the olive oil in a large skillet and add the carrot slices. Sauté 3 or 4 minutes, adding some salt and freshly ground pepper. Add 2 tablespoons chicken broth.

2. Cover and simmer over low heat until the carrots are tender, about 20 minutes. Add more tablespoons of broth during this cooking period to keep the carrots from sticking to the pan.

3. Turn up the heat, and sprinkle the sugar over the carrots. Stir until the sugar caramelizes and the carrots turn light brown. Add the marsala, and cook until it evaporates, about 3 or 4 minutes.

Serve after sprinkling with scallions.

SLICED POTATOES WITH OIL AND HERBS

Insalata di patate con olio alle erbe

Serves 4

Another classic because of its simplicity and taste. Make this ahead by several days to allow the potatoes to absorb the flavor of the oil, vinegar, and herbs. Be sure to take out of the refrigerator at least one-half hour before serving. This is best at room temperature.

1½ pounds potatoes, boiled with skins and then skinned and sliced thickly, about ¼ inch
4 tablespoons extra-virgin olive oil
1 tablespoon white wine vinegar
2 cloves garlic, minced
¼ cup of finely chopped herbs: fresh oregano, fresh basil, and fresh parsley
1 tablespoon chopped capers, drained and dried

1. As soon as the potatoes are put to boil, combine the remaining ingredients in a bowl and let sit until the potatoes are boiled, peeled, and sliced.

2. While the potatoes are still warm, add the remaining ingredients in the bowl. Toss lightly and well. The warm potatoes will absorb the dressing more so than if the potatoes were cold. Check, and if the potatoes appear dry, add a little more oil and vinegar. This may be made ahead and left at room temperature for about 3 hours

RED BELL PEPPER HALVES STUFFED WITH PINE NUTS AND GOLDEN RAISINS
Involtini di peperoni

Serves 4

Roasted and peeled bell peppers, a mainstay in almost every Italian kitchen, are prepared in as many ways as there are cooks, as least as far as the embellishments go. The inspiration for this filling comes from a cousin who once had a restaurant in Caserta, near Naples. The peppers can be made ahead and are delicious a day or two later, as long as they are at room temperature.

2 large red bell peppers
½ cup freshly made bread crumbs
4 anchovy fillets, minced
1 tablespoon capers
¼ cup pine nuts
¼ cup golden raisins
2 tablespoons finely chopped Italian parsley
2 to 4 tablespoons extra-virgin olive oil

1. Broil or grill the red peppers to char them until their skins blacken. Cool enough to handle. Remove charred skin, stems, ribs, and seeds. Cut each pepper in ½ lengthwise. Preheat the oven to 350°F.

2. Mix all other ingredients except the olive oil. Add salt if needed and freshly ground pepper. Add olive oil by the tablespoon to moisten the mixture.

3. Put a large tablespoon of filling in the center of each pepper ½, and then jacket the filling by raising the pepper sides to go over the filling. Carefully arrange the filled pepper halves in a pie dish or other appropriate baking pan, add a little more oil over the peppers, and bake 30 minutes.

ZUCCHINI PUDDING
Budino di zucchine

Serves 6 to 8

Puddings are quite popular everywhere in Italy, and zucchini lends itself well to this type of dish, as it is somewhat bland (and surely inexpensive when compared to other foods) and picks up the flavor of other food easily—in this instance, cream, butter, basil, and red peppers. As simple as this dish may be, the trick is to let the salted zucchini shavings stand in a colander for the required time, and to be sure that most of the watery liquid is squeezed out of them. Once you prepare this dish, you will want to cook it again.

2 cups grated zucchini, about 4 medium-sized zucchini
½ large red bell pepper, trimmed and cut into small dice
¼ cup finely chopped fresh basil plus 1 spray for garnish
3 eggs, room temperature
¼ cup all-purpose flour
2 tablespoons butter, melted
2 cups light cream or half and half

1. Wash the zucchini and cut off the ends, but do not peel. If the zucchini are small, grate the whole vegetable; if they are large, grate only the outside portion (cut them in ½, and remove the seeds). Grate the zucchini using the shredding side of a grater. Transfer the grated zucchini to a colander, sprinkle lightly with some salt, and let liquid drain from the zucchini 30 minutes. Press down on the gratings with your hands to extract as much liquid as possible. Transfer the zucchini to a bowl. Add the chopped red pepper and the basil. Preheat the oven to 325°F.

2. Beat the eggs well, and stir them into the zucchini mixture. Add the flour and stir again. Add the melted butter and the cream. Pour this mixture into a buttered 1½-quart glass or ceramic baking dish, and place the baking dish into a larger pan of hot water, forming a water-bath, or what the Italians call a *bagnomaria.*

3. Bake 1 hour, or until set. The end product will be a custard delicately flavored with fresh zucchini. Add the basil spray to the center of the baking dish and serve within 10 minutes.

BAKED CARAMELIZED ONIONS
Cipolle al forno

Serves 4

This is a prime example of the simplicity of Italian cooking, so easily duplicated in American kitchens. The onions, once cooked this way, will simply melt in your mouth.

4 medium onions, peeled
4 tablespoons extra-virgin olive oil
8 teaspoons dry bread crumbs, unseasoned

1. Preheat oven to 325°F.

2. Cut each onion crosswise to make 8 halves. Using about 1 tablespoon of oil, rub the ½ onions all over and set them in an oiled, shallow baking pan in a single layer, cut side up. Season liberally with salt and freshly ground pepper.

3. Using ½ of the remaining oil, spoon some onto each ½. Bake for 40 minutes. Remove from the oven for a minute to sprinkle a teaspoon of bread crumbs over each onion ½. Add more oil, and continue to bake until caramelized, about 40 minutes longer. These should be served warm.

POTATOES WITH OLIVE OIL
Patate schiacciate con olio di oliva

Serves 4 to 6

Do not mash these potatoes in a blender or processor, for they will get gummy. Americans add cream and butter only, as a rule; this Italian preparation adds good-quality olive oil and pecorino cheese with some cream. This can be made ahead and reheated in a warm oven.

3 pounds boiling potatoes, Yukon Gold preferred
¾ cup light light cream or half and half
½ cup extra-virgin olive oil
¼ pound pecorino cheese

1. Boil potatoes in a large pot up to 1 hour, or until tender. To test for doneness, pierce potato with a wooden skewer—if it goes through easily, the potatoes are done; if it meets resistance, the potatoes need further cooking. Drain and set aside to cool somewhat.

2. Peel the potatoes and return them to the pot in which they cooked. Mash them with a potato masher, incorporating the light cream. Put over low heat to keep warm.

3. Stir in the oil, a tablespoon at a time, being sure each spoonful is incorporated. Continue until all the oil is used. Season with some salt and freshly ground pepper.

4. Using the large holes on a cheese grater, grate enough of the cheese to make ½ cup. Add ½ of this amount to the potatoes and stir until the cheese is melted. Keep the potatoes warm, and just before serving, add the remaining ¼ cup of cheese over individual servings.

ZUCCHINI IN A HOT SAUCE, FARM STYLE

Zucchini piccante, alla contadina

Serves 4

It is un-Italian to peel zucchini, so don't give in to this American aberration. The peel adds color to the dish, but also adds a more defined form to the vegetable. Wash the vegetable well and, if you wish, scrape only a few lengths of the skin, so the zucchini appears striped; otherwise, leave completely unpeeled.

8 small zucchini, 1x5 inches each
1 cup freshly made bread crumbs
2 tablespoons red wine vinegar
6 tablespoons extra-virgin olive oil
2 anchovies, minced
1 tablespoon each capers, chives, and Italian parsley, finely chopped
Pinch of red pepper flakes

1. Rinse the zucchini well and trim the ends. Leave them unpeeled except for any small blemish. Bring a pan of water to boil, add the whole zucchini, and cook until tender, 10 to 15 minutes, depending on size. Add some salt to the water for the last minute or 2 of boiling. Drain and set aside.

2. Add the bread crumbs to a bowl and sprinkle the vinegar over all. Toss lightly but well. Let stand for 5 minutes or so. Add the olive oil, anchovies, capers, chives, parsley, and red pepper flakes. Mix lightly but well. Taste for seasoning and add salt if needed. Serve the zucchini whole, 2 per person, with a spoonful of the sauce over the zucchini. The zucchini should be warm and the sauce at room temperature.

FRIED ZUCCHINI SLICES
Zucchini in padella

Serves 4

In padella (cooked in the skillet) is a popular way to cook many things in Italy, especially vegetables; zucchini are a favorite cooked this way. Be sure to dry them well (use paper or cloth towels) after they are sliced; zucchini are so filled with water that you see the liquid even as they are sliced, and if they are not dried well, they will not fry well. As an extra touch, you can add a few drops of quality balsamic vinegar to the slices after they are salted and fried.

4 small zucchini, about 1 pound
½ cup all-purpose flour
4 tablespoons extra-virgin olive oil

1. Wash the zucchini and trim the ends. Slice into ¼-inch rounds. Dry them well.
2. Dredge them with flour, removing excess flour.
3. Heat the oil in a skillet, and sauté the zucchini on both sides, leaving plenty of space between each slice. Brown them lightly and transfer with a slotted spoon to paper toweling to drain. Sauté until all the slices are done. Salt the slices lightly before serving.

BAKED ZUCCHINI WITH MOZZARELLA

Zucchine e mozzarella al forno

Serves 4

4 small zucchini, 1x4 or 5 inches long
4 tablespoons extra-virgin olive oil
½ cup shredded mozzarella

1. Rinse and dry the zucchini. Cut off the ends. Hold each zucchini up on 1 end and slice off some of the outer skin. Do the same with the other side of the zucchini. Then slice the zucchini down the middle to get 2 slices, about ¼ inch thick by 4 or 5 inches long. Repeat with the other zucchini. Wipe slices dry.

2. Preheat the oven to 350°F.

3. Heat 2 tablespoons oil in a large skillet, add the slices, and sauté until nicely golden. Turn over, adding more oil if necessary, and sauté the other side. Oil a flat baking pan to hold the zucchini in 1 layer. Arrange them side by side, add some salt and freshly ground pepper over all, and carefully put the shredded mozzarella over the slices. Bake until the mozzarella melts, about 5 minutes. Serve as a *contorno*, on individual small plates.

BAKED CAULIFLOWER WITH SARDINIAN PASTA
Cavolfiori al forno con fregola

Serves 6

It would be best to make this with Sicilian pasta, known as *Freula Sarda* or *fregola*, if you can; but it is difficult to find in the supermarkets, so the best substitute would be small pasta such as tubettini, ditalini, or small shells—these are available in every grocery shop.

1 cup small pasta, such as tubettini, ditalini, or tiny shells, or Freula Sarda, Sardinian pasta
2 large heads cauliflower, trimmed and cut into florets
4 tablespoons butter
4 tablespoons all-purpose flour
3 cups milk, heated to boiling point
3 tablespoons finely chopped fresh oregano or 1½ teaspoons dried, crushed
Pinch of red pepper flakes
1½ cups freshly grated pecorino cheese
½ cup freshly made bread crumbs

1. If using pasta other than Sardinian, cook it in boiling water 3 minutes, drain immediately, and put into a bowl of cool water. Drain again just before using it in recipe.

2. Preheat oven to 375°F. Butter a 2-inch-deep baking pan, about 11x7 inches, and spread the precooked pasta on the bottom. Add the cauliflower florets over the pasta.

3. Melt the butter in a medium sauce pan over medium heat, and when it bubbles, stir in the flour, and stir all the time with a whisk or wooden spoon. Reduce the heat and stir for 2 to 3 minutes (cooking the flour this way removes the flour aftertaste of a sauce). Slowly add the hot milk, stirring most of the time until the mixture thickens, about 4 to 5 minutes. Remove from the heat.

4. Add 2 tablespoons of the oregano and the pinch of red pepper flakes. Add a liberal amount of freshly ground pepper. Stir in 1 cup of the pecorino cheese and stir to blend into the sauce. Check for salt seasoning; if you think it needs more, add some. Pour the sauce over the cauliflower. Then sprinkle the bread crumbs over the top.

5. Bake in the lower part of the oven 40 minutes (if the crumbs darken too much, cover the dish with foil). Remove the pan from the oven and sprinkle the remaining ½ cup of pecorino over the top. Continue cooking until the cauliflower florets are tender, about 30 to 40 minutes longer. To test for doneness, pierce a floret with a wooden skewer—if it penetrates easily, the florets are cooked; if it meets with resistance, cook a bit longer. When cooked and out of the oven, let stand 5 to 10 minutes, add the remaining oregano over all, and serve.

GRILLED HOT CHERRY PEPPERS
Peperoni rossi cotti alla griglia in sott'aceto

Serves 6

This preparation is more of a condiment than it is a vegetable and will, therefore, go with many other dishes in this book, especially grilled meats and poultry. It is spicy, so beware. It can be made with fresh cherry peppers, but the pickled state of the pepper, as called for in the recipe, is intoxicating.

12 pickled hot cherry peppers (red, green, or both)
2 or 3 slices Italian bread, 1 inch thick
⅓ cup extra-virgin olive oil

1. Cut out stems of peppers, as if coring tomatoes for filling. Opening should be wide enough to receive a 1-inch bread cube. Discard stems and seeds.

2. Brush both sides of bread slices with some of the oil, then cut the bread into 1-inch cubes. Toss peppers in remaining oil. Add some salt and freshly ground pepper. Toss well. Place 1 bread cube into each pepper. Thread 6 peppers on 1 of 2 skewers, from top to bottom, leaving almost no space between the peppers. Prepare the second skewer.

3. When the fire is ready, grill peppers for several minutes on each side, rotating until all sides show grill marks. Serve 2 per person.

ROAST POTATOES WITH CRUSHED FENNEL SEEDS
Patate arrosto con semi di finocchio

Serves 4

Usually, regular medium to large boiling potatoes are used; they are cut lengthwise in half and then again lengthwise three or four times.

16 small new potatoes, uniform in size, with clear skins
4 tablespoons extra-virgin olive oil
4 cloves garlic, peeled and sliced in halves
1 teaspoon dried fennel seeds, crushed

1. Pare the potatoes, rinse them in cool water, and dry completely with paper or cloth towels. Preheat the oven to 375°F.

2. Heat 3 tablespoons of the oil in a large skillet, large enough to hold the potatoes in 1 layer. Add the garlic halves and sauté them until they turn light brown, a minute or so. Immediately discard them. Add the dried potatoes and sauté them until they lightly brown all over. This may take 5 to 10 minutes depending on the size of potato. Shake the skillet often to rotate the potatoes so they will crust on all sides.

3. Transfer the potatoes and any oil remaining in the skillet to a baking container, again 1 that will hold the potatoes in 1 layer. Add the remaining tablespoon of oil and the crushed fennel seeds. Season with salt and freshly ground pepper. Cover the baking dish and bake until they become tender, 30 to 45 minutes. A good way to test for tenderness is with a long wooden skewer; insert it into a potato—it is tender if the skewer meets little or no resistance.

Chapter 5

FISH AND SEAFOOD

Italians love seafood. And it's no wonder. The thousands of miles of Italy's coastline that rim the eastern, southern, and western shores of the boot, and the hundreds of miles of coast around its many islands, are teeming with seafood. Wherever there is water, you will find fish and a fish market (*pescheria*). In Venice, the *pescheria* that is part of the colorful outdoor market at the famous Rialto Bridge, overlooking the Grand Canal, is one of the most extraordinary sights in all of Italy. In the very early morning as the barges come in, the variety of fish (and people) is astounding.

The fish market scene in Venice is duplicated in many cities and towns where the sea is a way of life and where most towns and cities have a fish specialty. South of Venice on the Adriatic coast lie the major fishing areas of Ancona, Porto Recanati, San Benedetto del Tronto, and Vasto, all famous for their fish dishes, especially their *brodetti*, made with mullet, cod, or dogfish (a species of small shark with firm, codlike meat). The western coast is no different. Indeed, all along the Ligurian and Tyrrhenian coasts from Genoa to Naples, there are extraordinary displays of seafood in the markets and wonderful fish dishes in the restaurants.. The fish dishes all over Italy may have the same name, but they vary from village to village, in fact, from home to home.

AGATA AND ROMEO'S SOLE FILLETS WRAPPED IN LEEKS
Filetti di spigola in sfloglie di porro

Serves 4

This dish is inspired by one that was created by one of Rome's top lady chefs, Agata Parisella Caraccio. She and her husband, Romeo Caracci, married some thirty years ago, share their passion for updated Italian cuisine, and showcase it at their restaurant on via Carlo Alberto. The restaurant was founded eighty years ago as a neighborhood *osteria* by Agata's grandmother. Today, it is an elegant restaurant, and a Roman institution.

4 fillets of fresh sole (1 to 1½ pounds and ½ inch thick); or any fresh filleted snapper of same thickness
2 leeks
1 pound brussels sprouts
4 tablespoons extra-virgin olive oil
2 shallots, peeled and minced
½ cup fish broth or bottled clam juice
1 teaspoon freshly chopped fresh thyme
2 tablespoons butter, cut in 4 pieces
4 radicchio leaves from center of head

1. Rinse the fillets and pat dry with paper toweling. Cut each fillet into 3 or 4 pieces, depending on the size of the fillet. Set aside.

2. Trim the leeks by cutting off the stem end; separate the leaves, cutting off the deep, dark green ends. Bring 2 cups water to boil in a large skillet, add some salt, and cook the leeks over medium heat to soften them, 3 or 4 minutes. Remove with a slotted spoon, reserving the juices in the skillet. Dry the cooked leaves and set aside.

3. Trim the stem ends of the brussels sprouts and remove outer leaves as necessary. Cut a cross ¼ inch deep with a sharp paring knife in the stem end of each sprout. Add these to the skillet and, over medium high heat, cook until tender, about 10 minutes. Stir several times, and when they are cooked, remove them with a slotted spoon.

4. Salt and pepper and then wrap each piece of sole with a leek leaf, and tie with a piece of kitchen string.

5. In a smaller skillet, heat 1 tablespoon of oil and sauté the brussels sprouts 3 minutes, seasoning to taste. Keep warm.

6. Heat 2 tablespoons of oil in a large skillet with a cover, add the shallots, and sauté for 2 or 3 minutes. Carefully add the sole bundles, the fish broth or clam juice, thyme, salt, and freshly ground pepper to taste. Bring the juices to boil, lower the heat, cover the pan, and simmer 6 minutes. Transfer the sole packets among 4 plates. Keep the heat under the juices to reduce the sauce, about 3 minutes. Add a piece of butter and stir to dissolve. Repeat until all the butter is melded into the sauce.

7. Toss the radicchio leaves with the remaining tablespoon of oil, adding salt and freshly ground pepper to taste. Arrange 1 leaf per plate, and add several brussels sprouts to the side. Spoon the reduced sauce over the fish and serve right away

FRESH BEANS WITH TUNA
Fagioli freschi al tonno

Serves 6

Classically simple, and Italian at its best, this combination of foods should be made ahead and allowed to marinate for several hours at room temperature. If using canned beans, put them in a colander and run cool water over them for several washings to rid them of salt.

2 pounds fresh cranberry beans, shelled and rinsed, or
2 cans (16 ounces) cannellini beans, drained
2 cans (6 ounces) tuna in oil; use an Italian brand such as Pastene or Genova
⅓ cup extra-virgin olive oil
1 tablespoon red wine vinegar
2 cloves garlic, minced
⅓ cup finely chopped red onion
1 tablespoon finely chopped Italian parsley
Pinch of nutmeg

1. Put the fresh beans in a large sauce pan and cover them with cold water. Add some salt. Bring to boil over medium-high heat, covered, and cook until al dente, about 20 minutes.

2. Drain the cooked beans and let reach room temperature. If using canned cannellinis, simply drain and add to all other ingredients. Combine the beans, cooked or canned, with all other ingredients. Add freshly ground pepper, and toss lightly but well. Serve at room temperature.

FRESH CLAMS WITH WINE IN PORTOFINO

Vongole in salsa di vino bianco alla Portofino

Serves 6 to 8

One evening, Puny (owner of the Ristorante da Puny in Portofino) and I discussed the matter of clams, and he knows all about them. Always purchase clams in the shell from a reliable source. Most clams keep their shells tightly closed when out of the water, so if you notice a shell is open, just tap on it—if there is a live clam inside, it will respond by swiftly snapping the shell shut. Discard any that are either unusually heavy (these are usually sealed with mud) or light—they are probably dead.

Many people place clams in a pot of cold water for several hours, sometimes along with a spoonful of cornmeal, in the hope that this will release the sand inside the shells. Puny believes the clams, unfortunately, lose most of their flavorful juice in this process. If you do this, he recommends that you strain the water through a sieve lined with a double layer of dampened cheesecloth or a coffee filter, to get rid of the sand, and pour the strained water into the dish you are preparing. Puny and I clean clams in about the same way. Put the clams in the sink and cover them with cool water, then scrub the clams all over with a stiff wire brush. Drain the water from the sink, making sure you rinse away any sand at the bottom, and refill with cool water. Let the clams soak for about five minutes. Repeat the soaking and scrubbing procedure 3 times; the last sinkful of water should be clear. Drain the clams and set aside until ready to use.

The creative, culinary Italian hand is evident by the addition of anchovies and capers (and, hopefully, you'll add the red chili pepper, too) to what otherwise would be just another good clam dish. It's difficult to improve on steamed clams and white wine, but in this preparation, my friend Puny shows how it can be done.

¾ cup extra-virgin olive oil
3 large cloves garlic, minced
5 anchovies packed in oil, drained and patted dry
1 tablespoon capers, drained
3 pounds small clams, such as littlenecks, in their shells, cleaned
1½ cups dry white wine
6 fresh, ripe, medium tomatoes, peeled, seeded, and cut into ½-inch dice
¼ cup finely chopped fresh Italian parsley
½ beef or vegetable bouillon cube
1 dried red chili pepper, optional

1. Heat the oil in a large, nonreactive pot over medium-high heat. Add the garlic, anchovies, and capers and sauté until the garlic just begins to take on a little color, about 2 minutes; do not let the garlic brown. Add the clams and the white wine and cook, uncovered, until some of the wine cooks off, about 5 minutes.

2. Add the tomatoes, parsley, bouillon cube, and the optional red chili pepper. Stir well, then cover tightly and cook until all the clams have opened, about 5 minutes more. Discard any clams that have not opened.

3. To serve, bring the pot to the table if at all possible. Spoon the clams into warm bowls, dividing evenly, but avoid any at the very bottom of the pot, because you might pick up any additional sand that has sunk there. Provide extra plates for the discarded clam shells.

FRESH TROUT ON THE GRILL
Trota alla griglia

Serves 4

For centuries, Italians and other Mediterranean people have cooked fish in the simplest way—better and healthier than other preparations. A few drops of good olive oil will make all the difference, and it seems now that Americans are getting the know-how of the way Italians cook.

4 fresh trout, slightly under 1 pound each, scaled, washed, and dried, heads and tails removed if you want
¼ cup finely chopped fresh Italian parsley
1 clove garlic and 1 tablespoon finely chopped scallions, minced together
¼ cup plus 2 tablespoons extra-virgin olive oil
8 thin slices of lemon, seeds removed
2 tablespoons fresh lemon juice
4 full sprigs fresh Italian parsley for garnish

1. Preheat the broiler or grill. Prepare the trout for grilling or ask your fishmonger to do this for you. If you have to do it yourself, simply scale each trout, rinsing well and drying them. Decapitate and de-tail as you prefer. With a sharp paring knife, cut 3 slashes in the skin of each fish.

2. Combine the parsley, garlic, and scallions, 2 tablespoons of the oil, and some salt and freshly ground pepper, and work this into the slashes. Put the 4 trout on an oiled baking pan and sprinkle 2 more tablespoons of oil over the trout.

3. Broil or grill the trout about 5 inches from the heat source. If using a grill with charcoal, be sure the coal is at the ashen stage (that is, gray, with the coals somewhat separated—there will be enough heat to cook these trout). Either broil or grill 3 or 4 minutes per side. To check for doneness, spear 1 trout with a wooden skewer. If the skewer penetrates the trout easily, it is done; if it meets resistance, it is not. When done, the inside of the trout should be opaque.

4. When the trout are done, transfer to individual plates and add a lemon slice where the head would have been and a lemon slice where the tail would be. Sprinkle lemon juice over all. Place a parsley sprig alongside the trout.

HOW TO CLEAN A WHOLE FISH

1. Cut off the pelvic, pectoral, and anal fins (all on the sides) with scissors; then snip off the dorsal (on the underbelly) fins.

2. Hold the fish by the tail with 1 hand, and scale the fish from the tail to the head, using a scaling knife.

3. Using a small, sharp knife, make a small incision from the vent (just forward of the anal fin) all along to the gill (just under the mouth), being careful not to cut into the entrails. Remove all the entrails and scrape away any remaining tissue.

4. Cut out the reddish gills by lifting the gill cover with 1 hand with scissors in the other. The reddish gill is underneath the gill cover. Do the same on the other side of the fish. Rinse the whole fish thoroughly under cool running water and dry with paper towels.

FRESH CODFISH, POTATOES, AND ONIONS
Merluzzo e patate

Serves 6

Merluzzo e patate, dried salted cod and potatoes (really, it's *baccala*) is a dish offered in Milan; in fact, salted cod appears in the cuisine of many of the other regions, each one having its special way to prepare it. The trouble with this dish, in my view, is the overnight soaking of the cod and the changing of the water in which it soaks three and four times. Even after overnight soaking, salted cod has a fairly strong taste. For the American table, fresh cod is used in this recipe—the taste is milder, yet the dish has all the components of the original Italian way of preparing it. Add a fresh green salad with a sliced tomato (if it is ripe) and the meal is complete.

¾ cup extra-virgin olive oil
4 medium onions, peeled, and sliced ¼ inch thick
2 cloves garlic, minced
1 bay leaf
6 tiny dried red chili peppers or ½ teaspoon red pepper flakes
1 teaspoon finely chopped fresh thyme or ½ dried, crushed
2 pounds fresh codfish, rinsed, dried, cut into 2-inch pieces
4 large potatoes, boiled, peeled, sliced ½ inches thick
1½ cups dry white wine
⅓ cup finely chopped fresh Italian parsley

1. Heat the oil in a large skillet. Add the onions and cook until they begin to turn color, about 5 minutes. Add the garlic, bay leaf, peppers, and thyme. Stir and cook 2 minutes.

2. Salt and pepper the cod pieces and add them with the potato slices, the wine, and ½ cup water. Cover the skillet. Bring to boil, lower the heat to get a steady simmer, cover the pan, and cook until the fish flakes and the potatoes are thoroughly heated, about 8 to 10 minutes. Sprinkle parsley over all and serve with a salad on the side.

FRIED, MARINATED SOLE IN SWEET AND SOUR SAUCE

Sogliole in sapore—"*sfogi in saor*"

Serves 6

The Venetian name for this dish is *sfogi in saor*. It is traditionally eaten for the great Venetian holiday, the Feast of the Redeemer, the third Sunday in July, with fireworks late in the evening after dinner. Simply put, this dish is made by flouring sole fillets, cooking them in olive oil, and covering them with lightly sautéed onions, carrots, celery, bay leaves, vinegar, and white wine. Pine nuts, raisins, and a couple of spices are also added. The dish marinates in the mixture for two days and is served cold.

6 fillets of sole, about 2 pounds
½ cup all-purpose flour
⅓ cup extra-virgin olive oil
1 onion, finely sliced
1 carrot, trimmed and cut into ¼-inch dice
1 stalk celery, trimmed, and cut into ¼-inch dice
1 cup white wine vinegar
1 cup dry white wine
2 bay leaves
¼ cup golden raisins
¼ cup pine nuts
Pinches of ground cinnamon, clove, and black pepper

1. Rinse and dry the fish fillets. Put the flour in a flat dish and lightly dredge the fillets in the flour, shaking off any excess. Set aside.

2. In a large skillet, heat the oil and sauté the fillets until lightly browned on each side, about 3 minutes per side over moderate-high heat. Remove to drain on paper towels. Sprinkle with salt to taste.

3. Using the same oil in the skillet, sauté the onion, carrots, and celery 5 minutes, stirring frequently. Add the vinegar and the wine, bring to boil, lower the heat, and simmer 5 minutes.

4. Arrange the fish fillets in a large, flat, earthenware container and pour the mixture over the fish. Add the bay leaves, raisins, pine nuts, and spices. Cover tightly and refrigerate for 2 days. This is to be served cold, but remove from refrigerator about ½ hour before you're ready to serve.

FRIED SOFT-SHELL CRABS IN THE VENETO
Moleche alla Veneziana

Serves 4

Soft-shell crabs appear in Venice at the end of April and the beginning of May. It is at this time of the year when the crabs are changing their shells, and they are so light that they float to the surface and are caught in shoals. Thousands of these *moleche*, as they are called in the Veneto, are caught, battered, and fried. They are dull green in color and about two inches wide. The whole crab is eaten, but properly clean it, as described below. In the Veneto, soft-shell crabs are usually deep-fried; an adjustment is made here to sauté them.

8 soft-shell crabs
2 eggs, well beaten with a pinch of salt
1 cup all-purpose flour
4 tablespoons olive or vegetable oil
Juice from 2 lemons
4 tablespoons butter
2 tablespoons finely chopped Italian parsley

1. Clean the crabs 1 at a time as follows: Place the crab, top side up, on a flat work surface. Cut off the protruding eyes. Turn the crab over, on its back, and remove the triangular-shaped apron. Lift the flaps on each side and remove the spongy gill tissue underneath. Rinse the crab in cool water and pat dry with paper towels.

2. Dip the crab in the beaten eggs and then dredge in the flour, which has had some salt and freshly ground pepper added to it.

3. Heat 2 tablespoons of oil in a large skillet and add 4 of the crabs. Cook over medium heat for 3 minutes or until the crabs are golden on 1 side. Turn and cook until golden on the other. The total time should be about 6 minutes, or a minute or 2 longer if the crabs are especially thick. Transfer the crabs to a platter. Heat the other 2 tablespoons of oil in the same skillet and repeat the process with the other 4 crabs. When all 8 crabs have been cooked, sprinkle them with the lemon juice.

4. Pour off any fat in the skillet and wipe it clean with a paper towel. Heat the butter in the skillet and let it brown. Pour this over the crabs also. Sprinkle the parsley over all.

SALMON IN PARCHMENT WITH SPINACH AND CARROT STICKS

Salmone al cartoccio con spinaci e carote

Serves 4

This is a fantastic presentation and a very tasty dish. Don't be put off by the use of parchment paper packages, or, as the Italians call this, *al cartoccio*; they are quite easy to make and easy to cook if you don't mind precooking the carrots.

1 salmon fillet, about 1½ pounds, skinned and boned, cut crosswise into 4 pieces
10 ounces fresh spinach, washed well with large stems removed
12 baby carrots, each about ½x2 inches long
3 tablespoons butter
1 teaspoon crushed dried fennel seeds
½ cup good Lungarotti white wine, such as Torre di Giano Riserva
2 large pieces of parchment paper, 16x24 inches (this will make 4 packets)

1. Prepare the salmon or ask your fishmonger to do this for you. Do not use the tail end of the fillet as it will not make an adequate serving. If you have to bone the salmon yourself, simply run your fingers down the center and you will feel the bones. Use a tweezers to pull out the bones. It is easier to do this before cutting the fillet into 4 pieces. Refrigerate, covered, until ready to use.

2. Be sure the spinach is well rinsed and dried. Put a number of leaves together and slice the spinach thinly, less than ¼ inch wide. Store in a plastic bag, tied, in the refrigerator until ready to use,

3. Trim the baby carrots if needed, cut in ½ lengthwise, and keep cutting lengthwise to make matchsticklike "batons." Steam them for several minutes. Do not fully cook, as they will cook further in the packet in the oven.

4. Bring the shorter ends of the parchment sheets together, fold, and cut in ½; this will give you 4 sheets, each 12x16 inches in size. Fold each of these sheets and, with scissors, cut the fattest, roundest heart shape you can place on that folded sheet. Start at the folded side about 2 inches

from the top and cut a curve around the corner. Do this in similar fashion on each of the next 2 corners (this means cutting only 3 corners). Lay open the hearts—you will need lots of counter space for this. Arrange a handful of spinach shreds in the center on the right side of the paper heart. Lay a piece of salmon on top of the spinach. Surround the salmon with some precooked carrot sticks. Add a tablespoon of butter on top of each salmon. Carefully spoon some of the wine over the salmon—use 2 spoonfuls without letting the wine run off the packet. Sprinkle each with some fennel seed, salt, and freshly ground pepper. Fold over the other ½ of the paper heart and bring the edges together. Starting at the top of the heart, crimp the edges and go all the way around to the end of the third side (it is not necessary to crimp the folded side) until the salmon and its contents are fully enclosed. These may remain at room temperature about 1 hour.

5. Preheat the oven to 475°F (very hot oven). Place 2 packets each on 2 baking trays. Be sure none of the parchment packages overlap the outer edge of the baking trays. Put both trays in the oven and bake 12 minutes. Remove the packets and carefully transfer each to a serving plate. The packets are opened at the table by each of the diners. Tear apart, with your hands, the top paper of the packet and spread wide, or cut it open with a scissors. The salmon and vegetables are eaten from the packet. Once the packet is opened, pass the following sauce. A spoonful of it may be put next to each cooked piece of salmon.

To make the sauce:

Horseradish, a relative of the radish, is a cylindrical root with a light skin that, when removed, is usually grated and served as a condiment, fresh or cooked, and often combined with mayonnaise, sour cream, yogurt, and so on. In Italy, it is seen in the markets in the spring to coincide with the Jewish holiday of Passover, when it is used as part of a celebratory meal. The user of fresh horseradish must be aware that the fresh product is considerably stronger than a bottled version. It makes an excellent accompaniment to salmon.

½ cup sour cream
1 tablespoon fresh lemon juice
Fresh or prepared horseradish to taste

1. Combine these ingredients to make a sauce, starting with a small amount of horseradish and increasing the amount, if you wish, to get the desired pungency. Add some salt and freshly ground pepper. Mix well. Refrigerate until ready to use.

POACHED SEA BASS AND SHRIMP IN WINE WITH SAFFRON, AS PREPARED BY FISHERMEN'S WIVES IN PORTO RECANATI

Branzino e gamberetti al Marchigiana affogati in vino bianco con zafferano

Serves 4

Saffron, originating in Persia, is one of the many foods introduced into Europe by the Arabs. At the time of the Crusaders, it was so popular that a special Office of Saffron was set up in Venice to handle the busy trade of it. Its history, however, as a condiment and medicine goes far back to Egyptian, Greek, and Roman times. It is cultivated today in France, Greece, Iran, Italy, Russia, South America, Spain, and the United States. In Italy, it is grown in Sicily, Sardinia, and Abruzzo and used in a variety of ways all over the boot. In Sardinia and Sicily, saffron is used in couscous dishes, obviously a connection to the Arabs. You cannot make the Sicilian dish of *pasta con le sarde* without it. The same is true for the *risotto alla milanese* of Milan. One would think it would be used in the many Abruzze fish soups, but it is not, although it is used in that way by the neighboring province of *Marche*.

It is best to buy saffron in strands, threads, or filaments rather than powdered, as it is more difficult to know whether the powder has good strength. Although a small amount of saffron is used here, it is important to the dish, as is the final touch of olive oil.

⅔ cup dry white wine
½ cup chopped, seeded tomatoes
⅔ cup fish broth, see page 379 or clam juice
⅓ cup finely chopped onions
1 teaspoon saffron threads
4 sea bass fillets or any snapper, about 1½ pounds
½ pound shrimp (about 8 large ones), peeled, deveined, and butterflied
2 tablespoons thinly sliced scallions
2 tablespoons extra-virgin olive oil

1. Over high heat, bring the wine to boil in a large skillet with a cover (large enough to hold 4 fish fillets) to reduce wine by ½, about 2 to 3 minutes.

2. Add the tomatoes, fish broth, and the onions, bring to a boil, and cook 1 minute.

3. Stir in the saffron and some salt and freshly ground pepper, and simmer 2 minutes to allow the saffron to dissolve into a lovely lemony-orange color.

4. Carefully place the fish fillets in the skillet. Do not overlap the fish. Cover the skillet and poach the fillets 3 minutes. Remove the cover, add the shrimp, return the cover, and cook an additional 2 minutes. Do not overcook the shrimp or they will toughen.

5. Serve immediately. Bring the covered skillet to the table. When you have everyone's attention, remove the cover. The escaping steam and the fresh fish aromas are breathtaking. (A woman in the village of Vasto, further south on the Adriatic, served it to me this way, and I have never forgotten the joy she showed in her presentation.) Transfer the fillets and some sauce to individual flat-type bowls, preferably with rims. Sprinkle the scallions over each fillet and spoon olive oil over each portion of fish.

GRILLED SWORDFISH WITH WHITE WINE AND SAGE

Pesce spada grigliata con vino e salvia

Serves 4

Swordfish is available in the United States, as it is in Italy, where it is enjoyed in a variety of ways, so you won't have to look far for swordfish. The fishermen of Bagnara (in Calabria) harpoon swordfish as did the ancient Greeks, and swordfish is a specialty of Messina also (in Sicily), where it is fried in olive oil with marjoram, or coated with bread and cheese and fried, or sautéed with tomatoes, onion, and celery in olive oil. In this menu, the fish is as simple as a recipe can be. It was inspired by one I enjoyed in Rimini, a pleasant resort town on the Adriatic where, in the early morning, its Piazza Cavour creates a lively fish market, where one can find almost any species of fish in the Adriatic Sea. The chefs go early to the market to get the freshest fish possible.

2 swordfish steaks, 1 pound each, about 1 inch thick
½ cup dry white wine
⅓ cup extra-virgin olive oil
2 tablespoons finely chopped fresh sage or 2 teaspoons dried, crushed
2 tablespoons finely chopped Italian parsley

1. Combine all ingredients in a large shallow glass or ceramic dish or platter and marinate at room temperature 1 to 2 hours, or marinate longer in the refrigerator, but not overnight. If refrigerated, allow fish to return to room temperature, about 1 hour.

2. When the grill fire is ready, grill the fish on 1 side by searing close to the heat and then raising the grill farther from the heat to complete cooking. Use the marinade to keep the fish moistened by brushing some of it on to the fish directly. Turn and grill the other side, searing first as before. Brush on some of the marinade. Total cooking time should be 8 to 10 minutes. Remove from the grill and add some salt and freshly ground pepper.

A FISHERMAN'S CHOWDER FROM FANO ON THE ADRIATIC
Brodetto Casalingo

Serves 8

The *brodetto* of the Marches, the old and rich fish chowder said to have been created in Athens, was spread by the Greeks throughout the Mediterranean. There is the *ciuppin* of Liguria, the *cacciucco* of Livorno, the *ghiotto* of Sicily, and the *cassola* of Sardinia as living examples of this Greek influence. Julius Caesar is supposed to have eaten a version of this chowder in Forlì, a province that is home to Rimini. The Italians say to make a good brodetto you need a good sense of smell—that you have to go to the seaside and take a breath of the sea air to determine whether it is a good fish day. Well, that's not exactly practical always, is it? The rules are given that this fish and that fish are essential to a good brodetto, but that doesn't hold up either, as each cook seems to have an idea about which kinds of fish are necessary. The one consistency among brodetto makers is that one of the fish used must be the *scorpena* or *scorfano*, a hogfish which is the French *rascasse*. In the United States, there is an American rascasse from Maine, and elsewhere there are varieties of rose fish (black bellied, white bellied), and either of these would make a good substitute for the scarpena. If you can't get these, then be sure to include the sea bass listed in the ingredient list below as the one essential fish to use.

¾ cup extra-virgin olive oil

2 leeks, white part only, carefully cleaned and thinly sliced

2 ribs celery, trimmed and thinly sliced on the diagonal

4 cloves garlic, minced

4 pounds various fish, such as flounder, any kind of snapper, sea bass (non-Chilean, as it is too oily), trout, and tilapia, cleaned and scaled, preferably with bone in, cut in large chunks, ready for cooking, with heads reserved

1 pound cleaned squid, left whole

¼ cup white wine vinegar

2 small onions, thinly sliced

2 cinnamon sticks

4 bay leaves

2 tablespoons finely chopped Italian parsley

16 slices bruschetta, see page 301

1. In a large sauce pan, heat ½ of the olive oil and sauté the leeks and celery until the leeks become opaque, about 5 minutes. Add the garlic and sauté 1 minute longer. Add the fish heads, the squid, and the vinegar; turn up the heat to cook off the vinegar, 3 or 4 minutes. Add some salt and freshly ground pepper and water to cover the heads. Bring to boil, lower the heat to a simmer, and cook 45 minutes, partially covered.

2. Remove the squid and set aside. Strain the sauce and set it aside. Discard the heads and other solids. Do not rinse the sauce pan in which the sauce cooked. When the squid have cooled, slice them across the body to make ⅓-inch-wide slices.

3. Heat the remaining oil in the same sauce pan and sauté the onion until it is opaque, about 5 minutes. Add the fresh fish pieces, cinnamon sticks, bay leaves, and 1½ tablespoons chopped parsley. Stir the fish in the sauce pan; add the cooked squid, and the strained liquid. Over medium heat, cook the fish until it begins to flake, about 15 minutes. Remove the bay leaves and the cinnamon sticks. Put 2 bruschetta slices in each of 6 bowls, spoon the fish over the bread and add the sauce. Dot with a little fresh parsley and serve a side dish of freshly steamed broccoli with olive oil and fresh lemon juice.

PEPPERY SHRIMP, ONE-TWO-THREE
Gamberi piccante, uno-due-tre

Serves 8 to 12

Once the shrimp are cleaned, this is one of the easiest dishes to make. It is also one of the best tasting. It is important to use fresh shrimp for the best results. Add the pepper flakes to the shrimp after they come out of the skillet to keep them red; otherwise they darken as they're sautéed with the shrimp. Also, the reason not to cook the garlic with the shrimp is to emphasize that the garlic should just turn color (or it gets bitter)—cooking it separately and then adding it to the already cooked shrimp provides better assurance that the garlic will be cooked properly.

2 pounds fresh shrimp (16 to 20 count per pound)
½ cup extra-virgin olive oil
Sprinkle of red pepper flakes
3 cloves garlic, minced
⅓ cup finely chopped fresh Italian parsley

1. Shell and devein the shrimp. Rinse them carefully in cold water. Pat them dry with paper towels.

2. Heat the oil in a large skillet and sauté the shrimp over high heat, uncovered, until they turn pink, about 5 minutes, stirring all the time. Season them with some salt and a liberal amount of freshly ground pepper. Remove the shrimp from the skillet and put them on a large platter. Sprinkle with the red pepper flakes.

3. Add the garlic pieces to the remaining oil in the skillet and sauté over high heat briefly, 1 to 2 minutes, stirring all the time. Do not darken the garlic pieces; they are to come off the heat as soon as they begin to turn color. Immediately, pour this over the shrimp on the platter and sprinkle the parsley over all. The shrimp should be served as they come off the stove. If they sit around too long, they begin to toughen.

FISH FILLETS, NEAPOLITAN FISHERMAN'S STYLE
Pesce alla pescatora

Serves 8 to 12

In Naples, the fishermen cook chunks of fish with skin and bones in this fashion. This has been adapted to use fish fillets instead. Cooking this the Neapolitan way will give more flavor, but I am convinced that Americans do not want to sit across from each other picking small bones out of their mouths—besides, there is the safety factor of not swallowing small fish bones.

2 pounds fish fillets (sole, flounder, snapper, bass, etc.)
Juice of 1 lemon
4 tablespoons extra-virgin olive oil
2 cloves garlic, minced
1 onion, finely chopped
3 cups fresh tomatoes, cored, blanched, peeled, seeded, and chopped, or 3 cups canned plum tomatoes put through a food mill
⅓ cup finely chopped fresh basil and Italian parsley
1 teaspoon dried oregano, crushed
½ cup dry white wine
8 to 16 pieces of crostini or bruschetti, see page 301

1. Rinse the fillets in cool water, dry them with paper towels, and put in a bowl with the lemon juice. Let marinate 15 minutes. Cut them into 3-inch pieces and set aside.

2. In a large skillet, heat the oil, add the garlic and onion, and brown lightly, about 8 minutes. Add the tomatoes, the herbs, and some salt, and cook over medium heat, uncovered, 15 minutes. Add the wine, and cook 7 or 8 minutes longer. Add the fish fillets and a liberal amount of freshly ground pepper, cover the skillet, and, over moderate heat, cook 5 minutes. The fish should be opaque when it is done. Serve over small or large crostini, but do not put the fish and its sauce over the bread until they are ready to be served and eaten.

SOLE, SHRIMP, AND SQUID, DEEP-FRIED, GAETA STYLE
Fritti misti di mare alla moda di Gaeta

Serves 4

Many people know the town of Gaeta for its great black olives, but it is also known for its fish dishes. Scampi from the Gulf of Gaeta are bigger than those in the Adriatic, and everyone has a special recipe for preparing them. One of the best dishes of the area is *fritti misti di mare*—a mixed fish fry—and here is one of the best recipes from the area.

To make a batter:
2 tablespoons olive oil
1 tablespoon white wine vinegar
2 egg whites
¾ cup all-purpose flour
7 tablespoons cornstarch
2 teaspoons baking soda
1 cup water

1. In a large bowl, combine the oil, vinegar, and egg whites with a whisk. Whisk until well blended.
2. Add the dry ingredients, whisking lightly but well Add the water a little at a time until all is well combined. Cover the bowl with plastic and let rest 20 minutes.

To deep-fry and serve the fish:
1 pound sole fillets, rinsed, dried, and cut into fingerlike pieces
1 pound cleaned squid, cut across the body into ⅓-inch-wide rings
1 pound shrimp, 16 to 20 count, shelled, deveined, rinsed, and dried
1½ cups all-purpose flour
Vegetable oil for deep-frying, about 4 cups
3 lemons, cut in wedges, ends cut off and seeds removed

1. Be sure to have the fish and seafood (dried with paper or cloth toweling), flour (in a flat dish), batter, and oil near the fryer.
2. It is best to do this in a deep fryer with a basket, but if you don't have 1, use a medium-size deep sauce pan and use a strainer or a slotted spoon to retrieve the fish. In either case, heat the oil until a piece of bread sizzles as quickly as it is put in the oil.

3. Dip each piece of fish first into the flour, shaking off any excess, then into the batter and into the oil. Do not crowd the fryer or sauce pan, as the fish pieces tend to stick together. Use a long fork to stir the pieces in the oil to keep them apart. Fry 1 minute and remove the basket or the strainer. Repeat this process until all the fish is fried. It is best to flour and batter the fish just before putting the pieces into the oil. Also, be sure the temperature of the oil comes back to the sizzle-bread stage (about 350°F) for each batch to be fried.

4. As the fried pieces are removed, place them on paper towels to drain. Add some salt and freshly ground pepper and serve with several wedges of lemon.

SHRIMP IN OLIVE OIL AND LEMON JUICE WITH ROSEMARY

Gamberi in salsa d'olio, limone, e rosamarino

Serves 4

Fresh lemon juice has the ability to quicken the intoxicating scent of rosemary on shrimp and some other fish. We all know what rosemary can do to lamb and other cuts of meat, but in this recipe the unusual touch is rosemary, with the help of lemon, on shrimp.

1 pound large shrimp, 16 to 20 shrimp per pound
½ cup extra-virgin olive oil
Juice of 1 lemon, about 3 tablespoons
½ teaspoon finely chopped fresh rosemary
4 sprigs of rosemary, each 3 or 4 inches long

1. Bring water to boil with some salt in a sauce pan and cook shrimp until pink, about 2 to 3 minutes after the water returns to the boil. Drain and rinse under cold water. Peel and devein the shrimp. Dry them well with kitchen toweling and put them in a glass bowl.

2. Combine the oil, lemon juice, chopped rosemary, and some salt and freshly ground pepper. Mix well and pour over cooled shrimp. Allow to marinate 20 to 30 minutes. Toss again.

3. Place a rosemary sprig on each of 4 plates. Carefully arrange 4 or 5 shrimp on each plate, slightly overlapping the rosemary and with each shrimp hugging another, side by side. Spoon some of the dressing over the shrimp and serve right away.

GRILLED EEL WITH WINE, BRANDY AND THYME
Anguilla arrostita al timo (in gratella)

Serves 6

Italians treat eel as a delicacy, and it is cooked all over Italy, especially in towns and villages along the hundred of miles of coastline. It may be stewed, baked, or grilled, or left in the sun to cook. In this part of Italy, Naples, townspeople enjoy the practice of cooking in ancient ways. Brindisi and Gallipoli both compete for the most ancient fish chowders, Greek style. One ancient way to cook eels (only newborn, tiny eels are used) is to put them in large basins of sea water and leave them in the sun until all the water has evaporated. A dash of vinegar is added and *ecco!* An eel dish is ready. Mostly, it is complemented by a variety of herbs such as bay leaves, rosemary, sage, or basil, as in the following recipe. When grilled this way, the flesh is sweet and firm. Eel must be freshly killed and skinned at once, and a fishmonger will do this. In the United States, conger eel, also known as sea eel, is common on the Atlantic coast.

6 pieces of eel, each 3 inches long, about 3 pounds total
1 cup dry white wine
3 tablespoons brandy
4 tablespoons extra-virgin olive oil
Juice of 1 lemon
1 tablespoon chopped fresh thyme or 1 teaspoon dried
2 tablespoons chopped fresh basil or 1 tablespoon dried

1. Rinse and dry the eel pieces and place them in a glass or ceramic dish in 1 layer.

2. Combine the wine, brandy, 2 tablespoons of the oil, lemon juice, thyme, and some salt and freshly ground pepper. Mix well and pour over the fish. Marinate in the refrigerator for 2 hours and be sure to bring to room temperature about ½ hour before grilling.

3. Split each piece of eel lengthwise and pat the basil in between the halves. Thread on 3 skewers, and when the fire is ready, grill 15 minutes, turning carefully and basting with the remaining oil. The eel is done when it turns white and a wooden skewer can be inserted with no resistance. Serve hot.

LOBSTER WITH SPICY HERBED TOMATOES
Aragosta fra diavolo

Serves 4

Italian lobsters have no claws and are different from Maine lobsters in other ways. The Italian ones are really spiny lobsters, more like those found on the Pacific Coast and in the Caribbean. From a basic cooking point of view, they can be treated alike. The Italian preparations are usually simple—some olive oil, lemon, herbs, salt, and pepper. The preparation given here is quite simple also, but cooking it *fra diavolo* means adding hot peppers, tomatoes, and cheese.

2 live lobsters, about 1½ pounds each
1 tablespoon each extra-virgin olive oil and butter
1 clove garlic, minced
2 large tomatoes, peeled, seeded, and chopped
3 tablespoons chopped Italian parsley
2 teaspoons finely chopped fresh oregano or ½ teaspoon dried
¼ teaspoon red pepper flakes
2 tablespoons freshly grated Parmesan cheese

1. Put a lobster on a cutting board and plunge the tip of a large, sharp knife between the eyes (this kills the lobster instantly and humanely). Immediately, cut down sharply in the direction of the tail, splitting the whole lobster in ½. With a paring knife, remove the intestinal tract; it looks like a thin vein running the length of the lobster. Also, remove the sandy sac just underneath the eyes. The coral, as this is known, is edible and delicious, so retain it for extra flavor. Repeat this procedure with the second lobster. Place them, cut side up, in a large baking dish. Set aside.

2. Preheat the oven to 350°F. Heat the oil and butter in a skillet and sauté the garlic until it turn light brown, 1 or 2 minutes. Add the remaining ingredients except for the cheese, and season with some salt and freshly ground pepper. Simmer over low heat until all is blended into a thick sauce, about 15 minutes. Pour this sauce over the lobster halves and bake until they are tender, about 20 minutes. Sprinkle with Parmesan cheese and return to the oven 2 or 3 minutes, just until the cheese melts. Serve right away.

GRILLED RED PEPPER SHRIMP
Gamberi piccanti alla griglia

Serves 4

A really delicious and easy dish, because it is prepared ahead and marinated—the grilling of the shrimp takes only a few minutes, and it is best to cook them just before you need them. It is always best to slightly undercook shrimp, for they have a tendency to toughen if overcooked.

1½ pounds medium shrimp (about 24), shells and tails left on
4 garlic cloves, minced
4 small, dried red pepper chilies, crushed
1 cup extra-virgin olive oil
3 lemons, cut into 8 wedges each
12 bay leaves, halved, or 24 small bay leaves

1. Wash and dry the shrimp, leaving the shells and tails intact. Place in a large glass or ceramic bowl.

2. In a small bowl, combine the garlic, 1 teaspoon salt, red pepper, and ½ cup of the oil and mix well. Blend in the remaining oil and pour over the shrimp, turning to coat all sides. Marinate in the refrigerator 4 hours; remove 1 hour before grilling. Drain, reserving the marinade.

3. Thread the lemon wedges, bay leaves, and shrimp alternatively on 4 skewers.

4. When the fire is ready, grill the shrimp for about 3 minutes on each side, brushing with the reserved marinade. Serve on the skewers. It is best to serve these directly from the grill, ready to be eaten.

SKEWERED TUNA GRILLED WITH LEMON AND OREGANO

Tonno alla griglia econ salsa di olio, limone, e origano

Serves 4

Although most of the food in Calabria is based on pasta and vegetables, there are a number of places along the coast where fish is a specialty. Fish here is best when it is prepared simply, the way the natives do. One special way of preparing tuna is to boil it in chunks and flavor it with oil, parsley, garlic, and hot pepper. Another way is to grill it—this is as simple as cooking can get, and it is delicious because of its simplicity.

2 pounds fresh tuna, at least 1½ inches thick
⅓ cup extra-virgin olive oil
Juice of 1 lemon, about 3 tablespoons
2 cloves garlic, minced
⅓ teaspoon red pepper flakes
¼ cup finely chopped Italian parsley
1 large sprig oregano, large enough to use as a brush during grilling

1. Prepare a wood fire, if possible; if not, charcoal will do. Ready the fire and let it reach the ashen stage. The goal is to get a red-hot fire with gray coals.

2. Cut the tuna into large chunks, preferably 1½ inches square. Wipe them dry and place them in 1 layer in a flat dish.

3. Combine the remaining ingredients, except the sprig of oregano. along with freshly ground black pepper and 1 teaspoon salt in a small bowl, and spoon over all the chunks of tuna, turning to cover all sides. Allow to marinate 15 minutes. Arrange them on skewers just before grilling them.

4. Put them on the grill and cook them quickly on all sides, always brushing or basting them with the oregano sprig dipped in the oil mixture. The whole grilling time will take 5 to 10 minutes, depending on how rare you wish the tuna to be. Serve on individual plates with some spaghetti.

SNAPPER OR TROUT IN VERNACCIA WINE
Triglie al Vernaccia

Serves 6

In Sardinia, the fish called for in this preparation is red or gray mullet, and sometimes trout. Mullets can be purchased in major cities, but, for most readers, this fish may be difficult to find. So snapper, red or most other kinds of snapper, does well. If you have difficulty finding vernaccia wine from Sardinia, substitute this: ½ sherry and ½ dry white wine.

3 whole snappers, about 1½ pounds each, or 6 trout
3 tablespoons extra-virgin olive oil
1 medium carrot, trimmed and finely chopped
2 cloves garlic, minced
1 teaspoon each finely chopped rosemary and oregano
¼ cup finely chopped Italian parsley
2 tablespoons grated lemon zest
4 cups Vernaccia wine, or 2 cups sherry plus 2 cups dry white wine

1. Ask your fishmonger to prepare the fish for cooking. The heads of the fish should stay on; snapper tails may be clipped.

2. In a very large skillet or large sauté pan in which the fish will fit in 1 layer, heat the oil. Add the carrot and cook 3 or 4 minutes or until the carrot pieces are tender. Add the garlic and cook 1 minute longer.

3. Add the rosemary, oregano, parsley, and lemon zest and lay the fish on top of them. Add some salt and a liberal amount of freshly ground pepper. Pour the wine carefully into the skillet or pan to cover the fish.

4. Cook over medium heat until the fish is flaky (use a wooden skewer and put it through the body of the fish—if it penetrates easily, the fish is cooked). Cook each side 10 to 15 minutes. Most of the wine should have evaporated. The total cooking time will be 20 to 30 minutes. One snapper will serve 2 people; or, if using trout, 1 per person. Serve the fish with whatever little sauce is left in the skillet.

SAUTÉED FRESH TUNA WITH AROMATIC HERBS
Tonno agli aromi

Serves 4

The sauce here is tasty and flavorful, and there will be more than you need to serve with the sliced tuna. Use any leftover sauce (it will keep refrigerated up to a week) as a delicious topping for small crostini or to be mixed with cooked 1/2 pound pasta, such as penne or small rigatoni.

1 thick tuna steak, about 1 to 1½ pounds
1 cup dry white wine
4 tablespoons extra-virgin olive oil
2 tablespoons each chopped parsley, basil, and mint
2 tablespoons butter
1 small onion, peeled and minced
1 large clove garlic, peeled and minced
1 carrot, trimmed, scrubbed, and finely diced
2 large tomatoes, peeled, seeded, and diced
1 tablespoon tomato paste

1. Rinse the fish and pat dry with paper towels. Put the steak(s) in a glass or nonmetal container that will hold the steak(s) in 1 layer, and pour in ½ cup of the wine. Sprinkle 2 tablespoons of the oil over all, along with pinches of the parsley, basil, and mint, and a liberal sprinkling of freshly ground black pepper. Turn the steaks over and let marinate in the refrigerator at least 1 hour. Remove from the refrigerator 10 to 15 minutes before sautéing.

2. Heat the remaining olive oil and the butter in a skillet, and sauté the onions about 3 minutes. Add the garlic and sauté 1 minute longer. Then add the carrots, parsley, basil, mint, tomatoes, tomato paste, the remaining ½ cup of wine, and some salt and freshly ground pepper. Cook over low heat until the sauce combines and thickens, about 12 minutes.

3. Drain the tuna steak and, in a second skillet, sauté on both sides over very high heat, 2 minutes per side. Then pour the onion and herb mixture over the fish and cook to marry the fish and sauce, 3 to 6 minutes, depending on how rare or well done you like tuna. Remove from the heat, let stand a couple of minutes, then slice and serve with some of the vegetable mixture.

TUNA IN ROASTED RED, ORANGE, AND YELLOW PEPPERS

Peperoni arrostiti con tonno

Serves 12

Canned tuna is stored in most Sicilian (and other Italian) pantries. Some people jar fresh tuna, but this seems to be a past household chore—one of the reasons being that delicious and high-quality canned tuna packed in olive oil is available. I noted in the introduction to this book that new cooks and others in Italy are defining the future by celebrating the past. They are creating small revolutions by redefining their own regional tastes. An example of this has to do with the traditional grilled pepper and tuna antipasto—one finds it in Sicily and all over Italy. I enjoyed a half roasted pepper wrapped around an ethereal tablespoonful of tuna mousse at the splendid restaurant Gener Neuv in Asti, a short distance from Turin, in the northern part of Italy, that I think works wonders at a Sicilian buffet which would ordinarily have had roasted peppers and canned tuna with other antipasti.

6 bell peppers, 2 red, 2 orange, and 2 yellow
4 tablespoons extra-virgin olive oil
4 cloves garlic, peeled and halved lengthwise
1 teaspoon red wine vinegar
3 cans (6 ounces) tuna packed in olive oil
2 sticks butter, softened
1 tablespoon cognac or brandy
2 tablespoons finely chopped fresh oregano or 2 teaspoons dried

1. With a damp cloth, wipe the peppers clean. Place them on a flat tray, and broil them slowly, under a low flame, until the skins are charred on all sides. Then put the peppers in a brown paper bag and set them aside to cool, 10 minutes. Shake the bag back and forth to help loosen the skins. When the peppers are cool enough to handle, remove the cores, peel off the skins, and remove the seeds. Cut them in halves and put them in a flat glass dish, like a pie dish. Pour the olive oil over the peppers, and add the garlic and the vinegar. Add some salt and freshly ground pepper. Toss lightly but well. Cover with plastic and leave at room temperature (for 4 or 5 hours) until needed.

2. Empty the cans of tuna, leaving the oil behind, in a food processor. Add the butter and the cognac or brandy. Add some salt and freshly ground pepper. Process to make a smooth puree.

3. Take a bell pepper ½ and lay it flat, inside-side up. Put a good tablespoon of the tuna mousse to 1 side of the pepper ½. Bring up the other side to cover the tuna, yet showing just a little of the tuna. Transfer to an attractive platter, 1 large enough to take 11 more halves. Repeat this procedure until all are done. Pour some of the leftover oil from the pepper dish or the canned tuna over the peppers and sprinkle the oregano over all. Add more salt and freshly ground pepper. This is to be served at room temperature and may sit out of the refrigerator for several hours.

SWORDFISH STEAKS WITH TWO SAUCES: BLOOD ORANGE AND CAPER/PARSLEY

Pescespada grigliato con due salse

Serves 12

The Strait of Messina (Calabria-Sicily), prized for its abundant swordfish and tuna—longer than 15 feet, provides these fish that are prepared in many ways. Often, the simplest preparation is the one most seen—a slice of it grilled simply with oil, lemon, and a selected herb. Italian gourmets will add special sauces, as provided here. If you don't have time for two sauces, choose 1. The swordfish takes little time to grill, so grill it just before serving.

Blood orange sauce, see below
Caper and anchovy sauce, see below
3 large swordfish steaks, each 1½ pounds (1 steak should serve 4 people)
6 tablespoons extra-virgin olive oil
3 tablespoons finely chopped fresh oregano, or 3 teaspoons dried, crushed
½ teaspoon red pepper flakes

To make the blood orange sauce:

The blood-red color of the flesh of the blood orange gives these sweet, juicy oranges their name. They are mostly imported from Mediterranean countries, Italy, particularly Sicily, being a major producer. They are small to medium-sized fruits with smooth or pitted skin that is sometimes tinged with red. If you can't find the blood oranges, use navel or Valencia and add a touch of tomato paste to achieve the red color.

1 blood orange, or 1 sweet orange (to make ¼ cup juice) and 2 tablespoons finely grated orange rind
Mayonnaise, double the recipe on page 42
1 teaspoon tomato paste or more, if using sweet oranges

1. Grate the orange for zest and set aside. Squeeze the orange for juice and set aside.

2. Prepare the mayonnaise, and blend in a little tomato paste at a time to color it. Add a tablespoon of juice at a time until you get a consistency like lightly whipped heavy cream. Fold in the orange zest.

To make the caper and anchovy sauce:

Capperi, as they are called in Italy, are the flower buds of a wild, Mediterranean, thorny climbing shrub and have been used as a condiment for thousands of years. They are preserved in brine or pickled in white wine vinegar. In Sicily, they are packed in whole salt, which should be rinsed off before using. Their use in Italy is widespread, as they are added to fish and seafood dishes, salads and vegetable sauces, and pizzas and pastas, such as in the famous Sicilian pasta dish *pasta colle sarde*. Try using pickled, brined, or packed-in-salt capers and your taste will prevail as to which type you will buy in the future. Capers should be rinsed, whether in brine or salt. Rinsing them before use softens their piquant, sharp flavor. They should also be dried before adding them to a preparation. The larger capers are cheaper than the smaller ones. There is no difference in taste, but the smaller ones seem to make a better garnish. Italians buy their packed-in-salt capers by the *etto*, which simply means they are sold loose; one etto equals three-and-a-half ounces. Once opened, capers packed in liquid should be kept refrigerated; they will last indefinitely, as will the ones packed in salt. This sauce is excellent over fish, cooked vegetables, meat, and poultry, all hot or cold.

2 anchovy fillets
½ cup white wine vinegar
3 tablespoons capers, rinsed, dried, and chopped
½ cup extra-virgin olive oil
2 tablespoons finely chopped Italian parsley

1. Place the anchovies and the vinegar in the food processor and process to a count of 10. Transfer the mixture to a large nonstick skillet.

2. Add the chopped capers and bring to a boil. Lower the heat, cover the skillet, and cook 5 minutes over low heat. With the help of a rubber spatula, transfer this mixture to a bowl.

3. Add the oil and beat with a wire whisk Add some salt and freshly ground pepper and the chopped parsley.

To grill and serve the swordfish:

1. Ready a wood or charcoal fire for grilling. Be sure the coals turn gray (the coal inside is red hot).

2. Combine the olive oil, oregano, and pepper flakes. Brush some of this on both sides of the fish.

3. When the fire is ready, grill the fish steaks 3 or 4 minutes per side, brushing on more of the oil mixture several times during the grilling period.

4. Remove from the grill, brush lightly with more oil, and add some salt and freshly ground pepper. Cut each steak into 4 portions. Put each of the sauces into bowls and serve with the fish.

SPICY SEAFOOD STEW IN SYRACUSE   SERVES 8

The famous geometrician Archimedes was born in 287 BC at Syracuse, one of Sicily's most prestigious cities of Magna Graecia, rivaling Athens at the time. Archimedes would forget to eat and drink—he was so absent minded. While taking a bath, he realized that any body immersed in water loses weight equivalent to that of the water it displaces. He was so delighted with his new finding, he jumped out of the tub and ran naked through the streets, bellowing "Eureka!" (I found it!). Italian cities are rich in such stories. The owner of the Archimede restaurant told that one to me on via Gemellaro in Syracuse, where I enjoyed fish dishes similar to the one given here.

The old town of *Siracuse* is on the island of Ortygio (right in the middle of the city), whose streets are rich with medieval and baroque palaces. When I was there in 2010 many of these buildings were covered with scaffolding; Sicilians are as eager to restore their heritage as others in Italy. On these narrow streets, there is restaurant after restaurant, and more of them are in the piazzas and squares, with menus filled with tuna and swordfish dishes. These fish are prepared as they are elsewhere along the coast—cooked in oil, tomatoes, onions, celery, olives, capers, and potatoes.

The addition of potatoes is really a nice touch, especially for a one-dish meal, as it readily provides the starch. Here is a version of one of them that uses shellfish. Syracuse raises shellfish, including oysters, and its *gamberoni rossi*— large, delicious shrimp (or crayfish)—are well known. Other cities in Sicily, notably Ragusa, Agrigento, Palermo, Messina, and Trapina, cook shellfish and crustaceans in the same way.

This particular seafood stew is my adaptation.

2 pounds shrimp (16 to 20 count), shelled, deveined (reserve the shells for making broth)
2 medium to large Idaho potatoes (about 1 pound)
½ cup extra-virgin olive oil
2 medium onions, finely chopped
4 cloves garlic, minced
2 tablespoons finely chopped fresh basil or 4 teaspoons dried
2 teaspoons finely chopped thyme
2 teaspoons saffron strands, crumbled
1 teaspoon red pepper flakes
4 whole cloves
2 cans (28 ounces) plum tomatoes, seeded, cut in small pieces, drained
1½ cups dry white vermouth, preferably Martini and Rossi
4 lobster tails with shells (about 2 pounds), each cut into 4 pieces with the shell on
2 pounds fillets of bass, grouper, cod, or other white fish, cut into 2-inch squares
2 tablespoons (or more) Sambuca
1 to 2 cups fish broth, see below

1. Rinse the shrimp well and dry them in paper towels. Set aside.

2. Peel the potatoes, cut in ½ lengthwise, and then cut them in ½-inch slices (these are fairly large slices of potatoes). Put them in a bowl of cold water until needed.

3. In a very large, stovetop-proof casserole with cover (or a large sauce pan), heat the oil. Add the onions and cook 5 minutes. Add the garlic, basil, thyme, saffron, pepper flakes, cloves, and some salt and freshly ground pepper.

4. Add the drained tomatoes and vermouth and bring to boil. Drain the potatoes and add them. Simmer, at a lower heat, covered, 20 minutes.

5. Add the shrimp, lobster, and white fish. Stir, bring to simmer, and cook 30 minutes, partly covered.

6. Add Sambuca 5 minutes before the end of cooking. When serving, spoon into individual large bowls and top with a piece of the lobster in shell, or serve in the casserole with the lobster pieces on top.

Nota bene: This stew is not a soup and therefore should not be too liquidy. It will make its own juice from the vegetables and fish. However, if you feel it is too dry for your taste, add a half cup at a time of the fish broth to increase the amount of liquid you wish to have.

<u>To make the broth:</u>
   Makes about 2 cups

Shells from the peeled shrimp
1 fish bouillon cube, chopped

1. Put the shells in a small sauce pan with a cover and add cold water just to barely cover them. Add the bouillon. Bring to boil over medium heat, lower the heat to get a steady simmer, cover the pan, and cook 30 minutes. Drain, squeezing as much juice as you can from the shells.

Chapter 6

POULTRY AND GAME

ROAST CHICKEN
Pollo arrostito

Serves 4 to 6

1 (3-pound) chicken, readied for roasting
3 tablespoons extra-virgin olive oil
2 tablespoons finely chopped rosemary
2 cloves garlic, peeled and halved
1 cup dry white wine

1. Preheat the oven to 425°F. Rub the chicken all over with the oil. Liberally salt and pepper the bird, inside and out. Add some rosemary and ½ the garlic to the cavity. Put the chicken in a roasting pan just large enough to hold the chicken.

2. Pour the wine in the pan, add the remaining garlic and rosemary, and bake 1 hour, until nicely browned. Baste frequently with the juices in the pan. To test for doneness, put a fork in the top of the thigh against the body, and if the juices run clear, the chicken should be done.

ROASTED ROSEMARY CHICKEN
Pollo arrostito al rosamarino

Serves 8

Another simple Italian preparation. Rosemary is a favorite herb with the Italians. All the houses I have rented in Italy always had bush after bush of rosemary. It is so wonderful to put a hand out the door and snip some fresh rosemary right off the bush.

2 whole chickens, 3½ pounds each
2 tablespoons good olive oil
12 small fresh rosemary sprigs
6 cloves garlic, peeled and thinly sliced

1. Preheat oven to 500°F. Rinse the chickens and pat dry. Cut off any excess fat. Rub the oil all over the outside of the chickens.

2. Insert some rosemary and garlic under the skin around the breasts and legs of each chicken and inside the cavities; do not break the skin.

3. Liberally salt and pepper the chickens inside and out.

4. Arrange the chicken breast side up in a baking pan and roast 20 minutes. Lower heat to 450 and bake 40 minutes longer or until the meat is moist and the skin crisp. Serve warm or at room temperature.

BLACK FOREST HAM AND SHALLOTS IN BAKED CHICKEN BREASTS
Rollatini di pollo, arrostitato

Serves 12

Italian like this artisanal preparation of stuffing the breast,

rolling and coating it, and baking it. It is a delicious dish.

12 boned chicken breast halves
Juice of 1 lemon
1 stick butter
½ cup finely chopped shallots
⅓ cup thinly sliced celery
12 medium-sized mushrooms, chopped fine
2¾ cups fresh egg-bread crumbs
4 tablespoons finely chopped parsley
12 thin slices Black Forest ham or equivalent
3 eggs
1½ cups flour
12 lemon wedges, seeded

1. Remove all the skin from the chicken breasts (be careful not to remove the fillets from the breasts), rinse, dry and put them in a shallow bowl. Add the lemon juice and let stand for 15 minutes. Drain, dry, and put each breast between 2 pieces of waxed paper. Pound lightly to flatten. Remove the top sheet of paper, and salt and pepper both sides of each breast.

2. Heat ½ of the butter in a large skillet and sauté the shallots and the celery for about 5 minutes. Add the mushrooms and cook another 5 minutes, stirring well. Remove the skillet from the heat, add ¾ cup of bread crumbs and the parsley (reserve 1 tablespoon for garnish), and mix well. Taste for seasoning and add salt and pepper if needed.

3. Arrange a piece of ham on each breast and divide the stuffing among them. Roll each breast, beginning with the smaller end. Secure with wooden skewers, 6 or 8 inches long, just as you would run a straight pin through a piece of cloth or paper.

4. In a bowl, beat the eggs. Roll each breast in the flour, then dip each in the egg, and then coat it completely in the remaining 2 cups of bread crumbs. Spread 2

tablespoons of butter in a baking pan and place the chicken in it. Dot with the remaining 2 tablespoons of butter. Bake in a preheated oven at 400°F for about 40 minutes or until the breasts are browned and cooked. To test for doneness, slice through 1.

5. To serve, imagine a telephone wire lined with birds, and arrange on a platter in that fashion. Be sure the skewers all point in the same direction. Sprinkle lightly with the chopped parsley and put the lemon wedges alongside the "birds." Or, if you prefer, remove the skewers and slice the breasts ½ inch thick, arranging pieces overlapping slightly on a large platter.

BAKED CHICKEN GARIBALDI
Pollo Garibaldi

Serves 2 to 3

This is easy to prepare and results in good-tasting food.

3-pound chicken, roasted at 375°F for 30 minutes
½ cup extra virgin-olive oil
2 cloves garlic, peeled and minced finely
1 red bell pepper, cored, seeded, and cut into small batons
1 onion, chopped coarsely
2 cups chicken broth
½ pound cremini mushrooms, wiped clean and sliced thinly
¼ cup red wine
¼ cup freshly grated Parmesan cheese
⅓ cup finely chopped scallions
½ cup toasted pine nuts

1. Prepare chicken and cool it. Then debone it and lay pieces in an ovenproof casserole.

2. Heat olive oil in large skillet and sauté garlic, red bell pepper, and onions until onions are translucent, about 5 minutes. Add chicken broth and salt. When sauce begins to boil, add mushrooms and red wine.

3. Put contents of skillet over the boned chicken in the casserole. Sprinkle Parmesan over all. Bake at 350°F for 30 minutes. Serve after topping off with scallions and toasted pine nuts.

CORNISH HENS WITH RICOTTA AND TARRAGON UNDER THE SKIN
Gallina stufata al dragoncello

Serves 6

It is best to prepare the hens with the ricotta mixture under the skins several hours ahead to allow flavors to develop. Keep the hens refrigerated, but take them out and leave at room temperature about one-half hour before broiling them. These hens may also be grilled following the same procedure as for broiling, but be sure the coals are gray to prevent flare-ups. Boneless chicken breasts with skins may be substituted for the half hens.

1 cup fresh ricotta cheese
3 tablespoons freshly grated Parmesan cheese
1½ tablespoons butter, softened
1 tablespoon finely chopped fresh tarragon or 1 teaspoon dried, crushed
2 medium cloves garlic, minced
3 Cornish hens, each about 1 pound, trimmed, split in halves lengthwise, rinsed, and dried
1 tablespoon extra-virgin olive oil

1. Combine the ricotta and Parmesan cheeses with the butter, tarragon, garlic, and pepper in a bowl.

2. Lay each hen ½ on a flat surface and carefully separate the skin from the flesh with your fingers, enough to allow you to put some of the ricotta mixture between. Do this with each of the remaining halves. Brush oil over both sides of each hen.

3. Preheat the broiler and line a broiler pan or a flat pan (such as a cookie sheet with a rim) with foil. Arrange the halves skin side down 4 to 6 inches below the heat source, and broil 12 to 15 minutes or until browned. Carefully turn over the halves with the skin side up and brown, about 10 to 12 minutes.

HERBED CHICKEN ON THE GRILL
Pollo al mattone

Serves 6

This is a special way to prepare chicken in Tuscany. Although a whole half chicken is grilled, and here it is suggested that each grilled half then be cut in two, it can be sliced in even smaller portions, almost small enough to be eaten by hand at a picnic.

2 chickens, about 3 pounds each, halved
2 tablespoons each finely chopped rosemary, thyme, basil, and mint
4 tablespoons finely chopped fresh Italian parsley
4 medium cloves garlic, minced
½ cup plus extra-virgin olive oil
For basting:
⅓ cup fresh lemon juice
⅓ cup extra-virgin olive oil

1. Taking care not to tear the skin, partially bone the chicken halves as follows: Cut off wing tips and remove drumstick bones and breastbones. Leave the wing bones, thigh bones, and ribs in place to retain shape. Wipe the chicken halves clean with a damp cloth. If you choose not to bone the chickens in this manner, ask your butcher to do it for you.

2. Combine the herbs, garlic, and ½ cup of oil to make a spreadable paste. Add more oil if you think it should be more spreadable. Add salt and freshly ground pepper. Coat the chicken halves with the paste, inside and out. Marinate, covered, overnight in the refrigerator. Bring chicken to room temperature before grilling.

3. If you have a flattop grill, wipe it clean and preheat it to 325°F to 350°F and lightly oil it. If you don't have a flattop, prepare your fire for the grill and let it come to a gray ash stage. Be careful not to disturb the herb coating when placing the chicken on the flattop or the regular grill. Top each piece with a heavy flat weight, such a brick wrapped in foil.

4. Combine the basting ingredients, adding some salt and freshly ground pepper. After the chicken has cooked 5 minutes, drizzle 1 teaspoon of the basting mixture, using a spoon, not a brush, to avoid breaking the herb crust. Baste again in the same way after another 5 minutes, and carefully turn over the pieces. Carefully replace the weights. Baste again after 5 minutes and again after 10 minutes, at which time the chicken should be done and off the grill. Cool and cut each chicken ½ in 2 or more pieces. This is very tasty at room temperature.

CHICKEN, KALE, AND CHICKPEA STEW

Pollo, cavolo nero, e ceci in umido

Serves 6

Italians enjoy used dried legumes (*legumi secchi*), and chickpeas, known as *ceci*, are quite popular. In the United States, these dishes are easy to prepare because of the availability of canned legumes, which do not need presoaking. In using these cans

of chickpeas, or cannellini or borlotti beans, or whatever, it is important to rinse the contents of the can under running water to flush away the high level of salt in these cans. Simply empty the contents of the canned food into a colander and run under cool water, tossing the legumes with your hands. Drain well and proceed with the recipe. This makes a good one-dish meal, and it is better if served with a crisp, fresh, green salad with a simple oil and vinegar dressing. Think of hearts of curly endive with thin slices of celery hearts for the salad.

2 tablespoons extra-virgin olive oil
1 large onion, chopped
1 green bell pepper, chopped
2 cloves garlic, minced
¾ pounds kale, chopped in 1-inch pieces
1 pound chicken breasts, cut into 1-inch pieces
1 can (28 ounces) plum tomatoes, undrained, chopped
2 cans (15 ounces each) chickpeas, drained
2 cups chicken broth, see page 377 , or 1 can (14½ ounces) low-sodium chicken broth
2 tablespoon tomato paste
½ teaspoon sugar
½ teaspoon each ground cumin, dried oregano, crushed red pepper flakes, and dried thyme
1 bay leaf
6 bruschetti, optional
6 tablespoons freshly grated Parmesan cheese

1. In a heavy sauce pan with a cover, heat the oil and sauté the onion and green bell pepper for 6 to 8 minutes. Stir frequently. Add the garlic and sauté 1 minute longer.

2. Stir in the kale and all the other ingredients except the bruschetti and cheese. Bring to a boil, then lower the heat to get a good, steady simmer. Partially cover the pot and simmer for 30 minutes or until the kale and chicken are cooked. Stir several times during the cooking. Serve over a piece of bruschetta if you wish. In either case, top each serving with a tablespoon of cheese.

BAKED MEAT-STUFFED TURKEY ROLL

Petto di tacchino ripieno al forno

Serves 8

The Spaniards brought turkey to Europe from America in the early sixteenth century. The Italians took to it quickly. It may be the most popular form of poultry in Italy today. Milan, in Lombardy, features a roast turkey at Christmastime, but turkey preparations appear all over the boot any time of the year. This stuffed and rolled turkey breast is an adaptation of Milan's roast turkey with its complex, yet delicious filling. This can be made ahead and served cold with a salad. Or serve it warm with some sauce, as in the following recipe.

2 pounds turkey breast, boned and skinned
3 tablespoons butter
2 tablespoons extra-virgin olive oil
1 pound Italian sausage, out of casing
1 carrot, finely chopped
½ onion, finely chopped
1 tablespoon each finely chopped rosemary and sage
6 ounces canned or jarred cooked chestnuts, coarsely chopped
12 walnut halves, coarsely chopped
4 tablespoons freshly grated Parmesan cheese
2 eggs, beaten
1 to 1½ cups white wine

1. With a sharp knife, cut part of the way through the turkey breast and open out the 2 halves, still attached. Pound the turkey with a mallet to get 1 large piece of meat. Your butcher should be willing to do this for you if you ask.

2. In a large skillet, heat 2 tablespoons butter and 1 tablespoon olive oil. Sauté, over medium heat, the sausage, carrot, onion, rosemary, and sage until the meat begins to brown, about 10 minutes. Add some salt and freshly ground pepper. Transfer this mixture to a large bowl to cool. Keep the skillet as is for a later step. Drain the sausage mixture and let the liquid fall into the skillet.

3. Add the chestnuts, walnuts, Parmesan, and eggs to the bowl with the sausage mixture and toss well. The stuffing should be slightly moist and not liquidy.

4. Spread the mixture over the turkey, leaving a ½-inch border all around. Roll up the turkey and tie it in 4 or 5 places across the roll, and once down the length, with kitchen string. Preheat the oven to 375°F.

5. Reheat the skillet that sautéed the sausage, adding the remaining butter and oil. When bubbly, add the turkey roll and brown over medium to high heat, rotating to brown all sides, about 12 to 14 minutes. Transfer to an ovenproof casserole with a cover.

6. Deglaze the skillet with ½ cup of the wine and pour over the turkey roll in the casserole. Add another ½ cup wine. Cover and place in the oven, and cook 20 minutes. Remove cover, add remaining wine, and cook, uncovered, 25 minutes longer, basting each 10 minutes of time.

7. Remove from the oven and let it sit about 10 minutes before slicing. Continue to cook the sauce to reduce it to your liking (thin or thicker). Serve slices of turkey after removing the string, with a little sauce to the edge of the roll slice. As a salad, use fresh or frozen green peas, thawed and cooked, with finely cut onions tossed with an oil and vinegar dressing.

Nota bene: If your butcher doesn't have a turkey breast of this size, use three smaller ones, each weighing about three-quarters of a pound. Slice each almost through so you have two pieces of breast attached at 1 side. Open up and flatten. Flattening is important because it increases the size of the roll—try to get an even thickness of about ⅓ inch. Repeat with the other two breasts. Lay the three pieces of turkey slightly overlapping 1 another with the shorter widths facing you (the longer lengths will go from your left to right). Join each overlap with a long wooden skewer (you will need two of them, and they can be removed easily after the roll has baked and is to be served). Arrange the filling over all and start to roll up, beginning with the side just before you. Tie in five places across the roll and once across the length.

QUAIL WITH HERBS AND TRUFFLE OIL
Quaglie al forno alle erbe, con olio di tartufo

Serves 4

When I was a boy, I used to hear all the time about shooting *quaglie*, quail, in Italy. My grandfather used to say that they were easy targets. These days I hear that most quail in Italy are farm raised, as they are in this country. They are very small birds and have a subtle, delicate, gamey flavor; they are small enough so one needs to serve two per person.

They are not always in the markets, and sometimes there isn't enough time to get them through mail order. Using Cornish game hens is a satisfactory substitute—one game hen can serve two people.

8 quail, ready for roasting
¼ cup finely chopped chives
¼ cup finely chopped basil
¼ cup finely chopped tarragon
½ cup finely chopped shallots
½ cup extra-virgin olive oil
1 tablespoon finely chopped rosemary
8 juniper berries, optional
2 bay leaves
4 tablespoons butter
8 paper-thin slices pancetta
1 tablespoon truffle oil

1. Ready the quail for cooking by rinsing and drying thoroughly. Set aside.
2. Combine everything else except the butter, pancetta, and truffle oil, and rub some of the mixture inside and outside the birds. Put the birds in a large plastic bag, pour in the herb/olive oil mixture, seal the bag tightly, and refrigerate overnight. Remove from the refrigerator 1 hour before cooking to bring them to room temperature.
3. Preheat the oven to 425°F. Melt the butter in a very large skillet and sauté the birds over moderate heat until lightly browned on all sides, 10 to 15 minutes. Transfer them to a baking pan, cover each bird with a slice of pancetta, and bake until done, about 15 minutes. Baste after 5 and 10 minutes, spooning some marinade over them. Remove from the oven and sprinkle truffle oil over the birds.

<u>To cook Cornish game hens in place of quail:</u>
2 Cornish game hens, quartered

1. Marinate as above, overnight, and bring to room temperature before baking. Sautéing them in a skillet, as for quail, is not necessary.
2. Preheat oven to 450°F. Place hen pieces in a baking dish and bake for 45 minutes, or until tender, following the procedure as in step 3 above.

TURKEY BREASTS BAKED WITH PROSCIUTTO AND CHEESE TO RESEMBLE A CARDINAL'S HAT

Petti di tacchino al forno alla cardinale

Serves 6

Here is a very good one-dish meal, because it is easy to make and also because boned turkey breasts are in most food markets—in fact, often they are sold sliced. Again, here is an Italian touch that may seem too cute for words, but it makes an attractive luncheon or light supper one-dish meal if accompanied by a beet salad or two or three slices of red ripe tomatoes that are dressed simply with oil, salt and pepper, and a couple of drops of balsamic vinegar. Either the beets or the sliced tomatoes will enrich the color of the cardinal's hat. Prosciutto di Parma is considered the best by many people, but there are others who give that accolade to the San Daniele ham The San Daniele come from the Fruili area in the northeast of Italy, where their pigs for this particular ham are kept outdoors and fed a diet of acorns, which results in the distinctive flavor. It imparts this flavor to the turkey, which is somewhat bland to begin with, therefore making a good food combination.

6 slices uncooked turkey breast, each about ¾ inch thick, about 1½ pounds
1 cup milk
6 tablespoons butter
3 or 4 teaspoons tomato paste
12 thin slices of mozzarella di bufala
6 thin slices prosciutto di San Daniele or di Parma
Juice of 1 lemon wedge
¼ cup finely chopped fresh chives

1. Put the slices of turkey in a flat glass dish large enough to hold the pieces in 1 layer. Pour the milk over the slices and let them rest 30 or 40 minutes at room temperature. Drain the turkey slices, pat them dry with kitchen paper towels, put each slice between 2 sheets of waxed paper, and pound them with a meat pounder to flatten them somewhat.

2. Melt 3 tablespoons butter in a large skillet and sauté 3 of the slices until they turn golden on both sides, a few minutes per side. Remove them to an ovenproof pan (such as a cookie sheet with a rim) and repeat this procedure for the remaining

3 turkey slices, beginning with melting 3 tablespoons butter and sautéing the other 3 slices. Add 1 teaspoon of the cooked melted butter to the tomato paste with 3 or 4 drops of lemon juice and stir well. Put the tomato paste mixture aside until needed. When all the slices are cooked, arrange them on the ovenproof pan, salt and pepper them, and put 1 slice of mozzarella on each turkey slice. The cheese should not overhang the turkey slice in any way—there should be a visible edge of border of turkey meat around the cheese.

3. Wrap a slice of prosciutto around each turkey/cheese slice and then put another smaller slice of cheese over the prosciutto wrapping. Broil just long enough to melt the mozzarella, about 2 to 3 minutes. Remove the pan from the broiler to put ½ teaspoon of tomato paste on the top of each piece. Return to the broiler to reheat, but be careful not to burn the tomato paste. Remove from the oven. Arrange the cooked turkey pieces on a platter and sprinkle the chopped chives over all, or put on individual plates, still sprinkling each with some chives.

CHRISTMAS CAPON WITH CONDIMENT FROM CREMONA

Cappone Natalizio con Mostarda di Cremona

Serves 8 to 12

The condiment *mostarda di frutta*, quite famous in Italy and becoming more popular elsewhere, is crystallized fruit of many kinds in a sauce flavored with mustard. It has been made in Cremona for well over a hundred years. It is usually served with sausages or roasted beef and pork. I think it is excellent with roasted capon, chicken, or turkey.

2 (6-pound) capons, readied for roasting
2 lemons
1 end piece of prosciutto, 2 or 3 ounces
2 small onions, finely chopped
2 medium carrots, trimmed and sliced in ½-inch pieces
4 celery ribs with leaves, trimmed and sliced in ½-inch pieces
2 cloves garlic, peeled, mashed with 2 teaspoons sage
4 tablespoons butter, softened
3 cups mixture of equal parts chicken broth and white wine)
1 jar (560 grams—about 2½ cups) mostarda di frutta: several good brands available in specialty food shops, e.g., Sperlari of Cremona, Italy

1. One day prior to serving, remove the giblets, necks, and livers from inside the capon. Save the livers for another use. Cut away all excess fat and discard. Put the birds on a platter with the giblets and necks next to it. Cut 1 of the lemons in ½ and rub as much of the cavities with lemon and its juice as possible. Cut the other lemon in ½ to rub outside the birds, squeezing the juice all over. Liberally salt and pepper the birds, inside and out. Chop the prosciutto coarsely and put inside the cavities with the onions, carrots, celery, garlic, and sage. Cover with plastic and refrigerate overnight. Remove the next day 1 hour before putting them in the oven.

2. Preheat oven to 400°F. Rub the butter all over the outside of the birds after moving the birds from the platter to a baking pan, remembering to add the necks and giblets to the pan also. Cover with foil and bake 1 hour. Remove cover and bake 1 hour more. Spoon the broth/wine mixture over the birds all during the roasting period, such as ¼ of the liquid at the beginning and remaining fourths every ½ hour until the liquid is gone. Baste with juices in the bottom of the pan until ready to remove from the oven.

3. The capons are cooked when a fork in the body/thigh part releases clear juice. If you want to use an instant thermometer, look for a reading of 170°F.

4. To serve, run a knife down each side of the breast bone, following the bone until you have cut out 2 breast halves. Remove the legs by cutting at the leg-thigh joints. Slice breast and thigh meat. Serve with the mostarda di frutta.

Nota bene:
Some Bolognese cooks will bone the bird and use the stuffing, as below, to stuff the deboned capon. It is then wrapped in cloth toweling and tied with string, put in a large pot with cold water, onions, carrots, celery, and salt, and simmered for two to two-and-a-half hours. It is then cooled and sliced. Or it may be baked as a stuffed, deboned capon. The point in cooking it in water is to provide the broth for the tortellini, which is usually the first course in a Christmas dinner in Italy. If you decide to use either one of these alternatives, and decide to stuff the deboned bird, you must decrease the amount of bread in the stuffing recipe by three cups.

A Special Stuffing
Il ripieno speziale

Serves 8 to 12

Italian stuffings use less bread than called for here, but almost always include the cured meats, ground fresh meats, nuts, cheese, parsley, and eggs. I like the stuffing to cook separately—it is a neater way to do it from all points of view, and you can cook more of it in a bowl than inside the bird. It is a great leftover dish, cold or reheated.

2 tablespoons butter
½ pound ground veal
½ pound ground pork
4 hard-boiled eggs, chopped coarsely
½ cup freshly grated Parmesan cheese
½ pound cooked ham, finely chopped
⅓ pound mortadella, finely chopped
¼ cup shelled pistachios
2 tablespoons each: finely chopped basil and Italian parsley
A good pinch of freshly grated nutmeg
4 cups prepared bread stuffing (e.g., Pepperidge Farm)
2 eggs, beaten lightly
½ cup marsala
1½ cups chicken broth

1. Preheat the oven to 350°F. Melt the butter in a large skillet over medium heat. When it bubbles, add the veal and pork, breaking it up with a wooden spoon. Sauté 6 to 8 minutes, stirring often. Transfer to a large mixing bowl.

2. Add the remaining ingredients. Toss with splayed fingers, lightly but well.

3. Liberally butter a large soufflé or other baking dish, about 9 inches in diameter, about 3 inches deep. Transfer the stuffing mixture to the pan and bake 1 hour.

Chapter 7

MEATS

*I*n large part, Italian food derives from the food of *la poverta*—the poor. For centuries the food has been based on bread (and pizza), soups, stews, rice, polenta, and vegetables. Many of these preparations used little meat because it was costly. Although almost every family had the proverbial pig tied to a piece of furniture in an otherwise barren room, every part of the pig was used once it was ceremonially butchered. When sausage was made, it was used sparingly in food, mostly as a flavoring agent.

But let this not mislead us. In the areas of Italy that had good pastureland, there was always beef, veal, goat, and lamb. Pork was always there, pastureland or not.

These days, every region is known for some of its meat preparations. For example, in Rome, oxtail stew is unchallenged as a native Roman creation. It is a stew of oxtail, cut into chunks, and simmered for a long time in beef broth, wine, and vegetables, especially celery. The same can be said for lamb, or, as the Romans call it, *abbacchio*, most notably at Easter time—a custom that has spread across the regions. Baby lamb, thirty to sixty days old, milk-fed, with never having tasted grass, is cooked with lots of rosemary. In Tuscany, *bistecca alla Florentine* (beefsteak) is world famous. The meat must be the right cut, the right thickness, the salt must go on at a certain time, as must the last rite of oil brushing.

Along with bistecca, the Florentines, and now most others in other regions, revere *arista alla fiorentina*—roast loin of pork. Each region has its own way of cooking it, and all are delicious. In Lombardy, veal and veal shanks are some of the favorite foods. Veal and lamb shanks, cooked Italian style, are now offered in restaurants all over the world. The richness of the Po Valley, as shown in Emilia-Romagna, produces outstandingly high-quality livestock and yields the veal, pork, and ham, along with the butter, cream, and vegetables. The area is also known for its production of prosciutto (and Parmigiano cheese). Nowhere can you find better *brodo misto*, a broth made of beef, and *gallina*, a hen, or *cappone*, a castrated chicken.

Just take a look at the Tamburini shop in Bologna, which has a wood-burning fireplace with a large spit turning over meats and poultry of all kinds. Look at the *salumi*—the salamis, *coppa, culatella, zampone* and sausages—and you'll think the mortadella is the largest you've ever seen, and it is. Parma, a place for foodies, is also the place where once a year almost two hundred people dine in the town hall to judge hundreds of the *culatello*, the heart of the prosciutto made from the center of the rump, a cured meat that many people prefer to prosciutto. Prizes are awarded by two juries of experts dressed in ermine-velvet robes. The winners kneel and swords touch their heads and they promise to make an equally good or better *culatello* for the next competition. And what makes the ragu of Bologna world famous? Surely its base of chopped prosciutto, beef, pork, chicken livers, and vegetables, slowly simmered in beef broth and wine.

Umbria competes with Rome for *porchetta* and Florence for *chiana* beef. The pigs in Umbria are fed on chestnuts, mushrooms, and truffles. The pork and salami of Norcia are so celebrated that most meals in Umbria and in other regions include a sampling. In southern Italy, the sausage known as *lucanica* or *luganega, soprassata* (pork sausage flavored with ginger), and the highly smoked sausage *capocollo* are now eaten in other Italian provinces. Although tuna and other fish overtake Sicilian food, Sicily is also known for lamb, pork, and beef, whereas in Sardinia, people thrive on spit-roasted pork, lamb, and goat (sometimes barbecuing them in the ground). Meat in Sardinia is more popular than fish. *La poverta* (the poor), as far as meat is concerned, seems to have disappeared.

BRAISED OXTAIL STEW
Coda alla vaccinara

Serves 8

This dish is unchallenged as a native Roman creation. It is a "stew" of oxtail, cut into chunks and simmered for a long time in beef broth, wine, and vegetables, especially celery. *Alla vaccinara* means "cowboy style." A fresh cucumber salad would make a sensible accompaniment for this rather rich Roman dish.

In my mind, this was probably a dish enjoyed by the young British noblemen who traveled to Italy on the Grand Tour that reached its culmination in the eighteenth century. The goal of the Grand Tour was to reach Italy, the touchstone of the classical past, where personal, intellectual, and civic identity could be forged. The Grand Tourists commissioned portraits of themselves in their traveling costumes or besides famous antiquities (the Colosseum or Mount Vesuvius, for example). One painter, Pompeo Batoni, executed more than two hundred portraits of British tourists. These tourists bought landscapes that captured their perceptions of the Italian countryside, and they collected antique sculpture, vases, and gems and refashioned the interiors of their homes into elaborate backdrops for the display of these objects. Grand Tourists stimulated the development of a full-scale tourist industry that still exists today, with its illustrated guidebooks, maps, travel diaries, postcards, and souvenirs. Think, then, of enjoying this one-dish meal with a view of Rome from Monte Mario, as did many of the Grand Tourists.

6 pounds oxtails, jointed
Olive oil
2 tablespoons all-purpose flour
½ pound pancetta or lean bacon, cut in small pieces
2 ounces prosciutto, finely chopped
2 bay leaves
2 carrots, sliced
4 cups sliced celery ribs
2 medium-sized onions, chopped
2 cloves garlic, minced
2 cups dry white wine
2 cups tomato puree from plum tomatoes (put through a food mill)
1 tablespoon finely chopped rosemary
2 to 3 cups beef broth
¼ teaspoon ground cinnamon

1. Soak the oxtail pieces in cool water for 2 or 3 hours. Drain and discard water. Pat dry with paper toweling.

2. Turn on the broiler. Lightly brush the oxtail pieces with olive oil and put them in a shallow baking tray. Salt and pepper them and broil 6 inches below the heating element to brown them, about 5 minutes per side. Sprinkle some flour over the meat, and set aside.

3. In a large sauce pan or casserole, sauté the pancetta or bacon and the prosciutto until some fat is rendered. Add the bay leaves, carrot slices, ½ cup of the celery, and the onion, and cook over moderate heat, uncovered, about 8 minutes, or until golden. Add the garlic after 6 minutes of cooking the onions.

4. Add the oxtail pieces and the wine and simmer, uncovered, until the wine evaporates. Add the tomatoes and the rosemary. Bring this to a boil, lower the heat, cover, and simmer 2½ to 3 hours. Add ½ cup beef broth every ½ hour or so until a sauce evolves.

5. Cook the remaining celery in boiling, salted water 10 minutes. Drain the celery pieces and add to the sauce pan or casserole 30 minutes before the end of the cooking time in step 4. Add the cinnamon and check for salt seasoning. Liberally add freshly ground pepper before serving.

GRILLED PORTERHOUSE STEAK
Bistecca alla fiorentina

Serves 6

Rib-eye or shell steaks may be cooked in the same manner as this porterhouse, being sure they are at least one inch thick or thicker. It is important to remember not to add salt before the meat cooks; rather, add it during the grilling process as described below. Be sure the meat is at room temperature before grilling it. This is surely one time you should seek the best meat possible. The simplicity of this dish is all the more reason to enjoy it. For the American table, this is a treat.

4 tablespoons extra-virgin olive oil
1 porterhouse steak, about 3 pounds, trimmed, at room temperature
4 cloves garlic, peeled and cut in ½ lengthwise
6 wedges fresh lemon, seeded

1. Build a charcoal fire and allow it to reach the gray ash stage. Gently tap the coals to shake off the ash. Move the coals slightly so they are about ½ inch apart to moderate the heat.

2. Using less than a tablespoon of oil, brush the steak lightly on both sides. Put the remaining oil and the garlic in a small sauce pan or skillet and heat until the garlic turns light brown. Do not let the garlic get darker. Remove from the heat, discard the pieces of garlic, and set the oil aside.

3. When the fire is ready, place the steak on the grill as close as possible to the heat source. Sear for 2 minutes on 1 side only to seal in the juices. Raise the grill about 4 inches from the coals and continue grilling until tiny bubbles of juice appear on top of the steak, 3 to 5 minutes, depending on the thickness of the steak. Turn over the steak with tongs and liberally add salt and freshly ground pepper.

4. Repeat grilling procedure for the second side, 2 minutes close to the heat source and raising the grill rack and grilling the steak a couple of minutes more to achieve a rare steak. A Florentine steak is never overcooked.

5. If you wish you to use a gas-fired grill, heat it and follow the same procedure for oiling, salting, and peppering the steak as above. Grill 5 to 7 minutes per side, depending on thickness. Be sure to let the steak rest for several minutes before slicing

6. To serve, let the steak rest a couple of minutes. Reheat the flavored oil. Slice the meat against the grain, put some slices onto each plate, and spoon some of the garlic-flavored oil over the meat. Add a lemon wedge to each serving; the lemon is to be squeezed over the meat as a final touch.

BEEF BRAISED WITH RED WINE AND SPICES

Brasato di bue al barolo

Serves 4

The vine has been established in Piedmont since Roman times, and its soil, tradition, and climate have been responsible, and still are, for producing some of Italy's best wines—*vini pregiati*—fine wines. One of these is Barolo, made of the Nebbiola grape; it is deep red in color, full, and fragrant. It spends at least three years in cask before bottling, and ages as well and as long in bottle as a good claret (longer than burgundy). They are expensive wines, and you may cringe at the price of a bottle in the United States, but using it in this dish will be special. If you decide to use it, you should also serve a bottle to drink with the beef. There are other good Italian reds to be used that cost less. Your wine merchant will tell you what else he has available.

2 onions, peeled and sliced
2 carrots, trimmed and sliced
2 inner ribs celery, trimmed and sliced
2 cloves garlic, peeled and sliced
1 bay leaf and 1 rosemary sprig
4 whole cloves
1 (3-inch) cinnamon stick
2 pounds beef top round in 1 piece, ready for cooking
1 bottle Barolo or other red wine
4 tablespoons extra-virgin olive oil
2 tablespoons tomato paste
¼ cup beef broth
¼ cup brandy or cognac
4 rosemary sprigs for garnish

1. Prepare the onions, carrots, and celery and put in a large bowl. Add the garlic, bay leaf, rosemary, cloves, and cinnamon.
2. Place the meat in the bowl and pour in the wine. Cover tightly and marinate overnight. Place in a refrigerator or in a very cool place. Remove from the refrigerator 1 hour before starting to cook. Drain the meat and reserve the marinade with vegetables and spices.
3. Heat the oil in a large stove-top casserole and brown the meat on all sides over high heat, uncovered, turning to brown. Complete browning the meat.
4. Add the reserved marinade of wine, vegetables, spices, and herbs. Cook 20 minutes, uncovered, over medium heat.
5. Combine the tomato paste with the beef broth and add to the casserole. Add salt and freshly ground pepper. Cover the casserole, lower the heat, and simmer until the meat is tender, about 2 hours.
6. To serve, remove the meat to a slicing board. Add the mixture in the casserole to a food processor and puree it. Also, put the puree through a sieve. Return the puree to the casserole, add the brandy, and reheat, cooking off some of the brandy, 4 or 5 minutes. Slice the meat for individual servings and spoon some of the brandied wine sauce over ½ of the meat on the plate. Add a rosemary sprig to the side of each serving.

MOZZARELLA MEAT LOAF
Polpettone di mozzarella

Serves 8

This is a moist, delicious meat loaf that can be served in many ways. It is an ideal one-dish meal in that it can be served warm or cold, in slices, with a composed green salad (include some cooked broccoli). Or slice it and make sandwiches of it between thin slices of Italian bread. Or serve it on top of a bruschetta with a warmed tomato sauce.

2 pounds ground chuck
2 links Italian sausage out of casing
2 eggs, beaten lightly
2 small onions, peeled, finely chopped
2 tablespoons finely chopped Italian parsley
1 clove garlic, minced
½ cup grated pecorino cheese
2 cups ¼-inch cubes fresh mozzarella
5 slices Italian bread, soaked in ¾ cup milk, squeezed dry
¼ cup chopped canned tomatoes

1. Preheat oven to 350°F. Combine the ground chuck with the sausage in a large bowl. Add the eggs, onions, parsley, garlic, pecorino and mozzarella cheeses, bread, and the tomatoes. Also add a generous sprinkle of salt and freshly ground pepper. With splayed fingers, toss the mixture lightly but blending well.

2. Transfer the mixture to a flat surface and, with your hands, shape it into a loaf (like a long loaf of Italian bread) and put it on an oiled baking sheet with a rim (a jelly-roll pan will do—this is to keep the meat juices from overflowing).

3. Bake 1½ hours. Remove from the oven and allow to cool about 10 minutes before slicing, or allow it to cool completely in order to serve it cold.

SICILIAN MEAT LOAF
Farsumagru o Falsomagro

Serves 12

In Sicily, this "meat loaf" (it is really a beef roll) is called *farsumagru* or *falsomagro alla Bellini*, after the great nineteenth-century Sicilian composer Vicenzo Bellini. Both the house in which he lived and the church in which he was baptized still exist on the picturesque, barrue Cruciferi Street in Catania. The meat loaf is really a stuffed beef roll, and versions of it exist elsewhere in Italy, so I have to believe that Signor Bellini did not create it—perhaps this is the way he liked it prepared.

2 pounds lean beef slice, in 1 piece, such as top round steak
2 small to medium onions, finely chopped
2 cloves garlic minced
1 pound ground beef and veal
2 links Italian sausage, out of casings
3 slices bacon, cut into small pieces
2 eggs, beaten
A good pinch of freshly grated nutmeg
¼ pound Parma ham, finely chopped
¼ pound pecorino cheese, grated on large teeth of cheese grater
½ cup finely chopped mint and Italian parsley
2 hard-boiled eggs, sliced
3 tablespoons olive oil
1 cup Sicilian red wine
2 cups beef broth

1. Ask your butcher to pound the slice of beef for you to make it rectangular in shape and to make small cuts along the edge to keep it from curling as it cooks. Explain to him what you plan to do with it—that is, stuff and roll it. It is easy enough to do this at home, and a meat pounder will facilitate the process. Set the slice of beef aside.
2. Combine ½ of the chopped onions with the garlic, ground beef, sausage, bacon, eggs, and nutmeg in a bowl. Add some salt and freshly ground pepper. With splayed hands, mix the ingredients until blended.
3. Spread the ground meat mixture over the beef slice, leaving about ½ inch free at the edges. Sprinkle the ham and cheese over the ground meat and do the same with the mint and parsley. Place the egg slices over all. Roll the meat from the larger end and tie securely with kitchen string.
4. In a large, elongated casserole, stovetop-proof and with a cover, heat the oil and sauté the remaining chopped onion 3 to 4 minutes or until the onion begins to brown. Carefully place the beef roll in the pan, and cook over medium heat to brown all sides. Add ½ cup of wine and cook, uncovered, until the wine evaporates. Add some salt and freshly ground pepper. Add the remaining wine and the broth, cover, and cook over low to medium heat for 1½ to 2 hours. This can be served warm or at room temperature. Remove the strings and slice.

PORK

ROAST LOIN OF PORK WITH ROSEMARY

Arista di maiale

Serves 6

If you ask anyone what is the favorite meat dish in Florence, you undoubtedly will get as an answer: *bistecca*—beefsteak. Or the answer might be *pollo alla diavolo*—chicken, split open, flattened, and grilled—somewhat similar to the chicken preparation of page __, except that this chicken dish is served with a ginger sauce. The third reply will surely be *arista alla fiorentina*—roast loin of pork. What makes the difference between roast pork in Florence and elsewhere is rosemary in its seasoning along with garlic and cloves. Another important difference is that it is basted with water and not oil.

This is a very old preparation and has been cooked this way since the fifteenth century. I learned to cook it in this manner from an adopted niece of mine, *la mia nipotina*, Ivana Fabbrizzio in Contignano (province of Siena), who emphasized again and again the importance of basting with water. It was wonderful to see her step outside the kitchen door and clip as much fresh rosemary as anyone would want or could use. Ivana always hung the day's laundry on a clothesline just outside the house, and I could catch a glimpse of her through the laundry pieces hung on the line, bending over to snip the rosemary. The road to Contignano winds uphill, affording views of an incomparable countryside. As you drive through acres of fields with wheat waving in the breeze, as if to the beat of a metronome, and get closer to the village, you see luxuriant gardens, olive-clad slopes, and lines of cypress trees, and there is always the ever-present clothesline of Ivana's *bucato* (laundry), soaking up the sun. Imagine this setting as you prepare this pork with rosemary.

4 pounds loin of pork, center cut
2 pieces rosemary, each 4 or 5 inches long, plus 2 teaspoons finely chopped
3 cloves garlic, minced
6 whole cloves
12 small new potatoes, peeled
1 can green peas or 1 (10-ounce) package, frozen

1. Preheat the oven 450°F. Make 8 or 10 slits in the meat and insert some chopped rosemary and garlic in each. Transfer to a baking pan and liberally add salt and freshly ground pepper all over the meat. Place 1 piece of rosemary on each side of the meat. Push the cloves into the meat. Add 2 cups water around the meat.

2. Roast 1 hour and 45 minutes to 2 hours, basting every 15 minutes or so. As the roast cooks and its fat melts, it will combine with the water. Use this liquid to baste the meat. After 45 minutes of roasting, add the potatoes. Add more water, if needed—the baking pan should always have some water in it. Add canned or frozen peas ½ hour before the pork is done

3. Remove from the oven, and let the roast stand 5 to 10 minutes. Slice and serve with potatoes and peas and a sliced beet salad.

BRAISED PORK TENDERLOIN WITH MARSALA SAUCE

Maiale arrosto con salsa al marsala

Serves 8 to 10

Most pork tenderloins sold in this country are packed in plastic to preserve freshness and are dated. Check the date. Inspect them after opening the package for any extra fat, and if there is any, remove it. This dish is simple and delicious—any leftover may be served cold with the sauce reheated.

2 pork tenderloins, about 3 pounds total
1 teaspoon large black pepper grains
2 tablespoons each butter and olive oil
4 large bay leaves
½ cup red wine vinegar
1 cup marsala wine
1 cup chicken broth
4 tablespoons butter

1. Trim the tenderloins, if necessary, and wipe clean. By hand, pat the pepper all over the tenderloins. In a heavy, large casserole with a cover (1 which will be able to cook on the stovetop), add the butter and oil and, when hot, sauté the tenderloins over high heat to brown all sides, about 10 minutes. Add some salt.

2. Add the bay leaves and the vinegar and cover immediately. Lower the heat to low-medium and cook 15 minutes. Uncover and remove the tenderloins to a plate. Add the marsala wine and the broth and, over high heat, reduce by ½, scraping up all the cooking residue from the bottom of the pan, 15 to 20 minutes. Remove the bay leaves. When the sauce is reduced, remove from the heat and whisk in 4 tablespoons of butter, 1 tablespoon at a time.

3. To serve, slice the tenderloins ½ inch thick, overlap the slices on a platter, and pour the sauce over the meat, but to the side. Do not cover the meat with the sauce. Or, put the sauce in a serving bowl and allow each diner to take some.

WHOLE ROASTED SUCKLING PIG, UMBRIAN STYLE

Porchetta alla Norciana

Serves 12

Umbria's food is special because of its pork products, in particular those found around Norcia, where Umbrian pigs feed on chestnuts, mushrooms, and truffles. The pork and salumi of Norcia are so celebrated that almost all meals in Umbria include a sampling.

The cooking of Umbria is honest and natural, somewhere between the extroverted gusto of nearby Lazio (Rome) and the refined simplicity of Tuscany (Florence). Condiments are used discreetly with an exception here and there, for example, with this tasty, peppery *porchetta*. In Perugia, as in Rome, one's culinary life starts with porchetta—in both places, the suckling pig is liberally salted and peppered and seasoned with a variety of herbs, not always including rosemary, which is a must in Rome. In Perugia and elsewhere in Umbria, wild fennel is always used in porchetta. The pig is either spit roasted or baked. Wherever one goes in Umbria, porchetta is in shops, in stalls, on streets, everywhere, waiting to be sliced and put between two pieces of bread.

1 whole suckling pig, 15 to 20 pounds, readied for oven roasting
4 large branches of fresh rosemary
Cloves from 1 whole garlic bulb, peeled, ⅔ left whole, ⅓ minced
1 fennel bulb with leaves, coarsely chopped
1 tablespoon dried fresh fennel seeds, crushed
1 cup olive oil
½ cup red wine vinegar
1 whole apple

1. Preheat oven to 350°F. Put the pig in a large roasting pan. Liberally salt and pepper the roast, inside and out. Place 3 of the rosemary branches in the cavity of the pig along with the whole garlic cloves, the fresh fennel, and ⅔ of the crushed fennel seeds.

2. Combine the oil and vinegar, the minced garlic, and the remaining fennel seeds, and use this mixture to brush on the roast all during the cooking. Baste the roast all over before putting it in the oven.

3. Bake for 5 to 6 hours, basting every 20 minutes or so. To test for doneness, insert a long wooden skewer into the roast—if it meets no resistance upon entering, the roast is done. Remove from the oven and, when cooled for 10 minutes or so, insert the apple in its mouth.

EGGS IN PURGATORY WITH GRILLED SAUSAGES

Uova in purgatorio e salsicce arrostite

Serves 4

This is a simple, peasant-type dish that is easy to prepare. Its roots are from southern Italy. The sausage used for this dish is traditionally called *luganega*; it is long and thin and made of pure pork. If you cannot find this type of sausage, a perfectly acceptable substitute is Italian sausage made in links.

1½ pounds luganega sausage or 8 links Italian pork sausage
2 tablespoons extra-virgin olive oil
½ cup finely chopped onion
¼ cup finely chopped green pepper
2 tablespoons chopped Italian parsley
2 cloves garlic, minced
1 can (16 ounces) Italian plum tomatoes, peeled and cut up
4 eggs, room temperature
4 large slices bruschetta, see page 301

1. If using the luganega, cut the long, thin sausage into 4 pieces, about 6 inches per serving, and form each piece into a coil. Secure with toothpicks that have been soaked in water for 20 to 30 minutes. Set aside. Ready a grill or broiler.

2. Heat the oil in a large skillet and sauté the onion and pepper 5 minutes, or until limp. Add the parsley and garlic and sauté 2 minutes longer.

3. Add the tomatoes, and season with some salt and freshly ground pepper. Bring the mixture to a boil, lower the heat, and simmer for 15 minutes.

4. While the tomatoes are simmering, grill or broil the coils of sausage, about 5 minutes per side, or until well cooked.

4. Break the eggs, 1 at a time, into a saucer, and slide them into the tomato mixture. Raise the heat slightly, cover the skillet, and poach the eggs until the whites are formed and the centers are semihard. If you wish, cook the eggs longer to a more solid state.

5. To serve, place a bruschetta in a large luncheon plate, and spoon an egg with some of the sauce onto each piece, adding more of the sauce to the side of the eggs. Add a coil of cooked sausage to each plate.

PORK, CABBAGE, AND BEANS IN CASSEROLE
Favata

Serves 6

Sheep, goats, and pigs are numerous in Sardinia. Pigs graze on acorns, and this feed makes the pork tasty. Acorns are plentiful because oak trees are the most common on the island, and they are forced to grow tall so that they can drop many acorns. Much of the pig is preserved, easy to do as salt is plentiful (half or more of Italy's salt supply comes from the Cagliari coastal flats). I have no way of making the comparison, but I've been told that the saltworks at Cagliari are the largest in Europe. Sardinians make excellent sausages and hams. One part of the pig, namely its foot, is featured in a well-known dish, *favata*, or *fava e lardu*, cooked with cabbage, fennel, and fava beans. Dried favas, limas, or butter beans require overnight soaking. If you have the time, this is the preferred way to prepare this dish. If not, there is an American shortcut of using canned or frozen beans, drained or thawed. Pork sausages and spare ribs are used in this updated version of the dish.

1½ pounds dried fava, lima, or butter beans; or 3 cans (16 ounces each) canned beans or 3 packets (10 ounces each) frozen
⅓ cup extra-virgin olive oil
6 Italian pork sausages, about 1½ pounds
6 pork spare ribs, in 1 piece, 1 to 1½ pounds
6 thin slices of pancetta or bacon, finely chopped
2 medium-size fresh fennel bulbs, trimmed and chopped including some of the pale green leaves
1 medium-size head Savoy cabbage, trimmed, core removed, and thinly sliced, as in coleslaw
2 medium-size onions, trimmed and thinly sliced
1 cup finely chopped plum tomatoes, without seeds, canned or fresh
1 cup freshly grated pecorino cheese

1. If using dried beans, soak overnight. Run your hands through them to be sure there are no stones or other foreign matter. Drain in a colander, and rinse again by holding colander under faucet. Set aside. If using canned beans, drain and rinse in cool water. Set aside. If using frozen beans, thaw and set aside in a bowl.

2. Heat the oil in a large heatproof casserole with a cover. Add the sausages and the spare ribs and brown them over medium heat, uncovered, moving the meat about in the casserole as each side browns. If using dried beans, add them now with enough boiling water to cover the meat and beans. Add everything else except the cheese, including some salt and a liberal amount of freshly ground pepper. Bring to boil, then lower the heat to achieve a steady simmer. Cover the casserole and simmer 2 hours. After 1 hour of cooking, check to see if more water is needed.

3. If using canned or frozen beans, brown the sausages and spare ribs as in step 2. Add all the other ingredients except the cheese with 6 cups water. Bring to boil, then lower the heat to achieve a steady simmer. Add some salt and a liberal amount of freshly ground pepper. Cover the casserole and simmer for 1½ hours. Add the canned or frozen beans to the casserole and cook 30 minutes longer. Check to see if more water is needed after 1 hour of cooking.

4. Remove the casserole from the oven. Transfer the ribs to a cutting board and cut into individual ribs. Put 1 rib in each of 6 shallow, rimmed soup plates. Add a sausage to each and a spoonful of the bean mixture. This should be served with grilled or broiled bread slices; see bruschetta on page 301. Sprinkle some pecorino over each dish and pass what remains.

VEAL

VEAL SCALLOPS WITH HAM AND SAGE
Involtini di vitello con prosciutto e salvia in umido

Serves 4

You may not have a mallet, so it is best to ask your butcher to pound the veal thinly for you. The prepackaged veal scallops offered in most supermarkets will not do here. If your supermarket has a special meat counter with a butcher, explain what you want.

1½ pounds veal scallopine, pounded thin
4 thin slices good-quality ham
4 full sage leaves
3 tablespoons extra-virgin olive oil
1 onion, finely chopped
2 carrots, finely chopped
1 celery rib, finely chopped
1 cup dry white wine
1½ cups chopped fresh or canned tomatoes

1. Place the veal slices on a flat surface and add a ham slice and then a sage leaf to each. Roll them up and secure with string or with a toothpick. If the slice is wide, use 2 toothpicks.

2. In a large skillet, heat the oil and sauté the onions, carrots, and celery until they become browned at the edges, up to 10 minutes. Add salt and freshly ground pepper.

3. Place the veal rolls in the skillet and brown them on all sides, 10 to 15 minutes. Add the wine and cook 4 minutes. Add the tomatoes and bring to a boil. (Cinzia, the resident cook described above, said most Italians would add ½ a bouillon cube, either chicken or vegetable, at this point—she said they do it all the time). Lower the heat and simmer to cook the veal and thicken the sauce, about 30 minutes. If you want to thin the sauce, add chicken broth by tablespoons.

VEAL SCALOPPINE WITH PEPPER GRAINS

Scaloppine di vitello con pepe in grani

Serves 4

Wherever Italian food is served, there are enticing food combinations of veal scaloppine. Veal of this cut marries beautifully with lemon, orange, marsala, vermouth, capers, tomatoes, cured meats, cheeses, and a wide array of herbs and spices. Cooking veal scaloppine that have been properly cut is one of the simplest things one can do in the kitchen, and one of the fastest. It is easy in the United States to buy this meat, plastic wrapped, in the refrigerated meat sections in supermarkets, but they are not properly cut. It is best to ask your butcher to cut the scaloppine from the top round, from the upper part of the hind leg, and to cut across the muscle's grain. Once cut in this way, they can be pounded properly. The reason for cutting across the grain is to keep the meat flat while it is sautéing. Here is a simple, elegant way to prepare them *all' italiana*.

1½ pounds of veal scallops, pounded to ¼-inch thickness
½ cup all-purpose flour
5 tablespoons butter
1 tablespoon extra-virgin olive oil
⅓ cup dry vermouth
2 tablespoons fresh lemon juice
2 teaspoons finely grated lemon zest

1. Just before sautéing the scallops, dust them with salt and 1 teaspoon coarsely ground pepper. Dip them into the flour and remove any excess. It is best to have as thin a coating of flour as possible.

2. Heat 3 tablespoons of butter and the oil in a large skillet over high heat. Brown as many pieces of veal as you can, 2 or 3 minutes on each side, using tongs to turn them. They should brown without burning. Remove the scallops to a serving dish, arranging them in 1 layer.

3. Quickly deglaze the pan with the vermouth and remaining butter, scraping up all the bits of brown particles clinging to the skillet. If the vermouth cooks off too quickly, add another tablespoon or 2. Pour this quickly over the scallops. Sprinkle all of them with some lemon juice and zest and serve right away.

ANGELA'S SUNDAY-BEST STUFFED BREAST OF VEAL
Petto di vitello facito all'Angela

Serves 10 to 12

My mother loved making this dish and our family enjoyed eating it. It was always served on a Sunday, the time of the major meal in our home. No excuses—everyone had to be seated at the table. It is an adaptation of the Ligurian veal dish—veal is a popular meat in this region—known as *cima alla genovese*. A breast of veal is filled with a stuffing of offal, vegetables, and nuts. There are a variety of ways to cook this dish, as you may imagine, and here it is filled with ground veal and pork, nuts, and cheeses—in other words, without the variety meats, which did not appeal to us as children.

You will need a large veal breast from an animal over one year old. Ask your butcher if he can accommodate you. He should bone it for you and create a pocket so it can receive a filling. Ask for the bones, as you can make a veal broth to use in this recipe.

1 (1-pound) Italian bread, 1 or 2 days old
1 cup milk
6 large eggs
1¼ pounds ground veal and pork
1 pound fresh ricotta cheese
1 cup freshly grated Parmesan cheese
½ cup finely chopped flat parsley
3 large cloves garlic, minced
⅓ cup golden raisins
⅓ cup pine nuts, toasted
1 (8-pound) breast of veal (see above)
1 cup veal or chicken broth
1 cup dry white wine
1 cup diced, canned tomatoes
1 large onion, thinly sliced

1. Preheat the oven to 450°F.

2. Break the bread into chunks and put them and their crumbs in a large bowl. Add the milk, toss to moisten the bread, and let stand 20 to 30 minutes. Squeeze the bread dry and set aside.

3. Whisk the eggs in a large bowl. Add the ground meat, ricotta and Parmesan cheeses, parsley, garlic, raisins, pine nuts, and some salt and freshly ground pepper. Add the bread and mix with splayed fingers. Combine these ingredients well but don't overdo. Do *not* mix in a food processor or other mechanical device.

4. Fill the pocket of the veal breast. Do not overstuff, as the filling will expand while it bakes. Secure the opening all the way by sewing with needle and thread.

5. Put the filled veal breast on a roasting rack in a large roasting pan and roast 30 minutes until the meat is browned. Remove from the oven and lower the heat to 300°F.

6. Add the veal or chicken broth, wine, tomatoes, and the onions to the roasting pan. Cover with foil and continue cooking 3½ to 4 hours. Remove the pan from the oven and let the veal rest, covered, 20 minutes or so. To serve, slice ½ inch thick and serve with a fresh, lightly dressed arugula salad.

VEAL CUTLET IN THE MILAN MANNER
Costoletta alla milanese

Serves 6

The true Milanese chop is the one with the bone, and the chop should be nicked with a knife on the outer edge so that, during cooking, it doesn't curl up. According to the Milanese, pounding the veal helps the crumbs adhere better. If the meat browns too quickly, the heat is too high.

6 veal chops with bone
Milk to cover the chops
2 large eggs
1 cup plain bread crumbs
½ cup butter
2 tablespoons vegetable oil
6 large lemon wedges, seeds removed

1. Trim any fat from the chops and be sure to nick them at the outer edge to prevent curling. Flatten each chop with a heavy knife or meat pounder to the thickness of a finger, as they do in Milan. Put the chops in a deep, nonreactive bowl or casserole and pour milk over them. Let stand for 1 hour to soften and tenderize the meat. Remove from the milk, discard the milk, and pat the chops dry with paper towels.

2. Beat the eggs in a flat-type bowl. Put the bread crumbs on a flat plate. Dip the chops into the egg and then into the bread crumbs.

Press the crumbs into the chops with the palms of your hands.

3. Heat ½ of the butter and a tablespoon of oil in a large, heavy skillet, large enough to hold 3 chops. When the butter is bubbly, add the chops and cook over medium-high heat until both sides are browned, 2 to 3 minutes per side. Lower the heat and cook longer to cook the insides, about 5 minutes. Remove the veal to a platter. Clean the skillet with paper towels, and cook the other 3 chops in the same way.

4. Serve with lemon wedges after salting and peppering the chops.

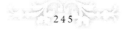

VEAL SHANKS, THE MILAN WAY
Fetta di stinco di vitello brasato alla Milanese

Serves 6

When all is said and done, it is again the Italians who use lemon peel most creatively. One of their Milanese dishes, *osso buco*, composed of thick pieces of veal shank braised in wine, vegetables, and tomatoes, is garnished, when it is served, with a colorful combination of finely chopped lemon peel, garlic, and parsley. This inspired mixture, called *gremolata*, transforms the osso buco, an essentially lusty dish, into a masterpiece. Imaginative cooks also use this garnish on other braised and sautéed veal dishes, and may even, on occasion, sprinkle it over broiled or sautéed fish. *Osso buco* means the "bone with a hole." To complete the experience of eating this dish, one must pick the marrow out of the bone and serve the osso buco with risotto, cooked the Milan way (see page 116).

2 celery ribs, trimmed
2 large cloves garlic, peeled
1 leek, white part and some tender green part
1 onion, peeled
1 large carrot, trimmed
3 tablespoons butter
1½ cups canned plum tomatoes (after putting through a food mill)
1 tablespoon finely chopped fresh basil or 1 teaspoon dried, crushed
½ cup all-purpose flour
6 veal shanks, each about 3 inches long, each tied with a string to hold the meat in place, about 4 to 5 pounds
4 tablespoons plus extra-virgin olive oil
1 cup dry white wine
1 cup beef broth
1 bouquet of 6 parsley sprigs, 2 bay leaves and 2 pieces lemon zest, 2x½ inch wide, tied together in a small bundle
Gremolata, see below

1. Pare the strings off the celery and wash thoroughly; also carefully wash the leek to be sure you rid it of its sand. Chop the celery, garlic, leek, onion, and carrot as finely as you can. Together, if chopped finely and firmly packed, it should make about a full cup. If there is a little more, do not be concerned. The Italians call this mixture *soffrito*.

2. Melt the butter in a heavy, deep casserole large enough to hold the 6 shanks snugly, and add the chopped vegetables (the soffrito). Cook over low heat, uncovered, stirring until soft, about 7 or 8 minutes. Do not brown.

3. Add the tomatoes and basil, raise the heat to high, and cook for several minutes to cook off most of the tomato juices and to thicken the mixture. Set the casserole aside.

4. Put the flour in a flat plate and add a liberal amount of salt and freshly ground pepper. Mix well. Put a shank into this flour mixture and coat evenly, shaking off the excess flour. Repeat with the other 5 shanks. In a large skillet, heat the oil (not quite to the smoking point) and sauté 3 of the shanks on all sides to brown them. As each piece turns golden, remove from the skillet and put it in the casserole on top of the soffrito. Add the herb bouquet. Continue until all shanks are browned. If more oil is need during the sautéing, add it a tablespoon at a time. Pour off any oil in the skillet, but return the skillet unwashed to the heat.

5. Add the wine and bring it to boil, scraping the bottom of the pan. As the wine evaporates, about 5 minutes or so, add the broth and bring just to boil. Then pour this over the shanks and vegetables in the casserole. Cover tightly, bring to boil, lower the heat, and simmer 1 hour until the meat is tender. If the casserole becomes dry, add more broth. The meat should appear as if it will fall off the bone. If this point has not been reached, simmer 5 to 10 minutes longer.

6. To serve, transfer the meat from the casserole to individual plates or on a large platter. Be sure the marrow does not fall out of the bone. Italians consider the marrow the essential reason for cooking veal shanks in this way. Taste the sauce and if it satisfies your taste, spoon some over the shanks; then add the gremolata. If the sauce needs more cooking, continue to cook, uncovered over medium heat.

To make the gremolata:
¼ cup finely chopped Italian parsley
1 tablespoon finely chopped lemon zest
1 tablespoon finely minced garlic

1. Combine these 3 ingredients, making sure the zest is as thinly peeled from the lemon as is possible. If this is made before the shanks are ready to be served, put in a small bowl and cover tightly with plastic wrap.

COLD VEAL IN A TUNA SAUCE
Vitello tonnato

Serves 8 to 10

There is a popular Milanese saying (in dialect), "Mai scoeud via l'acqua *del coverc,*" meaning "Never shake off the water on the cover." This simple expression just about describes the cooking of Milan and the rest of Lombardy: slow cooking, covered, for a long time. The only exception to this is the veal scaloppine that are quick fried. Osso bucco (lamb shanks), one of the most popular Lombardian preparations, is perhaps the best example of slow cooking. Another is one of my favorites, *vitello tonnato*, veal with tuna sauce—the veal is cooked about two hours in this typical Milanese style of cooking. Place yourself in the glass-roofed Galleria, a Milan landmark, just off the Cathedral Square, studded with cafes, restaurants, and ice cream parlors where women exchange fashion notes, men read the *Corriere delle Sera* newpapers, and others feast on this exquisite veal dish.

One of the reasons this is a favorite is that it may be made well ahead and refrigerated. I have had leftover veal prepared this way in the refrigerator for a week, still very delicious. There are many recipes available to make this dish. Some call for lots of wine; I would not use more than suggested here. Do not cook the veal in salted water, and use just enough water to cover the veal in the sauce pan. Some recipes require gobs of mayonnaise, and as good as homemade mayonnaise may be, if there is too much of it, you will find it gnawing. My solution is to puree the vegetables in which the veal cooked, adding some of the broth and adding the puree to the mayonnaise-type sauce. At no time are you to use commercial mayonnaise to make this dish.

1 medium carrot, chopped
1 rib celery, chopped
1 medium onion, chopped
4 parsley stems
1 cup dry white wine
1 cup extra-virgin olive oil
2½ pounds top round of veal
2 cans (6 ounces each) tuna packed in oil, drained
4 anchovy fillets, drained and dried
1 tablespoon plus 1 teaspoon capers, drained
1 egg yolk or hard-boiled egg yolk
Juice of 1 lemon
Light cream or half and half, optional
2 tablespoons finely chopped tarragon

1. In a large sauce pan (large enough to hold the veal, vegetables, and liquid comfortably), add the carrot, celery, onion, parsley stems, wine, 1 tablespoon olive oil, and water just to cover the veal. Bring to boil over medium-high heat, lower the heat, and simmer 15 minutes.

2. Carefully add the veal to the simmering water, bring again to boil, lower heat, and simmer 1½ hours. Let the veal cool in the broth. When cooled, remove the veal to a cutting board. Strain the broth, and place the vegetables, minus the parsley stems, into the bowl of a processor. Add 1 cup of the broth and puree. Set aside the remaining broth.

3. Add the drained tuna to the processor bowl (with the pureed vegetables) with the anchovies, 1 tablespoon capers, raw egg yolk or the hard-boiled yolk, and the lemon juice. Puree until smooth. With the motor running, add the remaining cup of the olive oil to the processor in a slow, steady stream, to incorporate it into the tuna sauce. Taste for salt seasoning, adding some if needed. If the sauce is too thick, thin with more of the reserved broth or add some light cream. The sauce should be like heavy cream in consistency.

4. Slice the veal into ⅛-inch slices. Put some of the sauce on the bottom of an oval ceramic or glass dish, approximately 9x14x2½ inches. Then arrange a single layer of the veal on top of the sauce. Spoon more sauce over the veal and repeat in this way until all veal slices are layered and sauced. If sauce remains, put in a small bowl and refrigerate it for later use as additional sauce for the veal. Cover the oval dish with plastic wrap and refrigerate overnight. Remove from the refrigerator at least ½ hour before serving. Add the tarragon to the top sprinkled with a teaspoon of capers. A salad of watercress, arugula, and curly endive, dressed simply with oil, vinegar, salt and pepper, and crisped pancetta bits, is appropriate.

LAMB

ROAST SUCKLING LAMB WITH GARLIC, OIL, ROSEMARY, AND POTATOES
Abbacchio con patate al forno alla casalinga

Serves 6

Abbacchio is very young, milk-fed lamb, usually about one month old, and is generally not available in the United States. A good substitute is "hothouse lamb," usually about three months old, but that is not easy to find. For this dish, you need young lamb about six months old, or you may opt for the alternative lamb dish offered following this recipe.

1 whole lamb, 12 to 14 pounds, prepared by butcher for roasting (see step 1)
¼ to ⅓ cup extra-virgin olive oil
24 large cloves garlic, peeled
1½ cups fresh rosemary leaves
3½ pounds small potatoes, scrubbed clean, washed, and dried
2 cups dry white wine

1. Ask your butcher to cut the lamb in 4, and to crack all the joints. Before baking, wash the pieces of lamb and dry them. Remove excess fat, but remember that some fat is needed to protect the meat when cooking it. Rub each piece of lamb with olive oil and set them in a large roasting pan, large enough to hold the potatoes also.

2. Make a number of slits into the lamb pieces with a sharp paring knife and insert slivers of garlic with some rosemary leaves. Sprinkle salt all over, with more garlic and rosemary, reserving some for the potatoes. The lamb should be set bone side down in the pan. Bake for 40 minutes.

3. While the lamb is roasting, cut each potato in 4. Put the pieces in a bowl and add the leftover oil and rosemary to the bowl and toss to cover the potatoes. Add them to the lamb. Pour the wine over the lamb and continue roasting 45 to 50 minutes. Romans like the lamb well done. Baste with the juices in the pan every 15 minutes or so.

4. Remove the roasting pan from the oven and transfer the lamb pieces to a platter. Allow to rest 15 to 20 minutes. Put the roast pan with the potatoes back in the oven to cook another 10 to 15 minutes, or until tender. When the lamb is to be served, spoon some of the pan juices over the meat and serve with some potatoes on the side.

ROSEMARY-SCENTED BUTTERFLIED AND GRILLED LEG OF LAMB
Agnello arostito alla rosamarina

Serves 6

1 leg of lamb (6 to 8 pounds), butterflied
1 cup extra-virgin olive oil
4 large cloves garlic, minced
¼ cup balsamic vinegar
6 tablespoons freshly minced rosemary leaves (or 3 teaspoons dried)
2 teaspoons freshly ground pepper

1. Ask your butcher to butterfly the leg of lamb and to remove as much fat as he can, including the thin, silvery membrane that envelops the leg. At home, wipe the leg with damp paper towels and remove any additional fat.

2. Combine all remaining ingredients in the bowl of a food processor and blend until the herbs and garlic are minced. Place the lamb in a nonaluminum roasting pan and pour the marinade over. Turn to coat all sides. Cover with plastic wrap and refrigerate overnight, turning occasionally. Remove from the refrigerator 1 hour before cooking.

3. This may be either grilled or broiled. If broiling, preheat the broiler and set the rack 5 to 6 inches below the heat source. Broil about 15 minutes per side, basting frequently with the marinade. If grilling, have the fire ready—meaning the coals should be gray—and grill the lamb on an oiled grid about 5 inches over the coals for 12 to 14 minutes per side, basting frequently. If you prefer your grilled or broiled lamb well done, add several minutes to each time given. Most importantly, let the lamb stand for 10 minutes, then cut across the grain in thin slices to serve. Because of the various thicknesses of the butterflied lamb, it will be possible to offer some meat well done and some rarer.

LAMB, PEPPER, AND PASTA CASSEROLE

Ragu di agnello e peperoni col pasta all'Abruzzese

Serves 4

Paolo Scipioni is a food authority in L'Aquila; he is a charming man and the owner of a prestigious restaurant called Tre Marie on the street of the same name in his city. He is the fifth generation in ownership of the restaurant, which is claimed by many to be the temple of Abruzzi cookery. In addition to the murals on the walls of the three dining rooms, I remember the chairs that were antique—not one of them had a nail in it; each part of the chair was held together by pegs. One midmorning, lingering over a Campari and soda and sitting on one of these chairs, Paolo described some interesting local dishes such as liver cooked with honey, *fegato dolce*, and liver cooked with hot peppers, *fegato pazzo*—meaning "crazy liver." He also described how the locals enjoy lamb, and he described this sauce as one of the most popular, especially when it is served with their chitarra pasta (squarish spaghetti which are cut by wires strung across a board). I have substituted another pasta similar in feeling and texture, as it is easier to make or buy in the United States.

1 pound lean lamb for stewing, preferably top round
4 tablespoons olive oil
2 cloves garlic, minced
2 bay leaves
½ cup dry white wine
3 large or 4 small ripe plum tomatoes, cored and diced
2 bell peppers, 1 red, 1 yellow, cored, ribs removed, sliced as thinly as possible
1 cup broth or water
1 pound macheroni alla chitarra or tagliarini, preferably homemade

1. Remove excess fat from the lamb and dice in ¼- to ½-inch pieces.

2. Heat the oil in a large skillet and add the garlic, bay leaves, and the diced lamb, and sauté over medium heat, uncovered, until browned, 15 to 20 minutes.

3. Add the wine and reduce it by ½, 5 to 7 minutes. Stir in the diced tomatoes. Add the sliced peppers, salt, and a liberal amount of freshly ground pepper. Cover the skillet, reduce the heat to low, and simmer about 2 hours, checking to see if a little broth or water may be needed. Remove and discard the bay leaves. Set aside or keep warm over very low heat.

4. In a large pan, bring 4 quarts of water to boil. Once it is boiling add a tablespoon salt. Then add the pasta. When cooked al dente, drain well and put it in the skillet. Toss well with the sauce and transfer it to a bowl if ready to serve now or to an ovenproof bowl until ready to serve (keep it warm, covered, in a low oven).

5. Serve this with a salad made of fresh baby spinach leaves with thinly sliced red or white onions with a slice of scamorza cheese on the side of the salad plate.

LAMB AND VEGETABLES, GREEK STYLE IN SOUTHERN ITALY
Spezzatino d'agnello

Serves 6

It has been said that the food of Italy is a function of its history. Over a period of thousands of years, invaders came and went, and some stayed. Each brought its customs, traditions, and eating habits; three, in particular, laid the foundation for Italian cooking—the Etruscans, the Greeks, and the Saracens. The Etruscans and the Greeks were there before the Saracens and divided the whole peninsula between them, with Etruscans taking over the north, the Greeks the south. In addition to the many Greek ruins that punctuate the southern Italian countryside, there are also remnants of Greek cooking. Here is an adaptation of a lamb stew, Greek style; instead of baking it in the oven, this is wrapped in foil and cooked on a grill.

2 pounds lean boneless shoulder of lamb, cut into 6 pieces
3 large cloves garlic, halved
6 small new potatoes, scrubbed and halved
6 whole mushrooms, stems trimmed, wiped clean
6 Italian frying peppers, stems, ribs, and seeds removed, halved
6 medium onions, peeled and halved
6 eggplant slices (1 inch thick), skin on, each slice cut into 3 pieces
12 canned plum tomatoes, drained, seeded, and coarsely chopped
3 tablespoons finely chopped fresh oregano or 3 teaspoons dried
12 tablespoons chicken broth
6 tablespoons extra-virgin olive oil

1. Cut 6 pieces of heavy-duty foil about 18 inches square, large enough to envelop the lamb and vegetables.

2. Place 1 piece of lamb on each piece of foil and top with a garlic ½. Add 2 pieces of potato, a mushroom, 2 pieces of pepper, 2 pieces of onion, 3 pieces of eggplant, and some tomatoes.

3. Sprinkle oregano over the mixture, adding some salt and freshly ground pepper. Also add 2 tablespoons chicken broth and 1 tablespoon oil. Wrap the foil by picking up 2 sides, the 1 closest to you and the 1 north of you. Bring them together and fold 2 or 3 times, leaving some air space in the packet. Fold in the ends tightly to avoid spills when the packets are turned over.

4. When the grill fire is ready, place all the packets on the grid, about 5 inches above the heat source. Cover the grill and cook 45 minutes (if using a grill without a cover, cook 55 to 60 minutes). After 25 minutes of cooking, carefully turn over the packets and cook for remaining time. Before serving, it is always best to open 1 packet to test for doneness.

OTHER

ROASTED RABBIT IN RED WINE
Coniglio arrosto al vino rosso

Serves 4

This recipe is for farmed rabbit; if you should use wild rabbit, marinate the pieces in a cup of red wine overnight before proceeding with the recipe. Discard the marinade.

2 tablespoons extra-virgin olive oil
1 medium onion, finely chopped
1 clove garlic, minced
1 small sausage link out of its casing
1 rabbit, 2½ pounds, cleaned and readied for roasting, cut into 8 pieces
2 tablespoons finely chopped fresh rosemary
1 cup red wine
½ cup vegetable broth

1. Preheat oven to 350°F. In an ovenproof casserole or baking pan, add the olive oil, onions, garlic, and sausage, and bake until the onions begin to brown, about 10 minutes, stirring 2 or 3 times.

2. Add the rabbit pieces, rosemary, and some salt and freshly ground pepper. Turn the rabbit pieces over to coat them with the oil and sausage. Bake 15 minutes longer.

3. Add the wine and bake, uncovered, until most of the wine has evaporated, about 40 minutes. As the wine cooks off, add some vegetable broth, a few tablespoons at a time, also basting the rabbit several times. Rabbit bakes in approximately the same amount of time as chicken, so the total baking time should be about 1 to 1½ hours. Cover with foil after the liquid has evaporated. Serve with polenta.

Chapter   8

SALADS

Italians are natural-born gardeners. They have green thumbs and love everything attached to a garden. I rarely have heard Italians complain about weeding, because they are so happy over the plant. One of the most amazing salads in Italy is found in Naples, called *insalata di rinforzo alla napoletano*. *Rinforzo* means "to reinforce"; what actually happens is this—a cauliflower salad is made with several other ingredients, but as it is eaten, more of the same vegetables, or even other leftover cooked vegetables, are added to "keep the salad going."

When I've been in Italy at someone's home, he or she has made the salads by picking from the garden. However, now in Italy as in the United States, supermarkets carry fresh most of the necessary ingredients to make salads. In the United States you may not be able to find the greens *misticanza*, as they are called in Italy—meaning mixed wild greens picked for a salad—but every supermarket I know in the United States has mesclun, a close cousin of *misticanza*.

Italians don't use as much salad dressing as do Americans, and they mostly use extra-virgin olive oil with a little vinegar, sometimes balsamic, or lemon. In restaurants, they are often dressed in your presence. The Italians are careful to dry their greens before adding oil and vinegar or lemon. A common error in this country is to rinse greens and not take time to dry them in a spinner or with paper or cloth toweling. Greens must be dried before applying any oil dressing. With few exceptions, such as the *puntarelle* salad in Rome, most Italians bring more composition to their salads by adding beets, tomatoes, and other vegetables and herbs. If a vegetable is *not* at peak ripeness, the Italian will shun it—in other words, they will not use pink, tasteless tomatoes. If they want to use a pear in a salad, it will be just ripe, or they omit it. They will not use overgrown green beans or aged broccoli florettes. Nowhere is the freshness of ingredients more important than in a salad.

ROASTED BEET SALAD WITH RED ONIONS AND DRIED FENNEL
Insalata di barbabietole arrostite

Serves 4

The leaves of small to medium-size beets can be used in several ways to keep up with the Italian parsimonious way with vegetables and some other foods. Most Americans discard them. An Italian will trim and sort them, rinse carefully and dry them, and add them to fresh green salads; or he will cook them as he does spinach.

8 medium-size beets, washed, left whole and untrimmed
6 tablespoons extra-virgin olive oil
½ teaspoon dried fennel seeds
1 red onion, peeled and thinly sliced
2 tablespoons balsamic vinegar
1 teaspoon sugar
4 radicchio leaves

1. Preheat oven to 375°F. Dry the beets and put them in a bowl. Add 1 tablespoon olive oil and toss to coat them. Place each 1 in a foil square, large enough to envelop it. Add salt, freshly ground pepper, and several dried fennel seeds. Wrap and place them directly in mid-oven.

2. Bake until they are tender, about 1 hour. Test for doneness by opening 1 package and inserting a wooden skewer into the beet. If it meets no resistance, the beet is cooked. Remove the beets from the oven, unwrap them, and discard the wrappings. Peel each beet when cool enough to handle and thinly slice into a bowl. Add the remaining oil, remaining fennel seeds, onions, balsamic, and sugar, and toss lightly but well.

3. Leave at room temperature until ready to serve, up to 3 or 4 hours. If longer than that (they may be made ahead by 2 or 3 days), refrigerate and bring to room temperature ½ hour before serving.

4. To serve, place a radicchio leaf on each of 4 plates and arrange beet slices and onions over the leaf. Spoon on whatever liquid may have accumulated in the bottom of the bowl. Adjust seasoning and add more salt and freshly ground pepper, if needed.

ROASTED CHICKEN SALAD IN ROUND LOAF OF ITALIAN BREAD

Insalata di pollo arrosto in pane

Serves 6

A boy of eight years in New York City had a weekly chore: carrying his grandmother's white enameled basin, filled with fresh yeasty dough, to the local Italian bakery. There, the grandmother, along with a dozen or other ladies, all clad in black, would turn out their dough and shape several loaves of Italian bread—a week's supply. They paid the baker a penny a loaf for peeling the loaves into the wood-burning oven and for retrieving them. The smell of that bread has lived with me for many years, and the experience of that "chore" instilled in me the deep desire for a good loaf of Italian bread. Here's a loaf filled with tasty roasted chicken salad.

Boned chicken pieces, cut in chunks, from a roasted 3-pound chicken, see page 208.

3 inner celery ribs with leaves, thinly sliced
3 scallions, thinly sliced
1 cup cubed pecorino cheese
½ cup chopped prosciutto or mortadella
2 bunches fresh arugula, washed, dried, and cut in 2-inch pieces
½ cup extra-virgin olive oil
3 tablespoons herbed white wine vinegar
Pinch of red pepper flakes
2 hard-boiled eggs, shelled, and cut into wedges
1 round loaf Italian bread, 8- to 10-inch diameter

1. Combine the chicken pieces in a large bowl with the celery, scallions, cheese, prosciutto, and the arugula. In a smaller bowl, combine the oil, vinegar, red pepper flakes, and some salt. Pour over the chicken mixture.

2. Slice the top off of the bread, reserving it, and remove the soft inner part of the bread. Reserve for another use or discard. Spoon about ½ of the chicken mixture into the bread container, garnish with the egg wedges, and put back the top of the bread that was cut off. This can keep at room temperature about 3 hours. Just before serving, remove the top of the bread and lean it against the loaf to show the salad. Have ready additional oil and vinegar if someone wants more. After the bread with chicken is cut in slices, add spoonfuls of the remaining chicken salad to the plate alongside of the bread.

SPRING GREENS WITH OIL, VINEGAR, AND MINT

Insalata di stagione con vinaigrette alla menta

Serves 6

Misticanza salad in Italy is determined by the farmer, who sows a variety of seeds together and harvests the small plants together. At times, this could mean as many as fifteen, more or less, varieties of greens and herbs sold together. Each farmer, and therefore each vendor at the markets, has his or her own specialty mixture. Customers usually get to know one or two venders and trust their combination. This kind of salad green mix is difficult to find in our supermarkets, but a close relative would be mesclun mixtures, and it would be wonderful if you were located near an open green market that sells fresh farm produce of this sort. A popular salad green, especially at Easter time in Rome and elsewhere, is a dandelion known as *puntarelle*. I've been in restaurants in and around Rome, and families on Sunday seem not to stop eating it. It is made with oil and vinegar and a touch of anchovy.

8 cups of fresh greens, such as baby dandelion or hearts of chicory, washed, dried, and torn into bite-size pieces
½ cup extra-virgin olive oil
2 tablespoons garlic-flavored red wine vinegar
1 anchovy

1. Place the greens in a large bowl.
2. In a smaller bowl, combine the oil and vinegar and mash the anchovy in it. Season to taste by adding salt, if needed, and freshly ground pepper. Blend well and pour over the greens. Toss lightly but well, and serve.

GREEN BEANS WITH PANCETTA AND SAVORY AS EATEN BY THE BENEDICTINE MONKS

Fagiolini con pancetta e santoreggio alla maniera dei Monaci Benedettini

Serves 6

Savory is a rather bitter herb vaguely like thyme, used in sausages, stuffings, and as a flavoring for beans and peas. A Mediterranean herb, it was valued for its affinity for green beans and its medicinal use. It was known by the Romans but enjoyed a rediscovery by the Benedictine monks who, as far back as the ninth century, cultivated it in the monastery gardens. This dish is updated in fancier Italian restaurants by wrapping the beans in pancetta slices and broiling them, a delicious idea.

1 pound fresh string beans, trimmed
¼ cup butter
2 sprigs fresh savory or 1 pinch dried
6 thin slices pancetta, about ⅓ pound

1. Cook the beans in salted, boiling water until tender, about 10 minutes. Drain and dry them with paper toweling.

2. In a large skillet, melt the butter, add the savory, and sauté the cooked beans quickly. Remove from the heat and cool somewhat, just enough to be able to handle them by arranging them in 6 bundles. Trim the edges to make uniform packets.

3. Place a pancetta slice on top and slightly around each bundle fitting it as if it were a wide belt.

4. Arrange the packets of beans with their belts of pancetta on a broil pan. Broil 5 or 6 inches under the heat source to brown and sizzle the pancetta, about 4 minutes.

FRESH FENNEL SLICES IN SALAD WITH WATERCRESS
Insalata di finocchio e crescione

Serves 8

Fresh fennel is a large white bulb with pale green, feathery leaves. The bulb should be snow white and firm when you buy it. A favorite in Italy way before it gained popularity in the United States, this anise-flavored vegetable is sometimes called sweet or Florentine (and sometimes Roman) fennel. Modern Italian fuss over it as much as did the ancient Romans.

3 large heads fresh fennel with some leaves
2 bunches watercress
6 tablespoons extra-virgin olive oil, preferably Tuscan
2 tablespoons herbed white wine vinegar
2 tablespoons capers, rinsed and dried
½ teaspoon sugar

1. Rinse and dry the fennel and trim, removing any blemished outer leaves. Cut each bulb in ½, and slice each ½ as thinly as possible. Chop very young, pale green fronds to include in salad. Put them in a large bowl.

2. Rinse and pick over the watercress. Cut off tough stems but leave watercress as sprays. Dry as well as you can and add to the salad bowl.

3. In a smaller bowl, combine the oil, vinegar, capers, sugar, salt, and a liberal amount of freshly ground pepper, and mix well. Pour into the bowl with the fennel and watercress. Toss lightly but well.

GENOVESE SQUID SALAD WITH VEGETABLES FOR LIGURIAN SAILORS
Insalata di calamari alla Genovese con verdure

Serves 6

Genoa, in the northern province of Liguria, is celebrated for its many fish preparations. This is easy to understand as the sea provides many of the raw materials of Genoese cooking. Two classic fish soups are *ciuppin*—a pureed soup similar to the French *bouillabaisse*—and *burrida*—a soup of various fish difficult to get in theUnited States. These soups are featured in Genoa's restaurants. Fish salads are also among the dishes offered. A famous one in Genoa is *cappon magro* (a Christmas Eve tradition), and it is delicious, but it is rather difficult to make at home as it requires a minimum of twenty-five ingredients. There is a delicious fish salad from this part of the world that is considerably easier to make and is presented here.

This squid salad was fashioned for Ligurian sailors who spent months away from home and on the high seas transporting spices to be traded. During these sea journeys, they yearned for the fresh-tasting vegetables and herbs they sorely missed during their dangerous and long sea voyages. I first tasted this squid salad at the home of the Ottolenghis.

1½ pounds cleaned squid, cut into ¼-inch rings
4 cloves garlic, minced
2 cups Italian red wine
1½ pounds new potatoes
12 ounces fresh green beans, trimmed and cut into 2-inch lengths
4 sun-dried tomatoes in oil, drained, and thinly sliced
7 tablespoons extra-virgin olive oil
3 tablespoons red wine vinegar
A good pinch of red pepper flakes
¼ cup thinly sliced fresh basil leaves or fresh marjoram

1. Warm the oven to 350°F. In a ceramic or glass baking dish, combine the squid, ½ of the garlic, and the wine, and cook, covered, about 50 minutes until the squid is tender.

2. Brush the potatoes clean and put them in a sauce pan. Cover with water, add a teaspoon of salt, cover, and bring to boil. Lower the heat, and simmer about 20 minutes until tender. Remove the potatoes but keep the water in the pan. Add the green beans and cook 5 minutes. Drain the beans.

3. Slice the potatoes ¼ inch thick and put them in a large mixing bowl. Add the warm beans and the sun-dried tomatoes. Add salt and freshly ground pepper.

4. Combine the oil, wine vinegar, the remaining garlic, and red pepper flakes, and pour over the salad. Drain the squid, discarding the wine mixture, and fold it into the salad. Check for salt and pepper seasoning. Sprinkle basil or marjoram over the salad. This dish is usually served warm.

LIGURIAN VEGETABLE SALAD
Condiglione

Serves 6

The Ligurians have a penchant for fresh green herbs and fresh vegetables, and here is a famous salad of the region. The desire for fresh herbs and vegetables dates to the region's history of seafaring—sailors on long voyages, subsisting on salt meat and dried beans, wanted and were given the freshest foods as part of the celebration of their homecoming.

1 can (6 ounces) tuna in oil
6 medium ripe tomatoes, peeled, cut into wedges
1 small cucumber, peeled and thinly sliced
2 shallots, peeled and thinly sliced
1 red, yellow, or orange bell pepper, seeded, ribbed, and thinly sliced
10 black olives, pitted and chopped
2 hard-boiled eggs, shelled and cut in wedges
1 teaspoon finely chopped anchovies
1 teaspoon dried oregano, crushed
¼ cup finely chopped fresh basil
1 clove garlic, minced
¾ cup extra-virgin olive oil

1. Add the ingredients from the tuna, including the oil from the can, to the boiled eggs in a large salad bowl or large platter.

2. In a small bowl, combine the remaining ingredients. Add salt and freshly ground pepper. Pour this mixture over the salad and toss lightly but well. Let the salad stand at room temperature about an hour before serving. Again, toss lightly, and serve.

SWEET SLICES OF TOMATOES WITH CHIVES

Pomodoro con cipolline

Serves 4

The tomatoes must be ripe and the skins must come off. Leave the tomatoes at room temperature for several hours and serve on separate small plates.

4 medium to large ripe tomatoes
2 tablespoons extra-virgin olive oil
2 teaspoons red wine vinegar
1 tablespoon sugar
⅓ cup finely chopped fresh chives

1. Core the tomatoes and blanch them in boiling water just long enough to loosen the skins, 30 seconds to 2 minutes, depending on ripeness. Drain tomatoes, run under cold water, and remove the skins. Slice as thinly as you can and arrange slices on a plate with little overlap.

2. Combine the oil and vinegar. Add salt and freshly ground pepper. Spoon over the tomatoes. Then, carefully sprinkle sugar and chives on them and allow to marinate at room temperature 20 to 30 minutes. To serve, arrange slices of tomatoes on 4 individual plates, overlapping them in a pattern with the sugared and chive side up.

ARUGULA AND TOMATO SALAD WITH LEMON DRESSING
Insalata di ricula al limone

Serves 6

Arugula, usually sold in small bunches, is a variety of greens made of flat, small leaves on long stems. It is often taken for dandelions. In Italy, its roots are almost always attached. Its mustardlike taste is distinctive, and the more mature, the stronger the taste. It is fun to grow because the leaves can be snipped at the base of the plant and in a few days there will be new growth. One can find it in most supermarkets these days, although it wasn't around some years ago until the popularity of Italian ingredients took hold in this country.

⅓ cup extra-virgin olive oil
3 tablespoons fresh lemon juice
½ teaspoons freshly grated lemon zest
1 teaspoon sugar
1 clove garlic, minced
8 cups arugula leaves, washed and dried
2 ripe medium tomatoes, trimmed, sliced into thin wedges

1. Whisk together the oil, lemon juice and zest, sugar, garlic, salt, and pepper until blended. Let rest 2 or 3 minutes to let the sugar dissolve.

2. Whisk the dressing again. Add the arugula and toss well. Add the tomatoes and toss lightly. Serve right away.

BABY SPINACH SALAD WITH OIL AND LEMON DRESSING

Spinaci in insalata con olio e limone

Serves 6

Olive oil and fresh lemon juice with freshly ground pepper and sea salt dresses more Italian salads than any other dressing. This is a heavenly salad if the spinach is young and tender and the dressing kept as simple as it is stated here. Trimmed, washed, and dried spinach may be prepared hours ahead and refrigerated in a plastic bag; remove from the refrigerator fifteen minutes and add the dressing just before serving.

1½ pounds young, fresh spinach
1 small celery heart with leaves, finely sliced
¼ cup finely diced red onion
¼ cup extra-virgin olive oil
2 tablespoons fresh lemon juice

1. Trim the spinach and remove outer leaves if they are large and blemished. Cut off stem ends and any stems that appear too large. Wash several times in cool water to rid the leaves of sand. When you are convinced they are clean, spin the spinach dry. Put it in a large bowl with the celery and onion.

2. In a small bowl, combine the oil and lemon juice. Add a liberal amount of freshly ground pepper and some salt. Pour over the greens and toss lightly but well. Serve right away.

CUCUMBERS IN MINT AND ICE
Centrioli con la menta

Serves 6

This is one time you don't have to drain and dry a vegetable.

Cucumbers are stacked high in the Italian markets and are used mostly in salads with oil, vinegar, and herbs. In our household, they were a staple, although my grandfather disliked them as much as zucchini—"they're nothing but water," he would say as my mother and grandmother continued to fill their antipasti plates and salad bowls with fresh, succulent cucumbers.

You'll find three basic types of cucumbers in the markets. The slicing cucumber is the most commonly seen in supermarkets—field grown, six to eight inches long, with dark green, glossy skins, usually waxed after harvesting for shelf life (be sure to remove all the waxed peel before using). The Kirby cucumber, a second variety, used for commercial dill pickles, is also sold fresh. The size is smaller, squatter, with lighter green skins. As a cucumber lover, I like these for their crispness, freshness, tiny seeds and thin skins. The third type, greenhouse or European-type cukes, are now widely available. You can't help noticing them in the markets, as they are sometimes almost 2 feet long (and usually covered in plastic). These are not only more expensive but somewhat bland. For this recipe, use the Kirby variety or small regular slicing cucumbers to avoid seeds—if your cucumber has large seeds, simply cut them away.

6 nicely shaped small Kirby cucumbers
1 tablespoon salt
6 large mint sprigs, 3 whole, 3 finely chopped
2 cups ice cubes

1. Slice off ends of the cucumbers and remove almost all of the skin with a vegetable peeler. Run the tines of a fork up and down the full length of the cukes. Cut in eighths lengthwise.

2. In a serving dish wide enough to hold the cuke lengths, combine them with the salt, chopped mint, and the ice cubes. Refrigerate for 1 hour or longer to crisp and scent the cukes.

3. Serve just as they are, but add the 3 sprigs of mint for garnish.

CURLY ENDIVE SALAD WITH FENNEL MATCHSTICKS IN FRESH HERB DRESSING

Insalata di'indivia riccia con finocchi a fiammifero

Serves 4

Curly endive is another name for chicory, a very popular Italian green—it is a head of ragged-edged, dark green leaves, which have a bitter, assertive taste. The inner leaves are yellow and white and have a milder taste. For this salad, use only the inner yellow and white leaves, and keep them crisp. The fresh fennel imparts a licorice or anise flavor. Note the dressing is simple Italian—oil and fresh lemon juice, heightened with lemon zest, some dill, and snipped fennel fronds. Add the dressing at the last minute, and if the greens were refrigerated, bring them out fifteen minutes or so before serving.

3 tablespoons fresh lemon juice
1 teaspoon grated lemon zest
⅓ cup extra-virgin olive oil
2 small bunches fresh curly endive, rinsed and dried
1 small fennel bulb, trimmed and sliced into matchstick shapes
1 teaspoon finely chopped fresh dill
1 teaspoon finely chopped fresh fennel fronds

1. Combine the lemon juice, zest, and some salt and freshly ground pepper in a bowl. Slowly add the oil, whisking until emulsified. Keep at room temperature until ready to dress the salad.

2. Place the endive and the fennel pieces in a large bowl. Add the dill and fennel fronds and the dressing; toss well and divide among 4 salad plates.

TRADITIONAL CAULIFLOWER SALAD IN NAPLES

Insalata di rinforzo alla napoletana

Serves 8 to 12

Rinforzo means "to reinforce"—what actually happens is this: a cauliflower salad is made with several other ingredients, but as it is eaten, more of the same vegetables, or even other leftover cooked vegetables, may be added to "keep the salad going." It is considered a holiday salad in Naples. It can be made ahead by a couple of days; in fact, it is better to do so to allow the flavors to develop.

6 tablespoons extra-virgin olive oil
2 tablespoons white wine vinegar
6 anchovy fillets, minced
2 tablespoons dried oregano, crushed
¾ cup coarsely chopped cured black olives (do not use canned California variety—these must be cured, either oil or brine)
¼ cup capers, drained and dried, chopped
1½ cups roasted red bell pepper strips
2 cloves garlic, minced
¼ cup finely chopped Italian parsley
1 large cauliflower head, trimmed of stem and tough outer leaves, cut into 1-inch florets
Juice of 1½ lemons and rind of ½ lemon

1. In a large bowl, combine the oil, vinegar, and anchovies. Whisk to make a smooth sauce. Then add the oregano, olives, capers, peppers, garlic, and parsley, and stir so the olives and peppers are well-coated. Set aside.

2. Bring a large pot of water to boil, add salt, the ½ lemon rind, ⅓ of the lemon juice, and the cauliflower florets. Cook 5 or 6 minutes until they are tender, drain immediately, and run cold water over them to stop cooking. Drain well and pat dry with paper towels.

3. Add the dried cauliflower, some salt and freshly ground pepper, and the remaining lemon juice to the salad. Toss lightly but well. Leave at room temperature for several hours to allow flavors to develop. If made 1 or 2 days ahead, and you may do that, refrigerate, but then bring the salad to room temperature by removing from refrigerator 1 hour before.

HEARTS OF ESCAROLE WITH RED PEPPER CONFETTI
Insalata di scarola con peperoni

Serves 8 to 12

The hearts of escarole are white and pale yellow and quite tender. It's difficult to buy just the hearts (they are available sometimes), so you may have to buy regular heads of escarole and peel away the green leaves, which can be used in other dishes, such as soups. This is a refreshing, tender salad and so pretty to look at. A classic dish in Naples is cooked escarole with raisins and pine nuts, called *scarole natale*, and I have adapted that idea to form this salad.

4 heads escarole, green leaves removed and reserved for another use
1 red bell pepper, cored, ribs and seeds removed, cut into tiny dice
¼ cup golden raisins, soaked in warm water ½ hour and then drained and dried
¼ cup pine nuts, toasted
⅓ cup finely chopped chives
⅓ cup extra-virgin olive oil
2 tablespoons herb-flavored white vinegar
1 teaspoon drained capers
½ teaspoon sugar

1. Prepare the escarole by removing the green leaves after trimming the stem end. When you reach the inside of the escarole, you will find tender leaves, white and pale yellow, with a tint of green. Pull these tender leaves apart. Rinse them and dry with paper towels or spin dry. Put in a large bowl as you complete preparing each head in this way. Add the red pepper "confetti," raisins, nuts, and the chives.

2. In a smaller bowl, combine the oil, vinegar, capers, and sugar with some salt and freshly ground pepper. Mix well and pour over the escarole. Toss lightly but well.

ROMAINE LETTUCE, WATERCRESS, AND SNOW PEAS WITH LEMON

Lattuga romana crescione e taccole al limone

Serves 6

The hearts of this lettuce as a rule do not need to be rinsed. However, check carefully before dressing them. Romaine lettuce is named for the Romans, who cultivated many varieties of lettuce. Although Americans often prefer the hearts of romaine, we should be aware of the fact that the outer, darker leaves of romaine have as much as six times more vitamin C and up to ten times more beta carotene as iceberg lettuce. (The same is true for arugula.) The addition of watercress and thinly sliced snow peas adds interest to the salad.

2 small heads romaine lettuce
1 bunch watercress, rinsed and dried
24 snow peas, about ⅓ pound, trimmed
½ cup extra-virgin olive oil
Juice from 1 lemon (about 3 tablespoons)
2 tablespoons finely chopped mint
1 clove garlic, minced

1. Remove outer green leaves from the heads of lettuce and discard or reserve some leaves for another use. Cut the hearts of this lettuce lengthwise in ½, and then again lengthwise in thirds to serve 6. Do the same with the second head of lettuce.

2. Put the watercress and the snow peas in a large mixing bowl.

3. In a smaller bowl, combine the oil, lemon juice, some salt and freshly ground pepper, mint, and the minced garlic. Mix well.

2. Arrange 2 lengths of romaine lettuce hearts on each of 6 plates. Spoon a little of the sauce over each strip. Add the remaining dressing to the bowl with the watercress and snow peas. Toss lightly but well. Add some of this to each plate over the lettuce hearts and serve.

GRILLED FENNEL SLICES WITH FRESH LEMON
Finocchi ai ferri

Serves 4

Fennel bulbs and their feathery leaves both impart a mild sweet flavor similar to licorice or anise. Because of its taste, fennel is also called anise in many markets, but actually, it is quite a different plant from the herb anise. In Florence, it is known as sweet fennel or *finocchio*. Italians have been enthusiastic about fennel for many years and cultivate it more than anyone else. The vegetable now appears in many US markets

2 large fresh fennel bulbs
6 tablespoons extra-virgin olive oil
½ cup chicken or vegetable broth
2 tablespoons fresh lemon juice
Pinch of dried fennel seeds

1. Trim the fennel by paring the bulb end and cutting the bulb from any branches. If possible, reserve 4 small sprays of the feathery green leaves for garnish. Cut both bulbs into thin slices, leaving each cutting attached to the bulb end. Do not fret if some cuttings are loose and unattached.

2. Heat 1 tablespoon oil in a large skillet and arrange the fennel slices in 1 layer. If this is not possible, repeat the procedure in order to cook all the slices. Pour some broth just to cover the slices. Simmer uncovered 20 minutes or until tender. Remove and drain the slices.

3. Brush a little more oil on the slices and transfer the slices to a heated grill or warmed broiling pan. Grill to achieve grill marks, or broil to brown the slices. Move them to a large plate or platter.

4. Combine the remaining oil, 4 tablespoons, and the lemon juice. Add the fennel seeds and some salt and freshly ground pepper. Mix well. Pour over the fennel slices and let marinate at room temperature up to an hour. If longer, refrigerate, but remove before serving by at least ½ hour. Distribute the fennel to 4 plates, with sauce over each portion. Add a spray of fennel feathers and serve.

CHICORY SALAD MIMOSA
Mimosa di cicoria

Serves 4

Chicory is also known as curly endive. The flavor is slightly bitter. The head forms a loose bunch of ragged-edged leaves on long stems. The outer leaves are deep green, whereas the leaves in the center are yellow and milder tasting. Use only the center leaves for this salad. If you can't find chicory, use arugula.

2 heads chicory, outer leaves removed for another use
2 tablespoons extra-virgin olive oil
2 tablespoons fresh lemon juice (½ lemon)
1 clove garlic, minced
2 hard-boiled eggs

1. Separate, wash, and dry the inner chicory leaves and put in a bowl. Add the oil, lemon juice, garlic, some salt, and freshly ground pepper. Toss the salad.

2. Shell the eggs and discard the whites. Mash the yolks finely and sprinkle over the salad. Serve right away.

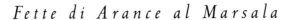

SLICED ORANGES WITH MARSALA
Fette di Arance al Marsala

Serves 4

Marsala is an important dessert wine with a particular virtue: it does not deteriorate after the bottle has been opened, so that one can be sure in any Italian cafe, restaurant, or home of having a glass of marsala in decent condition. Marsala is Sicily's most famous wine. Like sherry and port, it is a fortified wine and it bears some resemblance to Madeira in that one of its constituent parts is heated. Virtually all the production of marsala is in the hands of big companies, both those with English names and Italian, of which Florio is probably the most distinguished. All bottles of the real thing bear a numbered neck label showing the outline of the island of Sicily in red.

4 to 6 large eating oranges
⅓ cup marsala wine
2 tablespoons sugar
8 small fresh mint leaves

1. Peel the oranges and remove all the white pith. Thinly slice in rounds and discard any seeds. Arrange in a large dish, preferably a platter with a little depth to hold the wine.

2. Sprinkle first the marsala, then the sugar, over the oranges. Allow to marinate several hours at room temperature. Just before serving, garnish with the mint leaves.

SALAD OF ASSORTED LETTUCES WITH CAPERS AND TARRAGON
Insalata di lattuga con capperi e dragoncello

Serves 6

Many Italians pick dandelions from the wild before they start to flower. They love their pepper-tasting leaves, leaves that are long and indented, and they look like lion's teeth—this is why they are called *dente di leone* and also often called *cicoria di campo*, field chicory. Cultivated dandelion are available in many greengroceries and some supermarkets.

Arugula grows wild in the Italian countryside and it is cultivated, too, and appears in every supermarket in theUnited States. Lamb's lettuce, called *valeriana* in Italy, grows wild there, too, and it is a must ingredient in *misticanza* (a salad of mixed wild greens). You will see it in some shops as rounded leaves bunched together in a rosette shape—the smaller and rounder the leaves, the fuller the taste. If you are in an Italian market at the right time, you will see at least a dozen or more fresh salad greens. Italians like their salad greens simply dressed with olive oil and either vinegar or lemon juice, and after the main course, to cleanse the palate.

2 bunches fresh dandelion
1 large bunch fresh arugula
2 bunches lamb's lettuce
¼ cup finely chopped red onion
1 tablespoon chopped capers
1 teaspoon finely chopped fresh tarragon or ½ teaspoon dried
4 tablespoons extra-virgin olive oil
2 tablespoons fresh lemon juice
Pinch of sugar

1. Trim the lettuces from their roots and put them in several changes of cool water to clean them. Handle them with care, as they are fragile, especially the lamb's lettuce. Dry them carefully and well. Put them in a large salad bowl adding the red onion, capers, and tarragon.

2. In a small bowl, combine the olive oil, lemon juice, and sugar. Add some salt and freshly ground pepper. Stir well and pour over the lettuces. Toss lightly and well. Serve right away.

Chapter 9

CHEESES

It is almost impossible to think of Italian cuisine without cheese. Cheese is used in soups, main courses, and desserts, but perhaps it is best known when paired with pasta. In fact, it is rare to find a pasta dish without cheese (usually only the fish sauces avoid cheese). Fettuccine Alfredo is only one example of a cheese pasta dish, but a quick glance through these pages will show quickly how often cheese is served with pasta. Parmesan is surely the best known, the most popular, and probably the best tasting. It is fun, however, to experiment with other cheeses; we list some popular Italian cheeses available now in the United States.

ASIAGO: Comes from Vincenza, but also is made in Padua, Verona, and Trentome. A cow's milk cheese with a fat content of 30 percent, Asiago has the form of a small, flat wheel and has a somewhat sharp flavor. It can be eaten at the end of a meal and is very good grated on certain pastas. It is made in the United States in three forms: fresh (soft), medium, and old. It is less expensive than Parmesan and can be substituted in most pasta dishes except those which demand the delicate Parmesan touch.

BEL PAESE: From Lombardy, this is made from pasteurized cow's milk and has a fat content of approximately 50 percent. Its form is a rather thick disk, usually about eight inches in diameter and approximately two inches thick. Bel Paese has a mild, fruity flavor and is excellent with valpolicella wine. *Bel Paese* means "beautiful country," and the cheese is one of the best known and most popular of the Italian table cheeses. It is the trade name of one of a group of soft, mild, fast-ripened Italian cheeses. The first Bel Paese was made in Melzo, near Milan, marked larger than Rome. Although intended as a table cheese, Bel Paese also is good or for cooking. Its softness makes it an excellent melting cheese. A version of Bel Paese is now made in the United States in Wisconsin. It may be used in any recipe calling for mozzarella.

CACCIOCAVALLO: Its name means "cheese on horseback," and one theory is that the cheeses, which are tied in pairs and hung over poles to cure, look as though they were hung over a saddle. If the cheese is to be eaten straight, it is matured for two to four months, but if it is to be grated and used in cooking, it needs up to two months. The cheese has a smooth, firm texture and a pleasant, sharpish flavor; it keeps and travels well.

FIORE SARDO: Also known as pecorino sardo, this comes from Sardinia but also may be found in Latium and Campagna. It is made from sheep's milk and has a fat content of about 45 percent. Fiore sardo comes in small, cylindrical wheels with convex rims about eight inches in diameter and almost six inches high. It has a light, nutty flavor when young and much sharper taste as it is aged. It is excellent as a grated cheese or can be eaten at the end of a meal. It is similar to the other pecorinos, such as Romano.

FONTINA: This is one of the most delicious Italian cheeses. There are American imitations of this great Italian cheese, but they do not measure up to the original. The real fontina comes from the Piedmont's Val d'Aosta, a mountainous area just south of Switzerland. Fontina looks like a Swiss Gruyere; it has a rather light brown crust and comes in large wheels like Swiss cheese, but it doesn't have the network of holes. Fontina is made from cow's milk and has a fat content of 45–50 percent; the flavor is delicate, somewhat fruity, and it is excellent with the light, fruity wines of Piedmont. It is frequently melted, so it is excellent with pasta dishes, especially those which require cheese for stuffing and baking. When fully cured, it is hard, and used for grating.

GORGONZOLA: The most popular of the Italian blue cheeses, Gorgonzola is named after a village near Milan but is now mainly produced in and around Milan. Because Gorgonzola keeps and travels well, it enjoys an international reputation; it is unique for its creaminess.

White Gorgonzola, slightly more bitter in flavor than the blue, is highly appreciated in Italy. It can also be found in the provinces of Cuomo, Cremona, Milano, and Pavia. Gorgonzola is made from cow's milk and has a fat content of 45 percent. It comes in a cylindrical form up to twelve inches in diameter and often as high as eight inches. Very soft and tender, almost runny, it has a rather fully developed smell and a very savory taste. Gorgonzola can be used in sauces, with pasta, and at the end of the meal. It is excellent with a Barolo wine.

MASCARPONE: A soft and delicate cow's milk cheese with creamy, ricottalike consistency, this may be served as a dessert when mixed with sugar, coffee, cognac, or chartreuse. It is best in the autumn and winter. Good also in baked pasta dishes.

MOZZARELLA: A pure white, soft, smooth, and moist cheese made in pear, oval, square, or spherical shapes. It has a mild and creamy, delicate, and slightly sweet flavor; it is one of the most popular cheeses used in Italian cooking. Smoked mozzarella has been flavored by smoke, in many cases created artificially by chemicals instead of natural smoking over fire. It is delicious and works well in pasta salads.

PARMESAN: Grana cheese is the generic name of a group of Italian cheeses. The word *grana* means "grain" and refers to the grainy texture of the cheeses when they age. There are two types of grana cheeses, both commonly called Parmesan outside of Italy: Parmigiano-Reggiano and Grana Padano. One of the finest cheeses in the world, Parmesan has been made in Italy for more than nine hundred years. The full name is Parmigiano-Reggiano, and it comes from a small area of the country comprising Parma, from which it gets its name; Reggio-Emilia, where most of the cheese is produced; Modena; and certain sections of Bologna. It is made from mid-April to precisely November 11. Although Parmesan can be eaten fresh, it is best known as a hard grating cheese that has the quality of bringing out the essence of every other ingredient with which it is matched. It is a cheese that has never been duplicated outside of Italy. In the United States, Parmesan cheese made in the Midwest is being sold in most supermarkets, and Parmesan made in Argentina is finding its way into the delicatessen units of grocery stores; both are good, but we still prefer the Italian imported variety. Don't buy too much at a time, store it tightly wrapped in plastic in the refrigerator, and grate it each time you need it. This is extra work, but you'll appreciate the freshness of flavor and the moisture of newly grated cheese.

Parmesan cheese is made with cow's milk and has a fat content of 32 percent. It comes in large wheels with slightly convex sides, often up to eighteen inches in diameter and ten inch high. It is a hard, brittle, and crumbly cheese, very fruity to sharp in taste. It is the cheese most commonly ground to go with pasta, but it may be cut and eaten at the end of a meal.

PECORINO ROMANO: Pecorino is a generic name for all Italian cheeses made with sheep's milk. Pecorino Romano is a hard grating cheese used for pasta; pecorino da tavola is a sharp and pungent table cheese, but milder than the gratin pecorinos. Both have minimum fat content of 36 percent, and have a slightly smoky smell and a strong flavor with a sharp taste. They are excellent with full-bodied wines from the south and Sicily. They are used as grated cheeses with pasta and may also be enjoyed at the end of meals. Often, Romano is less expensive than Parmesan; but remember, it has more of a bite.

PECORINO SICILIANO: Also known as *canestrato* ("draining basket"), this is one of the most popular of the Sicilian cheeses. A strongly flavored cheese, it is molded in baskets and hardened sufficiently to be grated. It is made from sheep's milk with a minimum fat content of 40 percent and comes in cylinders with flat sides, often ten inches in diameter and as high as seven inches. It is like the pecorino Romano, again with a distinct smell characteristic of sheep's milk cheeses.

PROVOLONE: Provolone is associated with southern Italy, especially the Campania region. It is made from cow's milk and has a 44 percent fat content. With a smooth, glossy, golden rind and a dense, creamy white inside, provolone can taste delicate but sharp also, depending on its age. It is eaten generally with appetizers or at the end of a meal, but can also be grated and used with pasta.

RICOTTA: A white, creamy cottage cheese made from the whey from other cheeses such as provolone and mozzarella. It is on the borderline of being a cheese, but is an important ingredient in much of Italy's cooking, used as a filling for ravioli and many lasagne and cannelloni dishes, as well as for sweet dishes.

RICOTTA SALATA: This is a salty, dry, hard ricotta which is rather mild. It is grated and used as a seasoning. Because more liquid is drained away, it has the same consistency as feta cheese; it is not like ricotta.

ROMANO: See Pecorino Romano.

SCAMORZE: Somewhat like provolone, this cheese from the Campania region of Italy may also be found in Abruzzi and Molise. It is made from cow's milk and has a fat content of 44 percent. Its interesting gourd shape with a narrow neck is tied with a chord with four little loops on top; it is mostly seen hanging in Italian grocery and fancy delicatessen stores. Scamorze has a delicate, nutty flavor and a glossy, golden yellow skin. It may be eaten at the end of meals in pieces and also in some pasta dishes. It's best when fresh. In Italy there are some farms where scamorze cheese is still made from goat's milk by the traditional methods.

FRESH SEASONAL FRUIT AND ITALIAN CHEESES

Frutta di stagione e formaggi

Our markets sell small, dark purple plums sometimes labeled Italian plums. Romans love this kind of plum and irreverently call them "nun's thighs." Add some ripe pears, which are ideal with most cheeses, and be sure to serve some watermelon. In Rome, across the Tiber in the district known as Trastevere, when the weather is warm, there are stands filled with watermelon on ice. As for cheese, serve the two cheeses most often associated with Rome: pecorino Romano and fresh ricotta. The fresh ricotta can be sprinkled with sugar, espresso granules, and cinnamon, as it is in Rome, or eaten as is.

Pecorino Romano

Pecorino is a name given to all Italian cheeses made from sheep's milk. The best known, and the oldest, is pecorino Romano—so called simply because it was first made near Rome. It is hard grana cheese made in round shapes up to ten inches in diameter. This type of cheese can be aged up to one year; at that time it becomes brittle, hard textured, and is yellow-white in color. It has a sharp, piquant, pronounced aroma and taste. It is used as a grating cheese, sometimes in place of Parmigiano. *Pepato* is a pecorino spiced with peppercorns, making the flavor of the cheese more sharp. For a dessert cheese, it is better to use a younger pecorino Romano as it is softer, moister, and a little less assertive. It is delicious with a full-bodied red wine.

Cheese with Mixed Salad

Formaggio con insalata mista

Taleggio cheese: This cheese, a stracchino type, is semi-soft but supple and springy feeling to the touch. It is mild but rich in flavor, full and creamy. It is made from cow's milk and is ripened for about two months. The interior color varies from creamy white to light yellow. It is similar to Bel Paese and comes from the Taleggio Valley in Lombardy.

For the salad:
1 large bunch arugula leaves, rinsed and dried
½ head radicchio, rinsed, dried, and sliced like coleslaw
2 heads Belgian endive, trimmed and each cut into 4 lengths
2 shallots, peeled and minced
4 tablespoons extra-virgin olive oil
2 tablespoons fresh lemon juice
1 teaspoon finely chopped orange zest
1 teaspoon minced fresh thyme

1. Put everything in a large bowl and toss lightly but well.

CHEESE TRAY WITH MOSTARDO, PARMIGIANO-REGGIANO, SMOKED MOZZARELLA, AND ROBIOLA

Formaggi misti con mostarda

<u>Mostardo di Cremona</u>: Considered one of the most remarkable of Italian preserves. It is a fruit mustard made of whole fruits, such as pears, little oranges, cherries, apricots, plums, figs. Melon, and pumpkin pieces; they are preserved in a sugar syrup flavored with mustard oil. This is surely an original combination of ingredients with a delicious flavor. A spoonful of it may be served with a piece of Parmigiano as a separate course.

<u>Parmigiano-Reggiano</u>: Most cognoscenti agree that there is nothing more delicious than a piece of aged, pale-straw-colored Parmigiano. It is the perfect cheese to end any meal with bread or fruit, especially pears, or with a taste of mostardo.

<u>Smoked Mozzarella</u>: This cheese is delicious if it is made from buffalo's milk, but also because it is smoked. The color of it is pale beige to a light reddish brown. It is extra special when freshly grated black pepper and a dash of olive oil are added to the sliced cheese.

<u>Robiola</u>: Wrapped in paper to protect its freshness, this cheese is actually a stracchino made from creamy milk. It is matured for a short time, usually less than two months. It is often mistaken for taleggio (not a bad mistake, by the way). Robiola is a small, square-shaped stracchino, weighing between three and four ounces.

SPECIAL PROVOLONE FROM BARI
Burratina di Andria

This cheese is basically a family member of the southern Italian cheese provolone, straw white in color with a smooth texture and an oval or cylindrical shape. Regular provolone comes in many sizes, and you've probably seen them hanging from the ceilings in Italian delicatessens. However, this variety is quite small and comes from the village of Andria, near Bari on the Adriatic coast. It is made with a lump of butter buried in the center of the cheese, so that when it is cut, it looks like a hard-cooked egg yolk. It is available in specialty cheese food stores. If you can't find this, use the small, cylindrical-shaped fresh mozzarellas kept in brine—each weighs about one-third pound.

3 small burrantinas or mozzarella, each weighing about ⅓ pound—they resemble beggar's purses
10 long lengths of chives, 2 more than needed – in case you break one
8 very small Italian parsley sprays
1 large carrot, cut into very thin julienne strips 1½ inches long
8 teaspoons extra-virgin olive oil

1. Carefully cut off the rounded sides of each small cheese oval lengthwise so the slices will lay flat after slicing. Make 3 slices of each cheese oval. You will have an extra slice for another use.

2. Wrap the chive lengths in a moist paper towel and microwave for 10 seconds. This makes the chive flexible for tying around the neck of the oval cheese. Just make a knot in tying and cut off the ends to trim the "ribbon" lengths. Do this with each of 8 cheese slices. Place each in the center of 8 individual plates, preferably white ones.

2. Arrange a parsley spray next to each, along with 3 or 4 pieces of carrots, criss-crossing them. Add some salt and freshly ground pepper and sprinkle 1 teaspoon oil over each. Do not refrigerate. This should be served at room temperature.

RICOTTA CHEESE FRITTERS WITH GINGER AND ROSEMARY
Fritelle di ricotta

Makes about 16

There are many dessert fritters in Italy, and this comes from Sardinia, where they are usually dipped in flour, egg, and crumbs and then deep-fried. I have eliminated that step and go directly from tablespoons of batter to hot oil for browning both sides. The ricotta, ginger, and rosemary are essential, although any plain cookie can be finely crushed and substituted for the vanilla cookies used in this adaptation.

1 pound ricotta cheese
½ pound amaretti, finely ground
½ cup sugar
2 cups ground vanilla cookies
¼ cup finely chopped candied ginger
1 tablespoon finely chopped rosemary
2 tablespoons unbleached all-purpose flour
2 eggs, beaten
6 tablespoons honey
Vegetable oil for frying
Confectioners' sugar for dusting
Small sprays of rosemary for garnish

1. Wrap the ricotta in several layers of cheesecloth (or a cloth towel) and put into a colander. Allow to drain for several hours at room temperature. Unwrap and put in a large bowl.

2. Add the ground amaretti, sugar, ground vanilla cookies, ginger, rosemary, flour, and the beaten eggs. Mix well to make a fine paste.

3. Heat the oil in a skillet (the oil should be ½ inch deep), and when it is hot, carefully place 8 individual tablespoons of batter into the skillet and fry until they turn golden, 2 to 3 minutes. As they brown, transfer to paper toweling. Repeat until all the fritters are made

4. To serve, place 2 fritters on each of 6 plates, dusting them lightly with the confectioners' sugar. It is easiest to put some sugar in a small sieve, place the sieve over the fritter, and tap the sieve lightly so some sugar will fall through. Add a tablespoon of honey, on the side, to each plate, and a small sprig of rosemary for garnishment. These should be served as soon as possible after frying.

SELECTION OF ITALIAN CHEESES
Selezione di formaggi: asiago, provolone affumicato, e pecorino siciliano

The most attractive way to serve cheese is to buy good-sized chunks of it, meaning at least one-half pound per piece, and arrange them on an attractive flat tray, each cheese with its own knife. There are numerous garnishments one can use to catch the eye, such as a low bed of long, freshly cut chives as a base for the cheeses, or a large leaf, washed, dried, and oiled, and so on.

Asiago: This splendid cheese gets its name from the small, pine-tree-filled village of Asiago in northern Italy. Originally, this cheese was made solely with ewe's milk, but the rocky terrain of Asiago could not provide adequate land for the sheep to graze, thereby making the herds unable to keep up with the tremendous demand for this village's prize cheese. These days, Asiago is produced with pasteurized cow's milk in the neighboring village of Veneto, which has brought forth several different versions, the most popular being Asiago d'Allevo. Made partly from skimmed milk and either salted dry or immersed in brine, this "aged" Asiago has a buffed-yellowish appearance, unmistakable sweet smell, and tiny, evenly distributed holes with a deep, dark-colored rind. It is often eaten as a dessert cheese if it is not too mature. After six months, the semi-matured cheese (*asiago da taglio*) develops a more piquant, saltier flavor and can still be eaten on its own. If the cheese is more than twelve months old, it is really only suitable for grating and cooking.

Smoked Provolone—*Provolone affumicato*: Straw white in color with a smooth, supple texture and an oval or cylindrical shape, provolone is a southern Italian cheese. It can be found hanging from the ceiling in almost all Italian food stores and in many delis in theUnited States. In the south of Italy, buffalo milk is often used, and the cheeses are also smoked. But it can be made from different types of milk and rennet; the strongest versions use goat rennet, which produces a spicy flavor. One interesting variety of provolone is called *provolone burrino*, and it comes from Calabria. It is made by enclosing a lump of unsalted butter in the center of the cheese, so, when sliced, it appears as a large, hard-boiled egg. If smoked provolone is not available, then look for a mild, fresh, unsmoked one, for once it becomes strong, it is better to be used in cooking, as in pizza and pasta preparations.

PECORINO SICILIANO—CANESTRATO:

All cheeses in Italy made with sheep's milk are called pecorino. They vary considerably in flavor and texture, all the way from soft and mild to hard and strong. The pecorino made in Sicily is also known as *canestrato* and is available all year for eating because of the stabilized nature of the cured cheese. In Sicily, it is usually sold unwrapped, and the cheese itself bears traces of the draining basket (*canestro* is the name of the draining basket). There is an interesting variety of it in Sicily that is studded with whole black peppercorns called *pecornio pepato*—you can imagine the peppery jolt in taste.

Chapter 10

BREADS AND PIZZAS

Bread is always served to accompany food in Italy. In fact, it often constitutes one of the dishes of the meal in the form of a *bruschetta* or *crostini*, toasted bread canapes; *pancotta*, a bread soup; *panzanella*, a bread salad; or a pizza. In some parts of Italy, such as in Florence, a *fettunta*, an appetizer, plays a more important role than pasta. Grilled or toasted bread rubbed with garlic, painted with olive oil, and sprinkled with coarse salt is called fettunta. It becomes a bruschetta when a topping is added, such as roasted bell peppers, chopped olives, or chopped fresh tomatoes and basil.

Bread is important to the Italian. It is toasted, buttered, and jammed for breakfast, added to soups to absorb the tasty sauces, and serves as a base for anchovies, tomatoes, tuna, salamis, mushrooms, olives, beans, and artichokes. And chicken liver. It is used as stuffing for vegetables, meats, fish, and poultry. It is gratineed for toppings of pasta and oven-baked vegetable dishes. I like it best when it is used as a device to mop up any Italian sauce.

Each region of Italy has a style of bread, and the repertoire goes beyond focaccia, flatbread, pizzas, and ciabattas. It doesn't matter what they are called, really; the ingredients (and shapes) in making these breads are unending. In Maremma (Tuscany), for example, there is a *schiaccia di ricotta*, an oval-shaped flatbread made with sheep's milk ricotta and dried fennel seeds. Further south, there is the same dough studded with pork cracklings. And still, there are breads made with raisins, olives, figs, nuts, marjoram, mascarpone, basil, and so on. There are large batches of bread dough used to make cheese focaccias and braided breads scented with rosemary. The cheese breads may use taleggio, stracchino, fontina, fresh mozzarella, or almost any other cheese.

On a daily basis, almost everyone in Italy buys or bakes bread. The country Tuscan bread is made without salt, since it is always served with salty cured meats. Southern Italian breads not only contain salt, but also have olive oil as an ingredient—a perfect combination with tomatoes. One of my favorites is *pane integrale*, a whole-wheat bread cooked classically in a wood oven. All Italian breads are firm textured with real crusts. The texture and flavor will of course depend on the type of flour and seasonings used, but nowhere will you find the soft, cottonlike, white sandwich textured bread one finds in US supermarkets.

Since bread is so important to the Italian table and needs to be replicated for the American table, I have chosen to include four basic breads: (1) a generic country loaf, (2) the popular smaller loaf called *ciabatta* (meaning "slippers") which can be cut into slices or cut across its length and stuffed with all kinds of foods as one might do with focaccia, (3) *focaccia*, not only popular all over Italy but in other countries, especially the United States, and (4) a crisp scented flatbread which is easy to make if one has the roller-type pasta machine.

Nota bene:

<u>Measuring flour</u>: It is important to aerate the flour before measurements are made—this simply means to transfer cupfuls of flour from their sack to a large bowl and then lightly stir the flour with a spoon to break up any clumping or packing of flour that occurs after packaging it. After the flour is "fluffed," spoon it into the measuring cup and level it off with a straight edge.

<u>Testing for the rise:</u> Put two fingers into the dough—if the indentations remain, the dough is properly risen; if the indentations disappear, the dough needs more rest to rise properly.

A COUNTRY LOAF
Pane casereccio

Makes 1 (2-pound) loaf

This is the typical bread one sees all over Italy, although let me assure you that the variations are many. This is a basic loaf that can be eaten with soups, used in soups, used to make bruschetta, used to dip into peppered oil, and eaten with pasta, which is not uncommon in Italy. This is one of the breads that are always brought to you in a restaurant and for which you are charged on your bill under the listing *coperto*. In the United States, you will use it in these ways but you will also toast it for breakfast, laden with butter and jam, and you will make sandwiches with it. It requires a starter, or sponge, or, as they call it in Italy, a *biga*. I like to make this in an electric mixer, but it can be done by hand.

For the starter, sponge, or biga:
1 cup warm water, 105°F
1 teaspoon sugar
2 packets (¼ ounce each) plus 1 scant teaspoon active dry yeast
1½ cups unbleached all-purpose flour plus 2 tablespoons for dusting

1. Pour the warm water in the large bowl of an electric mixer that has a paddle arm, and add the sugar. Sprinkle all of the yeast over it and blend on low speed until the yeast is dissolved.

2. Add 1½ cups flour and on low speed, stirring until smooth. With a rubber spatula, scrape down sides of the bowl. (It is best to stop the machine while doing this and start again immediately after scraping.) When the mixture is blended (only a matter of 2 or 3 minutes), remove the bowl from its stand. Sprinkle the 2 tablespoons of flour over the top and cover with a moistened cloth kitchen towel. (Take a clean, dry, cloth towel, wet it completely with water, squeeze it dry, and shake it out.) Let this rest for a minimum of 1 hour. Or you may refrigerate this overnight. Before proceeding to make the dough, check to see that this mixture is bubbly and tacky.

For the dough:
1 cup warm water
4 cups unbleached all-purpose flour
1 tablespoon good olive oil for the bowl

1. Add the warm water to the biga. Combine 1 cup flour with 1 tablespoon salt, mix well, and add it to the bowl. On low speed, stir with the paddle arm to mix. Add another cup of flour, and continue on low speed until blended. Add the third cup of flour, continue on low speed to mix and blend. All of this in step 1 should take 2 or 3 minutes. The dough will be quite sticky and tacky.

2. Put the remaining flour (1 cup) on a flat work surface and make a large well in it. Turn out the dough with the help of a rubber spatula and start kneading the bread, bringing in a little of the flour from the well (as in making pasta) until all the flour has been absorbed by the dough. You will notice that midway through this procedure, the dough becomes easier to knead. The kneading should take about 8 minutes. Form the dough into a ball.

3. Use the olive oil to coat a large bowl, and place the ball of dough in it, moving the ball around to coat all sides with oil. Cover with a moist cloth kitchen towel, and let the dough double in size, up to 60 minutes.

4. Lightly flour a work surface. Turn out dough onto it (it should fall out in 1 piece without the help of a rubber spatula, but if the spatula is needed, use it). Punch down the dough simply by kneading it 2 minutes. Shape the dough into a 15-inch elongated loaf, gently rolling it with the palms of your hands to the desired length. Line a large bake sheet (a cookie pan with sides works well for me) with parchment paper and transfer the loaf to it, laying it diagonally across the pan to gain the longer length of the pan. Again, cover with a moist cloth kitchen towel. Let it rest until it about doubles in volume, up to 60 minutes.

5. Preheat the oven to 500°F. (If using tiles or a bake stone, preheat either for a minimum of 30 minutes before putting on the loaf). Make 3 or 4 slashes on the diagonal on top of the loaf using a razor blade or very sharp knife, cutting almost ½ inch deep. As soon as this is put into the oven, spray liberally with water, and repeat the spray after 3 minutes, and again after 6 or 7. Bake at this high temperature 10 minutes. Lower the temperature to 425°F and bake until the bread is browned and sounds hollow when tapped on its backside, 40 to 45 minutes.

6. Cool the loaf on a rack and then wrap in a large dry kitchen towel.

CIABATTA, THE ITALIAN SLIPPER BREAD
Makes 2 loaves

Ciabatta, in Italian, means "slipper," and this bread is shaped more or less like a slipper. It is made with olive oil and often flavored with herbs, sun-dried tomatoes, or olives. The whole loaf can be cut from one end to the other and filled with meats, cheeses, tomatoes, olive oil, and whatever you wish to make a delicious sandwich. It is delicious sliced, toasted or not, for breakfast, and, if warmed, it is a perfect accompaniment to cheese.

½ teaspoon active dry yeast
3 tablespoons warm milk
¾ cup water, room temperature
2 teaspoons extra-virgin olive oil
1 cup biga, see below, made the day before
2½ cups unbleached all-purpose flour

1. Stir the yeast into the milk in the large bowl of an electric mixer with a paddle arm. Leave until puffy, about 10 minutes.

2. Add the water, oil, and the biga, and blend with the paddle arm. Combine the flour and 2 teaspoons coarse or sea salt and add to mixer. Stir with paddle attachment 2 to 3 minutes.

3. On low speed, let the paddle knead the dough 2 minutes. Raise to medium speed and knead 2 minutes more. Transfer to a lightly floured surface (adding as little flour as is possible) and knead by hand to make a smooth, springy dough.

4. Form a ball and place it in an oiled bowl, cover with a moist cloth kitchen towel, and let rise until doubled, about 1¼ hours. The dough will be bubbly and sticky.

5. Fit parchment paper into a baking pan large enough to receive the 2 loaves. Cut the dough in 2. Pat each into a small, flat rectangle, then stretch each into a large rectangle, about 5x10 inches. Place the 2 doughs on it and make dimples in each with your fingers. Cover with a moist cloth kitchen towel and let rise until puffy—almost 2 hours (the dough will not quite double but shall in the oven).

6. Preheat the oven to 425°F. Bake until done, about 20 to 25 minutes, spraying 3 times with water during the first 10 minutes of baking. Cool on racks.

To make the biga:

This will make a little over two cups. Use what you need and keep the remainder in the refrigerator, covered, up to three days.

¼ teaspoon active dry yeast
1 teaspoon sugar
¼ cup warm water
1 cup water, room temperature
2½ cups unbleached all-purpose flour

1. Stir the yeast and sugar in the warm water in the large bowl of an electric mixer and let stand until the mixture becomes puffy, about 8 minutes.

2. Stir in the remaining water and then the flour, 1 cup at a time.

3. Mix at low speed 2 minutes using the mixer paddle arm.

4. Remove to a lightly oiled bowl, cover with a moist cloth kitchen towel, and let rise at room temperature, 6 to 24 hours. Biga will triple in volume and still be wet and sticky when ready. Cover well and refrigerate until needed.

FOCACCIA

FOCACCIA WITH FRESH SAGE, OLIVE OIL, AND SALT
Focaccia col salvia, sale, e olio

Makes 1 flat 14-inch round or 11x17-inch rectangular loaf

This seasoned focaccia bread showcases sea salt, sage (salvia), and extra-virgin olive oil. In Florence, it's called *schiacciata*, in Bologna *piadina*, in America *focaccia*. No matter the name, this lightly seasoned pizza dough bread makes an especially delicious change from grilled bread. It is put on the table and eaten with and without other food. In Italy, a whole focaccia from a bakery weighs several pounds and is sold by weight, cut into manageable pieces. Various ingredients can be worked into the dough or serve as a topping—cheese, ham, olives, onions, oregano, pancetta, or rosemary. Compare the one presented here with the one served on Good Friday in Apulia, *focaccia del Venerdi Santi*—it is topped with anchovies, capers, chicory, fennel, and olives. For other occasions, it may be flavored with sun-dried tomatoes or herbs, but one of my favorites is the simple one with sea salt, an herb, and extra-virgin olive oil.

It seems to me that no one in Liguria eats regular bread. Focaccia reigns here, and it is present everywhere in this region, almost always herbed, or with olives, or just plain. This is a basic recipe, and feel free to change the herb to one you wish.

1 envelope active dry yeast
1 teaspoon sugar
1 cup warm water
3 to 3½ cups unbleached all-purpose flour
26 fresh sage leaves, 20 finely chopped, 6 left whole
¼ cup plus 2 tablespoons extra-virgin olive oil

1. Sprinkle the yeast and the sugar over the warm water and stir. Let stand 10 minutes.

2. Place 3 scant cups flour in a large bowl and make a well in the center. Add the yeast mixture, the chopped sage leaves, ¼ cup olive oil, and 1 teaspoon coarse salt. Work in the flour until a dough forms, then turn the dough out onto a floured work surface and knead until smooth and elastic, about 10 minutes, adding more flour as needed. Place the dough in a clean bowl, cover with a moist cloth kitchen towel, and let rise until doubled in volume, about 1 hour.

3. Punch the dough down, arrange in a ball form, and put back in the bowl. Let rise again until doubled in volume, about 1 hour.

4. Brush a 14-inch pizza pan or an 11x17-inch jelly-roll pan generously with olive oil. Gently punch down the dough, fitting it in the pan, and brush all over with the remaining olive oil. Arrange 6 sage leaves in a decorative fashion to express your creativity. Sprinkle with 1 teaspoon of coarse salt. Let rise for 30 minutes.

5. Preheat the oven to 450°F. Bake the focaccia until nicely browned, about 15 minutes. Serve warm.

SEMOLINA FLATBREAD WITH ROSEMARY

Makes 12 strips, 3 to 5 inches wide by 12 to 16 inches long

These thin slices of crispy bread will keep in a crisper for up to two weeks. They can be served with antipasto, soups, and main courses. Some say they originate from the Greek phyllo, others from the Sardinian sheet music bread; no matter, these are now so easy to make because of the pasta machine and can be made days ahead.

2 cups semolina flour
2 cups unbleached all-purpose flour
2 tablespoons finely chopped fresh rosemary
1 cup and 2 tablespoons water
5 tablespoons extra-virgin olive oil and more for brushing

1. Combine the flours, 1½ teaspoons sea salt, and the rosemary in the bowl of a processor. Pulse 4 or 5 times.

2. With the machine on, pour the water and oil through the feed tube and stop just as a ball of dough is formed. Rest 2 minutes and pulse on and off for about 30 seconds, only until the dough is smooth. Do not overwork the dough.

3. Remove dough from bowl. Shape into a ball, cover with plastic, and refrigerate 60 minutes.

4. When ready to bake, preheat the oven to 450°F. Divide the dough into 12 even-sized pieces. Keep them well covered. Lightly flour your hands and flatten a piece of dough just enough to get it through the widest opening of the pasta maker. Run it through the rollers again and then decrease the opening size by 3 notches; roll through the dough and repeat once again. Think of making large lasagna strips. As each strip is rolled out, lay it on a lightly oiled cookie sheet or other baking sheet. Repeat until all pieces are rolled. Bake flatbreads about 8 to 9 minutes. Check at 8 minutes for doneness. The flatbread should appear lightly browned at the edges, with 1 or 2 blisters. Remove from oven.

5 As they come out of the oven, cool a minute or 2, lightly brush oil on them, and then sprinkle lightly with coarse salt.

Crostini

Crostini, basically, are Italian canapes consisting of "toasted" slices of bread, spread with various toppings such as shrimp butter, truffles, or liver pate. They are not as large as bruschetti, as they are used differently. Crostini are smaller and thinner pieces of bread that are buttered or oiled and baked until they become pale golden. Then they can be spread with pates and so on. They can also be cut into various shapes: rounds, squares, triangles, ovals, and stars.

GRILLED BREAD WITH OIL
Bruschetta

Once a poor man's dish, grilled garlic bread has become even more popular now that it is called by its Italian name, *bruschetta*, which comes from *bruscare*, meaning to roast over coals. I still like to grill the bread over a charcoal fire or a gas-fired grill, though it is much easier to broil it. Bruschetta is always made with fresh garlic, even when the bread is not roasted over coals. Ideally, bruschetta should be made with *pane integrale* (Italian whole-wheat bread), which is now available in many specialty food shops, not just Italian bakeries.

4 slices (each 1 inch thick) Italian bread, preferably whole wheat
2 large cloves garlic, peeled and cut in ½
2 tablespoons extra-virgin olive oil

1. Preheat the grill or broiler.

2. Place the bread slices on the grill or broiler rack and grill until crisp and golden brown, 1 to 2 minutes per side.

3. Rub the cut side of the garlic over 1 side of each piece of toast, preferably the side that last faced the heat source.

4. Carefully brush the oil liberally over the garlic side of the toasts. Sprinkle with salt and pepper and keep warm until ready to serve, no more than 1 hour.

Nota bene: *Crostini* are smaller, thinner pieces of bread that are used for canapes. They may be fried in butter (and oil, if you wish), or put on a baking try and baked dry at 350°F, 12 to 15 minutes. They can be broiled also, but you have to stand by all the time to be sure they do not burn. These dry pieces of bread can receive cheeses, peppers, olive pastes, and any other suitable food for a canapé.

FRESH BREAD CRUMBS
Pangrattato

Makes about 2½ cups

Although supermarket shelves are filled with Italian-style bread crumbs, it is best to use homemade crumbs. If you don't have Italian bread, use a rich white bread and crumb it in a food processor. You can vary the herb and spice flavoring to your liking. If you're not going to use them in the next week or two, freeze them.

4½-inch slices Italian bread, crusts removed, to make 2½ cups crumbs
2 tablespoons finely chopped parsley
2 tablespoons extra-virgin olive oil
2 tablespoons butter

1. Cut bread into 1-inch pieces and put in processor. Pulse on/off about 1 minute to make fine crumbs.

2. Add parsley, salt, and freshly ground pepper to crumbs, Toss well. Set aside.

3. Heat oil and butter in a large skillet. When bubbly and hot, add the crumb mixture and sauté, stirring frequently, until the crumbs take on some color and become crisp, about 10 to 12 minutes.

4. Use immediately or when cooled, or store in an airtight jar, refrigerated, until needed.

FOCACCIA WITH MARJORAM AND OLIVE OIL
Focaccia col maggiorana, sale e olio

Makes 1 flat 14-inch round or 11x17-inch rectangular loaf

This seasoned focaccia bread showcases sea salt, marjoram (*maggiorana*), and extra-virgin olive oil. In Florence, it's called *schiacciata*, in Bologna *piadina*, in America *focaccia*. No matter the name, this lightly seasoned pizza dough bread makes an especially delicious change from grilled bread. It is put on the table and eaten with and without other food. In Italy, a whole focaccia from a bakery weighs several pounds and is sold by weight, cut into manageable pieces. Various ingredients can be worked into the dough or serve as a topping—cheese, ham, olives, onions, oregano, pancetta, or rosemary. Compare the one presented here with the one served on Good Friday in Apulia, *focaccia del Venerdi Santi*—it is topped with anchovies, capers, chicory, fennel, and olives. For other occasions, it may be flavored with sun-dried tomatoes or herbs, but one of my favorites is the simple one with sea salt, an herb, and extra-virgin olive oil.

It seems to me that no one in Liguria eats regular bread. Focaccia reigns here and it is present everywhere in this region, almost always herbed, or with olives, or just plain.

1 envelope active dry yeast
1 teaspoon sugar
1 cup warm water
3 to 3½ cups all-purpose flour
2 tablespoons freshly chopped marjoram
¼ cup plus 2 tablespoons extra-virgin olive oil
2 teaspoons coarse salt

1. Sprinkle the yeast and the sugar over the warm water and stir. Let stand 10 minutes.

2. Place 3 scant cups flour in a large bowl and make a well in the center. Add the yeast mixture, 1 tablespoon marjoram, ¼ cup olive oil, and 1 teaspoon coarse salt. Work in the flour until a dough forms, then turn the dough out onto a floured work surface and knead until smooth and elastic, about 10 minutes, adding more flour as needed. Place the dough in a clean bowl, cover with a towel, and let rise until doubled in volume, about 1 hour.

3. Punch the dough down, arrange a ball form and put back in the bowl. Let rise again until doubled in volume, about 1 hour.

4. Brush a 14-inch pizza pan or an 11x17-inch jelly-roll pan generously with olive oil. Gently punch down the dough, fitting

it in the pan, and brush all over with the remaining olive oil. Sprinkle with 1 teaspoon of salt and the remaining tablespoon of marjoram. Let rise for 30 minutes.

5. Preheat the oven to 450°F. Bake the focaccia until nicely browned, about 15 minutes. Serve warm.

SEMOLINA FLATBREAD WITH ROSEMARY

Makes 12 strips, 3 to 5 inches wide by 12 to 16 inches long

These thin slices of crispy bread will keep in a crisper for up to two weeks. They can be served with antipasto, soups, and main courses. Some say they originate from the Greek phyllo, others from the Sardinian sheet music bread; no matter, these are now so easy to make because of the pasta machine and can be made days ahead.

2 cups semolina flour
2 cups unbleached all-purpose flour
2 tablespoons finely chopped fresh rosemary
1 cup and 2 tablespoons water
5 tablespoons extra-virgin olive oil and more for brushing

1. Combine the flours, 1½ teaspoons sea salt, and the rosemary in the bowl of a processor. Pulse 4 or 5 times.

2. With the machine on, pour the water and oil through the feed tube and stop just as a ball of dough is formed. Rest 2 minutes and pulse on and off for about 30 seconds, only until the dough is smooth. Do not overwork the dough.

3. Remove dough from bowl. Shape into a ball, cover with plastic, and refrigerate 60 minutes.

4. When ready to bake, preheat the oven to 450°F. Divide the dough into 12 even-sized pieces. Keep them well covered. Lightly flour your hands and flatten a piece of dough just enough to get it through the widest opening of the pasta maker. Run it through the rollers again and then decrease the opening size by 3 notches; roll through the dough and repeat once again. Think of making large lasagna strips. As each strip is rolled out, lay it on a lightly oiled cookie sheet or other baking sheet. Repeat until all pieces are rolled. Bake flatbreads about 8 to 9 minutes. Check at 8 minutes for doneness. The flatbread should appear lightly browned at the edges, with 1 or 2 blisters. Remove from oven.

5 As they come out of the oven, cool a minute or 2, lightly brush oil on them, and then sprinkle lightly with coarse salt.

Crostini

Crostini, basically, are Italian canapes consisting of "toasted" slices of bread, spread with various toppings such as shrimp butter, truffles, or liver pate. They are not as large as bruschetti, as they are used differently. Crostini are smaller and thinner pieces of bread that are buttered or oiled and baked until they become pale golden. Then they can be spread with pates and so on. They can also be cut into various shapes: rounds, squares, triangles, ovals, and stars.

FOCACCIA WITH MARJORAM AND OLIVE OIL

Focaccia col maggiorana, sale e olio

Makes 1 flat 14-inch round or 11x17-inch rectangular loaf

This seasoned focaccia bread showcases sea salt, marjoram (*maggiorana*), and extra-virgin olive oil. In Florence, it's called *schiacciata*, in Bologna *piadina*, in America *focaccia*. No matter the name, this lightly seasoned pizza dough bread makes an especially delicious change from grilled bread. It is put on the table and eaten with and without other food. In Italy, a whole focaccia from a bakery weighs several pounds and is sold by weight, cut into manageable pieces. Various ingredients can be worked into the dough or serve as a topping—cheese, ham, olives, onions, oregano, pancetta, or rosemary. Compare the one presented here with the one served on Good Friday in Apulia, *focaccia del Venerdì Santi*—it is topped with anchovies, capers, chicory, fennel, and olives. For other occasions, it may be flavored with sun-dried tomatoes or herbs, but one of my favorites is the simple one with sea salt, an herb, and extra-virgin olive oil.

It seems to me that no one in Liguria eats regular bread. Focaccia reigns here and it is present everywhere in this region, almost always herbed, or with olives, or just plain.

1 envelope active dry yeast
1 teaspoon sugar
1 cup warm water
3 to 3½ cups all-purpose flour
2 tablespoons freshly chopped marjoram
¼ cup plus 2 tablespoons extra-virgin olive oil
2 teaspoons coarse salt

1. Sprinkle the yeast and the sugar over the warm water and stir. Let stand 10 minutes.

2. Place 3 scant cups flour in a large bowl and make a well in the center. Add the yeast mixture, 1 tablespoon marjoram, ¼ cup olive oil, and 1 teaspoon coarse salt. Work in the flour until a dough forms, then turn the dough out onto a floured work surface and knead until smooth and elastic, about 10 minutes, adding more flour as needed. Place the dough in a clean bowl, cover with a towel, and let rise until doubled in volume, about 1 hour.

3. Punch the dough down, arrange a ball form and put back in the bowl. Let rise again until doubled in volume, about 1 hour.

4. Brush a 14-inch pizza pan or an 11x17-inch jelly-roll pan generously with olive oil. Gently punch down the dough, fitting it in the pan, and brush all over with the remaining olive oil. Sprinkle with 1 teaspoon of salt and the remaining tablespoon of marjoram. Let rise for 30 minutes.

5. Preheat the oven to 450°F. Bake the focaccia until nicely browned, about 15 minutes. Serve warm.

THE FLAT BREAD OF EMILIA-ROMAGNA
Piadine

Makes 8 small rounds of bread

One sees *piadine* snack stands all over the region. The flatbread is eaten with meals or as snacks, often sandwiched with salami, prosciutto, Swiss chard, spinach, or cheese.

3¼ cups all-purpose unbleached flour
⅓ teaspoon baking soda
4 tablespoons good lard, cold
⅔ cup warm water
2 tablespoons olive oil for cooking

1. Preheat the oven to 225°F. In the bowl of a processor, combine the flour, 1 teaspoon salt, and baking soda. Process to a count of 4. Add the lard and process to a count of 25. Add the water and process to a count of 5—only to blend in the liquid (like cooked oatmeal). Turn dough onto a lightly floured work top.

2. Knead 5 or 6 times to gather into a ball. Cut the ball into 8 pieces and roll each to a 7-inch circle.

3. Cook, 1 at a time, on a griddle, in a heavy cast iron skillet, or in a stainless steel skillet with a copper bottom (to distribute heat evenly). First add a teaspoon of oil to the selected cooking vessel, put pan over high- moderate heat, place a piadina in it, and cook about 2 minutes. Turn over and cook the other side 30 to 60 seconds. When done, remove bread from the griddle or skillet, put it in a baking dish, cover with foil, and place in the oven to keep warm.

4. Repeat to finish "baking" the bread. Serve it warm, whole, or cut into wedges.

TWO PIZZAS

Pizza reached the height of its popularity during the *Borboni* (Bourbon) rule in the Kingdom of the Two Sicilies, of which Naples was the capital. It was the food of the *lazzeroni*—of the people. Pizza is a simple food in that it has no mystical or religious meaning as do many other Italian foods. It does not represent money, or power, or fertility. It is the ultimate fast food, ancient for sure, but with such appeal in modern times. It has grown in popularity outside Naples and Italy for these reasons, and also because anyone can add anything to it once a dough is made. No other food is so egalitarian.

Making and serving a pizza can seem like an easy task, and it is, but there are some preparation steps to pay attention to. For example, if a pizza dough fails, it is most likely because the water added was too hot. It is better to err on the cool side, as kneading the dough will help it rise later. Also, kneading the dough should be thorough. In other words, knead the dough until it is smooth and satiny. The dough, while kneading, needs to rest every once in awhile, so knead and rest, knead and rest. To achieve a crisp cooked pizza, it is best to use a pizza stone and pizza paddle. They are available in shops that sell kitchen equipment. See sources on page 383. In adding toppings to the dough, be sure liquids and juices have been strained out of the particular toppings—if using ricotta or mozzarella, put them in a colander with cheesecloth and let them drain for a half to one hour before using. If applying tomato sauce, use just a thin coating of it on the dough, and always brush some oil on the top of the dough before adding anything else. Pizza should be eaten as it comes out of the oven (after a few minutes' rest), and the best way to cut it is with a pizza wheel. If pizza has to be reheated, put some slices on the stone which has been preheated in the oven at a temperature of 400°F. Do not cover it, as it will become mushy.

To make pizza dough:
3 cups unbleached all-purpose flour
1 tablespoon sugar
1 packet rapid-rise yeast (¼ ounce)
1¼ cups lukewarm water, no warmer than 105°F
2 tablespoons garlic-flavored oil, see below

To make the dough in the processor
1. Put the flour, 1 scant tablespoon salt, sugar, and yeast granules in the bowl of the processor. Pulse to a count of 4.

2. Combine the water and the oil and feed it into the bowl through the feed tube. Stop as soon as a ball of dough is formed. Let this dough rest 2 minutes.

3. Process dough for 1 minute, but stop the machine every 15 seconds for a few seconds. (This 1 minute of processing takes the place of manually kneading the dough).

4. Turn the dough out on a lightly floured surface and form a ball. Put it into a bowl that has been lightly oiled. Turn the dough over to coat it, cover with a moist cloth kitchen towel, and let it rise in a warm, draft-free place. Let it rise to 2 times its size, about 40 to 60 minutes. To test for rising, put 2 fingers into the dough—if the indentations remain, the dough is properly risen; if the indentations disappear, the dough needs more rest to rise properly.

5. Turn out the dough, form it quickly into a ball, and return it to the bowl for a second rise (this is important—do not shortcut this step.) When properly risen the second time, turn it out into the pizza pan (with some cornmeal to loosely cover the bottom), and use your hands and fingers to fit the dough into the pan. If properly risen, it will stretch into place easily. If the dough resists, give it a rest for a minute or 2 and continue fitting it into the pan. Preheat oven to 450°F. Add the topping, let the pizza sit uncooked for a couple of minutes, and then bake 15 minutes.

To make dough manually:
1. Combine the dry ingredients, add the water and the oil, and mix with a wooden spoon. When it becomes difficult to move the spoon, start kneading with floured hands on a lightly floured surface. Knead for 5 minutes, rest for 2, knead 5 minutes, and rest for 2 until a smooth, satiny dough is achieved.

2. Place in an oiled bowl, cover with a damp towel, and allow dough to rise in a warm place until twice its size. Punch down the dough and put it back in the bowl for another rise. To test for proper rising, put 2 fingers into dough—if the indentations remain, the dough is ready for the next step; if the indentations disappear, the dough is not ready and should be left to rise further.

3. Fit the dough in a pizza pan with a little cornmeal strewn over the bottom of the pan. Do this with your hands—do not use a rolling pin. (When the dough has risen properly, it will stretch easily to the rim of the pan—if there is any resistance, let the dough rest a minute or 2 and then proceed.) Preheat oven to 450°F. Let the dough rest again 5 minutes before adding any topping. Add topping, put in to bake until golden and crispy, about 15 minutes.

SWEET PEPPER PIZZA WITH RICOTTA SALATA

Pizza con peperoni e ricotta salata

Minced garlic, or even thinly sliced garlic, put on top of the pizza before baking will usually darken or burn and become bitter. Some pizza makers like to add finely minced fresh garlic to the topping of a pizza after it has come out of the oven, but raw garlic dominates the other flavors in the topping and will "burn" the inside of one's mouth. The best way to get a good garlic flavor is by adding some drops of garlic-flavored oil to the topping. Here are two pizzas built on this principle which are totally delicious, easy to make, and provide a fabulous one-dish meal. Just add a fresh green salad with your favorite salad dressing.

2 tablespoons extra-virgin olive oil for sautéing peppers

2 bell peppers, 1 red, 1 yellow or orange, cored, ribs and seeds removed, and cut into thinnest slivers possible

¼ pound grated ricotta salata

1 tablespoon each finely chopped fresh oregano (or 1 teaspoon dried, crushed), fresh parsley, and fresh chives

1 (14- to 15-inch) pizza dough (see above), ready to receive a topping

1 tablespoon garlic-flavored oil, see below

1. Heat the olive oil in a large skillet over low heat and add the peppers. Toss lightly but well. Cover, and gently sauté until the peppers become soft, about 15 minutes.

2. In a small bowl, combine the grated cheese and the herbs and toss lightly but well.

3. Preheat oven to 450°F. Brush some of the garlic-flavored oil over the pizza. Arrange the peppers on top, covering the pizza, and sprinkle the herb-flavored cheese overall. Spoon 1 tablespoon of the garlic-flavored oil over the pizza. Liberally add freshly ground pepper over all. Put in the oven and bake until golden and crisp, about 15 minutes.

BROCCOLI RAPE AND GOAT CHEESE PIZZA
Pizza con broccoli rapa e formaggio di capra

This is a favorite of mine. The combination of flavors is divine. The proper way to prepare broccoli rape is described on page 64; please take a minute to read this.

¼ pound goat cheese, crumbled
¼ pound mozzarella, cut into smallest dice or grated through large teeth of a cheese grater
1 tablespoon finely chopped fresh rosemary
2 tablespoons plus garlic-flavored oil, see below
1 (14- to 15-inch) pizza dough, see above, ready to receive topping
1 bunch broccoli rape, trimmed, steamed, and cut into ½-inch pieces, including stalks, drained and dried
Pinches of red pepper flakes, optional

1. Combine the 2 cheeses and the rosemary and a liberal amount of freshly ground pepper. Toss lightly but well. Set aside.

2. Brush some of the garlic-flavored oil over the pizza dough and carefully arrange the cooked and cut broccoli rape over the surface of the pizza.

3. Preheat oven to 450°F. Sprinkle the cheese over the broccoli and dot with more garlic-flavored oil (about 1 tablespoon). Add the optional red pepper flakes, if you wish. Bake until golden and crisp, about 15 minutes.

To make garlic flavored oil:
15 large cloves garlic, peeled
1 cup extra-virgin olive oil

1. In a small sauce pan, add the garlic and oil, and, over very low heat, cook over the lowest simmer possible until the garlic turns golden; this could take up to 20 minutes. If not ready to use, cool and then put into a small jar just large enough to hold the garlic and oil, and refrigerate. If ready to use, drain and use the oil. If refrigerated, the oil must always be brought to room temperature.

AN OPTIONAL THIRD TOPPING: ARTICHOKES, MORTADELLA, AND FONTINA
Pizza con carciofi, mortadella, e fontina

Canned artichokes work well here, and it is not necessary to buy those packed in olive oil. If they are packed in water, rinse them several times to wash away the saltiness, and dry them well before combining with the other topping ingredients. If they are packed in oil, simply drain them well; do not rinse them.

1 can (13¾ ounces—5 to 7 count) artichoke hearts, finely chopped
¼ pound thinly sliced mortadella, finely chopped
½ cup finely shredded fontina cheese
2 tablespoons garlic-flavored oil

1. Preheat oven to 450°F.
2. Combine these ingredients with 1 teaspoon salt and freshly ground pepper, and spread them over the pizza dough before putting it into the oven. Bake until golden and crispy, about 15 minutes.

Chapter 11

DESSERTS

A meal in Italy usually ends with a strong espresso. Restaurants, however, seem to always offer desserts, probably for the American and other tourists. All over Italy we see beautiful and exciting pastry shops. Invariably, if you stand in front of one sweet shop, you will surely go in and buy cookies or whatever appeals to you. Italians keep their shops going because they buy from them. They like their sweets either midmorning or midafternoon or late at night, unless it is an important holiday. Then, the sweets are rolled out, many of them being homemade, such as the *zeppole* in Naples, the fritters in Treviso, the biscotti in Prato, the *gialetti* (sweet semolina cookies with *grana* and honey), the apple streudels in Bergamo, and the *croccante di meringa, pinoli e mandorle*—meringue cookies made all over Italy. Then there are all kinds of gelati, the thousands of *torta di nonna*—cakes made by Grandma—the fruit compotes, the vast majority of puddings, and various tarts. However and whenever sweets are eaten, Italy is dessert country. Ask any nun you run into, she'll tell you her favorite confection.

CAKES

MARIA MICHELE'S SPECIAL CHEESECAKE

Torta di formaggio alla Maria Michele

Makes 1 (9- or 10-inch) cake

Maria loves this cake, and she makes it several ways. She will add the slightest bit of candied lemon or orange peel, or a piece of vanilla bean, or a spoonful of a liqueur to alter the taste of the cake to her mood.

2½ pounds fresh ricotta
5 eggs
1½ cups sugar
1 teaspoon finely chopped candied lemon zest (or orange) or ½ finely grated fresh vanilla bean or 1 tablespoon fruit brandy

1. Preheat the oven to 400°F. Process the ricotta until it is smooth.

2. Beat the eggs, sugar, and 1 of the flavors until well blended. Add this to the ricotta a tablespoon at a time.

3. Butter a springform pan and line the bottom of it with parchment paper. Pour the filling into it and place it in the oven. Immediately turn the oven down to 350°F. Bake 30 minutes. The cake will still be soft in the middle. Turn off the oven and leave the cake in the oven 15 minutes. Open the door and let the cake sit in the opened oven 15 minutes longer. This should be served warm.

ORANGE RING CAKE, IN A MODERN MANNER
Ciambellone all'arancia

Serves 8 to 10

Ciambellone is a Florentine orange-flavored cake that is usually served at teatime. It has been enjoyed by the Florentines for many years and one can still find it in some pastry shops, but I had difficulty finding it. Perhaps it is not as popular as it used to be. Here is an updated version that is very tasty at teatime, or as a dessert, served with a dollop of whipped cream. The secret of this cake lies in the syrup.

To make the cake:
1 cup butter, softened
1 cup sugar
4 egg yolks, room temperature
1 cup sour cream
2 tablespoons finely chopped orange zest
2 cups all-purpose flour
1 teaspoon each baking powder and baking soda
4 egg whites, room temperature

1. Preheat oven to 325°F. Cream the butter and sugar until well blended. Add the egg yolks, sour cream, and the zest. Beat until light and fluffy and until a ribbon is formed when the beaters are raised.

2. In a large bowl, sift together the flour, baking powder, and soda. Fold this into the butter and sugar mixture. Beat the egg whites until stiff, but not dry, and fold them into the mixture.

3. Pour the batter into an oiled (use vegetable) and floured 9-inch tube pan. Bake 1 hour. Remove the cake and let it sit 15 to 20 minutes. When the pan is cool enough to handle, very carefully loosen around the edge of the cake with a sharp knife, and invert the cake onto a cake platter.

To make the syrup:
Juice of 1 orange
Juice of 1 lemon
¾ cup sugar
¼ cup orange liqueur

1. Gently boil these ingredients in a small saucepan until the mixture turns to syrup, about 5 minutes.

To assemble and serve:
Syrup, above
Cake, above,
1 cup heavy cream, whipped
4 thin slices of orange, seeded, cut in halves

1. Spoon the syrup over the cake and let it soak in. Serve ½-inch slices with whipped cream and a ½ orange slice.

CHOCOLATE MOCHA RICOTTA CAKE
Torta di ricotta al cioccolate

Serves 6 plus

Ricotta is used in cooking all over Italy in both sweet and savory preparations. *Ricotta* means "recooked" because the remaining whey from hard cheeses with some fresh milk is heated to produce a white curd cheese—a cheese with a wonderfully soft texture. When ricotta is freshly made, it is usually put into baskets to drain—the basket shape and markings are known as *cestelli*, meaning little baskets.

In Italy, cheesecake is made in every *pasticceria*. The Italians love it. They love ricotta so much so, they eat it fresh with some honey and thyme (see page 366). If at all possible, try to find a cheese shop near you that makes fresh ricotta—it is surely a different product than the one in plastic containers on supermarket shelves.

15 ounces whole ricotta
½ cup sugar plus 1 tablespoon sugar
¼ cup flour
2 eggs plus 2 egg whites
1 teaspoon vanilla extract
6 tablespoons cocoa powder plus extra for dusting
1 tablespoon espresso granules
1 tablespoon butter

1. Put several thicknesses of cheesecloth into a colander and place the ricotta in it. Cover with more cheesecloth. Weight it lightly and let sit in a bowl in the refrigerator for 3 hours to drain. (This may sit overnight, but be sure the ricotta is covered.)

2. Preheat the oven to 350°F. Add the drained ricotta, ¼ cup of sugar, flour, 2 whole eggs, vanilla, cocoa powder, and espresso granules in a processor bowl and combine until smooth. Do not overprocess. Empty this mixture into a large bowl and set aside.

3. Using 1 tablespoon butter, coat a springform pan (6 inches) and sprinkle 1 tablespoon of sugar over all. Turn pan over slightly; tap it gently to remove any excess sugar. Set this aside.

4. Combine the egg whites and ¼ cup sugar in a large bowl; place it over simmering water and whisk for several minutes until the sugar is dissolved. Off the heat, beat with an electric hand mixer for about 10 minutes or until the whites form stiff peaks. Carefully fold about ⅓ of the meringue into the ricotta, then another ⅓, and then the final ⅓. Transfer to the prepared bake pan. Bake until the center is firm, about 40 minutes. Remove from the oven, set on a cooling rack for 15 or 20 minutes, remove ring, dust with cocoa powder (be sure to use a small strainer to do this), and serve.

LEMONY APPLE CAKE
Torta di mele al limone

Serves 6 to 8

This cake is from Liguria, and it is best if it is served warm. It calls for a dollop of whipped cream, and you should whip the cream with some lemon zest to get the true Ligurian taste of freshness.

9 tablespoons butter, melted
1½ pound apples (Golden Delicious, Cortland, or Rome Beauty), peeled, cored, and sliced
Zest and juice from 1 lemon
¼ teaspoon lemon extract
4 eggs
¾ cup confectioners' sugar plus 1 teaspoon for sprinkling
1¼ cups all-purpose flour
1 teaspoon baking powder
½ cup heavy cream, whipped

1. Preheat oven to 350°F. Use 1 tablespoon of melted butter to grease a 9-inch, 10-inch, or 11-inch springform pan. Put the apple slices in a bowl and pour on the lemon juice. Add the lemon extract. Toss well.

2. Put the eggs, sugar, and lemon zest (reserve a pinch for the whipped cream) in a bowl and whisk until the mixture becomes thick and mousselike, up to 5 minutes. The whisk should leave a trail.

3. Combine ½ of the flour, the baking powder, and some salt and sift it over the whisked eggs. Pour the remaining 8 tablespoons of melted butter to the sides of the bowl, and fold with a rubber spatula. Sift the remaining flour and fold that in also. Add the lemony apples and fold in carefully. Pour this mixture into the prepared pan.

4. Bake about 60 minutes or until a wooden skewer comes out clean. (Check after 50 minutes if using the larger pan.) Remove from the oven and let rest for 10 minutes. Remove the sides of the springform pan. Sprinkle with the confectioners' sugar (using a small strainer). Serve the cake warm with whipped cream to which has been added some lemon zest.

SAMBUCA FLAVORED COCOA ROLL
Torta di cioccolato con Sambuca

Serves 4

This will serve more than four people, but it will keep in the refrigerator for up to three days. It may also be frozen up to one month.

6 eggs, separated
1 cup sugar
6 ounces dark sweet chocolate
3 tablespoons Sambuca plus 1 tablespoon for whipped cream
3 tablespoons cocoa powder
1 cup heavy cream

1. Whip the egg yolks with ¾ cup sugar until they form a ribbon when the beaters are raised. Preheat oven to 350°F.

2. Slowly melt the chocolate in the top of a double boiler pan just until it is smooth. Add the Sambuca, stir to combine, and allow to cool until it is lukewarm. Blend into the yolk mixture.

3. Beat the egg whites until they hold firm peaks, and fold them into to yolk/chocolate mixture.

4. Butter a cookie sheet, about 9½x13½ inches. Cover the bottom with waxed paper and butter the waxed paper. Spread the batter over this, smoothing it with a rubber spatula. Bake 10 minutes, reduce heat to 300°F, and bake 5 minutes. Check for doneness by inserting a toothpick into the cake; if it comes out dry, the cake is cooked. Do not overcook the cake. Remove from the oven and cover with a damp towel.

5. When the cake is cool, remove the cloth and loosen the cake from the baking sheet. Dust with 1½ tablespoons of cocoa, using a small sieve. Turn the cake out onto another piece of waxed paper, and carefully peel off the buttered waxed paper from the bottom (which is now on top); be careful not to tear the cake.

6. Whip the heavy cream with the remaining 1½ tablespoons cocoa powder, ¼ cup sugar, and 1 tablespoon Sambuca. Spread this over the cake evenly and roll up jelly-roll style. Sprinkle with more cocoa powder before slicing and serving.

A RICH VENETIAN NUT CAKE
Stranglapreti

Serves 6 plus

It is a common practice in Italy to devise amusing nicknames for food, often poking fun at the clergy. *Strangolapreti* means, literally, "priest stranglers." According to most Italian men, the explanation for this is simple: priests love to eat and they eat a lot. This term is also applied to pasta preparations of many kinds, all over Italy. Legend has it that a priest who loved a certain spinach dumpling gobbled them down so fast he choked to death. Let's hope this is not the case with this rich nut cake.

½ cup golden raisins
½ cup rum
1 sponge cake, crumbed (see below)
½ cup diced, candied peel (lemon or orange)
½ cup of each: walnut pieces, chopped almonds, and pine nuts
1 cup sugar
½ cup water
2 tablespoons butter for baking pan
1 cup heavy cream, whipped

1. Put the raisins and rum in a small bowl and marinate 30 minutes. Preheat oven to 350°F. Crumb the sponge cake by cutting it into 1-inch pieces and processing briefly to make large crumbs.

2. In a large bowl, add the crumbed sponge cake, candied peel, nuts, and the soaked raisins and any rum in the small bowl. Mix lightly with splayed fingers.

3. Combine the sugar and water and, over medium heat, bring to boil. Stir frequently until the sugar is dissolved. Pour some of this into the large bowl, and mix again in order to bring the mixture together. Add the remaining syrup to do this.

4. Liberally butter an 8- or 9-inch springform pan, and put the mixture in it. Use a rubber spatula or your hands to press and smooth out the mixture. Bake 30 minutes. Cool, slice, and serve with whipped cream.

TO MAKE THE SPONGE CAKE:
Makes 1 (9-inch) cake

This cake is called by the French word *genoise*, but in actuality, it is a cake from Genoa, and that name should be *genoese*; in other words, Italians feel the French named the cake after the Genoese, for that is where the cake came from. Many people simply call it sponge cake.

4 eggs
⅔ cup sugar
1 cup sifted all-purpose flour (sift flour and then measure)
½ cup (8 tablespoons) butter, melted and cooled

1. Preheat the oven to 350°F. Put the eggs and sugar in a rounded bowl and beat with an electric mixer. Put the bowl over simmering water, without touching the water, and continue to beat until the mixture is warmed and doubled in volume, about 5 minutes. Remove from the simmering water and keep beating until the mixture has cooled.

2. Fold in the flour and the butter. It is best to do this with a rubber spatula. Do not overwork the mixture—the goal is simply to incorporate the flour and butter. Transfer, with the help of the spatula, to a well-buttered 9-inch cake pan, and bake until the center feels firm, about 40 minutes. Invert and turn out onto a flat dish.

APOLLINARE'S CHOCOLATE ROLL WITH ZABAGLIONE SAUCE

Salame di cioccolata con salsa allo zabaglione

Serves 10

Andrea Scotacci says he changes his menus frequently but this dessert remains on all of them. "Per certo, e molto dolce ma e molto delizioso," says Andrea (For certain, it is very rich but very delicious). Massimo and Simone, two of Andrea's assistants, made a number of suggestions. Use tea biscuits (*biscotti da te*), said one, or use short pastry biscuits (*biscotti di pasta frolla*), said the other, to make it even richer. They both agreed that butter cookies called *frollini* or cat's tongue cookies (*lingue di gatto*) would be good choices. These young men were making this dessert for one hundred wedding guests the next day.

4 ounces plain cookies, such as vanilla wafers, to make 1 cup ground
⅔ cup slivered almonds, toasted
9 ounces very good chocolate, such as *val guanaja* (bittersweet), broken into 1-inch chunks
1½ sticks butter
3 tablespoons rum
2 small egg yolks, room temperature
Zabaglione sauce, see page 364

1. Put the cookies in the bowl of a food processor and blend until the cookies look like uncooked oatmeal (count to 10). Transfer to a bowl. Process ½ of the almonds and grind them finer than oatmeal. Transfer to a small bowl and set both bowls aside.

2. Put a sauce pan filled ⅓ of the way with water to simmer. Put all the chocolate in a bowl that will sit over simmering water in the sauce pan. The bottom of the bowl must clear the water by several inches. Add ½ stick of butter and all the rum. Put the bowl over simmering water and stir until the chocolate melts. Remove the bowl from the heat, and turn off the heat source.

3. Fold in the egg yolks and the remaining butter, a tablespoon at a time. When this is combined and melted, add all, except for a scant ¼ cup ground cookies. Fold in the remaining (unground) toasted almond slivers. Cover and refrigerate for about 1 hour, or until the chocolate mixture becomes almost firm, but malleable.

4. Lightly oil a large piece of parchment or waxed paper, at least 12x16 inches. With the help of a rubber spatula, transfer the chocolate mixture to the paper and form a log or salami, 9 to 10 inches long. Mold each end to appear salamilike and wrap tightly and securely. Put in a large plastic bag folded over 1 or 2 times, and freeze for several hours, up to 5 hours, until solid.

5. The chocolate roll must come out of the freezer 1 full hour before serving. To serve, combine the ground almonds and the remaining crushed cookies on a fresh piece of parchment or waxed paper. Roll the "salami" to cover completely. When the roll has stood at room temperature for about 1 hour, serve either the whole "salami" on a large white platter with garnishment of your choice, or serve ½-inch-thick slices on individual plates. Pass the sauce separately. Rewrap any leftover roll and refrigerate if it will be used in a day or so, or refreeze and use much later.

GRAND GALLIANO CAKE
Torta al liquore Galliano

Serves 4 to 12

This cake has a lovely texture and is deliciously moist. You must carefully spoon the syrup into the cake. It seems a bit tedious, but it doesn't take that long. This cake, covered with plastic and left at room temperature, will hold well for several days.

1 cup sugar
1 cup butter (2 sticks), softened
4 eggs, separated, at room temperature
1 cup sour cream
2 tablespoons minced orange zest
2 cups all-purpose flour
1 teaspoon baking powder
1 teaspoon baking soda
Grand Galliano liqueur syrup, see below

1. Cream the sugar and butter together until well blended. Add the egg yolks, sour cream, and orange zest, and beat until the batter is light and fluffy and a ribbon forms when the beaters are raised.

2. Preheat oven to 325°F. Grease and flour a 9-inch tube pan. Sift the flour, baking powder, and soda into a large bowl. Stir into butter mixture. Using clean beaters, beat the egg whites until stiff but not dry; fold into the mixture.

3. Pour batter into the prepared pan. Bake until a tester inserted in center comes out clean, about 1 hour. Remove and let cool 15 minutes. When the pan is cool enough to handle, very carefully loosen the cake around the edge with a sharp knife and invert onto a plate. Drizzle hot syrup over the warm cake, letting each tablespoon soak in. All of the syrup should be spooned into the cake.

To make the syrup:
⅓ cup Liquore Galliano
Juice of 1 orange
Juice of 2 lemons
¾ cup sugar

1. In a small nonaluminum saucepan, combine all ingredients and bring to boil. Lower heat and simmer until the sugar is dissolved and the liquid is syrupy, about 5 minutes. Continue as in step 3 above.

SICILIAN CREAM CAKE
Cassata alla siciliana

Serves 12

The two main Sicilian desserts are *cannoli* and *cassata*. There are many versions of both, and as many as there may be of cassata, each variation always includes candied fruit. I have enjoyed many good eating experiences in Sicily, and one I remember especially well has to do with desserts in the town of Erice, a town that rises 2,500 feet above the Trapani harbor. The Antica Pasticceria del Convento concocts sinfully good sweets. In addition to the cassata presented here, I remember eating (a free sample) a cookie called *brutti ma belli* (meaning "ugly but oh so good"). If I remember correctly, I was told they are made all over Italy, different versions, of course.

Erice has a medieval character. The streets are very narrow and cobblestoned. The walls are thick stone. In winter, the town is enshrouded in mist and cold—in the summer months and on a clear day, the view reaches all the way south to North Africa. It is one of the best places for views, cookies, and cassata.

1½ pounds fresh ricotta or cottage cheese
2 cups sugar
1 teaspoon vanilla
2 tablespoons tangerine or orange liqueur
5 squares (5 ounces) bitter chocolate, crushed into small bits
½ cup finely diced candied fruit
¼ cup whole pistachio nuts
1 recipe sponge cake, page 324
Confectioners' sugar for sprinkling

1. Put the ricotta, sugar, vanilla, and liqueur in a food processor and process until smooth, about 15 seconds. Transfer to a bowl and fold in the chocolate, fruit, and the pistachios. Mix well.

2. Cut the sponge cake into ½-inch slices and line a 10-inch rounded glass bowl with some of the slices. Add the creamed ricotta mixture over the sponge cake pieces and pat it down with a rubber spatula. Cover with the remaining slices of sponge cake. Make a cardboard cutout the same size as the top of the cake inside the bowl. Cover the cardboard with plastic wrap and press the plastic side of the cutout on top of the cake. Weight it with 1 or 2 cans of food. Put in the refrigerator, minimum 4 hours, or overnight.

3. When ready to serve, remove the cake from the refrigerator and turn it over onto a large platter or plate, holding the cardboard and bowl steady and securely. Remove the bowl, sprinkle the cake with confectioners' sugar, and serve. I like to be able to see the pattern of the turned-over cake slices through the confectioner's sugar.

TARTS

ROMAN WILD CHERRY TART
Crostata di visciole

Serves 6 to 8

Traditional pastry making in Rome dictates that fruit tarts are made almost invariably with jam from sour cherries—called *visciole*. There are two main types of cultivated cherries, sweet and sour. In the United States, sweet cherries are cultivated in far greater numbers than sour cherries. The best-known sour variety is called Montmorency, and most of those grown are usually canned or frozen for use as pie fillings or sauces. (Bing cherries, by the way, are sweet cherries.) Sour cherries come from mostly eastern and midwestern states, and during the summer you may find local harvests at farmers' markets and local roadside stands, if you want to make your own sour cherry jam. To make this tart on a year-round basis, it's far simpler to buy a good brand of sour cherry jam, such as Crosse & Blackwell or Smucker's.

As a rule, most people in Italy do not make their own pastries, as their custom is not to end a meal with a sweet dessert. Instead, they will purchase elegantly made pastries at a local *pasticceria* and eat them either in the afternoon with a café or perhaps on very special holidays. Italians generally want fresh fruit and cheese for dessert. The American sweet tooth dictates something sweet at the end of a meal.

2 cups all-purpose unbleached flour
½ cup sugar
8 tablespoons butter, softened
2 eggs
1 teaspoon vanilla
½ teaspoon lemon zest

1. Sift the flour, sugar, and a pinch of salt together and put on a work surface. Make a well in the center. Put the butter, eggs, vanilla, and lemon rind in the well and incorporate these ingredients with your hands. Do not add any water. Knead lightly for a short while—it will be smooth. Shape into a ball, wrap in waxed paper, and chill for 30 minutes. Cut the dough in 2 pieces, 1 a little larger than the second (about ⅔ and ⅓).

2. Preheat oven to 375°F. On a floured board, roll the larger piece into a pie crust (it helps to do this between 2 pieces of waxed paper) to fit a shallow 9-inch tart pan with a removable bottom. Trim neatly. Roll out the smaller piece into a 10-inch

circle and cut it into strips about ½ inch wide.

3. Spread the jam over the dough in the tart pan. Arrange dough strips in a lattice pattern, trimming the edges neatly at the rim of the tart pan but firming the dough into the bottom crust. Brush the lattice strips with the beaten egg and bake about 40 minutes or until the pastry is golden.

4. When the tart has cooled a bit, put the confectioners' sugar in a small strainer and, with the help of your finger swirling around in the strainer, dust the tart lightly.

Nota bene: (1) If you wish to make the pastry in a food processor, the butter must be cold and cut into bits; use one egg only, and add two tablespoons dry white wine. Process flour and butter together until crumbly. Then add the egg, sugar, a pinch of salt, and the wine. *Important:* When processing, bring the dough just to the point where it begins to form a ball. Remove from bowl of processor, bring together with your hands quickly, cut dough two thirds and one third, wrap each piece separately, and chill for one-half hour. (2) This crostata can be made with a prepared pastry pie crust, such as Pillsbury, treating the pastry as in the above recipe. But you must make two adjustments: Use only one cup of jam, and bake at the same temperature for only twenty-five minutes.

FIG AND PINE NUT TART
Crostata di fichi e pinoli

Serves 8

The food shops all over Italy inspire most people to want to cook, even if they may not want to cook on a holiday. If you are in an Italian home, cooking will happen. In fact, this is an easy way to learn something about Italian food. We bought some fig preserves—they are always so beautifully made and packaged—and decided to create this tart. Once home in the United States, we recreated it with a prepared pastry crust and enjoyed it also. In Italy, this is usually made with a heavier crust, called *pasta frolla*. The recipe for that crust is added below if you choose not to use the one suggested.

½ cup butter, room temperature
½ cup plus 2 tablespoons confectioners' sugar
3 egg yolks and 1 egg white
1 cup plus 2 tablespoons ground almonds
1 cup plus 2 tablespoons pine nuts, toasted
1 prepared pie crust, preferably Pillsbury
½ cup fig preserves or jam
1 cup whipped cream

1. Preheat the oven to 325°F. In an electric mixer, cream the butter and the sugar until fluffy and the color has paled. Add 1 yolk at a time with some of the ground almonds until all is incorporated. Add the egg white and mix until thoroughly blended. Remove the bowl. Put the pine nuts in a small skillet over medium heat and toast the nuts by allowing them to become slightly golden, 3 to 4 minutes, stirring most of the time. Keep your eye on this to avoid burning them. Fold in the pine nuts with the help of a rubber spatula.

2. Fit the pastry according to the manufacturer's directions into a 9-inch tart pan with a removable bottom. Carefully spread the fig preserves on the bottom of the pastry.

3. Spoon the butter and nut mixture into the tart pan. Bake for 30 minutes. Test for doneness by inserting a wooden skewer in the center of the pie; it is done if the skewer comes out clean. If not, cook a few minutes longer.

4. Allow to cool 10 to 15 minutes. Remove the side of the tart pan by pushing up from below, but leave the tart on the bottom base. Serve with whipped cream, if desired.

TO MAKE PASTA FROLLA—ITALIAN PASTRY

Makes 2 rounds for 8-, 9-, or 10 inch tart pan

2 cups all-purpose unbleached flour
2 tablespoons sugar
4 ounces plus 1 tablespoon butter, cut into tiny squares, kept cold
1 egg
1 egg yolk
1 teaspoon vanilla
2 to 3 tablespoons cold white wine

1. Place the flour, sugar, and a pinch of salt in the bowl of a processor with the steel blade.

   Pulse 2 or 3 times. Sprinkle the butter pieces over the flour and pulse 5 times until the mixture resembles coarse meal,

2. In a small bowl, combine the eggs, vanilla, and 2 tablespoons wine. Pour this mixture into the feed tube with the motor on, stopping as soon as the dough gathers on top of the blade. If it appears too dry, add the remaining tablespoon of wine. Do not let it form a ball or the pastry will toughen.

3. Transfer the pastry to a lightly floured work surface and knead only slightly, just to bring the dough together and to overcome the stickiness. Cut the dough in ½.

4. Pat one half into the buttered tart pan, cover with plastic, and chill until it is ready to be filled as in the above recipe. The pastry should chill about 1 hour, and not more than overnight. Wrap the remaining dough in plastic or waxed paper and refrigerate, but bring to room temperature at least 30 to 40 minutes before using. Roll it out to fit another tart or to make strips for lattice work.

Nota bene: If you want to make this by hand, the butter has to be room temperature. Follow the steps as by processor except bring the ingredients together on a work surface; for example, mix flour, sugar, and salt, create a well, pour in the liquids, and bring together to form a dough and knead at little as possible. Pat one half into pan and chill and wrap remaining pastry for later use.

ALMOND CHEESE TART
Torta di formaggio alle mandorle

Serves 6 to 8

This cheese tart should be made a day ahead so the flavors have time to blend. It will serve more than four people, but the cake keeps well for several days.

1 package (8 ounces) cream cheese, room temperature
4 ounces (½ an 8-ounce container) mascarpone cheese, room temperature
⅓ cup plus 2 tablespoons sugar
2 small eggs, beaten
½ tablespoon vanilla extract
1 teaspoon grated lemon zest
¼ teaspoon almond extract
½ cup almond slivers, toasted
1 baked pastry crust, see below
¼ cup sour cream

1. Preheat oven to 350°F. Combine cream and mascarpone cheeses and the sugar in a large bowl. Whip until smooth. Beat in the eggs, vanilla extract, lemon zest, and the almond extract. Whip again to combine all ingredients.

2. Spread ¼ cup of toasted almonds in the bottom of the cooked crust. Carefully spread the filling into the crust. Bake until the cheesecake is puffed and the center is firm to the touch, about 40 minutes.

3. Remove the cheesecake from the oven and spread the sour cream evenly over the top. Sprinkle with the remaining ¼ cup of toasted almonds. Cool on a rack for 1 hour. May be refrigerated overnight.

To prepare the crust:
1½ cups unbleached flour
⅓ cup confectioners' sugar
¼ teaspoon baking powder
8 tablespoons chilled butter, cut into small dice
1 egg yolk

1. Preheat oven to 350°F. Sift the flour with the sugar, baking powder, and a pinch of salt onto a work surface. Make a well in the center and add the diced butter into it. Add the egg yolk. Using your fingertips, or a pastry blender, bring the ingredients together to form a dough.

2. Fashion the dough together and press it into a deep 9-inch fluted tart pan with a removable base. Bake 12 minutes and remove to cool before adding the filling.

BRANDIED HAZELNUT TART
Crostata di nocciole al cognac

Serves 8 to 12

In Italy, hazelnuts are used in all sorts of confectionery. Probably best known is its use in *baci* (kisses) from the chocolate manufacturer Perugina in Perugia. The "kiss" contains a whole hazelnut in the center of the chocolate piece. But they are also used in the Italian nougat *torrone* and in a delicious fondant chocolate from Piedmont called *gianduiotti*. As children, we used to buy hazelnuts strung as necklaces at various celebrations. I wish I could tell you that this tart has a long Italian history and that it was made famous by an Emilian or other Italian baker, but I can't. It is something I've concocted in my kitchen, which is Italian, heart and soul. I use it for special occasions, Christmas being one.

For the pastry:
1 cup hazelnuts, ground
2 tablespoons all-purpose flour
4 tablespoons sugar
3 tablespoons butter, melted

1. Preheat the oven to 375°F. Blend all the ingredients in a bowl, adding about ¼ teaspoon salt. Press this into a 9-inch tart pan with a removable base, covering the bottom and sides. Bake 10 to 15 minutes, until it is golden. Remove from the oven and set it on a rack to cool. Then remove the shell from the pan but keep it on the base.

For the filling:
4 egg yolks, room temperature
½ cup sugar
1 tablespoon lemon juice
3 tablespoons brandy
1 cup heavy cream, whipped

1. In the top of a double boiler, combine the yolks and sugar, and cook over simmering water, stirring constantly with a wire whisk, until the mixture thickens to the consistency of mayonnaise, about 10 minutes. This is important; if the yolks and sugar are undercooked, the filling will not solidify. Remove the top saucepan from the heat, add the lemon juice, and stir well. Add the brandy and stir again. Allow the yolk mixture to cool to room temperature.

2. Fold the whipped cream into the cooled yolk mixture. Pour the filling into the pastry shell and refrigerate the tart until it is set, at least 2 hours.

3. This tart will keep nicely overnight. When you are ready to serve it, decorate with rosettes of whipped cream, topping each with a hazelnut.

GREEN TOMATO JAM TART WITH ZABAGLIONE AND WHIPPED CREAM
Crostata di marmellata (pomodori verdi) con zabaglione

Serves 8 to 10

If you have ever wondered what to do with green tomatoes, here is the perfect answer, for this jam makes a perfect tart. The jam is very easy to make, but you will need green tomatoes. Importers of Italian specialty foods will be able to get jars of this jam for you from Italy.

To make the pastry:
2½ cups unbleached all-purpose flour
¼ teaspoon baking powder
2 large eggs and 1 large egg yolk
½ cup sugar
1 tablespoon whole milk
1 scant teaspoon finely minced lemon zest
½ cup (8 tablespoons) soft butter

1. Sift the flour with the baking powder into a bowl and make a well in the center. In another bowl combine the whole eggs, the extra yolk, sugar, milk, and the lemon zest. Pour this into the well. Add the soft butter and, with a fork or with your fingers, bring some of the flour into the liquid and butter mixture. Continue until all the flour is incorporated to make a dough. Turn the dough onto a work surface and knead until it is smooth. Wrap in waxed paper and put it in a cool place for 1 hour of rest. If you refrigerate it, it will become too hard and will be difficult to roll out.

To make the green tomato jam:
2 pounds green tomatoes
1 lemon
2 cups sugar
¼ cup honey

1. The tomatoes should be really unripe. Core them and cut each in ½. Then cut each ½ into very thin slices, as thinly as you can cut them. Put them in a heavy, nonreactive saucepan.

2. Cut thin zest strips down the length of the lemon, all around, and cut each piece of zest into very thin strips, as thin as possible. Put into the sauce pan. Remove and discard as much as you can of the remaining pith, cut off the ends, and slice the lemon in ½. Remove all seeds and thinly slice the lemon halves, as thin as possible. Add these to the sauce pan along with the sugar, honey, and ¾ cup water. Bring to boil, lower the heat, and simmer, uncovered, 1 hour, stirring frequently. Be careful not to burn the bottom of the pan. The jam should be thick (it will thicken more when it cools) but simmer on very low heat 10 to 15 minutes longer if needed. Let cool.

To make the tart:

1. Preheat the oven to 375°F. Divide the dough in 2 pieces in these approximate sizes—⅓ and ⅔. Cover the smaller piece, and on a floured work surface, roll out the larger to fit a 9-inch tart pan with a removable base. Roll out as thinly as possible (even if too large for a 9-inch pan), being sure you can lift and fit it into the tart pan. Trim the pastry neatly.

2. Use 1½ cups of jam to spread on the bottom pastry. Keep any remaining jam in a clean Ball jar with clean lids in the refrigerator for up to 6 weeks. On a floured work surface, roll out the smaller piece of dough as thin as possible to make a circle at least 10 inches in diameter. Cut lattice strips about ½ inch wide. Arrange the dough strips in a lattice pattern over the jam, trimming the edges neatly at the rim of the tart pan and firming the dough into the bottom crust. Bake until golden, about 40 minutes.

3. Allow the tart to cool. To serve, put a teaspoon or 2 of confectioners' sugar in a small strainer and, with the help of your finger swirling around in it, dust the tart lightly with the sugar.

Nota bene: This can be made with a pastry pie crust such as Pillsbury, treating the pastry as in the recipe. But you must make two adjustments: use only one cup of jam, and bake at the same temperature for twenty-five minutes only.

DESSERTS

COOKIES

FAMOUS COOKIES FROM SIENA
Ricciarelli di Siena

Makes 16 to 20

When I was in Ilaria and Georgio Miani's sixteenth-century house, *Buonriposo*, which is situated in the soothing, undulating hills of the Val d'Orcia (an area recently made more famous by the filming of *The English Patient*), it was only a short drive to Siena, where I could feast on fabulous cookies called *ricciarelli*. One can buy them in many pastry shops, but San Domenico's on Via del Paradiso made the ones I liked best. I also found more in Pienza, Montalcino, Montepulciano, and other villages around Siena. They seem to be the regional cookie in these parts; eating one proves why. They are cookies one would expect to find in heaven. They are fairly easy to make, and they were a treat in the afternoon with coffee or tea or an iced drink. While enjoying these in the pergola on a sunny afternoon, we were happy to look across the wheat fields and the clay hills and the landmark eleventh-century tower on the hill below—to look across the sky at sunset and see the towns of Montalcino, Pienza, Montepulciano, and Radiocafani perched on their hilltops and dream about this confection.

2 egg whites, room temperature
7 ounces pure almond paste, such as Odense or Betty Crocker
1 cup confectioners' sugar
1 teaspoon almond extract
2 teaspoons minced orange zest
Confectioners' sugar for dusting

1. It is easiest to whip the egg whites in a mixer with a balloon whisk. Be sure the bowl is absolutely clean. These egg whites are not to be beaten to the soft stage, or to peaks—they are simply beaten to become foamy, but they should triple to quadruple in volume; they will not be pure white as in meringue—if they get to that stage, they have been whipped too much. Set aside.

2. Preheat the oven to 275°F. Line 2 baking sheets with parchment.

3. If the almond paste is in a block or formed like a sausage, it should be cut in ½-inch cubes and then put in the bowl of a processor and pulsed until softened. It should look like a smooth paste.

4. Add the cup of confectioners' sugar and the foamy egg whites and mix until smooth. Add and blend in the almond extract and zest.

5. By teaspoonfuls, drop the mixture onto the parchment sheets, spacing them at least 1 inch apart. Bake until they become a very light tan or beige and firm to the touch, about 25 minutes.

6. Be sure to cool on the baking sheets. The cookies should cool completely before removing them; if they are not cool, some of the bottoms will stick to the parchment. Sprinkle with confectioner's sugar before serving. If storing them, place them in airtight containers.

COUSIN GIUSEPPE'S MERINGUE COOKIES

Croccante di meringa, pinoli, e mandorle

Makes about 24

This is a delicious, crunchy cookie that keeps well if stored in a tight container, so they can be made days ahead. It is a variation of the famous Siena cookie, as the flavor is somewhat similar, but the crunch makes the cookie a totally different confection. They can be eaten by themselves, or with some fresh berries, or as a base for ice cream. I am the "Cousin Giuseppe" referred to in the name of the recipe. I made these cookies for cousins in Caserta, the city northeast of Naples, famous for the Reggia di Casertaa, the eighteenth-century Bourbon palace with gardens, often called the Versailles of Italy. The palace has 1,200 rooms and the gardens are spread over 250 acres. This is a grand place for this cookie.

2 cups almond slivers
½ cup pine nuts
1½ cups sugar, divided ¾ and ¾ cups
½ cup confectioners' sugar
1 teaspoon finely grated orange zest
3 egg whites, room temperature
½ teaspoon cream of tartar
½ teaspoon almond extract
Confectioners' sugar for dusting

1. Put the almonds and pine nuts in the bowl of a large processor and process them (should look like a very fine sand). Transfer the mixture to a large bowl.

2. Add ¾ cup of sugar, the confectioners' sugar, and the orange zest to the bowl with the almonds and combine them well with the help of a rubber spatula.

3. In a very clean bowl of an electric mixer, add the egg whites and start to whip, preferably with a balloon whisk. When the egg whites are frothy, add the cream of tartar. When they have tripled in volume but are still somewhat soft, add the remaining ¾ cup of sugar, a heaping tablespoon at a time. When the whites are reasonably stiff and shiny, add the almond extract. Transfer to the bowl of dry ingredients and fold in the whipped egg whites. Combine slowly, carefully, and thoroughly.

4. Fit parchment paper into 2 baking trays—jelly-roll pans work well here. By teaspoonfuls, place mixture onto parchment, leaving 1½ inches in between cookies. Arrange 12 or 15 cookies in each bake tray. Flatten each with the back of a clean and wet teaspoon—each should be about ½ inch thick.

5. Preheat the oven to 350°F. Bake 1 tray at a time, 8 to 10 minutes. Do not brown them. Remove from the oven, let cool before moving them off parchment, and dust with confectioners' sugar before serving.

ENRICHED AND CRISPED VANILLA/ALMOND COOKIES
Bocconcini alle mandorle

Makes about 80 cookies

There are probably more cookies made with almonds in Italy than any other one ingredient; these cookies explain why. They are sort of like American "icebox" cookies, as the ingredients can be pulled together, rolled as in the directions, wrapped, and stored in the refrigerator until ready to be sliced and cooked.

½ pound blanched almonds
½ pound unsalted butter, room temperature
1 cup sugar
2 large eggs, room temperature
½ teaspoon pure vanilla
2½ cups all-purpose flour

1. Put the almonds in the bowl of a processor (if the processor is small, do this in batches) and chop the almonds. Do *not* overprocess. Set aside.

2. Cream the butter and add the sugar by tablespoons. It is best to do this in an electric mixer with a paddle; if not, do this by hand with a wooden spoon.

3. Add the remaining ingredients and form a dough. Divide the dough in ½ and roll each into 2-inch-thick logs. Wrap them carefully in waxed paper and refrigerate them overnight, or 2 nights if you wish.

4. Liberally butter 2 large baking trays. (If you use both logs of cookie dough, you will have to bake 2 times. If you decide to bake only once, keep the unused dough in the refrigerator for a day or 2, or freeze if not ready to use soon.) Before baking, preheat oven to 350°F. Remove the dough logs from the refrigerator, slice as thinly as possible, and place the slices on cookie sheets, leaving 1 inch space in between. Bake until edges crisp, about 12 to 15 minutes, depending on thickness of cookie.

FRUITS

CANTALOUPE MELON BALLS IN HONEYDEW PUREE

Misto di due meloni

Serves 4

In the sixteenth century, interest in cooking in Italy was growing, and the clergy were at the forefront in participating—in fact, the popes themselves expressed interest. It has been reported that because of this, the tiny melon used by the ancient Romans became the one we know today as cantaloupe. It is claimed that it was developed on papal property near Rome called Cantaloupe. Here is the perfect follow-up to a bowl of freshly cooked pasta.

1 cantaloupe
Juice of ½ lemon
½ honeydew melon
4 tablespoons honey
8 raspberries or strawberries

1. Cut the cantaloupe in ½. Discard the seeds. With a melon baller, cut melon balls out of both halves and put them in a bowl. Add the lemon juice and a pinch of salt. Toss to coat the balls.

2. Cut the honeydew melon in slices and remove the outer skin, cutting far enough into the melon slices to avoid any unripe parts. Coarsely chop the skinned slices and puree them in a processor. If the melon is too watery, spoon some of the liquid away and discard. Fold in the honey.

3. To serve, spoon some of the honeydew puree into oversized red wine goblets. Add some cantaloupe balls, and 2 raspberries or strawberries to the top, and serve.

FRESH SUGARED RED AND WHITE GRAPES, VIN SANTO, AND BISCOTTI
Confetti di uva fresca con vin santo e biscotti

Serves 4

These sugared grapes may be made a day ahead and refrigerated until needed.

8 small clusters of grapes, 4 red, 4 white
2 egg whites, beaten until frothy
½ cup sugar

1. Dip grape clusters into egg whites, coating completely. Pour the sugar into a wide saucer and press the grapes lightly into it.

2. To serve, put 1 of each color grape cluster on a plate. Serve with a glass of vin santo and pass some biscotti.

PEACH "COBBLER" FROM THE COUNTESS D'ORBICCIANO

Dolce di pesche al forno alla "Contessa d'Orbicciano"

Serves 4 to 6

Warrie Price, my friend who has a house just outside Lucca, was born in Texas instead of Italy. To compensate, she is an Italianophile of high order and lives a lifestyle more Italian than American. Her home, Le Tre Case, is filled with Italian antiques and artifacts down to the silverware and linens. Her plantings of rosemary and sage alongside her home seem larger than others in Italy, and the Italian umbrella on the other side of her house seems larger than most and it is Italian. Her kitchen, though modern in every way, has the appearance that it has been there for hundreds of years—for example, a special place to cut fresh Lucca bread on a worn breadboard, and below, a gathered skirt of a fine Italian print fabric to cover several utility shelves. She concocted this fabulous dessert in Italy because she says the peaches taste better.

2 to 3 cups of sliced fresh peaches without skins
2 cups sugar, separated into cups
1 stick butter, melted
2 teaspoons baking powder
¾ cup all-purpose flour
¾ cup milk

1. Combine the peaches and 1 cup sugar in a bowl, toss, and set aside.

2. Put the butter in a baking dish, such as an 8-inch-wide and 3-inch-deep soufflé dish. Preheat oven to 350°F.

3. Combine the remaining cup of sugar with the baking powder, ¼ teaspoon salt, flour, and milk in a bowl and stir well. Pour this "batter" into the soufflé dish with the melted butter in it and *do not stir*. Carefully spoon the peaches and their juices into the batter and, again, *do not stir*.

4. Place the filled soufflé dish on a larger baking sheet with a rim and put in the oven to cook for 1 hour. Remove from the oven, let rest a few minutes, and serve with ice cream. (The cooked dough will have risen to the top of the dish. and it will seem like a cobbler.)

CHESTNUT PUREE WITH SWEET WHIPPED CREAM WITH CANDIED ORANGE STRIPS

Purea di castagne con arance caramellizzate e panna montata

Serves 4

Italians would normally boil fresh chestnuts to puree them, but whole cooked chestnuts are easier to handle and are available in most food specialty shops. If the puree is too thin, it will not pass through the food mill properly. The chestnuts may be cooked one or two days ahead, but do not put them through the food mill until just before serving. The candied orange strips make this a delightful dessert.

½ cup milk
2 tablespoons cocoa
½ cup sugar
15 ounces cooked whole chestnuts, canned or jarred
¼ cup dark rum
½ cup heavy cream
¼ cup confectioners' sugar
Candied orange strips, see page 352

1. Heat the milk and stir in the cocoa and sugar.
2. Add the chestnuts and cook over medium heat to heat them thoroughly, 6 to 8 minutes. Remove from the heat.
3. Add the rum and mash thoroughly. Pass the mixture through a food mill to fall on a plate.
4. Whip the cream and confectioners sugar, and add it to the top of chestnut puree. Carefully place about a tablespoon of candied orange strips over the cream.

DESSERTS

FRESH ORANGE SLICES WITH SLIVERS OF ORANGE ZEST
Arance con scorza

Serves 6

The vin santo wine used here is an Italian term used for strong, sweet white wines. Actually, this sweet dessert wine is made all over Italy, but wine experts prefer those from Umbria, Tuscany, Trentino (near Venice), and Urbino (in the province of Marche). The grapes (varying from one region to the next) are dried on straw after the vintage and not pressed until as late as the following Easter. Since it is made in Holy Week, it is called vin santo. It is then aged in cask for four to six years and produces a scented, luscious, delicate amber-colored dessert wine. This dish can be made ahead by as much as six or eight hours before serving. Refrigerate it, and remove from the refrigerator one-half hour before serving.

6 large oranges or 8 smaller ones with good, clear rinds
⅔ cup sugar
½ cup vin santo
½ cup fresh orange juice
1 cup fresh raspberries or 1 (10-ounce) package frozen, thawed

1. With a vegetable peeler, remove the rind from 3 oranges, taking as little pith as possible. Peel all the oranges. Cut the rinds without the pith into the thinnest strips and set aside. Discard the other rinds or save for another use.

2. Slice the peeled oranges crosswise, remove any seeds, and arrange, overlapping the slices, on a large platter.

3. Over low heat and without stirring, cook the sugar in a sauce pan until it turns dark brown around the edges. Remove from the heat and add the wine, orange juice, and the zest. If the sauce appears too thin, cook a while longer. Then remove from the heat to cool, and pour over the fresh orange slices. This may be made ahead by 6 or 8 hours and refrigerated. Remove the oranges about ½ hour before serving, and add some raspberries, fresh or frozen, atop the oranges.

FRUIT COMPOTE WITH CITRUS SAUCE

Composta di frutta con salsa agli agrumi

Serves 4 to 6

The citrus sauce in this recipe makes the dish. The first citrus fruit to be introduced in Italy was the citron in the third century; the lemon appeared in the seventh, the bitter orange in the tenth, and the real orange in the fourteenth. No Italian kitchen is complete without a bowl of lemons and oranges. They are used to brighten *antipasti (appetizers)*, *primi (first course)s*, *second (second courses)*, *contorni (vegetables or side dishes)*, and *dolci (sweets)*.

For the compote:
8 fresh strawberries, hulled and sliced
1 ripe pear, peeled, seeded, and cut into ½-inch pieces
1 small banana, peeled and thinly sliced on the bias
½ cup fresh blueberries, stemmed, rinsed, and dried
1 cup diced fresh pineapple

1. Combine all the fruit, toss well, and distribute among 4 large red wine goblets.

For the citrus sauce:
1 cup fresh orange juice
¼ cup fresh lemon juice
1½ cups sugar
1 tablespoon marsala wine

Combine the above ingredients. Pour it over the fruit in the glasses. Refrigerate until ready to use. Remove from the refrigerator 20 to 30 minutes before needed.

FRESH FIGS WITH KIRSCH
Fichi alla Veneziana

Serves 6

This simple way to serve figs is the way they are served in the famous Hotel Gritti in Venice. They elegantly peel the figs after trimming the ends, cut them in halves, and pour the kirsch over them. I like not to peel them—simply run quickly under cool water, pat dry, trim them, and then cut in halves.

18 fresh ripe figs
6 tablespoons kirsch

1. Ready the figs for serving by running under cool water and drying with paper or cloth towels. Trim the ends and cut each fig in ½. Plan 3 figs per person (6 halves). Arrange the fig halves, cut side up, and carefully spoon some kirsch over them. Let them stand this way about 10 minutes before serving. These must be at room temperature.

BAKED STUFFED PEACHES WITH AMARETTI, ALMONDS, AND MASCARPONE
Pesche ripiene

Serves 6

Italians love peaches, fresh, peeled, sliced, and served in wine, or combined with wine and baked. I have made these with a good quality of preserved peaches and found that they work, perhaps not as well as fresh peaches, but they still make a fine ending to a lunch or other meal. Here's a favorite recipe of mine. If you can't find Italian amaretti, use American-made macaroons, but reduce the number of them to eight.

6 ripe peaches, halved and pitted
6 blanched almonds, finely chopped
12 amaretti, crushed
½ cup sugar
⅓ cup unsweetened cocoa
10 tablespoons dry white wine
12 teaspoons mascarpone cheese

1. Preheat oven to 325°F. With a melon baller, remove a bit of the flesh from the inside of each peach ½. Put the flesh in a bowl with the almonds, amaretti, ¼ cup sugar, cocoa, and 2 tablespoons wine. Mix well.

2. Fill the cavities of each peach ½. Carefully place 1 teaspoon mascarpone on top of each filling and place the peach halves in a buttered baking pan. Add the remaining wine to the pan and sprinkle the remaining sugar over all.

3. Bake in a preheated oven 30 minutes until the peaches are tender. To test for doneness, spear the peach with a wooden skewer. If the skewer penetrates easily, the peach is cooked. Remove from the oven and serve warm.

STRAWBERRIES IN BALSAMIC WITH FRESH MINT AND WHIPPED CREAM
Fragole con balsamico, menta, e panna montata

Makes 8 to 12

Leave four or five berries unhulled (but rinsed) to lay on top of the others. At Christmastime, they are especially colorful and in tune with the colors of the season. This preparation is best if it can be brought together one hour before needed and left at room temperature. Berries and balsamic may seem a strange combination, but you will find that the taste of the vinegar disappears when it gets overpowered by the taste of the berries, and the acidity brings out the taste and sweetness of the fruit.

2 pints ripe strawberries, all of them rinsed and all but 4 of them hulled
2 tablespoons high-quality balsamic vinegar
1 tablespoon sugar
¼ cup finely chopped fresh mint

1. Combine the strawberries, balsamic, and sugar in a bowl. If any of the berries are extra large, cut them in ½. Toss lightly but well. Let stand at room temperature 30 to 60 minutes. Longer will make the berries too soft.

2. To serve, pick out the ones with the stems and place them on top. Sprinkle mint over the berries.

Nota bene: For Christmas especially, Italians will offer a bowl of beautiful oranges and other fresh fruit, a tray of roasted chestnuts, a hunk of Parmigiano-Reggiano, some home-baked holiday cookies, or chocolates. You may wish to do the same.

FRESH BERRIES WITH ALMOND CREAM

Fragole di bosco e mirtilli con crema di mandorle

Serves 6

Another perfectly simple Italian dessert. Adding almond extract to whipped heavy cream is like a whiff of an exotic perfume, and adding this to fresh berries is heaven sent. Do not overwhip the cream—keep it light and fluffy—and do try to get the wild strawberries; They are filled with flavor and worth the extra cents.

2 cups fresh wild strawberries, trimmed
2 cups fresh blueberries, stems removed
1 cup heavy cream
1 teaspoon almond extract

1. Remove the stem ends of the strawberries but do not wash them. Check them over and wipe with a kitchen towel if necessary. Put the blueberries in a colander after removing their tiny stems, and run under cool water, tossing with your hand to freshen all the berries. Drain well and dry. Set both berries aside.

2. Whip the cream and the almond extract until some cream can stand on the beater when it is lifted. Do not overwhip.

5. To serve, apportion the berries to each plate and spoon some of the sauce over each serving. Do not cover the berries with the sauce. The berries should be seen.

PEARS COOKED IN WINE WITH MASCARPONE

Pere cotte in vino bianco con mascarpone

Serves 4

Mascarpone is a fresh cheese originally from Lombardy in the north of Italy, but now it is found all over Italy and in most supermarkets in the United States. Often it is served just as a dessert cheese with fresh fruit and sugar. Here is a dessert I like to make utilizing mascarpone. Pears are baked all over Italy, also in red wine, but white wine is used here as it does not compete as much with the mascarpone, as might the red. Mascarpone is added to the center of each cooked pear and served warm.

4 pears for cooking, peeled, stems intact
1½ cups dry white wine
⅓ cup sugar
4 whole cloves
Pinch ground cinnamon
4 tablespoons mascarpone cheese, softened

1. Preheat oven to 350°F. Put the pears, stem end up, in a small baking dish (the pears should be able to stand up in the pan). Pour the wine over the pears. Sprinkle the sugar over all. Add the cloves and sprinkle the cinnamon over the pears.

2. Bake about 30 to 35 minutes, until the pears are tender. Test for doneness with a wooden skewer. If the skewer penetrates easily, the pears are cooked. The liquid should be syrupy. Remove from the oven and cool a bit. Cut each pear in ½ and scoop out the seeds with a melon baller. Lay 2 halves on each of 4 dessert plates and add ½ tablespoon mascarpone to each center. Spoon the syrup in the baking dish over each pear. Add another pinch of cinnamon and serve while the pears are warm.

CARAMELIZED ORANGES
Arance caramellizzate

Serves 6

There are many versions of this dessert, and most of them call for slicing the oranges. I like them left whole, dipped in the syrup before it caramelizes the orange strips, and served whole with caramelized orange strips on top. This is a special dessert.

6 oranges, zest from 3 oranges, sliced as thinly as possible and all 6 oranges carefully peeled with no pith
9 ounces sugar
⅔ cup water
2 tablespoons kirsch or brandy

1. Prepare the oranges, slice the zest, and put aside.

2. Combine the sugar and water in a sauce pan and bring to boil, stirring most of the time. Make a syrup to completely dissolve the sugar. If the sugar reaches to the top of the sauce pan, quickly remove the sauce pan from the heat source and, as the syrup recedes, put back on the heat.

3. Add the kirsch or brandy after 7 minutes of cooking the syrup. Cook 1 minute longer and remove from heat. Dip each orange in the syrup for 2 minutes apiece. Remove and place on a plate. Reserve the syrup in the sauce pan.

4. Put the strips of orange peel in a sauce pan and cover with water. Bring to boil, lower the heat, and simmer 10 minutes. Drain well.

5. Cook the drained zest in the syrup until caramelized.

6. To serve, place an orange on a plate and top with the candied zest.

ROASTED FIGS WITH ALMONDS AND CHOCOLATE

Fichi Mandorlati

Makes 25 pieces

In Bari and Calabria, neighbors of Naples, desserts are associated with ancient traditions and contain many delicious ingredients, such as figs and honey, almonds, and dried fruits, which are exported to places all over the world. Some people say the dried figs of Bari, packed in square straw boxes, are the best from anywhere. They are large, dark, and moist, packed with a faint roasted flavor. Fennel seeds and almonds are added for additional flavor. Bay leaves are added to the boxes, also for flavor. Typical of these desserts is the one presented here, but only the best quality figs should be used. These can be made several days ahead of the time of serving.

25 whole, unblanched almonds
25 dried figs that are moist
½ cup diced candied peel
2 tablespoons dried fennel seeds
2 ounces bittersweet chocolate, broken into small pieces
⅔ cup cocoa
⅔ cup confectioners' sugar
25 bay leaves

1. Preheat the oven to 350°F. Bake the almonds 12 minutes. Set aside.

2. Trim off any stalks on the figs and carefully cut the figs on 1 side to create a pocket. Stuff each fig with a roasted almond, a couple of pieces of peel, 2 fennel seeds, and a small piece of chocolate. Close the pocket by pressing them shut with your fingers. Transfer them to a baking sheet and bake until they darken a bit, about 15 minutes.

3. Combine the cocoa and sugar in a shallow dish, and as soon as the figs are removed from the oven, roll them in the cocoa mixture and place each fig on a bay leaf. Pack the figs with the bay leaves in an airtight container. Serve 2 or 3 per person, and pass more of them if you wish.

ASSORTED MELONS WITH CAPRINI CHEESE
Melone e caprini

Serves 6

This cheese is a goat cheese from southern Italy. It does not travel well and will be difficult to find. However, it is found in bottles of flavored Italian olive oil (usually with herbs and chilies). If you have trouble finding it, try some fresh ricotta on the side of the melon slices. Here is a chance to have a fruit and cheese dessert.

6 thin slices of canteloupe, trimmed, seeds removed
6 thin slices of honeydew melon, trimmed, seeds removed
6 thin slices of watermelon, trimmed, seeds removed
6 small wedges of caprini
¼ cup finely chopped fresh mint
12 to 18 small bread squares, toasted

1. When cutting the melons, keep the crescent shapes for the cantaloupe and honeydew melons. For the watermelon, cut a thin triangle, 3x3x3 inches.

2. Arrange the crescent-shaped melons, side by side, on a large, shallow dessert plate, and lay the watermelon triangle against the 2 crescents. Add some salt and freshly ground pepper. Place the cheese to 1 side, but touching the melons. Sprinkle the mint over the melons, and pass a plate of crisped bread squares to be used with the cheese.

ROASTED GRAPES WITH A SLICE OF CACIOCAVALLO

Uva cotta in forno con caciocavallo

Serves 4

There are several places in Calabria, notably Catanzaro and Verbicaro, where they bake grapes in a preparation called *panicielli d'uva passa*, which means that small bunches of grapes are wrapped in cedar or chestnut leaves and are then baked. My friend and mentor, Georgianna Orsini, has given me an idea that works really well here. I like it because it eliminates the difficult task of finding cedar or chestnut leaves.

1 pound red grapes, rinsed and drained well
Olive oil for baking pan
4 slices caciocavallo cheese

1. Remove the grapes from their stems and put them on an oiled baking tray—a pizza pan will do. Preheat the oven to 350°F and bake the grapes 1 hour or until they begin to caramelize (the grapes will begin to collapse). Remove from the oven.

2. To serve them hot or lukewarm, simply spoon some on individual plates and add a slice of cheese next to the grapes.

PEACH SOUP WITH RASPBERRIES AND TOASTED PANETTONE FINGERS
Zuppa di pesche e lamponi con fette di panettone tostate

Serves 6

This is a modern touch, brought about by young restaurateurs who want to preserve the old flavors, but present them in new light. The good news is that the "soup" can be made with frozen peaches, which are available in every U.S. supermarket. And these days, I find panettones in the same markets.

2½ pounds ripe peaches or 2 (10-ounce) packages frozen peaches
¾ cup sugar
3 tablespoons fresh lemon juice
¼ cup good-quality marsala
1 orange, peeled, pith removed, sliced across the segments to make wheels
1 pint fresh raspberries
12 (½x½-inch-thick) slices panettone, toasted

1. If using frozen peaches, thaw them and drain in a colander. When fully drained, cut them into 1-inch pieces. If using fresh peaches, peel them and remove the pits. Cut them into coarse pieces and put either frozen or fresh in a food processor.

2. Add the full amount of sugar to the fresh peaches, or only ¼ cup to the already sweetened frozen and thawed peaches. Add the lemon juice and the marsala. Process to thoroughly puree the mixture. Transfer to a bowl. Refrigerate until ready to use. When ready to serve, spoon puree into rimmed soup plates. Arrange an orange slice in the middle of each and toss some raspberries overall. Pass the panettone slices.

APRICOTS WITH AMARETTI CRUMBS AND CREAM

Albicoche agli amaretti sbriciolati

Serves 6

This is a dessert that will fit almost any occasion. If the apricots are fresh, it will be sublime. But jarred or canned apricots fare well here with the help of the liqueur and wine. If you cannot get amaretti cookies, crush a few vanilla cookies as a substitute.

12 apricots, preferably fresh, cut in halves, stones removed, or 12 canned apricot halves, drained
½ cup hazelnut liqueur (reserve 1 teaspoon for the cream)
½ cup white wine, such as chardonnay
⅔ cup sugar
½ cup heavy cream
12 amaretti (Italian macaroons), crushed with a rolling pin

1. Place the apricots, either fresh or canned, cut-side down in a skillet. Add the liqueur (except for the reserved teaspoon) and wine. Sprinkle the sugar over all and cook over medium heat until the fresh apricots are cooked through, about 8 to 10 minutes, or the canned ones are heated through, 3 or 4 minutes, and the sauce has become syrupy. Remove the apricots and cook down the sauce to about ½ its original volume. Let cool.

2. Add the teaspoon of liqueur to the cream and whip to soft peaks.

3. Arrange 4 apricot halves on dessert plates, spoon over the sauce, add whipped cream to the side overlapping 1 apricot, and sprinkle the amaretti crumbs overall. Serve right away.

PUDDINGS

ORANGE PANNA COTTA WITH BLUEBERRY SAUCE

Panna cotta di arancia con salsa di mirtilli

Serves 6

Panna cotta is a pudding and very Italian, with its origins in Piedmont. It has a light, subtle flavor, and these days, Italians serve it everywhere with all sorts of fruit sauces, or just plain, sliced fruit. This tasty version uses an orange flavor in the pudding with a blueberry sauce. It can be made a day ahead and unmolded as you need it.

To make the molds:
2 tablespoons orange liqueur
2 tablespoons water
1 packet unflavored gelatin
6 ounces cream or mascarpone cheese, softened
6 ounces sour cream
½ cup sugar
1 teaspoon vanilla
¾ cup heavy cream

1. Combine the orange liqueur, water, and gelatin in a small sauce pan and let sit 5 minutes. Put over heat and simmer slowly, stirring all the time, until the gelatin is dissolved, about 1 to 2 minutes.

2. In the bowl of an electric mixer, beat the cheese until it is light and fluffy, about 3 minutes. Put the machine on low speed and add the sour cream, sugar, vanilla, and the gelatin mixture, and combine well. Slowly add the heavy cream. When all of this is well combined, distribute among 6 (½-cup) molds that have been lightly sprayed with nonstick cooking spray. Cover with plastic wrap and refrigerate for several hours until they are firm. They made be made ahead by 2 days. This dessert is for 4, but 6 molds are made in case there is difficulty in turning 1 out or another problem arises. If there are any extra, they are good the next day, so save a little of the sauce.

3. To serve, dip the mold very quickly into hot water, or wrap a warm cloth around the mold to loosen it from its edges. Turn each mold out onto individual dessert plates and add the sauce, covering 1 side

of the mold and letting it run into the plate. Add 2 fresh blueberries to the top of each and serve.

To make the sauce:
1 cup fresh blueberries, stemmed, rinsed, and drained (reserve 12 berries for garnish)
½ cup freshly squeezed orange juice
2 tablespoons orange liqueur
⅓ cup sugar
2 teaspoons finely grated orange zest

1. Put the berries in a sauce pan and add the orange juice, orange liqueur, and the sugar. Bring to boil, lower the heat, and simmer 5 minutes, stirring most of the time. The sugar should dissolve. Remove from the heat, and let reach room temperature before putting over the molds. When the sauce has been added to the mold, top with 2 berries, and carefully sprinkle some of the orange zest over everything on the plate.

TIRAMISU WITH AMARETTO FROM CAFFE POLIZIANO IN MONTEPULCIANO
Tiramisu con amaretto (Caffe Poliziano, Montepulciano)

Serves 6 to 10

Tiramisu has been claimed by the Venetians, but the dish is popular all over Italy and in the United States, so much so that it is no longer claimed to be regional. Everywhere in Italy, each cook puts his or her own imprint on the dish, and I recall one version quite clearly. After a delightful meal at the restaurant Diva e Maceo, in the center of Montepulciano, we decided on a dessert after all, after having refused it at the restaurant (the only reason being we were too full of food). Our *passegiata* led us to a nearby coffee house and restaurant called Caffe Poliziano (people of Montepulciano are called *poliziani*). The view of the hillside was fantastic from the *caffe*, as was the tiramisu (which means "lift me up").

This is a no-fail recipe and a delicious one. I find it is good the next day, if any is left over. Some shops sell Savoie biscuits in the shape of lady fingers. If you find these, use them instead of other lady fingers, as they are already dried out.

16 to 20 (7 to 8 ounces) dried ladyfingers ("toast" them or dry them out in the oven, 250°F for about 30 minutes)
3 eggs, separated
½ cup sugar
1 tablespoon espresso or strong black coffee
8 ounces mascarpone cheese
¼ cup amaretto liqueur
2 cups strong black coffee
¼ to ⅓ cup cocoa

1. Prepare the ladyfingers. Combine the yolks, sugar, 1 tablespoon of espresso or coffee, and the amaretto, and beat 2 to 3 minutes. Add the mascarpone and whip until the mixture is smooth.

2. Beat the egg whites nearly stiff and fold into the yolk mixture.

3. Moisten ½ of the ladyfingers with coffee, and arrange them in a glass or ceramic dish or bowl. Do this by quickly dunking ½ of each ladyfinger into the coffee and quickly laying it in the bowl. If you don't move quickly and carefully, the ladyfinger will disintegrate.

4. Carefully add ½ of the mascarpone mixture over the entire layer of ladyfingers. Sprinkle ½ of the cocoa over all.

5. Repeat with the remaining fingers, mascarpone mixture, and the cocoa. Cover and refrigerate for a minimum of 3 hours or overnight. Serve by first sprinkling some cocoa (through a small sieve) onto individual dessert plates, and then spooning some of the tiramisu over it.

APPLES AND PEARS WITH GINGER IN A MILAN CHARLOTTE

Mele e pere allo zenzero in charlotte alla milanese

Serves 6

There is an old dessert in Milan that is made in a ring mold by placing buttered and sugared pieces of French bread in the bottom of the mold, layering the bread with apples, raisins, and pine nuts, and again more sugared and buttered bread on top. When it is cooked, some rum is added and set aflame. I have updated this dessert by lining small timbales with thin bread pieces, filling them with apples and pears, baking them, and turning them out. They are as pretty as a picture and delicious. Lining the timbales with the bread is quite simple—think it through before attempting it, and you'll see how easy it is. No rum, no flambé. That is too French for my Italian taste.

To make the filling:
3 Fuji apples, peeled, cored, and sliced fine
3 pears, peeled, cored, and sliced fine
4 tablespoons butter
1 cup sugar
4 tablespoons finely chopped candied ginger
4 tablespoons fresh lemon juice

1. Combine all the ingredients in a large skillet or sauce pan and cook over low heat, stirring frequently, until the fruit is tender, about 20 minutes.

To make the molds:
The size mold (timbale) used here is 2¼ inches deep; bottom diameter is 2 inches, top diameter is 2⅝ inches. This is a 5-ounce timbale.

12 slices Pepperidge Farm thin sliced white bread, crusts removed
1 stick butter, softened
Filling, see above
½ cup heavy cream, whipped
2 tablespoons softened Gorgonzola
2 tablespoons finely chopped candied ginger

1. Preheat oven to 350°F. Butter 6 slices of thin bread and cut each in 4 equal pieces. Cover with plastic and set aside.

2. Lay the remaining 6 slices on a flat work surface. Using appropriate-sized round cutters, cut 2 rounds, 1 for the bottom and top of each timbale. If you don't have the right size cutters, improvise. Glasses that are 2 inches wide at the mouth and 1-ounce bar (jigger) glasses can be used to cut the bread into rounds. Liberally butter the inside of each timbale, and liberally butter the 6 smaller and 6 larger rounds of bread.

3. Place a small round of bread in each of the 6 timbales, buttered side down in the mold. Then take 4 buttered squares and place them inside the mold, buttered side against the mold, to fit around the inside.

Simply lay 1 next to the other, and they will fit. Then spoon in some of the apple and pear mixture almost to the top of the mold. Place a larger bread round, buttered side up, in the top of each mold covering the apple and pear filling. Set the 6 molds in a small baking dish and bake 45 minutes. The bread should be golden; if not, bake 5 to 10 minutes longer. Remove from the oven and let rest 5 minutes or so. With a sharp paring knife, insert it into the mold between the bread and the outer rim of the mold and go around the mold to help loosen the "charlotte." With the help of a cloth napkin, turn out each mold to the center of a dessert plate.

4. Combine the whipped cream and the Gorgonzola by swirling the cheese into the whipped cream. Do not try to combine them completely. Spoon some of this sauce to the side of each timbale. Sprinkle some ginger confetti over the plate, and serve.

CREAM WITH LEMON AND BRANDY
Crema al limon

Serves 4

This simple dessert is an example of the fine Italian hand and its use of lemon. The zest and the lemon juice must be fresh.

1 pint heavy cream
1 tablespoon finely minced lemon zest
½ cup confectioners' sugar
1½ tablespoons fresh lemon juice
1 ounce brandy
8 chocolate curls for garnish

1. Whip the cream until it makes peaks. Fold in the lemon zest with the help of a rubber spatula.

2. Fold in the sugar, 2 tablespoons at a time. Add the lemon juice and again fold gently. If it should need additional whipping, do so with a wire whisk. Fold in the brandy.

3. Fill 4 stem glasses with the cream mixture and refrigerate for a minimum of 2 hours to allow the flavors to blend. Before serving, add 1 or 2 chocolate curls to the top.

ZABAGLIONE FROM BASSANO DEL GRAPPA

Zabaglione da Bassone del Grappa

Serves 4

The Ponte degli Alpini is a Palladio-designed bridge that crosses from the ceramics-thriving city of Bassano del Grappa into the old town. At the town edge of the bridge is the famous Nardini grappa distillery. It has been in operation since the eighteenth century, for grappa was invented here. The alcoholic content of grappa, a brandy, is about 40 percent. It is distilled from the pressed skin and seeds of grapes left after making wine. It can taste like raw alcohol when new, but as it ages, its taste is more refined—and as it ages, its cost goes up.

The more expensive grappas come in beautifully designed hand-blown bottles. It is rarely used in Italian cooking, but it can be used for flambéing and for preserving berries. Many Italians preserve berries this way; later, they eat the berries and then have a small glass of the flavored grappa as a *digestivo*. In this recipe, grappa is used to flavor the egg and wine mixture to make a zabaglione, and, of course, it is served over a variety of fresh berries.

1½ pints of fresh berries (raspberries, strawberries, blueberries, et al., singly or together)
4 egg yolks
¼ cup sugar
½ cup dry white wine
¼ cup grappa

1. If the berries have been refrigerated, bring to room temperature. Put 8 berries aside for garnish. Arrange some or all of the berries on 4 plates. Set aside to receive the warm zabaglione when it is made.

2. Combine the yolks and the sugar in the top pan of a double boiler (the boiling water should not touch the bottom of the pan with the yolks). With the top pan off the heat, heat the eggs and sugar until the mixture is thick and lemony in color. Bring the boiling water in the bottom pan to a simmer.

3. Put the top pan over the bottom one and whisk constantly until the mixture thickens and foams, about 10 minutes. Add the wine and grappa, a little at a time, but whisk constantly to increase the volume of the egg mixture. It should be thick enough to coat a spoon. Spoon immediately over the berries; add 2 berries onto each and serve.

SWEET SEMOLINA DIAMONDS WITH GRANA AND HONEY

Gialetti, "zaleti" con grana e miele

Makes about 36 cookies

Semolina flour, made from durum wheat, is the basis of many pastas. Here, it is combined with sugar and all-purpose flour to produce a slightly sweet, crunchy, rum-raisin cookie.

1 cup light rum
1 cup seedless golden raisins
4 egg yolks, room temperature
1 cup sugar
2 cups all-purpose flour
1½ cups semolina flour
1 cup (2 sticks) butter, melted and cooled
1 teaspoon vanilla
Grated zest from 1 lemon
½ cup pine nuts
2 tablespoons confectioners' sugar
8 to 12 thin shavings of Grana cheese
4 tablespoons acacia honey

1. Combine rum and raisins in a small bowl and set aside for several hours (or overnight, if you wish) to plump. Drain raisins, reserving liquid. Pat raisins dry.

2. Preheat oven to 375°F. Generously butter baking sheets. Beat eggs and sugar in the bowl of an electric mixer until a slowly dissolving ribbon forms when beaters are lifted, about 6 or 7 minutes.

3. Combine the flours and gradually mix into egg mixture. Blend in the melted butter, vanilla, lemon zest, and the reserved raisin liquid and some salt to taste. Turn dough out onto a floured surface. Knead until smooth, about 5 minutes (or do this in a mixer with a dough hook). Sprinkle raisins and pine nuts over dough and continue kneading just until incorporated.

4. Lightly flour work surface again and roll dough out to thickness of ⅓ inch. Using a very sharp knife, cut dough diagonally into 2-inch-wide strips—then cut diagonally in opposite directions to form diamonds.

5. Transfer diamonds to baking sheets, spacing evenly. Bake until cookies are lightly colored, about 20 minutes. Cool and store in airtight container. To serve, arrange 2 or 3 cookies on a plate. Sprinkle with confectioners' sugar before. Add 2 pieces of Grana and a tablespoon of honey placed next to the cheese.

RICOTTA WITH HONEY AND THYME SAUCE
Ricotta al miele e timo

Serves 4

Ricotta is widely used in Italian cooking for both savory and sweet dishes. It is considered a fresh cheese and does not have the depth of other Italian cheeses in spite of its excellent texture. It therefore is a candidate for seasoning, such as honey, as in the following recipe, or pepper, nutmeg, fresh chopped herbs, and, in fact, other cheeses, such as Parmigiano-Reggiano, in lasagnas and ravioli. In sweet dishes, it is perhaps best known for its use in cheesecakes (Italians love cheesecakes, and every Italian cook has a recipe), and it is often combined with fruit.

Ricotta means "recooked"; the leftover whey from hard cheeses is reheated with some milk to make a soft white curd cheese. It is a cheese most Americans like because it has a fat content of only 20 percent. Almost all supermarkets carry ricotta in whole, skim, or fat-free versions, but unfortunately none of them have the taste or texture of those sold as fresh ricotta in special Italian markets. Look for an Italian food store in your neighborhood—it will be worth the search, especially if the ricotta is to be used in this dessert. The honey and fresh thyme with the ricotta here are an unusually good combination of food, and a poetic touch of Italian ingenuity.

2 cups of fresh ricotta
1 cup wildflower honey
2 teaspoons fresh thyme leaves, including small flowers
4 small sprays of thyme

1. Divide the ricotta onto 4 dessert plates.
2. Heat the honey in a small sauce pan until it liquefies, about 4 minutes. Spoon or pour some honey on each of the 4 servings.
3. Sprinkle the thyme leaves and flowers over the honey, arrange a thyme spray on each plate alongside the ricotta, and serve.

DESSERTS

PANETTONE BREAD PUDDING
Budino di panettone

Serves 8 to 12

Panettone, a rich, buttery bread supposedly first made in Milan, is the most popular holiday bread in Italy. It is a household staple at Christmastime, and in this country it is available all year long in many supermarkets. Bread pudding made with pannettone is made all over Italy, and each area, city, village, and town claims the origin of this buttery, sweet, brioche-type bread.

16 slices pannettone, 2 inches wide by ½ inch thick by 6 inches high
1½ sticks butter, cut into 6 pieces
¾ cup honey
½ cup dark rum
6 large eggs
¾ cup sugar
1½ cups heavy cream
4½ cups milk

1. Preheat oven to 375°F. Butter an oval glass or ceramic baking dish 15x10x3 inches. Arrange the slices of pannettone on the bottom to cover, overlapping as necessary.

2. In a small sauce pan, melt the butter over low heat, then add the honey and rum. Raise the heat and stir all the time. The mixture should bubble and thicken. Remove from the heat and pour over the bread, spreading it as evenly as you can.

3. Beat the eggs and the sugar until well-combined. Slowly add the cream and then the milk to bring it all together. Be sure the mixture is well mixed. Pour over the bread.

4. Bake for 20 minutes, lower the heat to 325°F, and bake 20 minutes longer until the bread has a golden color and the pudding is set.

CHOCOLATE SOUFFLÉ WITH FIG PRESERVES

Budino di cioccolato con marmellata di fichi

Serves 4

This "soufflé" is baked in a shallow dish rather than the traditional deep mold. This is a bit of magic and is a delightful dessert. Different jams and preserves may be used, although in the southern part of Italy, figs are preferred. Be careful and follow the directions when beating the egg yolks and whites.

Soft butter to grease the baking dish, 1 to 2 tablespoons
4 eggs, separated, room temperature
¼ cup sugar
¼ cup Dutch process cocoa powder
2 tablespoons orange liqueur
8 tablespoons fig preserves
1 tablespoon powdered sugar

1. Position the baking rack in the upper ⅓ of the oven and preheat to 375°F. Butter a 9x14x2-inch glass oval gratin or baking o the whites (which may also be metal or enamel).

2. Beat egg yolks in a large bowl of an electric mixer until pale yellow and slowly dissolving ribbons form when the beaters are lifted, 6 to 8 minutes. Beat egg whites in another bowl until soft peaks form. Beat in the sugar to the whites, about 1 tablespoon at a time. Add the cocoa to whites about 1 tablespoon at a time and continue beating until stiff but not dry. Gently fold yolks into egg white mixture, then fold in liqueur.

3. Spoon fig preserves into the prepared baking dish in mounds, spacing evenly. Pour the egg mixture over and smooth with a spatula. Bake until the "soufflé" is puffy, about 15 minutes.

4. Sprinkle with powdered sugar and serve immediately, including 2 portions of preserves with each serving.

ICE CREAM

PURPLE PLUM (NUN'S THIGHS) ICE CREAM

Gelato di Prugne

Serves 4 to 6

One type of purple plum is irreverently called "nun's thighs" in Italy (I understand the irreverence started in Rome), and it makes a wonderful ice cream which is sold all over Italy. These plums flood our supermarkets in summer, and you can cook the plum pulp and freeze and save it for making ice cream anytime you wish.

3 cups skinned, pitted, diced, purple plums (6 to 8 plums)
¾ cup sugar
2½ cups milk
½ cup heavy cream, whipped
8 edible nasturtiums

1. In a medium saucepan, combine the nun's thighs (plums) and the sugar and cook over medium heat 6 or 7 minutes, until the sugar is dissolved and the plums are soft. Transfer this mixture to the food processor and pulse to a count of 10, until it is smooth. Strain this mixture, discarding the solids, and measure 2¼ cups puree. Cover and refrigerate to chill completely.

2. Put the milk and 1½ cups of the chilled plum puree in the ice cream machine and freeze according to the manufacturer's instructions. When the ice cream is formed, transfer to a freezer container, such as a plastic container with a lid, and put in the freezer for at least 1 hour.

3. If serving the iceNacnich@cs.com cream on its own, that is, without the peach dish included in this menu, then combine the remaining plum puree with the whipped cream. Do not overcombine—try to keep it streaked—and serve the ice cream with the streaked-plum cream and a nasturtium to the side of each serving.

ICE CREAM WITH SAMBUCA AND ESPRESSO

Gelato con sambuca ed espresso

Serves 6

Simple and elegant. This is a dessert you can use again and again.

Add a little more Sambuca and espresso granules if you wish.

1 quart vanilla ice cream
6 tablespoons Sambuca
⅓ cup instant espresso granules

1. Place 2 small balls of ice cream in each plate or glass. Pour 1 tablespoon Sambuca over each serving and dust with instant espresso.

MOSCATO SORBET
Sorbetto di moscato

Makes 1 quart

Sweet dessert wines are made all over the boot of Italy, and they are available in the United States at most wine shops. On New Year's Day, when promises are made to start the new year in the right away, it seems in order to present a lighter dessert. This sorbet can be a perfect way to end this meal. If you feel you want to add a confection, say, a cookie, see pages 337. Remember that alcohol does not freeze, so the wine must be boiled slowly—this will let the alcohol "cook off." Later, before the sorbet is finally frozen, a little more moscato wine will be added to reinforce the sorbet's flavor.

1½ cups water
1½ cups sugar
4 cups Moscato wine, plus 3 tablespoons chilled
3 tablespoons fresh lemon juice (1 lemon)

1. Make a simple syrup by combining the water and the sugar in a small sauce pan, bringing the mixture to boil, lowering the heat, and simmering until the sugar is completely dissolved, 3 to 4 minutes. You should not see any sugar crystals in the water. Remove the pan from the heat; it is important that this be completely cooled.

2. Pour the 4 cups of wine in another sauce pan. Bring this to boil, lower the heat, and simmer about 15 minutes to reduce the wine to a little under 3 cups. Again, remove from the heat and allow to cool sufficiently.

3. Put both the syrup and the reduced wine in the container of an ice cream maker. Add the fresh lemon juice and freeze according to the manufacturer's instructions. When the sorbet develops a thick, smooth consistency, about 20 minutes later, add the 3 tablespoons chilled Moscato wine. Continue to operate the ice cream maker until the sorbet has formed. Transfer to a plastic container with a lid and put in the freezer, if not using immediately. To serve, transfer the frozen sorbet to the refrigerator about 1 hour before needed—this will make it easier to scoop.

PINEAPPLE ICE WITH STRAWBERRY SAUCE
Sorbetto al pompelmo con salsa alle fragole

Serves 6

Sorbets are always welcomed desserts when a main course is strong enough and there just isn't room for a rich dessert. Fresh fruit makes delicious sorbets, although you will need an ice cream maker. When sorbet is made ahead and frozen, it needs time out of the freezer to "soften" a bit before serving.

3¾ cups unsweetened pineapple juice
1½ cups sugar
1 tablespoon unflavored gelatin, softened in ⅓ cup water
1½ tablespoons fresh lemon juice
Strawberry sauce, see below
12 (1-inch) squares fresh pineapple

1. In a nonaluminum sauce pan, bring 1½ cups pineapple juice to boil. Reduce heat to low. Add the sugar and the gelatin mixture and cook until both the sugar and gelatin are dissolved. Remove from the heat and let cool.

2. Add the lemon juice and the remaining pineapple juice. Refrigerate until well chilled. Transfer to an ice cream maker and process according to the manufacturer's directions.

3. Spoon some strawberry sauce onto individual plates or into goblets. Top with a scoop of sorbet and 2 pieces of fresh pineapple.

To make strawberry sauc (about 3 cups):
2 (12-ounce) bags frozen unsweetened strawberries, thawed
½ cup sugar
¼ cup strawberry preserves

1. Puree all ingredients in a processor and strain through a fine sieve.

TANGERINE SORBET WITH LEMON LIQUEUR

Sorbetto al mandarino con liquore di limone

Serves 4 plus

A wonderful combination of citrus flavors. Most sorbets, when made ahead and frozen, become hard (almost too difficult to scoop). Be sure to remove from the freezer ten minutes or so before you're ready to serve.

½ cup water
¾ cup sugar
1 cup fresh orange juice
1 tablespoon fresh lemon juice
1 teaspoon grated tangerine zest (about 2 small tangerines)
¼ cup lemon liqueur, such as Ramo d'Oro
1 cup Asti Spumante

1. Put the water and the sugar in a pan and bring to boil over medium heat, stirring frequently. Transfer to a bowl.

2. Add all the other ingredients and mix well.

3. Pour into the container of an ice cream mixer and follow the manufacturer's directions. When the sorbet has reached the desirable consistency, move into containers and freeze until needed.

BLUEBERRY ICE WITH MELON BALL SPEARS

Granita di mirtilli con palline di melone

Serves 4

In addition to its beauty as a dessert, this blueberry ice and melon combination is delicious. All of it can be made ahead. Bring the ice out of the freezer ten minutes or so before you're ready to serve, to soften it a little.

1½ cups water
1 cup plus 2 tablespoons sugar
1½ pints fresh blueberries, picked over, rinsed, and drained
3 tablespoons fresh lemon juice
Melon ball spears, see below
4 mint sprigs

1. In a sauce pan, combine the water and sugar and bring to boil. Lower heat and simmer, stirring frequently, until the sugar is dissolved. Transfer to a nonaluminum bowl and set over ice water to chill for 1 hour, stirring occasionally.

2. Meanwhile, put the blueberries through a food mill in batches. Add the puree to the cooled syrup. Stir in the lemon juice. Cover with plastic and refrigerate for several hours.

3. Freeze in an ice cream maker according to manufacturer's instructions. Freeze until ready to serve.

4. To serve, place a scoop of the ice on each plate and lay a melon ball spear alongside. Garnish with a mint sprig.

<u>To make the melon ball spears:</u>
20 melon balls (from cantaloupe, honeydew, or any other melon of your choice)
¼ cup grappa
16 fresh blueberries

1. Marinate the melon balls in the grappa 30 minutes or so. Drain. Thread on 4 long bamboo skewers, alternating melon balls and blueberries, using 5 melon balls and 4 blueberries on each.

Chapter *12*

BASICS

A BASIC MEAT AND POULTRY BROTH

Brodo Misto

Makes about 3 quarts

When Italians use broth, they will usually combine meat and poultry to achieve a more complex and richer taste. In Italy, this is sometimes considered a holiday broth, in addition to the broth made with a capon. It may be used in soups, stews, pasta sauces, and for risotti. Keep in mind, however, that Italians will often use water as the primary liquid in making a dish—for example, in Naples they add water to vegetables to make a vegetable soup or minestrone. At one time I asked a Neopolitan why water, and his reply was that nothing is to interfere with the taste of the vegetables.

4 pounds beef and veal bones, including some beef shank, beef, or veal marrow bones and neck bones
1½ pounds chicken legs, thighs, and other parts
4 quarts of water
5 onions, each cut into 8 pieces
5 ribs celery with leaves, coarsely chopped
5 carrots, each coarsely sliced
1 can (14 ounces) Italian plum tomatoes, drained and chopped or 3 large tomatoes, coarsely chopped
¼ cup coarsely chopped Italian parsley

1. Rinse the meat and poultry and put it in a large stockpot with the water. Bring to a boil over medium-high heat and cook uncovered 20 minutes. As foam comes to the top of the pot, skim it off.

2. Add the vegetables, 3 teaspoons coarse salt, and 2 teaspoons freshly ground pepper, and return to boil. Bring to a simmer by reducing heat, and cover the pot partially. Cook until the meat falls off the bones, about 3½ to 4 hours.

3. Let broth cool, remove the meat and bones, and strain through 2 or 3 layers of dampened cheesecloth. Discard the bones and meat and refrigerate the broth. The fat will congeal during the night, so in the morning, remove the top layer of fat. It will come off in large pieces like broken, thin chocolate. Refrigerate for several days or freeze for several months. Always bring to boil before using it in a recipe.

CHICKEN BROTH
Brodo di pollo

Makes about 2½ quarts

Italians do not always agree on broth-making techniques; perhaps this is why there are so many recipes. But they do agree that a soup bone should be cracked before it goes into the soup pot and that parsley stems are more important to the broth than their leaves.

3 pounds chicken parts, including wings, backs, gizzards, necks, and other bones
1 pound veal marrow bones, cracked
3½ quarts water
2 carrots, sliced coarsely
1 large leek, washed carefully, cut into thin slices, including green parts
8 parsley stems without leaves, chopped coarsely
1 large sprig fresh thyme or 1 teaspoon dried

1. Put the chicken and veal in a large stockpot, add the water, and bring to boil over medium-high heat. Boil 10 minutes, skimming off the foam as it appears.

2. Add the carrots, leeks, parsley, thyme, and 1 teaspoon each of salt and pepper. Bring to boil, uncovered. Reduce the heat to achieve a steady simmer and cover pot partially. Simmer for 2 hours.

3. Strain the broth through 2 or 3 layers of dampened cheesecloth. Discard the bones and meat and everything else in the strainer. Put the broth in the refrigerator and leave overnight. The fat will congeal, making it easy to remove it the next morning. Keep refrigerated several days or freeze for 4 months, but always bring to boil before using.

VEGETABLE BROTH
Brodo vegetale

Makes about 2½ quarts

A Neapolitan chef (who prefers to be called a cook) working at the famous L'Ortica restaurant in Rome said that only water should be used to make vegetable stock, and the vegetables must be fresh and simmered a long time (over an hour). Do not be tempted, as some cooks are, to add a light chicken- or other meat-flavored broth to make a vegetable one.

1 pound cremini or other mushroom, wiped clean and coarsely chopped, including stems
4 ribs celery with leaves, thinly sliced
4 large carrots, trimmed, thinly sliced
2 medium boiling potatoes, rinsed well, cut into 1-inch pieces with skins on
1 large leek, carefully rinsed, thinly sliced
4 cloves garlic, unpeeled, cut in halves
¼ cup chopped Italian parsley stems (without leaves)
1 teaspoon freshly ground pepper
3½ quarts water

1. Put everything in a large stockpot and bring to boil over high heat. Bring to simmer by reducing heat, and cook, uncovered, 1½ hours.

2. Line a sieve with several layers of dampened cheesecloth and strain the stock. Discard the cooked solids and refrigerate the broth overnight. Remove the congealed fat the next morning. Keep in the refrigerator for several days, or freeze for 4 months, but always bring to boil before using.

FISH/SHRIMP BROTH
Brodo di pesce e gamberi

Makes about 6 cups

The addition of uncooked shrimp shells in making a fish broth can add a lot of flavor. This is especially useful if the fish dish being prepared includes shrimp—for stews, brodettos, and soups—then reserve the shrimp shells and add them as in the recipe. However, if you do not want the flavor of shrimp in the broth, simply eliminate the shrimp shells and double the nonoily fish ingredient by making it two pounds instead of one and continuing with the recipe.

Shells from 1 pound uncooked shrimp
1 pound fish bones from nonoily fish (heads should be included but the gills should be removed), cut into small pieces
1 medium onion, coarsely chopped
2 ribs celery, including leaves, coarsely chopped
8 whole black peppercorns
2 small bay leaves
7 cups cold water
1 cup white wine
1 fish bouillon cube, optional

1. Put all the ingredients in a sauce pan and bring to boil over medium-high heat. Lower the heat, bring to a steady simmer, and cook 30 minutes. Strain. If to be stored, cover tightly and refrigerate up to 3 days, or freeze 1 to 2 months.

Nota bene: I try not to use bouillon cubes because of their high sodium content. I have seen, however, many Italian chefs add a touch of bouillon, be it chicken, beef, mushroom, fish, or vegetable. Italians seem to like salt more than Americans. If you want more flavor in the broth, add ½ bouillon cube first, then add more if needed.

HOMEMADE CAPPUCCINO
Cappuccino

Serves 6

Not many people own an espresso coffee machine, but it is possible to brew a fairly decent cup of cappuccino without one. Espresso coffee is sold in bean, grain, and granule form in most supermarkets across the United States. Choose one of these, heat and whip some milk dust with cocoa, and you will produce an exciting cup of homemade cappuccino.

6 regular-size cups brewed espresso
2 cups whole milk
1 tablespoon quality cocoa powder

1. Make the espresso by 1 of the methods mentioned above and keep warm.

2. Heat the milk in a small saucepan and whip with a wire whisk until it becomes frothy. This will take constant whipping and may take up to 5 minutes.

3. Pour the hot espresso into regular coffee cups, filling about ⅔ full. Immediately add the frothy milk to each cup. Dust with cocoa powder by putting the cocoa in a small sieve and tapping it lightly to dust over each cup. Serve immediately.

FRUIT VINEGARS
Aceto insaporito alla frutta

When I was visiting my cousins in Modena, after the lunch with Lucia, I paid a visit to her mother, Angela, at their home. Lucia's mother is my mother's niece. She teaches cooking in Modena. When I entered, the smells of vinegar and fruit were everywhere. Since I love anything vinegary, I thought, "What a way to greet me!"

Angela was knee deep in fruit: peaches, oranges, and raspberries. She crushed each one separately, and had to cut some of the peaches and oranges into smaller bits, plus making some zest of the orange peel. She put each different fruit in a large, nonreactive bowl and covered the peaches with red wine vinegar and the raspberries and the oranges, separately, with white wine vinegar. She carefully covered each bowl with plastic and left them in her kitchen to marinate for three days. She then boiled each mixture four or five minutes, removed them from the heat, and sieved the vinegar into bottles. She wanted me to take some of them home to the United States, but I said I was happy to know how she did it, and this is the way I learned to make and enjoy fruit vinegars. They are, at times, a pleasant relief from the constant use of balsamic, which seems to have taken over the United States.

SOURCES

Agata and Valentina
1505 First Ave.
New York, NY 10021
Telephone: 212-452-0690
Salt-packed anchovies, salted capers, and a wide variety of Italian products, including San Marzano tomatoes

The Bakers Catalogue
135 Route 5 South
Norwich, VT 05055
Telephone: 800-827-6836
www.kingarthureflour.com

Bel Canto Foods
1300 Viele Ave.
Bronx, NY 10474
Telephone: 718-497-3888
Pastas, oils, vinegars, olives, cheeses, grains, flours, and polenta

Bridge Kitchenware
563C Eagle Rock Ave.
Roseland, NJ 07068
Telephone: 800-274-3435
www.bridgekitchenware.com

Broadway Panhandler
65 E. Eighth St.
New York, NY 10003
Telephone: 866-266-5927
www.broadwaypanhandler.com

Butte Creek Mill
PO Box 1
Eagle Point, OR 97524
Telephone: 541-826-3531
Fax: 541-830-8444
Buckwheat flour, unbleached white bread flour, and semolina

Chef's Catalogue
PO Box 620048
Dallas, TX 75262
Telephone: 800-338-3232
Fax: 800-967-3291
Kitchenware, appliances, and cutlery

Club della Fattorie
Piazza dei Martiri della Liberta 2 Pienza, Italy
Fax: 0587-748-150

Dried porcini mushrooms, capers, balsamic vinegars, extra-virgin olive oils, pasta, preserves, candied fruits, cookies, chocolate, and honey

D'Artagnan
280 Wilson Ave.
Newark, NJ 07105
Telephone: 800-DARTAG or 973-344-0565
Fax: 973-465-1870
www.dartagnan.com
Pates, sausages, smoked delicacies, foie gras, organic game and poultry, and mushrooms

Dean and Deluca (New York store)
800-221-7714
www.deandeluca.com
Extension 221 for oils, spices, truffle oil, vinegars, coffees, olives, preserves, nuts, saffron, truffles; extension 247 for cheeses (scamorza, taleggio, caciocavalla for grating)

A. G. Ferrari Foods
14234 Catalina St.
San Leonardo, CA 94577
Telephone: 877-878-2783
www.agferrari.com
Oils from Lazio, Tuscany, Liguria and Sicily; wide selection of Italian pastas (from Naples, Marche, Gragnano, in Campagna, Lombardy, Emilia-Romagna, Sardinia, Abruzzi, Piemonte, Puglia, Basilicata); flavored oils, herbs from Italy; San Marzano tomatoes, saffron, rice, beans, polenta, stone-ground flours,

salamis, cheeses, honey, cherry and other jams, and torrone

Formaggio Kitchen
120 Essex St.
New York, NY 10002
244 Huron Ave.
Cambridge, MA 02138
Telephone: 888-212-3224
Fax: 617-547-5680
www.formaggiokitchen.com
Cheeses and oils from all over Italy; flavored oils; pastas and rices; biscotti; mostarda di cremona and other condiments; cherry and other fruit jams and honey from Sardinia

Kalustyan's
123 Lexington Ave.
New York, NY 10016
Telephone: 800-352-3451
www.kalustyans.com

Lobel's of New York
1096 Madison Ave.
New York, NY 10028
Telephone: 800-565-2357
www.lobels.com

Mackenzie
1027 Wilso Dr.
Baltimore, MD 21223
Telephone: 800-858-7100
Fax 800-858-6547
www.mackenzieltd.com

Leg and rack of lamb, salmon, lump crabmeat, soft-shell crabs, artisanal balsamic vinegar, Ravida Sicilian olive oil, Cergnola olives, whole bean espresso coffee, and coffee grinders

Manganaro Foods
488 Ninth Ave.
New York, NY 10018
Telephone: 800-472-5264 and 212-563-5331
Fax: 212-239-8355
Wide assortment of Italian products, including cured meats

Melissa's/World Variety Produce
Telephone: 800-588-0150
www.melissas.com

Napa Style, Inc.
801 Main St.
St. Helena, CA 94574
Telephone: 866-766-6272
www.napastyle.com
Preserves, pasta flour, cocoa powder, honey, rice, spices, polenta, coffee, and herbs

Niman Ranch
Telephone: 866-808-0340
www.nimanranch.com

Penzeys Spices
Telephone: 800-741-7787
www.penzeys.com

Salumeria Biellese
376-378 Eighth Ave.
New York, NY 10001
Telephone: 212-736-7376
www.salumicuredmeats.com

Salumi Artisan Cured Meats
309 Third Ave. S
Seattle, WA 98104
877-223-0813
www.salumicuredmeats.com

Viansa
PO Box 35
Vineburg, CA 95487-0035
Telephone: 888-875-5057
Fax: 707-935-4731
www.viansa.com
Oils, vinegars, sauces, spices, condiments, mustards, preserves, and nuts

Vinny's Deli and Pasta
14 East Main St.
Pawling, NY 12564
Telephone and fax: 845-855-1922
Pastas, imported cheeses, oils, vinegars, olives, cured meats, and fresh mozzarella

John Volpi and Co.
5254 Daggett Ave.
St. Louis, MO 63110
Telephone: 800-288-3439, ext. 3332
www.volpifoods.com

Zingerman's
422 Detroit St.

Ann Arbor, MI 48104
Telephone: 888-636-8162
Fax: 734-477-6988
www.zingermans.com
Oils, chocolates, vinegars, spices, artichokes in oil, lemon oil, truffle oil, salamis, salt-packed anchovies and olives, and wild cherry jams

INDEX

Almonds,
    Amaretti and, Baked Stuffed Peaches, 346
    Cheese Tart 331
    and Chocolate, Roasted Figs with, 351
    Cookies, Enriched and Crisped Vanilla, 338
    Cream, Fresh Berries with, 348
    Peppers with, Basilicata Style, 35
Amaretti (Italian macaroons)
    and Almonds, Baked Stuffed Peaches, 346
    and Crisped Leeks, Asparagus and Leek Soup with, 46
    Crumbs, Apricots with Cream and, 355
Amaretto, Caffe Poliziano's Tiramisu, 358
Anchovies,
    Capers and, Grilled Eggplant with, 3
    Hot, Mortadella and Fontina Canapes, 26
    Sauce
        Caper/, Swordfish Steaks with, 202
        Grilled Peppes in, Roasted Olives, 18
Angel Hair Pasta, in Custard Mold, 95
Appetizers,
    Roasted Peppers and Eggplant Puree, 14
Apples
    Cake, Lemony, 319
    Pears with Ginger in Milan Charlotte, 359

Apricots with Amaretti Crumbs & Cream, 355
Artichokes
    Cooked in a Saucepan, 128
    Mold, Individual, with Taleggio Sauce and Sage, 151
    Mortadella and Fontina Pizza, 313
Arugula
    Tomato Salad with Lemon Dressing, 267
Asiago Cheese, 288
Asparagus
    Grilled, and Parma Ham Salad, 20
    with Oil, Vinegar and Hard-Cooked Eggs, on Radiccio, 16
    Soup
        and Leek, with Crushed Amaretti and Crisped Leeks, 46
        Pietro Tecchhio's, 53
    Vegetable Rainbow of Zucchini, Carrots, Broccoli Rabe and, 154

Bacon Omelet with Parsley, 7
Bari
    Special Provolone cheese from, 286
Basil
    Pesto, Spaghetti with Chef Gilberto

Pizzi's, 52
  Spaghetti with Clams, Cherry Tomatoes and, 75
Basilicata
  Style Peppers with Almonds, 35
Beans
  Baked, from Piedmont, 141
  Fava
    Country Style, 129
  Green
    Benedectine Monks' Pancetta and Savory with, 262
    with Onion Sauce, 150
  Marinated Cannellini, with Oregano and Crisp Salami, 33
  with Tuna, 174
  in Tuscany, 136
  White, with Mushrooms, 136
Beef, Braised in Red Wine and Spices, 231
Beet Salad, Roasted, with Red Onions and Dried Fennel, 259
Bel Paese cheese, 280
Berries, Fresh, with Almond Cream, 348
Biga (starter for bread), 293
Biscotti, Almond, with Fresh, Sugared Red and White Grapes and Vin Santo, 340
Blueberry
  Ice with Melon Ball Spears, 372
Bologna
  Lasagna Baked with Meat Sauce, 82
  Ragu, 71
Bouillon cubes, 377
Brandy
  Cream with Lemon and, 361
  Grilled Eels with Wine, Thyme and, 194

Bread crumbs,
  Toasted, Pasta with Mascarpone, Sage and, 88
Breads
  Flat, of Emilia-Romagna, 308
  Italian Slipper, 295
  Pudding, Panettone, 365
  Round Loaf of Italian, Roasted Chicken Salad in, 260
  Toasts, with Truffles, 28
Broccoli
  Baked with Prosciutto, 143
  and Cauliflower, 132
  Cooked in Garlic-Flavored Oil, 64, 152
Broccoli Rabe
  Braised, Lasagna Squares with, 64
  and Goat Cheese Pizza, 312
  Spicy Polenta with Cheese, Sausages and, 124
  Vegetable Rainbow of Zucchini, Asparagus, Carrots and, 154
Broths,
  Chicken, 375
  Fish, 377
  Homemade Tortellini in, 54
  Meat and Poultry, 374
  Parmigiano in, and Poached Eggs, 50
  Seafood, 377
  Vegetable, 376
Bruschetta, 25
Brussels Sprouts, Sole Fillets Wrapped in Leeks with, 172
Butternut Squash with Cinnamon, 147

Cabbage
  Pasta with, Cheese and Potatoes, 74

Pork, and Bean Casserole, 239
Savoy, with Fresh Lemon, 140
Caciocavallo cheese,
Roasted Grapes with, 361
Cakes
Cheesecake, Maria Michele's Special, 316
Chocolate Mocha Ricotta, 318
Grand Galliano, 325
Lemony Apple, 319
Orange Ring, 317
Sambuca-Flavored Cocoa Roll, 321
Sicilian Cream, 326
Sponge, 322
Venetian Nut, 321
Calabria
Onion Soup with Potatoes from, 57
Canapés
Crostini for, 300
Hot Anchovy, Mortadella and Fontina, 26
Cannelloni alla Peppino's (Piacenza), 86
Cantalope
Melon Balls in Honeydew Puree, 339
with Prosciutto, 8
Capers
and Anchovies, Grilled Eggplant with, 3
Anchovy Sauce, Swordfish Steaks with, 202
and Chive Sauce, Fried Zucchini with, 144
and Tarragon, Salad of Assorted Lettuces with, 277
Capon
Christmas, with Condiment from Cremona, 222
Stuffing for, 223
Caponata, 2
Cappuccino, 378
Caprini Cheese
Assorted Melon with, 352

Carpaccio
of Sea Bass with Herbs, 10
Carrots
with Marsala, 157
Salmon in Parchment with Spinach and, 182
Spaghettini with Clams, Wine and, 92
Vegetable Rainbow of Zucchini, Asparagus, Broccoli
Rabe and, 154
Casseroles
Lamb, Pepper and Pasta, 252
Pork, Cabbage and Bean, 239
Cauliflower
Baked, with Sardinian Pasta, 166
Broccoli and, 132
Salad, Traditional, 271
Celery, Glazed, in Mustard Sauce, 153
Charlotte, Apples and Pears with Ginger in Milan, 339
Cheesecake, Maria Michele's Special, 316
Cheeses, *See also specific cheeses* 280-1
Spicy Polenta with, broccoli rabe, and Sausages, 124
Sweet macaroni with, 61
Tart, Almond, 331
Tray, with Mostardo, 285
Turkey Breasts, Baked with Prosciutto and, 220
Two, Tagliatelle Baked with, 89
Cherry Tart, Wild, 327
Chestnut Puree, with Sweet Whipped Cream and Candied
Orange Strips, 342
Chicken
Broth, 375
Herbed, on Grill, 214
Kale, and Chickpea Stew, 216
Livers, Tuscan Style Risotto with, 113

Risotto, with Vegetables, Venetian Style, 123
Salad, Roasted, in Round Loaf of Italian Bread, 260
Chickpea Stew, Chicken, Kale and, 216
Chicory, *See also* Endive
    Hearts and Radicchio, Scallops and Pancetta on, 39
    Salad Mimosa, 275
    and Smoked Mozzarella on Grill, 131
Chili, Spaghetti with Garlic and, 97
Chives
    and Capers Sauce, Fried Zucchini with, 144
    Tomatoes with, 266
Chocolate
    Almonds and, Roasted Figs with, 351
    Mocha Ricotta Cake, 318
    Roll with Zabaglione Sauce, Apollinare's, 323
    Soufflé, with Fig Preserves, 366
Chowder, Fisherman's, 187
Christmas
    Capon with Condiment from Cremona, 222
Cinnamon, Butternut Squash with, 147
Clams
    Spaghetti with Cherry Tomatoes, Basil and, 75
    Spaghettini with, Carrots and Wine, 92
    with Wine in Portofino, 175
Cocoa Roll, Sambuca-Flavored, 320
Codfish, Fresh, with Potatoes and Onions, 179
Cookies
    Cousin Guiseppe's Meringue, 337
    Semolina Diamonds with Grana and Honey, 363
    From Siena, Famous, 335
    Vanilla-Almond, Enriched and Crisped, 338
Cornish Hens
    with Ricotta and Tarragon, 213
Cornmeal. *See* Polenta
Country Loaf, 292
Crabs, Fried Soft-shell, 181

Cream
    Almond, Fresh Berries with, 348
    Apricots with Amaretti Crumbs and, 355
    Cake, Sicilian, 326
    with Lemon and Brandy, 361
    Pasta Bows with Mushrooms, Fresh Spinach and, 109
Cream, Whipped
    Chestnut Puree with Sweet, and Candied Orange Strips, 342
    Green Tomato Jam with Zabaglione and, 333
    Strawberries in Vinegar Balsamic, with Mint and, 347
Cucumbers
    with Mint, 269
    Sauce, Rotelle Pasta Salad with, 99

Desserts
    Apricots with Amaretti Crumbs and Cream, 355
    Chocolate Roll with Zabaglione Sauce, Apollinare's, 323
Duck, Stewed, Lentils with, 18

Eels,
    Grilled, with Wine, Brandy and Thyme, 194
Egg Pasta, 104
Eggplant
    Grilled, with Capers and Anchovies, 3
    and Pasta, Timbale of 100
    Rigatoni with, in Creamy Curry Sauce, 98
    And Roasted Peppers Puree Appetizer, 14
Eggs. *See also* Omelets
    Hard-Cooked, with Asparagus, Oil, Vinegar, on Radicchio, 16
    Poached, Parmigiano in Broth and, 50
    in Purgatory with Grilled Sausages, 238
    With Tuna Mayonnaise, 41

INDEX

Endive, Curly, and Fennel Matchstick Salad, with Fresh Herb
    Dressing, 270
  Hearts of, with Red Pepper Congetti, 212
Espresso, Ice Cream with Sambuca and, 368

Fennel,
  Dried, Roasted Beet Salad with Red Onions and, 259
  Fresh
    with Parslied Oil and Vinegar, 31
    Slices, in Salad with Watercress, 263
  Grilled, with Frsh Lemon, 274
  Matchstick Salad, Curly Endive and, with Fresh Herb
    Dressing, 270
  Mold, with Herbs, 148
  Seeds, Roasted Potatoes with, 169
Fettuccine with Soked Salmon all' Orsini, 68
Figs
  with Kirsch, 345
  and Pine Nut Tart, 329
  Preserves, Chocolate Soufflé with, 366
  Roasted, with Almonds and Chocolate, 351
Fish. *See also specific fish*
  Broth, 377
  for chowder, 187
  Cleaning, 13 (NOTE)
  Fillets, Neopolitan Fisherman's Style, 190
Flatbread, Semolina, with Rosemary, 299
Flour, measuring, 292 (NOTE)
Focaccia
  with Fresh Marjoram and Olive Oil, 303
  with Fresh Sage, Olive Oil and Salt, 297
Foie Gras with Hazelnuts, 4
Fondue,
  Val d'Aosta's Fontina, with Steamed Vegetables, 11

Fontina cheese, 11
  Artichokes, and Mortadella Pizza, 313
  Fondue, with Steamed Vegetables, 11
  Hot Anchovy, and Mortadella Canapés, 26
  Polenta and, with Tomatoes and Roasted Red Peppers, 115
Food processor,
  Pastry in, 328 (NOTE)
Frittata with Pancetta, Pasta and Peas, 32
Fritters, Ricotta Cheese, 287
Fruit. *See also specific fruit*
  Compote with Citrus Sauce, 344
  Fresh, Seasonal, Italian Cheeses and, 284
  Vinegars, Lucia's Mother's, 379

Garlic,
  and Chili, Spaghetti with, 97
  Flavored Oil, Broccoli Cooked in, 64, 152
  Octopus with Wine, Oil, Parsley and, 12
  Pasta with Ginger and, 96
Ginger,
  Apples and Pears with, in Milan Charlotte, 359
  Pasta with Garlic and, 96
Gnocchi
  Ricotta, with Light Picante Tomato Shrimp Sauce, 76
  Roman Style, 62
Goat Cheese and Broccoli Rabe Pizza, 227
Gorgonzola cheese, 280
Grand cheese, 281
  Semolina Diamonds with Honey and, 363
Grapes
  Fresh, Sugared Red and White, with Vin Santo and Almond
    Biscotti, 340
  Roasted, with Caciocavallo, 353

Grappa, 16, 362
Greens, Spring, with Oil, Vinegar and Mint, 261
Gremolata, 246
Grills, cooking on, 131

Ham, *See also* Prosciutto
    Capocollo, 26
Ham (*cont.*)
    Parma
        Mortadella and Pickled Vegetables, 22
        Saffron Sauce, Tagliatelle in, 78
        Salad, Grilled Asparagus and, 20
    Veal Scallops with Sage and, 241
Hazelnuts
    Baked Mushrooms, with, 133
    Foie Gras with, 4
    Tart, Brandied, 332
Herbs. *See also* Spices; *specific herbs; specific spices*
    Aromatic, Sauteed Tuna with, 199
    Baked Pasta with Zucchini and, 67
    Carpaccio of Sea Bass with, 10
    Chicken, on Grill, 214
    Dressing, Curly Endive and Fennel Matchstick Salad with, 270
    Fennel Mold with, 148
    Quail with, Truffle Oil, 219
    Sliced Potatoes with Oil and, 138
    Tomatoes, Lobster with, 195
Honey
    Ricotta and, with Thyme, 364
    Semolina Diamonds with Grana and, 363
Honeydew Puree, Cantaloupe Melon Balls in, 339

Ice Cream
    Purple Plum, 367
    with Sambuca and Espresso, 368

Ices
    Blueberry, with Melon Ball Spears, 372
    Pineapple, with Strawberry Sauce, 370

Jam, Green Tomato, with Zabaglione and Whipped Cream, 333

Kale
    Chicken, and Chickpea Stew, 216
    Soup, 47
Kirsch, Figs with, 345

Lamb, 250
    Pepper and Pasta Casserole, 252
    Rosemary-Scented, Butterflied and Grilled Leg of, 251
    and Vegetables, Greek Style, 254
Lasagna
    Baked with Meat Sauce, Bologna Style, 82
    Chiara's, with Meat Sauce, 71
    Squares with Braised Broccoli Rabe, 64
Leeks
    and Asparagus Soup, with Crushed Amaretti and Crisped
        Leeks, 46
    Sole Fillets Wrapped in, with Brussels Sprouts, 172
Lemon
    Apple Cake, 319
    and Brandy, Cream with, 361
    Dressing
        Arugula and Tomato Salad with, 267
        Oil and, Baby Spinach Salad with, 268
    Fresh, Grilled Fennel with, 274
    Fresh, Savoy Cabbage with, 140
    Juice, Shrimp in Olive Oil and, with Rosemary, 193
    Liqueur, Tangerine Sherbet with, 371

Romaine Lettuce, Watercress and Snow Peas with, 293
Sauce, Spaghetti with, 63
Skewered Tuna Grilled with Oregano and, 197
Spinach with Oil and, 156
Lentils,
Soup, 51
Stewed, with Duck, 18
Lettuces
Romaine, Watercress and Snow Peas with Lemon, 273
Salad of Assorted, with Capers and Tarragon, 277
Liguria, xiii, 38, 74, 264, 265
Liqueurs, *See also specific liqueurs*
Lemon, Tangerine Sherbet with, 371
Lobster with Spicy Herbed Tomatoes, 195
Lombardy, 50, 111, 217, 226, 280, 349

Macaroni
Sweet, with Cheese, 61
The Marches, 187
Markets, open, xiv, 43
Marsala
Carrots with, 157
Sauce, Braised Pork Tenderloin with, 236
Sliced Oranges with, 276
Mascarpone
Pasta with, Sage and Toasted Bread Crumbs, 88
Pears Cooked in Wine with, 349
Mayonnaise, Tuna, Eggs with, 41
Meat Loaf
Mozzarella, 232
Sicilian, 233
Meat mallet, or pounder, 217
Melon. *See also specific melon*
Assorted, with Caprini Cheese, 352
Ball Spears, Blueberry Ice with, 372

Milan
Charlotte, Apples and Pears with Ginger in, 359
Manner, Veal Cutlet in, 245
Risotto, 116
Veal Shanks, 246
Minestrone soup, Emilia Mastracci's, 44
Mint
Cucumbers with, 269
Spring Greens with Oil, Vinegar and, 261
Strawberries in Balsamic Vinegar, with Whipped Cream and, 347
Mortadella,
Artichokes and Fontina Pizza, 313
Fontina, and Hot Anchovy Canapés, 26
Parma Ham, and Pickled Vegetables, 22
Mostardo, Cheese Tray with, 285
Mozzarella cheese, 281
Baked Zucchini with, 165
Dried, 382
Pasta Bows with Fresh Spinach, Cream and, 109
White Beans with, 136

Naples, 38, 92, 103, 190, 257, 271
Nutmeg, 5, 54, 84
Nuts, *See also specific nuts*
Cake, Venetian, 321
Fruit, cheese and, 347

Octopus with Wine, Garlic, Oil and Parsley, 12
Oil
Garlic-Flavored, 312
Broccoli Cooked in, 152
Truffle, Quail with Herbs and, 219
Focaccia
with Fresh marjoram and, 303

with Fresh Sage, Salt and, 297
Shrimp in, and Lemon Juice with Rosemary, 193
Whipped Potatoes with, 162
Olives, Roasted, Grilled Peppers in Anchovy Sauce with, 38
Omelets. *See also* Frittata with Pancetta, Pasta and Peas
    Bacon, with Parsley, 32
Onions
    Baked Caramelized, 161
    Dried Fennel and Red, Roasted Beet Salad with, 259
    Fresh Codfish, Potatoes and, 199
    Sauce, Green Beans with, 150
    Soup, with Potatoes, Calabrian, 57
Oranges
    Caramelized, 350
    Panna Cotta, with Blueberry Sauce, 356
    Ring Cake, 317
    Slices
        with Marsala, 276
        with Slivers of Orange Zest, 343
    Strips, Chestnut Puree, with Sweet Whipped Cream and Candied, 342
Oregano,
    and Crisp Salami, Marinated Cannellini Beans with, 33
    Skewered Tuna Grilled with Lemon and, 197
Osso Buco (veal shanks), 246
Oxtail Stew, Braised, 227
Oysters
    Baked, Taranto Style, 36
    Shucking, 37

Pancetta,
    Frittata with Pasta, Peas and, 32
    and Savory, Benedictine Monks' Green Beans with, 262

and Scallops on Chicory Hearts and Radicchio, 39
Pane integrale, 25, 292, 301
Panettone
    Bread Pudding, 365
    Fingers, Peach Soup with Raspberries and, 354
Parchment paper, 182, 294, 316, 324, 339
Parma, xiii, 20
Parmesan cheese, 281
    Custard Tart, 17
Parmigiano in Broth, and Poached Eggs, 50
Parmigiano Reggiano, 285
    With Cheese Tray, 285
Parsley
    Bacon Omelet with, 7
    Octopus with Wine, Garlic, Oil, and, 12
    Oil, Fresh Fennel with Vinegar and, 31
Pasta, xxviii, 10-12. *See also specific pastas*
    Baked, with Zucchini and Herbs, 67
    Bows, with Fresh Spinach, Mushrooms and Cream, 109
    with Cabbage, Cheese and Potatoes, 74
    egg, 84
    Eggplant and, Timbale of, 100
    Frittata with Pancetta, Peas and, 32
    with Ginger and Garlic, 96
    Lamb, and Pepper Casserole, 252
    with Mascarpone, Sage and Toasted Bread Crumbs, 88
    Salad, Rotelle, with Cucumber Sauce, 99
    Sardinian, Baked Cauliflower with, 166
    Spinach, 84
    Stars of Italy with Two Sauces, 23
Pasta machine, 60, 71, 81, 103, 105
Pastry, 69
    Italian, 330
    Making, 69, 78

INDEX

Peaches
    Baked Stuffed, with Amaretti and Almonds, 346
    "Cobbler" from Countess d'Orbicciano, 341
    Soup, with Rapberries and Toasted Panettone Fingers, 334
Pears
    Apples and, with Ginger in Milan Charlotte, 359
    Cooked in Wine with Mascarpone, 349
Peas
    Frittata with Pasta, Pancetta and, 32
    Green, Grandomother's Way, 138
    and Rice Soup, Doge's, 118
    Snow, Romaine Lettuce, Watercress and, with Lemon 273
Pecorino cheese, 66, 73, 74, 97, 124
    Pasta with, Cabbage, and Potatoes, 74
    Spaghetti with Black Pepper and, 66
Penne Pasta
    with Cognac from Citta di Castello, 91
    with Pork Tomato Sauce, 94
    in Timbale, 69
Pepper,
    Black, Spaghetti with Pecorino Cheese and, 66
    Grains, Veal Scaloppine with, 242
    with Almonds, Basilicata Style, 35
    Grilled, in Anchovy Sauce with Roasted Olives, 18
    Grilled Hot Cherry, 68----168
    Lamb, and Pasta Casserole, 252
    Pizza, Sweet, with Ricotta Salata, 310
    Red
        Hearts of Escarole with, 272
        Roasted, Polenta and Fontina Cheese, with Tomatoes and, 115
        Shrimp, Grilled, 196
        Stuffed with Pine Nutes and Golden Raisins, 159
    Tuna Roasted in Orange, Yellow and, 200
    Roasted
        and Eggplant Puree Appetizers, 14
        with Prosciutto, 9
    Stewed Sweet, 145
    Yellow, Soup, Cibreo's, 48
Perugia, 29, 237, 352
Pesto, 23, 64, 73
    Basil, Spaghetti with Chef Gilberto Pizzi's, 73
Pie, Country Spinach, 5
Pienza, xiii, 134, 335
Pig, Whole Roasted Suckling, Umbrian Style, 237
Pine Nuts
    Red Bell Peppers Stuffed with Golden Raisins and, 159
    Tart, Fig and, 329
Pineapple Ice, with Strawberry Sauce, 370
Pisa, xiii
Pistachios, 223
Pizza,
    Artichoke, Mortadella and Fontina, 313
    Broccoli Rabe and Goat Cheese, 227, 312
    Dough, 225
    Sweet Pepper, with Ricotta Salata, 310
Pizzi, Gilberto, 73
Plum, Purple, Ice Cream, 367
Polenta, xii, 111
    in Bergamo, 117
    and Fontina Cheese with Tomatoes and Roasted Red Peppers, 115
    Layered, Baked, Venetian Style, 119
    Spicy, with Cheese, Broccoli Rabe and Sausages, 124
Poor Boy Wraps, Swiss Chard Stalks in, 134
Pork. *See also* Ham; Pancetta; Pig; Prosciutto
    Cabbage, and Bean Casserole, 239

Roast Loin of, with Rosemary, 234
Tenderloin, Braised, with Marsala Sauce, 236
Potatoes
Calabrian Onion Soup with, 57
Fresh Codfish, Onions and, 179
Pasta with Cheese, Cabbage and, 74
Roasted, with Crushed Fennel Seeds, 169
Sliced, with Oil and Herbs, 158
Whipped, with Olive Oil 162
and Zucchini Soup from Franco Ricatti, 56
Poultry. *See* Capon; Chicken; Cornish Hens
Poultry and Meat Broths, 374
Preserves, Fig, Chocolate Souffle with, 366
Prosciutto
Broccoli Baked with, 143
Cantalope with, 8
and Cheese, Turkey Breasts Baked with, 220
with Roasted Peppers, 9
Provolone cheese
from Bari, Special, 286
Smoked, 288
Pudding
Panettone Bread, 365
Zucchini 160
Puree
Chestnut, with Sweet Whipped Cream with Candied Orange Strips, 342
Honeydew, Cantalope Melon Balls in, 339
Roasted Peppers and Eggplant, Appetizer, 14

Quail with Herbs and Truffle Oil, 219

Rabbit, Roasted, in Red Wine, 255
Radicchio, xiv, 13, 16
Asparagus with Oil, Vinegar and Hard-Cooked Eggs on, 16
Chicory Hearts and, Scallops and Pancetta on, 249
Marinated and Sauteed, 39
Ragu, Bologna Style, 71
Raisins, Golden, Red Bell Peppers Stuffed with Pine Nuts and, 159
Raspberries, Peach Soup with Toasted Panettone Fingers and, 354
Ravioli, Bergamo Style, 107
Restaurants
Al Cancelleto Verde, 2
Antico Osteria del Teatro, 86
Apollinare, 323
Ar Galletto, 66
Caffe Poliziano, 358
Cibreo, 48
Coccorone, xii
Gritti, 345
Il Cantinori, 131
Le Tre Vaselle, 29
L'Ortica, 376
Orsini, ix, 42, 353
Peppino's, 86
Ristorante da Puny, 175
Tre Marie, 252
Rhubarb, Marinated Salmon with, 29
Rice, 44
and Pea Soup, Doge's 118, 111
Ricotta, xxix
Cake, Chocolate Mocha, 318
Cheese Fritters, 287
Cornish Hens with, and Tarragon, 213
Gnocchi with Light Picante Tomato Shrimp Sauce, 76
and Honey with Thyme, 364
Salata, Sweet Pepper Pizza with, 310
Rigatoni with Eggplant in Creamy Curry Sauce, 98

INDEX

Risotto
    Chicken, with Vegetables, Venetian Style, 123
    with Chicken Livers, Tuscan Style, 113
    Milan Way, 116
    Shrimp and Bass, with Saffron, 121
Riviera, Italian, xiii, 46, 32
    Vegetable Soup from, 52
Robiola on Cheese Tray, 285
Rome, ix, xiii, 4, 12, 23, 56, 61, 66, 89, 92, 109, 136, 152, 172, 225, 226, 227, 237, 258, 261, 284, 327, 339, 367, 376
Rosemary
    Roast Loin of Pork with, 234
    Scented, Butterflied and Grilled Leg of Lamb, 251
    Semolina Flatbread with, 299
    Shrimp in Olive Oil and Lemon Juice with, 193

Saffron, 116, 204, 382
    Parma Ham, Sauce, Tagliatelle in, 78
    Poached Sea Bass in Wine with, 184
    Shrimp and Bass Risotto with, 121
Sage,
    Grilled Swordfish with White Wine and, 186
    Individual Artichoke Mold with Taleggio Sauce and, 151
    Pasta with Mascarpone, Toasted Bread Crumbs and, 88
    Veal Scallops with Ham and, 241
Salad Dressings
    Herb, Curly Endive and Fennel Matchstick Salad with, 270
    Lemon, 12, 63, 140, 156, 193, 197,
        Arugula and Tomato Salad with, 267
        Oil and, Baby Spinach Salad with, 268
Salads
    Arugula and Tomato, with Lemon Dressing, 267

Of Assorted Lettuces with Capers and Tarragon, 277
Bread *
Cauliflower, Traditional, 271
Chicory, Mimosa, 39
Curly Endive and Fennel Matchstick, with Fresh Herb Dressing, 270
Fresh Fennel Slices in, with Watercress, 263
Genovese Squid, with Vegetables, 264
Ligurian Vegetable, 265
Mixed, Cheese with,
Parma Ham, Grilled Asparagus and, 20
Roasted Beet, with Red Onions and Dried Fennel, 259
Roasted Chicken, in Round Loaf of Italian Bread, 266
Rotelle Pasta, with Cucumber Sauce, 99
Spinach, with Oil and Lemon Dressing, 156, 268
Spring Greens with Oil, Vinegar and Mint, 267
Salami,
    Oregano and Crisp, Marinated Cannellini Beans with, 33
Salmon
    Marinated, with Rhubarb, 29
    in Parchment with Spinach and Carrots, 182
    Shrimp and Smoked, in Sweet and Sour Sauce, 15
    Smoked, Fettuccine with, all' Orsini, 68
Sambuca
    Flavored Cocoa Roll, 320
    Ice Cream with Espresso and, 368
Sardinia, 66, 166, 184, 187, 198, 226, 239, 299, 305
Sauces, See also Pesto; Ragu, Bologna Style
    Anchovy
        Caper, 202
    Besciamella, 64, 70, 72, 83, 95, 148, 151
    Blood Orange, 202
    Blueberry, Orange Panna Cotta with, 356

Buttery Tomato, Tagliatelle with, 80
Caper and Chive, Fried Zucchini with, 144
Citrus, Fruit Compote with, 344
Creamy Curry, Rigatoni with Eggplant in, 98
Cucumber, Rotelle Pasta Salad with, 99
Hot, Zucchini in, Farm Style, 163
Italian Green, Vegetable Matchsticks in Bundles with, 139
Lemon, Spaghetti with, 63
Light Picante Tomato Shrimp, Ricotta Gnocchi with, 76
Marsala, Braised Pork Tenderloin with, 236
Meat
    Chiara's Lasagna with, 71
    Lasagna Baked with (Bologna Style), 82
Mustard, Glazed Celery in, 453
Onion, Green Beans with, 150
Parma Ham-Saffron, Tagliatelle in, 78
Pork Tomato, Penne with, 94
Rhubarb, 29
Strawberry, Pineapple Ice with, 370
Sweet and Sour, 15
Sweet and Sour, Shrimp and Smoked Salmon in, 29
Taleggio, Individual Artichoke Mold with, and Sage, 151
Tuna, Cold Veal in, 248
Two, Pasta Stars of Italy with, 23
Two, Swordfish Steaks with, 203
Zabaglione, Apollinare's Chocolate Roll with, 323
Sausages, *See also* specific sausage
    Eggs in Purgatory with Grilled, 238
    Spicy Polenta with Cheese, Broccoli Rabe, and, 124
Savory, and Pancetta Benedictine Monks' Green Beans with, 262
Scallops and Pancetta on Chicory Hearts and Radicchio, 39

Sea Bass
    Carpaccio of, with Herbs, 10
    Poached, in Wine with Saffron, 184
    and Shrimp Risotto, with Saffron, 121
Seafood, 41. *See also* specific seafood
    Broth, 377
    Stew, Spicy, 204
Sherbet, Tangerine, with Lemon Liqueur, 371
Shrimp
    and Bass Risotto, with Saffron, 121
    Grilled Red Pepper, 196
    in Olive Oil and Lemon Juice with Rosemary, 193
    Peppery, One-Two-Three, 189
    Sauce, Light Picante Tomato, Ricotta Gnocchi with, 76
    Shells in broth, 377
    and Smoked Salmon in Sweet and Sour Sauce, 15
    Sole, Squid and, Deep Fried, Gaeta Style, 191
Sicily, 202, 204, 289, 326
    Cream Cake, 326
Snapper or Trout, in Vernaccia Wine, 198
Soffrito (vegetable mixture), 246
Sole
    Fillets, Wrapped in Leeks with Brussels Sprouts, 172
    Fried Marinated, in Sweet and Sour Sauce, 180
    Shrimp, Squid and Deep Fried, Gaeta Style, 191
Sorbet. *See* Ices; Sherbet, Tangerine, with Lemon Liqueur
Sorbet, Muscat, 369
Souffle, Chocolate, with Fig Preserves, 366
Soups. *See also* Broths; Chowder, Fisherman's
    Asparagus
        and Leek, with Crushed Amaretti and Crisped Leeks, 46
        Pietro Tecchio's, 63
    Bread, 291-311
    Calabrian onion, with Potatoes, 57

Cibreo's Yellow Pepper, 48
Emilia Mastracci's Minestrone, 44
Fish, 184, 204
Kale, 47
Lentil, 51
Peach, with Raspberries and Toasted Panettone Fingers, 334
Potato and Zucchini, from Franco Ricatti, 56
Rice and Pea, Doge's, 118, 111
Vegetable, from Riviera, 52

Spaghetti
 with Chef Gilberto Pizzi's Basil Pesto, 73
 with Clams, Cerry Tomatoes and Basil, 75
 with Garlic and Chili, 97
 with Lemon Sauce, 63
 with Pecorino Cheese and Black Pepper, 66
Spaghettini, with Clams, Carrots and Wine, 92
Spices, *See also specific spices*
 Braised Beef in Red Wine and, 231
Spinach
 Fresh, Pasta Bows with Mushrooms, Cream and, 109
 with Oil and Lemon, 268
 Pasta, 84
 Pie, Country, 5
 Salad, with Oil and Lemon Dressing, 268
 Salmon in Parchment with Carrots and, 182
Squash. *See specific squash*
Squid
 Salad, Genovese, with Vegetables. 264
 Shrimp, and Sole, Deep Fried, Gaeta Style, 191
Steaks
 Oliviero's Style Porterhouse, 229
 Swordfish, with Two Sauces: Blood Orange and Caper/Anchovy, 202
Stew
 Braised Oxtail, 227

Chicken, Kale, and Chickpea, 216
 Spicy Seafood, in Syracuse, 204
Strawberries
 in Balsamic Vinegar, with Mint and Whipped Cream, 347
 Sauce, Pineapple Ice with, 370
Stuffing, Special, 223
Swiss Chard Stalks in Poor Boy Wraps, 134
Swordfish
 Grilled, with White Wine and Sage, 186
 Steaks, with Two Sauces: Blood Orange and Caper/Anchovy, 209

Tagliatelle
 Baked, with Two Cheeses, 89
 with Buttery Tomato Sauce, 80
 In Parma Ham-Saffron Sauce, 78
Taleggio cheese, 151
Tangerine Sherbet, with Lemon Liqueur, 371
Tarragon
 Capers and, Salad of Assorted Lettuces with, 277
Tarragon (*cont.*)
 Cornish Hens with Ricotta and, 213
Tart
 Almond Cheese, 331
 Brandied Hazelnut, 332
 Fig and Pine Nut, 329
 Parmesan Custard, 17
 Wild Cherry, 327
Thyme
 Grilled Eels with Wine, Brandy, and, 194
 Ricotta and Honey with, 364
Timbale
 of Eggplant and Pasta, 100
 Penne Pasta in, 69
Tiramisu with Amaretto from Caffe Poliziano, 358

Tomatoes
    and Arugula Salad with Lemon Dressing, 267
    Cherry, Spaghetti with Clams, Basil and, 75
    with Chives, 266
    Jam, Green, with Zabaglione and Whipped Cream, 333
    Polenta and Fontina Cheese with Roasted Red Peppers and, 115
    Slow-Cooked Roasted Plum, 130
    Spicy Herbed, Lobster with, 195
Tortellini, Homemade, in Broth, 54
Trout
    on Grill, 177
    or Snapper, in Vernaccia Wine, 198
Truffles
    Bread Toasts with, 28
    Oil, Quail with Herbs and, 219
Tuna
    Beans with, 174
    Mayonnaise, Eggs with, 41
    Roasted in Red, Orange and Yellow Peppers, 200
    Sautéed, with Aromatic Herbs, 199
    Skewered, Grilled with Lemon and Oregano, 197
Turkey
    Breasts, Baked with Prosciutto and Cheese, 220
    Roll, Baked Meat-Stuffed, 217
Tuscany, xiii, 12, 47, 82, 113, 136, 214, 225, 292

Umbria, xi, xii, xiii, 18, 23, 28, 91, 226

Veal
    Angela's Sunday-Best Stuffed Breast of, 243
    Cold, in Tuna Sauce, 248
    Cutlet, in Milan Manner, 245
    Scallops with Ham and Sage, 241
    Scaloppine with Pepper Grains, 242
    Shanks, Milan Way, 246
Vegetables. *See also specific vegetables*
    Lamb and, Greek Style, 254
    Matchsticks in Bundles, with Italian Green Sauce, 139
    Pickled, Parma Ham, Mortadella and, 22
    Steamed, Fontina Fondue with, 11
The Veneto, 16, 111, 121
    Fried Soft-shell Crabs in, 181
Venice, xiii, 10, 20, 112, 119, 121, 171, 345
    Open markets in, 112
Verona, 146, 279
Vin Santo wine, 340, 343
Vinegar, Balsamic, 347
    Strawberries in, with Mint and Whipped Cream, 347
Vinegars
    Fresh Fennel with Parslied Oil and, 31
    Lucia's Mother's Fruit, 379

Watercress
    Fresh Fennel Slices in Salad with, 263
    Romaine Lettuce, Snow Peas and, with Lemon, 273
Wine,
    Clams with, in Portofino, 175
    Grilled Eels with Brandy, Thyme and, 194
    Octopus with, Garlic, Oil and parsley, 12
    Pears Cooked in, with Mascarpone, 349
    Poached Sea Bass in, with Saffron, 184
    Red
        Beef Braised in, and Spices, 231
        Roasted Rabbit in, 255
    Spaghettini with Clams, Carrots and, 192
    Vernaccia, Snapper or Trout in, 198
    White, Grilled Swordfish with, and Sage, 186

INDEX

Zabaglione
    from Bassano del Grappa, 362
    Green Tomato Jam with, and Whipped Cream, 333
    Sauce, Apollinare's Chocolate Roll with, 323
Zucchini
    Baked, with Mozzarella, 165
    Baked Pasta with Herbs and, 67
    Fried, 164
    with Capers and Chive Sauce, 144
    in Hot Sauce, Farm Style, 163
    and Potato Soup from Franco Ricatti, 56
    Pudding, 160
    Vegetable Rainbow of Carrots, Asparagus, Broccoli Rabe and, 154

CPSIA information can be obtained at www.ICGtesting.com
Printed in the USA
LVOW111945110313

323713LV00008B/504/P